This book places the plays of Aristophanes in their contemporary context and tries to answer the question: What aspects of Greek, and especially Athenian, culture did the comedies of Aristophanes bring into play for their original audiences? It makes particular use of the structural analysis of Greek rituals and myths to demonstrate how their meanings and functions can be used to interpret the plays which are themselves shown to be constructed according to similar patterns. This information is then used to suggest ways in which twentieth-century audiences may read the plays in terms of contemporary literary theories and concerns: modern interpretation is thus grounded in ancient ways of thinking. This is the first book to apply the techniques of structural anthropology systematically to all the comedies. It differs from earlier studies in that it does not impose a single interpretative structure on the plays, either individually or as a group, but argues that each play operates with a range of different structures, and that groups of plays use similar structures in different ways.

Students and scholars of Aristophanes and of ancient Athenian society and its myths and rituals will find this work valuable to them. All Greek is quoted in translation and the book is written to be accessible to readers from a variety of disciplines.

ARISTOPHANES

ARISTOPHANES

MYTH, RITUAL AND COMEDY

A. M. BOWIE

*Lecturer in Literae Humaniores in the University of Oxford
and Fellow of The Queen's College*

 CAMBRIDGE
UNIVERSITY PRESS

Published by the Press Syndicate of the University of Cambridge
The Pitt Building, Trumpington Street, Cambridge CB2 1RP
40 West 20th Street, New York, NY 10011-4211 USA
10 Stamford Road, Oakleigh, Melbourne 3166, Australia

First published 1993
Reprinted 1994, 1995
First paperback edition 1996

Printed in Great Britain at the University Press, Cambridge

A catalogue record for this book is available from the British Library

Library of Congress Cataloguing in publication data

Bowie, A. M.
Aristophanes: myth, ritual, and comedy / A. M. Bowie.
p.   cm.
Includes bibliographical references and index.
ISBN 0 521 44012 2 (hardback)
1. Aristophanes – Criticism and interpretation.   2. Greek drama
(Comedy) – History and criticism.   3. Mythology, Greek, in
literature.   4. Ritual in literature.   I. Title.
PA3879.B84   1993
882'.01–dc20
92-39415 CIP

ISBN 0 521 44012 2 hardback
ISBN 0 521 57575 3 paperback

SE

To Peter

φίλῳ ὄντως βεβαίῳ

CONTENTS

PREFACE

There is a lively, sometimes acrimonious, debate current about how far modern methods of criticism should be applied to Classical texts created centuries, millennia even, before the theories were a twinkle in a critic's eye. This book offers a mediation between the positions for and against the use of modern methods, by arguing that the study of texts in terms of their own times is not an alternative to the use of modern methods, but a necessary prerequisite of it. In an attempt to recreate something of the ways in which the ancient Athenians may have received and reacted to the plays, which can then be used as the basis for contemporary readings, it applies the methods of structural anthropology to the study of the dramas. It is hoped that one advantage of this procedure will be that it offers the possibility of avoiding the uncritical reading back into the fifth century of contemporary attitudes to war and peace, city and country, wealth and poverty, sexuality and so on, and of grounding our interpretation of the texts in Athenian thought-patterns. The study is offered also as a means of opening up new questions in the study of Aristophanes: it does not claim in any way to be a full treatment of the author, nor that this is the only way to read him. It is part of a widespread attempt to show how aspects of ancient culture can be elucidated by structuralist methodology, which is a mode of thought not, after all, entirely alien to the Greek tendency to view things in terms of polarities and analogies.

A number of choices about presentation have been made in the interests of economy. Most controversially, perhaps, I have decided, because this is not a close linguistic study and is designed for non-specialist as well as specialist audiences, to dispense with the original Greek: the translations lay no claim to particular elegance but are meant as a guide for those with no Greek. In the footnotes, I have not aimed at completeness of reference to ancient and modern works, but have cited the more recent works in which further bibliography, ancient and modern, can be found. Similarly, I have not felt it necessary to refer constantly to standard dictionaries and lexica on matters of Greek religion and mythology, nor to repeat material from the commentaries on the plays. I have also kept cross-referencing to an absolute minimum, so where there are no footnote references accompanying a discussion of a particular aspect of Greek culture, the index should be consulted for the main treatment(s). Since I wish the book to be accessible to non-specialists, I have also at times given details on Greek matters which are rather more widely known now than when the book was first begun: I must ask colleagues to bear with me.

The book has been in preparation for more than a decade, and many debts have therefore been contracted. Apart from patient and sceptical audiences, I would like to mention, in particular, Peter Bayley, who helped me escape the typewriter, transfer to the word-processor and save a great deal of time; and, for reading varying amounts of the text with an attention to detail for which I am deeply grateful, Jan Bremmer, Nan Dunbar, Richard Hunter and Richard Seaford. I hope they will not be held responsible for what is found herein. Lastly, I would like particularly to single out Christiane Sourvinou-Inwood, to whom I owe a very great deal, not simply for her willingness to read and comment on the material, but more especially for her encouragement and guidance, which has been invaluable throughout the book's composition.

Oxford, July 1992   AMB

ABBREVIATIONS

CA   J. U. Powell (ed.), *Collectanea Alexandrina*, Oxford 1925.

CAF   T. Kock (ed.), *Comicorum Atticorum Fragmenta*, Leipzig 1880–8.

CAG   *Commentaria in Aristotelem Graeca*.

CPG   E. L. Leutsch & F. G. Schneidewin (eds.), *Corpus Paroemiographorum Graecorum*, Göttingen 1839–51.

EGF   G. Kinkel (ed.), *Epicorum Graecorum Fragmenta*, Leipzig 1877.

EM   T. Gaisford (ed.), *Etymologicum Magnum*, Oxford 1848.

FGH   F. Jacoby (ed.), *Fragmente der griechischen Historiker*, Berlin and Leiden 1923–57.

FHG   C. Müller (ed.), *Fragmenta Historicorum Graecorum*, Paris 1841–70.

GG   E. Schwyzer, *Griechische Grammatik*, Munich 1939–53.

IC   F. Halbherr & M. Guarducci (eds.), *Inscriptiones Creticae*, vol. I, Rome 1935.

IG   *Inscriptiones Graecae*, Berlin 1873– .

KG   R. Kühner, *Ausführliche Grammatik der griechischen Sprache*, vol. II rev. by B. Gerth, Hanover 1898–1904.

LGRM   W. H. Röscher (ed.), *Ausführliches Lexicon der griechischen und römischen Mythologie*, 8 vols., Berlin and Leipzig 1884–1937.

LSJ   Liddell and Scott, *A Greek–English Lexicon*, 9th edn rev. by Sir Henry Stuart Jones & R. McKenzie, Oxford 1940.

OCT   Oxford Classical Texts Series.

PCG   R. Kassel & C. F. L. Austin (eds.), *Poetae Comici Graeci*, Berlin and New York 1983– .

PMG   D. L. Page (ed.), *Poetae Melici Graeci*, Oxford 1962.

P. Oxy.   *Oxyrhynchus Papyri*, London 1898–   .

RE   *Paulys Real-Encyclopädie der klassischen Altertumswissens-*
            chaft, Stuttgart 1894–   .

SEG   *Supplementum Epigraphicum Graecum*.

SH   H. Lloyd-Jones & P. Parsons (eds.), *Supplementum Hellenis-*
            ticum, Berlin and New York 1983.

SIG   W. Dittenberger (ed.), *Sylloge Inscriptionum Graecarum*,
            3rd edn., Leipzig 1915–24.

TGF   *Tragicorum Graecorum Fragmenta*, Göttingen 1971–   .

The text of Aristophanes used is the OCT. Occasional reference is
made to the editions of Aristophanes by F. H. M. Blaydes, B. B.
Rogers and L. van Leeuwen. Comic fragments are numbered according to *PCG*, where the poet has been edited in those volumes, and
CAF where not (these have 'K.' after the reference). Other abbrevia-
tions are from LSJ, *L'Année Philologique* or will be obvious.

A complete translation of the plays is available in three volumes
by D. Barrett and A. H. Sommerstein (Penguin, Harmondsworth
1964–78). This is very readable but inevitably somewhat free.
Sommerstein provides a more faithful translation in his editions of
the plays (Warminster 1980–   ; cf. Bibliography).

I

Introduction

In Beethoven's *Fidelio*, after the prisoners have been locked away for
the night, Leonora, disguised as a young man, descends with the
jailer Rocco to the cell where her husband Florestan is imprisoned, in
order to help kill and bury him as ordered by Pizarro. As they
prepare the tomb, Rocco gives Florestan a little wine, and permits
Leonora to give him a piece of bread she has been carrying for two
days. Leonora eventually scotches Pizarro's plan, and, in a blaze of
light in the prison courtyard, Florestan is recognised for who he is by
the Minister; Pizarro is led away and the prisoners receive their
freedom.

  An anthropologist, seeking to explore the meanings that lie
behind or structure such a story, might note the bread and wine and
wonder whether this symbolism of the Last Supper is more important than seems to be the case at first sight. Further reflection might
prompt a suggestion that one should see in the release of the expiring
Florestan something of Christ's harrowing of Hell and resurrection:
Christ was in Hell for three days, and this is the third year that
Florestan has been in the dungeon. The release of the prisoners will
then be the redemption of mankind that follows Christ's triumph
over death. Rocco, 'the rock', points to St Peter, the rock on whom
Christ's church is built, and also the keeper of the keys to heaven.
Leonora's adopted name is indicative of the faith she preserves and
which leads to the resurrection of her husband. Pizarro makes a
respectably devilish figure or even a Pilate in his official capacity.
There is in the opera, therefore, a certain broad similarity between
elements in the tale of the death and resurrection of the saviour
Christ and the tale of the deathlike imprisonment and salvation of
Florestan, a similarity which is supported by individual expressions
in the text, such as the Prisoners' 'O Heaven! Salvation!'

Obviously, this Christian reading of the opera is not here presented as 'the' meaning of the opera, but rather as one way of understanding it in terms comprehensible and significant at the time it was written. Nor does the reading necessarily represent the intended meaning of the author, of libretto or score. Beethoven seems to have been particularly concerned with the idea that injustice could be defeated by firm belief in human values, and Bouilly's *Léonore ou l'amour conjugale* was written at the time of the French Revolution, but the politically delicate nature of the tale caused him to set it in the Seville of 150 years earlier. Furthermore, the story is based upon an actual event in Bouilly's judicial career. Moral and political factors are naturally in play too. Finally, the present ending of the opera was not the original one (which took place in the dungeon), but the result of Treitschke's revision of the libretto for Beethoven's third attempt at making a success of *Fidelio* in the theatre, so that the 'resurrection' idea may be said to become really striking only in this last version.

Again, there is no claim that there exists any simple one-to-one correlation between the two stories. We have spoken of Florestan in terms of Christ, but Christ was not saved by faith. Florestan could therefore equally be read as standing for man saved by faith, with echoes again of the sacrifice of Christ in the bread and wine. Peter, unlike Rocco, was not the key-holder of Hell, and so on. There does however seem to be present in the story a Christian 'code', which illuminates the story in a number of ways, and gives the opera a significance which, for a Christian culture, is deeper than that of a simple tale of a husband saved by his transvestite wife. If our student of the opera is unaware of this Christian code, then he or she will of course be able to understand the story and to discuss the moral and political factors involved, but will be missing a crucial aspect of the opera for an audience brought up with a knowledge of the mythology and ritual surrounding the person of Christ. With such knowledge, the anthropologist will be able to interpret the opera using the Christian filters, which should mean that the interpretation approximates more to that of the nineteenth-century audience, and is given further protection from anachronism: it can be argued that the interpretation, even if it is one that not all in the audiences arrived at, plausibly situates the opera in the cultural milieu of its time. Indeed, this would be so, even if we take the extreme hypothetical position in which no-one in 1814 or later thought of the opera in such Christian terms: the reading could justified on the grounds that, given the cultural conditions of the time, it was available as a way of looking at the opera.

It is the aim of this book to consider the plays of Aristophanes in ways similar to that sketched here for *Fidelio*.[1] It will attempt to situate the plays of Aristophanes in their cultural context, and try to answer the basic question: What aspects of the Greek and especially the Athenian thought-world did these comedies bring into play for their original audiences? Just as we concentrated on the religious symbolism of *Fidelio*, the analyses of Aristophanes' plays will make most use of ritual and mythological material, partly because there is so much explicit use made of Greek myth and ritual in the comedies, and partly because, as with the story of Christ, we can reconstruct a good deal of the significances of these myths and rituals in Greek culture generally and so assess their meaning in the narrower area of Aristophanic drama. Since this book has no desire to be purely antiquarian, it hopes then to use this information to suggest ways in which twentieth-century audiences may read the plays in terms of contemporary literary theories and concerns, whilst at the same time avoiding some of the pitfalls that attend interpretations whose neglect of the circumstances in which the plays were produced can result in their being disagreeably anachronistic.

The idea of connecting comedy to myth and ritual is not of course new. Zielinski in 1885 related Old Comedies to 'Märchen', which he reconstructed, but these reconstructions were largely hypothetical and there is little or no evidence for their independent existence in Greece. The most famous attempt was that of Cornford in *The Origin of Attic Comedy*, first published in 1914. The difference between this study and Cornford's is that he tried to construct a single ritual structure which could be found to inform all the plays: 'The plays, under all their variety and extravagance, have not only a unity of structure, but a framework of traditional incidents, which cannot, I believe, be otherwise explained than as the surviving fabric of a ritual plot.'[2] The plot, which turned out to be very similar to that posited by Murray for the origin of tragedy, was the Frazerian one involving a conflict between figures representative of the powers of

---

[1] For reasons of space, I leave the fragmentary plays for separate treatment elsewhere. Cf. Moessner 1907.   [2] Cornford 1914: vii.

fertility and death, of good and evil, of Summer and Winter, etc. Attic Comedy was thus a kind of fertility ritual: 'All the varieties that we shall pass in review symbolise the same natural fact, which, in their primitive magical intention, they were designed to bring about and further by the familiar means of sympathetic or mimetic representation – the death of the old year and the birth or accession of the new, the decay and suspension of life in the frosts of winter and its release and *renouveau* in spring.'[3] In the conflict (*agon*), the good spirit is slain, dismembered, cooked and eaten in a communal meal and then brought back to life rejuvenated to be married to the Mother Goddess. Cornford related this ritual plot to the Phallic ceremonies which Aristotle said were the starting point for comedy, and claimed to be able to explain the origins of the main elements of Attic comedy in terms of these ceremonies. The rite began with a procession of Dionysiac worshippers, who paused for the sacrifice, and the *agon* of the plays was 'the beginning of the sacrifice in its primitive dramatic form – the conflict between the good and evil principles';[4] the parabasis reflected the *komos*-hymn of the Phallic procession with its invocation of the good spirit and expulsion of the evil; the part of the play between parabasis and exodos was the slaying, eating and revival of the good spirit in the communal sacrifice; the end of the play represented the marriage. The ritual of comedy thus consisted of the following elements: Fight, *Agon*, Sacrifice, New King (or Zeus), Cooking, Feast, Marriage (Courtesan or Bride), *Komos*. In *Acharnians*, for instance, the Fight is the pelting of Dicaeopolis and the conflict between the two halves of the Chorus; the *Agon* is Dicaeopolis' plea for peace that converts one half of the Chorus; the Sacrifice is the threat to the coal-basket, and the Megarian's daughters who are offered for sacrifice; Dicaeopolis is obviously the New King; the last quarter of the play concerns the Cooking of Dicaeopolis' feast, and the Feast motif is repeated in the invitation to Dicaeopolis to dine; the Marriage is represented by the two Courtesans at the end and the *Komos* is sung as the actors leave.

As can be seen from this example, the original plot has undergone not inconsiderable dismemberment itself, and indeed Cornford was able to make it fit some of the plays only by notable special pleading. It is, for instance, usually very hard to see in the scenes after the parabasis the killing, eating and rebirth of the good spirit;

[3] Ibid. 53.   [4] Ibid. 103.

and in some plays, the hero has actually defeated his opponent before the parabasis is sung, so that it does not look like the defeat of the evil spirit; the scenes of feasting are also usually celebrations of the victory rather than a revivifying of the hero. Furthermore, although elements from this 'ritual-plot' are found in Greek ritual practice, we have no evidence for any rite in Athens such as Cornford describes. The nearest to the idea of the dying and reviving god would be the rites of Adonis, but these were a foreign import and not one of the official city festivals. It is also perhaps a little unlikely that comedy should have laboured to preserve the details of this plot in every one of its plays. Rather than trying to reduce all the plays to a single schema, therefore, this study tries to see what different structures inform and illuminate the different plays.[5]

The principal method of analysis to be used is that of structural anthropology, whose use in Classical studies, largely for tragedy rather than comedy, was pioneered by the French structuralists such as Louis Gernet, Jean-Pierre Vernant, Pierre Vidal-Naquet and Marcel Detienne.[6] This method assumes that one can analyse a culture by looking for certain patterns of thought which are used to construct, order and talk about the world, and which will appear in a variety of cultural contexts, such as myths, festivals, literature, painting, sculpture and so on. The method, which owes something to theories of language and especially those of Saussure, thus works not by trying to comprehend the 'meaning' of individual items in a culture, but by considering the items in their various relationships with other items, in what are usually referred to as 'structures' of thought. What this sort of analysis is doing in essence is trying to map out the 'grammar' of Greek culture. Just as the grammarian may seek in the myriad sentences of a language the underlying rules and structures, so the analysis works out the different ways the culture represents the world and tries to discern the underlying patterns, their varieties and their meanings. Stories, such as those for instance of young men engaged on rites of passage, which may appear to be very different on the surface, can often be shown to be conveying very similar messages at a deeper level, and the elements that make up the stories

---

. [5] Similar criticisms may be made of Thiercy's use of the initiatory schema (1986: 301–27), and Pappas's of the *komos* (1987). Frye 1957: 163–86 presents a more general 'myth' of comedy.

[6] Their writings are easily approached in Gordon 1981, with Buxton's useful introduction (ix–xv).

may also be found to be repeated in works of art and initiation rituals. Similar patterns may then be detected in comparable rites, such as those for initiation into mystery cults, for instance. The fact that the pattern is found in different cultural activities lends some support to the idea that it represents a way of thinking, or a piece of the mental furniture of the culture. Once the pattern is established, one can return to the individual examples of it and see how they also differ in significant ways. In the *Fidelio* example above, we distilled the structure of the story of Christ's redemption of mankind; it was distorted and fragmented in various ways, but still recognisable and significant for the interpretation of the opera.

As the case of *Fidelio* showed, there are inevitably problems about the notions of 'similarity' between the structures and the plays. In some cases, the similarity and so relevance of a myth or ritual will be obvious and even incontrovertible, but in others readers may feel that the claimed relationships are to say the least tendentious. To some extent, this is inevitable: the Rohrschach ink-blot tests are instructive precisely because different people discover different similarities in them. In any system where the grouping of features is important, there will always be disputes about whether certain features, which do not fulfil the necessary criteria in a clear fashion, belong in a particular group. Furthermore, the more one works at the relationship between two things, the more the points of contact that appear; the reader, meeting the claims for the first time, can be less impressed. On the other hand, it is also true that the similarities may have been more obvious to those, like the original audiences of Aristophanes' plays, to whom the different features were even more familiar than they are to the researcher who indulges in this method of analysis. This problem does not, of course, mean that the method is fundamentally flawed: there are cases of clear similarity. There will be times therefore when it will be thought that I have pressed my argument too far, but, since the purpose of this book is to open up as many questions as possible, I have left in cases where scepticism has been expressed but where I think that a sufficient element of similarity remains to suggest that the myth or ritual can illuminate the play.

There are two further major problems, which are linked together. This structural method of analysis is often accused of discussing the works of a particular period but taking its evidence from a wide chronological spread, and counting almost anything convenient as a 'myth'. To some extent, this is inevitable, because we have only very patchy evidence for particular types of myth or ritual at particular times: the same is sometimes true of linguistic studies, in that later usages must be used to explain earlier ones in the absence of relevant contemporary data. However, as Buxton puts it, 'in practice, the matter does not present itself as a cut-and-dried choice between "chronology" and "structure"; it is rather a matter of *how much* to privilege chronological considerations at the expense of structural ones, or vice versa'; a middle course needs to be steered.[7] Furthermore, the meanings and functions of mythical and ritual features of a culture obviously change, but, especially in religious matters, there is a strong element of conservatism, so that the description of a rite taken from a later period *need* not be seriously misleading but may perhaps represent an old tradition preserved at the shrine, and an interpretation based on it need not be false for an earlier time. The meaning, use or details of a myth may change, but often its basic structure will be preserved, giving a possible glimpse of an earlier function. The method of analysis must be refined by the provision of further evidence and by debate, and this book is an attempt to contribute to that debate.

The question of what counts as a 'myth' is also a thorny one.[8] Burkert defined it as 'a traditional tale with secondary, partial reference to something of collective importance'.[9] Some myths, of course, were newer than others and so not strictly traditional, but then new tales very often take their pattern from existing ones, so that we are still dealing with a traditional structure. It is for this reason that one feels it not improper to use stories from, say, 'literary' sources such as Hellenistic writings. The Athenians came across 'myths' of various forms in a wide range of contexts, such as schools, dramatic and poetic competitions, paintings on walls and vases, religious rites, and, no doubt, grandmother's knee. Not all of these may have qualified as myths, even in Burkert's broad formulation, but they are all, where we have them, evidence for how the Greeks talked about the world. Thus, 'myth' in this book will inevitably cover a wide spectrum of different kinds of story and discourse.

Old Comedy makes use of these myths and rituals in a variety of different ways. In some cases, there is no doubt where one should

[7] 1980: 26.   [8] For an orientation, cf. Bremmer 1987: 1–9.   [9] 1979: 23.

look. *Thesmophoriazusae* needs to be discussed in terms of the festival whose name it bears, and any account of the play must be able to show what it is that links reference to that festival to the Euripidean tragedies which also provide a large part of the play's matter. In the same way, the Chorus of *Frogs* consists of the Eleusinian Initiates, many others of whom were in the audience, so that the function of any Eleusinian echoes is going to be crucial. Where a play has some of its action take place not at a festival but during the period of a festival, again I presume that the references to that festival are significant, as in the case of *Acharnians*, which moves from the Rural Dionysia of Dicaeopolis' house early in the play to the Choes day of the Anthesteria at the end. The meanings and functions of these festivals in Athenian religious and social life enable us to understand something of the attitudes to Dicaeopolis' actions which the play is provoking: the contrast between the usual significance of the Rural Dionysia and Dicaeopolis' is one way in which questions are raised about the merits of his private treaty; the mythology of the Anthesteria functions similarly. Similarly, in *Ecclesiazusae*, the fact that the women plan their action at the Scira and their new communistic regime is inaugurated with a parody of the Panathenaic festival seems to suggest that the play needs to be considered in part in terms of the festivals, like Scira and Panathenaea, that surrounded the new year. It will emerge that a particularly common technique in Aristophanes is to juxtapose reference to these city festivals to the actions of his heroes, so that the ideology of the city is contrasted with the deeds of the main characters, often to the discredit of the latter.

At other times, no specific festival or myth will be referred to and so we may have to have recourse to a particular type of festival. Here it can be difficult to know whether an individual festival or myth is in question or whether we should discuss the play in terms of the general type of festival or myth with which it appears to have affinities. Such a problem occurs in *Lysistrata*. The women seize power in the play, so that myths dealing with 'women in power' are the obvious parallels. One in particular, that of the Lemnian Women, is especially close in structure and details, and Aristophanes and a number of other dramatists wrote plays on this myth. The question is thus raised whether *Lysistrata* is to be taken as actually based upon this one myth, rather than on ideas found in this type of myth generally. A good case could be made for the Lemnian myth as the model for *Lysistrata*, but since I am not trying to write literary history, I am not over-concerned whether it was or not. I prefer to take the myth as one of a number of possible correlates to the play. Perhaps, in the minds of some spectators, it was the dominant one, but since we can no more know this than we can be sure whether Aristophanes was using the myth as his model, I am happier to treat it as the myth which allows us to construct a particularly clear view of what the play is doing with the mythical idea of 'women in power'. It would, of course, be possible exhaustively to compare the play to all other such myths, but the restriction to one gives a more manageable account of what is involved in comprehending this aspect of *Lysistrata*. What I give therefore is an account of the intertextual relations between this play and its closest congener in myth and ritual, which must stand for the wider treatment.

Other plays have plots that relate to obvious myth-types. *Birds* is naturally treated in terms of the myths (and indeed rituals) that concern city-foundation, and it is the distortion in the structures of such myths which conveys something of the nature of Nephelococ-cygia. With other plays, the relevant myth-types are not so immediately apparent. This is the case with the trio *Knights*, *Wasps*, *Clouds*,[10] in which myths of transition turn out to be a crucial structure, in different ways. In these cases, though specifically Athenian versions are going to be especially important, the whole genre of status-transition myths and festivals can be instructive. Here again, the 'normal' pattern that is evinced by the city's rituals and their accompanying myths is used to provide a commentary on the actions of the plays.

It should be clear from what has been said that this book is concerned with audience reception rather than authorial intention.[11] It cannot be stated too clearly that it is no part of its function to detect the 'views' of Aristophanes. He is dead and cannot tell us what he himself thought, and much of the literary theorising of this century has shown the grave, if not insoluble, problems attaching to the attempts to disengage some kernel of 'what the author really

[10] The chronological sequence of the plays is followed in this book, except that, in order to discuss two of these plays in the more illuminating order, I have taken the fact that our version of *Clouds* post-dates the production of *Wasps* as an excuse for transposing them.

[11] The most influential statement of the opposite case, that Aristophanes has clear political and other preferences, is de Ste Croix 1972: appdx xxix.

thought' from all the things that appear on the page. The contradictory pictures of 'Aristophanes' that have been drawn from his texts,
which make him, for instance, for and against intellectual activity, or
a conservative and a democrat (radical or mild), may suggest that the
attempt to gauge his views is doomed, and the very contradictions
suggest that there may be more interesting things to say of the plays.
Not infrequently too one can see that the 'Aristophanes' constructed
by those who would know his views bears no small likeness to the
author of the study in question. The fact that Aristophanes often
juxtaposes virulent criticism of the city and its works with pictures
of other possible political situations even less appetising in various
ways suggests that attempts to restrict the meaning to some single
message may be doing little justice to the complexity of the dramas,
while reinforcing the view that Aristophanes is an author of much
humour but little substance.

   Furthermore, these plays were part of one or other of the two
city festivals, the Lenaea and City Dionysia, at which dramas were
performed. The city displayed itself in various ways either to itself,
at the Lenaea, or also to representatives from many other cities, at the
Dionysia, where there was also the exposition of the year's tribute,
the awarding of crowns to the city's benefactors and the parading in
full armour of the orphans of those who had died in war.[12] The public
nature of these dramas might therefore suggest that their function in
the city was not principally for one man to lecture the audience, but
rather that they were part of that displaying of the city to itself; that
the audience was more important than the author. The dramas
examined the nature of the city and its ways of representing itself, in
positive and negative ways.[13] Whether ultimately the plays deconstructed the discourse the *polis* used of itself, leaving it problematic,
or whether the plays act like a religious rite themselves in which
order is restored out of disorder,[14] is still debated, but one would
perhaps expect some positive contribution from the plays to the
general activity on the city's behalf that constituted the festivals.
This contribution is ambivalent, as is fitting, in comedy, but this may
be not because Aristophanes really had doubts about the city, but
because it was comedy's job to make fun of the city, for a variety of
reasons such as entertainment through extreme behaviour, control

---

[12] See especially Pickard-Cambridge 1988: 57–125.
[13] Cf. e.g. Goldhill 1986, 1987, 1991: 167–221; Hall 1989.   [14] Cf. Easterling 1988.

through mockery, avoiding divine envy at the splendour of the city's self-presentation, examining problems in a less sombre manner than tragedy and so on. The plays, in other words, may not have been propagandistic for a particular political position, but may have worked to raise the audience's consciousness of the problems facing them, whilst at the same time permitting types of humour and behaviour that were not permitted at other times. Which plays were to be performed was not left to the playwrights, but was decided by city officials to whom the plays were submitted. Unfortunately, we know nothing of the criteria used by the archons to choose the plays, but it may have been the case that plays with too idiosyncratic concerns would not have been chosen.

None of this rules out the possibility that an author may have expressed his own views, but it suggests that viewing the plays from the perspective of the *polis* is an essential proceeding, and perhaps one with a greater hope of success than that which tries to distil an individual's ideology from a complex set of texts, which, when analysed more closely, seem to be resisting just such an analysis. If we consider comedy from this perspective of its role in the city, we begin to see that it could have had a function which is recognisable from other cultures in which humour plays a part in religious contexts.[15] Summing up cross-cultural studies of humour in ritual, Apte wrote: 'drama is both entertaining and educational. Humor plays a significant role in dramatization and is often the primary mode of entertainment, especially in preliterate societies.'[16] Obviously, such cross-cultural evidence cannot *prove* anything about Aristophanes' comedies, because there are naturally differences between cultures within the broad similarities, but they do give us a possible perspective against which to check our own perceptions of what is likely in his case.

Apte lists the following as the typical properties of ritual humour, all of which, if we consider the dramatic characters rather than the generality of the audience, are to be found in Old Comedy: an absence of social control, behaviour contrary to established cultural norms, sexual and scatological elements, burlesque of rituals, people in authority and foreigners, and an appearance of disorder and chaos. It is generally the case that the performers, in a more or less structured way, interact with the 'audience' in various

[15] For what follows, cf. Apte 1985: 151–76; see now Halliwell 1991.   [16] Ibid. 155.

types of abnormal behaviour, one of whose functions is, as I would claim it is in the case of Aristophanes, not the expression of personal feelings (though this may happen) but the reversal of normal life which the ritual is designed to create, the better to re-establish that normality afterwards. In Attic comedy, the interaction between the performers and the audience is restricted by the conventions of the theatre: the suspension of control takes place on a specially privileged stage rather than in a more unstructured manner as at, say, Carnival, but the effect is similar.[17] This mockery of the normal ways of city life, the cross-cultural evidence suggests, can thus be stimulated more by the conventions of particular rituals than by a genuine desire to tell the people they are going wrong. A brief consideration of Apte's categories will make this point clearer.

'Contrary behaviour' tends to be manifested in two main ways: transvestism and sexual inversion, and status inversion. In Aristophanes, transvestism is usually ridiculed, as is the case either with the effeminate god Dionysus or individual effeminates in the city: sexual behaviour that breaches a social norm for masculine conduct is brought on stage to be publicly mocked. At the same time, the mockery of transvestism may be mitigated by the fact that transvestism is a feature of various rites of passage, so that realisation that the character may be embarked on such a rite prevents one taking the mockery as simply critical of transvestism or effeminacy. Laughter at contrary behaviour is a fundamental feature of Attic comedy, and personal animus need not always be involved. Furthermore, cross-dressing by the male actors lies at the heart of Attic drama, where all actors were men.

Apte's account of the use of status reversal is also familiar: 'Individuals with status often become the butt of caricature, pantomime, parody, and burlesque and are ridiculed especially if they have overused their authority and power. Such spoofs are often carried out by people with low social status and without authority and power.'[18] If comedy represents a period of licence in which politicians may be ridiculed, the choice of target may not be determined by deeply held political convictions but by the comic mileage that may be extracted from a particular character: did all comic poets who made hay with Pericles sincerely see him as bad for the city?

---

[17] Cf. Goldhill 1991: 167–88, who argues against the uncritical application of Bakhtinian categories to Athenian comedy.   [18] 1985: 157.

Cleon's personal characteristics, if for these we may trust Aristophanes and Thucydides (who are hardly attempting to produce
balanced accounts), may have accounted for his popularity with the
comedians as a good butt. Again, Aristophanes regularly represents
the comic poet and the comic hero as people of ordinary or even
rather low status. This may be because he wanted to identify with
the common man, but it may also, as it is elsewhere, be a traditional
feature of such humorous performances that those not normally
prominent in society are assigned a role at the special periods in
which this kind of humour is displayed.[19] Ordinary farmers and
women are thus made the heroes and heroines of the plays, and the
former are often from outlying demes, not necessarily because
Aristophanes was particularly interested in their plight, but perhaps
because this enabled normally marginalised aspects of the socio-
political geography of Attica to occupy the foreground for the period
of the comedies, in which normality is reversed and distorted: the
centre is asked to look at itself from the margins, and vice versa.

As was the case in a number of other Greek festivals, often of
Dionysus and Demeter, comedy makes much use of sexual and
scatological language and behaviour. So it is elsewhere: the clowns of
the Pueblo Indians, for instance, will pretend to eat excrement from
people kneeling in prayer.[20] It does not seem that the victims are
chosen for any other reason than that they are engaged in a serious
activity, mockery of which is traditional on certain days.[21] Furthermore, the practice of burlesquing ritual has been found among many
peoples. Clowns may interfere with the holy acts, or the rites are
ridiculed through a parallel burlesqued performance: the *fariseos* of
the Yaqui Indians 'shiver and scrape imaginary filth from their legs
whenever the name of Mary or God is mentioned'.[22] Normally
private activities are publicly displayed at a time formally set apart
for this purpose.

The status of those entrusted with ritual humour obviously
varies greatly. Apte lists as two of the most important determinants
'the type of ritual involved and its significance for participants and

---

[19] This factor was perhaps enhanced in Athens by a deliberate desire to define comedy as
   different from its more august older sibling, tragedy; though cf. Silk 1988 for the unwisdom
   of always so defining comedy against tragedy.   [20] Cf. Apte 1985: 158.
[21] For this type of festival in Christian European societies, cf. e.g. U. P. Burke 1978: 178–204.
[22] Cf. Apte 1985: 159.

for the community at large' and 'the fundamental religious ideology underlying the ritual(s)'. There is too a difference between calendrical rituals and rites of passage: 'it appears that, in rituals of the latter type, humor-generating activities are generally undertaken by relatives or friends of the individuals going through the ritual or by people who are connected with the ceremony itself in some way';[23] whereas in the former, the activities are performed by people professionally or officially endowed with responsibility for the festival, such as ritual clowns. In Athens, we have already seen that the choice of play was made by city officials, and only those capable of composing plays could contribute. Furthermore, the comic playwrights appear to have been men of substance, not simple farmers, so that the dramas and those responsible for their writing and production were not marginal to the city but of its centre: once again I would argue that the concerns of the plays would not necessarily have been the individual concerns of the playwright, but concerns of relevance to the city as a whole, which it was the task of the comic playwright to address, whatever he may have thought privately.

Aristophanic comedy is therefore to be discussed in this book as a public art form, that does not so much lecture or preach at its audience, as offer it ways of looking at itself. Where present-day satire usually concentrates on prominent figures, and the audience enjoys seeing these traduced in various ways without itself being involved directly in the satire, Aristophanes also regularly makes fun of the audience itself. Sometimes this is done directly, by having a character called 'Demos' ('The People') on stage, as in *Knights*, but more often indirectly, by having one or more of the leading figures represent aspects of Athenian self-definition. Thus, in *Wasps*, Philocleon the insane juror confronts those in the audience who had served on juries with a picture of themselves. This is, of course, grotesque and distorted, but calculation of the extent of that distortion is left to the individual jurors: can they honestly say that there is nothing of themselves in Philocleon? The same is true of *Clouds*: are the audience the uneducable Strepsiades in their attitudes to philosophy? At other times again, unflattering pictures of the city and its behaviour act as the background to the heroes' attempts to change the world, as in *Acharnians* and *Birds*, but here the possibility is left

---

[23] Ibid. 162.

open that there may be worse things than the Athenian democracy: the audience must look and compare.

One might say, therefore, that comedy holds up a miraculous mirror to the audience, which does not simply reflect, but refracts and distorts in a kaleidoscopic manner. Comedy was performed under the gaze of the god Dionysus, so it will be instructive finally to compare comedy's mirror with that operated by another aspect of Athenian life connected with Dionysus, vase-painting on vessels to be used at symposia.[24] These vases regularly depict sympotic and other scenes of greater or lesser propriety, involving men, Dionysus and his satyrs. Current research on these vases and cups suggests that the pictures are not mere decoration, but played a central role in the articulation of the meaning of the symposium and in the control of the behaviour at it, and so in the process of thinking about the city and one's place in it. 'Wine is the mirror of the soul',[25] and attitudes to wine and the symposium act as a metaphor for political attitudes. Frontisi-Ducroux describes the process with the vases as follows:[26]

> when the vase, even as it presents itself to be looked at – offering the banqueter selected representations of the city, its activities, and its models – begins to look back at the drinker, to fix his eyes with its own, the serene relationship of the spectator to the image becomes troubled, and the one-way relation of subject to object is inverted. It is especially in the sphere of Dionysus that this confusion takes place – indeed, this is the function of the god.

Thus, as I have suggested, Attic comedy, which addresses itself to the ordinary spectator and his ways, could not be regarded by the Athenians simply as amusement at others' expense: it is there to trouble their complacency by the implication that what they are laughing at may be themselves.

The drinking-cups frequently display the face of Dionysus, often as a mask and sometimes flanked by two enormous eyes, looking straight into the eyes of the drinker, posing to him questions about his behaviour and reminding him of the power for possession

---

[24] For what follows, cf. Bérard et al. 1989 (esp. Frontisi-Ducroux 1989); Lissarrague 1990. I hope to treat this subject at greater length elsewhere.

[25] A. fr. 393; cf. Alc. 333; Theognis 499f. Compare the depiction of an obscenely riotous satyr or a drunken man in the tondo of a cup, so that the drinker sees this figure as it were in a mirror.   [26] 1989: 151.

and disruption that the god deploys.[27] Other vases use the face of a satyr:[28]

> ... the hilarity of the companions of Dionysus certainly express[es] the liberating madness that imposes itself on whoever receives the god and throws into question, with him, the categories of the organized world, breaking down the barriers separating animal from man, man from god, obliterating social roles, sex, and age. But when a bestial and hairy face with horse's ears turns toward the spectator and with its widened eyes looks deeply into his own, the confrontation can only be disquieting. The drinker who finds a necessary experience of alterity in the wine also discovers in himself his least divine part, sees the awakening of the animality nestled in the heart of the civilised. The satyr ... presents man with the image of his hidden desires, of the savagery he holds in check, the exhibition of a truth quite different from his official identity.

Does Aristophanic comedy not work in the same way? The plays offer a Dionysiac liberation by their abolishing of many of the restraints normally in force in Athens, making lavish use of obscenity, pillorying the prominent, bringing on-stage things and people normally repressed; a release of pent-up and unexpressed emotions is achieved comparable to that produced by the wine drunk at the festival. At the same time, however, though in comedy the figures on stage are not actually satyrs, their grotesque dress, phalli and masks render them similarly only half-human.[29] They also portray the wilder and more disorganised sides of the spectators, offering them the picture of men who behave in ways that are not only liberating but also disruptive and not in the interests of the city as a whole. These figures may be the violent choruses of *Acharnians*, sure of the correctness of their views, or the Wasps, who, it is implied, are the mere foolish dupes of the demagogues; they may be women with an admirable programme for the city. The comic heroes can contrive to make peace-treaties against the wishes of the rest of the city, or to overthrow the divine order, as does Peisetaerus in *Birds*, in a display of autocracy that has frightening consequences for a city that values its democracy. Like the vases, therefore, and indeed tragedy with its superhuman heroes, the plays offer a vision of release from constraints, but also show where it can lead if

---

[27] Compare perhaps the King's Eye in *Acharnians* and the suggestions he is used to make?

[28] Frontisi-Ducroux 1989: 156.

[29] On the functions and meanings of satyrs see Seaford 1984: 1–48.

unchecked; like wine, they offer the possibility of altered perception, of seeing oneself in another guise, as beast, woman, godlike
hero, foolish old man, sophist etc. Summing up her discussion of the
use of the full-frontal mask for sympotic satyrs, gorgons and flute-
players, Frontisi-Ducroux writes as follows:[30]

> through masks whose stares force the drinker to face supernatural
> powers, and human faces in which he sees reflected various
> possible versions of himself, the frontal representation of the vases
> suggests a visual exploration of the frontiers of the human con-
> dition, of the maximum difference of the divine, of bestiality or of
> the beyond, of certain forms of an otherness internal to humanity.

So too comedy has its masks, flutes, half-human beings and the wine
of the festival, whose Dionysiac combination serves to shake the
viewer out of his normal condition, in order to let him see himself as
he does not normally see himself.

Frontisi-Ducroux goes on, emphasising the muteness of the
mask:[31]

> It expresses what it has to say to men in the silence of its glances
> and by resonances radically opposed to articulated language: the
> strange lowing of rhombes in the Dionysiac cult, the satyrs'
> inhuman groans, the piercing yelps of gorgons in mythic tales, and
> always and everywhere, the disturbing sound of the flute, whose
> music, incompatible with the voice and singing, has the function of
> evoking all that cannot be said.

In comedy, the process is made more explicit. Language is now used,
and, at moments of actual address to the members of the audience,
the mask looks full-frontally at the man it is addressing, or at the
whole audience, in passages like the parabasis. Comedy thus puts the
questions implied by the vases more explicitly into words; like the
vases, they are not preaching but probing, demonstrating excesses,
warning perhaps, but leaving the answers to the spectators.

[30] 1989: 163.   [31] Ibid. 163f.

2

Acharnians

The 'Unjust' and 'Just' Cities

Acharnians is traditionally labelled one of Aristophanes' 'peace-plays', in which the poet bemoans the Athenians' addiction to war and entices them with a more alluring picture of the benefits of peace.[1] The war certainly forms the background to the action, in that it is the cause of the difficulties of the countryman in the city (32–6) and of the individual in the Assembly (37–9), but there is a danger of distortion of the play if one talks of war and peace as its 'main' subject. Is it without significance that the prologue, which, as we shall see, regularly announces more or less openly the main ideas of a play, does not mention peace until Dicaeopolis has finished his more general complaints about the paucity of pleasures in Athens and the disorderly conduct of business in the Assembly? Aristophanes no doubt holds back the mention of peace because he does not wish to let the cat of his comic idea out of the play's bag too soon, but the subjects with which Dicaeopolis begins are not therefore to be ignored. By concentrating on this one aspect of the play, however, there is a danger that its other structural concerns will be obscured. A reconsideration of the function of mythological and ritual reference in the play will show that it is in fact dealing with a much greater range of questions of central importance to the city, in particular the relationships between state and individual, between city and deme, and between city and country.[2]

[1] An exception is Forrest 1963, which provoked de Ste Croix 1972: 363–71. That this play has a particular message is argued now by MacDowell 1983 and Foley 1988 (cf. 46 n. 53). On Aristophanes and politics, cf. Gomme 1938; Heath 1987a; Edmunds 1987a; Cartledge 1990: 43–53; Henderson 1990.

[2] This opposition is a popular one in the discussion of comedy; see however Osborne 1985a on

18

To examine what *Acharnians* has to say about these relationships, we shall consider it first in terms of the opposition, suggested
by the pattern of the play itself, between Athens and the new world
of Dicaeopolis. This opposition implies that, as in a simple diptych,
the hybristic disorder of Athens is replaced, in a manner traditional
to comedy, by a paradigmatic world of peace and delight. We shall
then look at how the use of the myth of Telephus and of references to
Athenian festivals introduces substantial modifications to this
picture.

Acharnians displays affinities with the opposition between the
Just and Unjust Cities found in Hesiod's *Works and Days*.[3] In the
former, they 'give straight judgments to visitors and to their own
people', who thus prosper; they have peace not war, famine not
blight, and 'feast on the crops they tend'; 'the womenfolk bear
children that resemble their parents'; they do not sail, 'but the grain-
giving ploughland bears them fruit'. In the Unjust City, 'they occupy
themselves with violence'; a city may suffer because of a bad man;
they have disaster, famine and plague; the women do not give birth;
Zeus destroys their city and ships.

If the contrasted worlds of *Acharnians* are less strictly sundered
than those of Hesiod, the play works with the same ideas. As in
Hesiod's Unjust City, Athens before Dicaeopolis' treaty is a city in
which violence is regular, just treatment hard to come by, visitors
like the Megarian starving, sexuality disordered and political man-
agement in the hands of two classes opposed to the mature citizens
presumed to be the natural masters – the young and the foreign. In
Dicaeopolis' private world, there is peace and plenty; visitors are, if
not exactly given 'straight judgments', at least welcomed and to
some extent fed, family life is untroubled and sexuality appears more
'normal'.

Similarities in the structuring of the start of the drama and of
the part after the parabasis suggest that a comparison is to be made
between the types of society found in the two halves. Each part

the problems of its use in the discussion of Attica; for instance, 'Town and country fail to be
important blocks either to act in or think with precisely because locality is made so
important . . . It remains one of the paradoxes of this study that Athens, thought of as a mass
democracy and one with a strong city base, should emerge as a polis with no abiding city'
(188). See further Osborne 1987: 93–112.

[3] *Op.* 225–47, tr. M. L. West; cf. 109–201 for the myth of Ages; for further parallels, M. L.
West 1978: 213.

begins with Dicaeopolis alone, and the marking out of boundaries, of the assembly with the sacrificial pig that creates the sacred space (44),[4] and of Dicaeopolis' agora through the erection of the boundary-markers (719). There are then two scenes with foreigners speaking in foreign accents, involving Pseudartabas and the Odomantes, and the Megarian and the Boeotian. In each case, there is an address to people or things long desired but not seen for six years, to Phales (263ff.) and to the Copaic eel (885ff.). The pig is repeated from the purification of the Assembly in the sale of the Megarian's daughters as piglets, and these girls are a reflection of Dicaeopolis' daughter at the Rural Dionysia. Garlic also features, in the theft by the Odomantes and the price of the Megarian's children. These repetitions not only emphasise the fact that a new start is being made, but also aid comparison of the worlds of the two parts.

The most notable characteristic of Athens at the start of the play is violence and violent reaction to anything that is disapproved of.[5] The tone is set by Dicaeopolis in his opening words, where two out of three of the first eighteen lines contain one or more words expressive of strong emotion, some highly poetic.[6] As soon as the Prytaneis and Assemblymen arrive, finally driven in by the dye-stained cord, they begin fighting for the front seats (40–2), and Amphitheus' attempt to get expenses for his peace-mission provokes his summary expulsion by the Scythian Archers. Dicaeopolis' protest at this is curtly disallowed (59, 64). Sensible communication is scarcely possible because the basic conventions of Assembly debate are not being observed – an orator lists the orderly assembly of Boule and Ecclesia among the benefits of a law-abiding society,[7] – and the Prytaneis apparently do not even wait for the Assembly to express its displeasure at what Amphitheus is saying before ejecting him, as appears to have been the custom.[8] When Theorus leads in the band of Odomantean mercenaries, Dicaeopolis' aspersions on their prowess cause them to dispossess him of his garlic (163f.). The Acharnians who pursue Amphitheus on his return from Sparta and attack

---

[4] *Eccl.* 128 and Aeschin. 1.23 with their scholia; Jacoby on Istrus, *FGH* 334 F 16 (3b Suppl. 1.639f.); R. C. T. Parker 1983: 21.   [5] Bowie 1982a: 32–7.

[6] See however Dover 1987: 224–37 for the problems of the idea of 'poetic' words in this passage; on such words in Greek, Bowie 1981: 139–78, and 1979: 123–161 for a perhaps overbold attempt to use the concept in criticism. For the strength of Athenian feeling at enforced evacuation from their demes, cf. Thuc. 2.16.2.   [7] [Dem.] 25.20.

[8] Pl. *Prot.* 319C.

Dicaeopolis are a fearsome lot: 'tough old men, hard as holm-oak, stout Marathon-fighters, with hearts of maple' (180f.); they need but one sniff of Amphitheus' *spondai* ('treaty-wine') before they give chase (179). When they discover Dicaeopolis celebrating his Rural Dionysia, their reaction is to stone first and ask questions afterwards (292ff.). Such a proposal to stone him is contrary to Athenian law: 'there is no indication that stoning was ever a legal punishment in Athens. The instances of community stoning mentioned can only be classified as lynching.'[9] To get them to listen, Dicaeopolis is himself forced threaten the life of their kinsman, the coal-scuttle (325ff.), thus paying them in their own coin, and they lend him their ears only on condition that a chopping-block is conveniently to hand (355ff.).[10]

The significance of these violent scenes involving the Chorus can be summed up in their attitude to Amphitheus. It is ironic that men who claim once to have kept up with Phayllus, an Olympic athlete (211–14), should use the word *spondophoros* (216) of one to whom they are offering violence. *Spondophoros* was the official term for those who announced through the cities the truce declared during such festivals as the Eleusinian Mysteries[11] or Olympic games:[12] 'During this truce there was to be peace throughout the land, no one was permitted to bear arms within the sacred territory, and all competitors, embassies, and spectators travelling to Olympia were regarded as under the protection of Zeus and sacrosanct.'[13] Breaking this truce could be costly, even to the Spartans.[14] This point is emphasised by the fact that Amphitheus is closely associated with the Eleusinian Mysteries through his genealogical links with Demeter, the goddess of the Mysteries, and two heroes who played an important role in Eleusinian myth and cult: Triptolemus, the Attic hero who introduced to men the art of agriculture given him by Demeter,[15] and Celeus, king of Eleusis, who entertained the goddess

---

[9] Bonner & Smith 1930: II 277 quote Plut. *Sol.* 12, schol. *Knights* 447 (Cylon), and Hdt. 9.5, Dem. 18.204 (Lycidas and wife stoned spontaneously after proposing submission to the Persians); cf. Barkan 1935.

[10] *Akouein* is densely used: 292–306, 5 times; 322–4, 4 times; 335–7, twice. Cf. 370ff.

[11] Aeschin. 2.133; *SIG*³ 1019.6.

[12] Pi. *Is.* 2.23 with schol.; also Thuc. 5.49.1. *Spondophoros/-ein* seems to be a technical term at this time, though used more generally later.   [13] Gardiner 1910: 43; cf. 141f., 201f.

[14] Thuc. 5.49–50.4 (420).

[15] Aristophanes' genealogy for Triptolemus is unparalleled, cf. Simon 1960; Richardson 1974: 194–6; Kearns 1989: 201.

when she was searching for Persephone (47–54).[16] The Acharnians'
attacks on a man whose attributes recall the great pan-Hellenic
festivals when a sacred truce stopped warfare and Athens' own
Eleusinian festival thus emblematise the disordered state that Athens
is in.

In his long *apologia pro pace sua*, Dicaeopolis lays his emphasis
on the extreme reactions of the Athenians in the war. Any small item
of goods would be declared Megarian and sold forthwith (515ff.),
and an exchange of prostitute-stealing, which cost Aspasia two girls,
provoked Pericles into a cosmic act of revenge, whereas the Megarians had merely repaid one theft with another:[17] 'then in his rage
Olympian Pericles flashed lightning, thundered, stirred up Greece,
made laws that were dashed off like drinking-songs' (523ff.; cf. 530–
2). A bravura coda of nine lines of genitives vividly depicts the city-
wide mobilisation that the slightest instance of Spartan sanctions-
breaking would bring (546–54). It is not surprising, therefore, that
the Chorus resort to the standard Athenian reaction in calling out the
belligerent Lamachus, gorgon and all (557ff.), to have Dicaeopolis
suppressed and beaten. He too, after a violent reaction and a
characteristic refusal to listen to a beggar (593), exits unrepentantly
vowing to maintain hostilities against the Peloponnesians for ever
(620–2). That only half of the Acharnians support this course of
action is a cause for hope for the future.

The disturbed nature of Athenian politics is further exemplified by the influence barbarians have over the demos. This has been
prefigured by Amphitheus' expulsion from the Assembly by the
Scythian Archers, foreign troops who policed the Assembly.[18] At
least this is at the behest of the Athenian Herald; later matters get
worse. First, there is the transparently named Pseudartabas, whose
'Persian' is clear enough in 104 to reveal his villainy,[19] but who is still
invited into the Prytaneum, despite the fact that Dicaeopolis exposes
the embassy as a surreal charade, composed of Athenian effeminates
disguised as eunuchs (110ff.). The presence of this barbarian mon-

[16] Richardson 1974: 177–9.

[17] Whether or not this passage parodies the start of Herodotus' *Histories*, the historian's
doubts about the wisdom of using such pretexts for war are, in the context of this play,
notable (cf. 1.4.2).

[18] This dominance by outsiders is reflected in Dicaeopolis' claim that the city's problems are
not the fault of all the citizens, but of the activities of certain 'foreign devils' (518).

[19] Brixhe 1988.

ster, with his single eye (94–7) like the Cyclopes or Arimaspi at the ends of the world,[20] holding sway in the Assembly and Prytaneum, the centre of Athenian political life,[21] and persuading the Athenians to accept his arrant nonsense, shows how much the world has been turned upside-down: bushy-bearded men parading as eunuchs add to the confusion (115–21). The Odomantes go similarly unchecked when they steal Dicaeopolis' garlic, despite being foreigners (168), and, unlike the Greeks, circumcised, as is twice pointed out (158, 161).[22] The Prytaneis take no notice of this barbarian usurpation of influence over Athenian citizens (55, 167), and well might Dicaeopolis appeal in despair to the ancient name of the city, *Kranaa* (75). It has come to the point where the distinction between Athenians and barbarians, so firmly established in Athenian law, is breaking down, as is shown by the grant of citizenship to the son of Sitacles, king of the Thracian Odrysi; this son now wants to 'eat sausages at the Apaturia', that is, to become fully Athenian through initiation at the festival where the sons of citizens were registered as members of their phratries (145–7).[23]

Further evidence for Athens' debased condition is to be found in the relations between the old and the young. Traditionally in Greek society, the young did the fighting whilst the old deliberated on policy at home and abroad: the Greek word *presbeus* means both 'old man' and 'ambassador'. In *Acharnians* this position has been reversed. While the younger generation suffer the luxurious hardships of embassies, Dicaeopolis puts his life at risk as a soldier (68–72):[24]

> *Ambassador.* And then we suffered as we crossed the Caystrian plains under canopies, lying luxuriously in carriages – it nearly killed us.
> *Dic.* I was in fine fettle then, as I lay in the rubbish by the rampart!

He makes the same point to Lamachus at 614–17, and gives as his reason for making peace that 'I saw grey-beards in the ranks, but young men like you shirking service' (600f.). It was also traditional in

[20] Hdt. 3.116; Strabo 1.21; Plin. *NH* 7.9f; A. Gell. 9.4.6.   [21] Miller 1978.

[22] Circumcision was not a Greek practice. Herodotus disapproves of it on aesthetic grounds (2.37.2; cf. *Wealth* 267) and lists its practitioners (2.104.2–4; no Thracians, and Thracians are not depicted as circumcised on Greek vases (Dover 1978: 129 n. 10)).

[23] The phratries were the older divisions of the Athenian citizenry which were much more exclusive than the newer demes: 'they show an obsession with membership problems' (Osborne 1985a: 73).   [24] The same complaint in Andoc. 4.22.

Greece for children to look after their parents: *sophrosune, eutaxia,*
and *aischune* ('proper and orderly conduct' and 'respect') on the part
of the young towards their parents and elders are the three things
which one author says maintain the safety of the city.[25] But in Athens
now the young hound the old through the courts with the confusing
rhetorical subtleties of the Sophists (676–91), in a way that reminds
one of Dicaeopolis' rough treatment in the courts at Cleon's hands
(371ff.). Service at Marathon counts for nothing (692–702) and it is
pathetic to see a man like Thucydides, son of Melesias, beset by one
such as Euathlus, who unites in himself the two groups usurping
power in the state: he is both young and a Scythian bowman
(703–12).[26]

The faults of the young do not stop here: they are also addicted
to unnatural sexual practices.[27] The two eunuchs are the perverts
Cleisthenes and Straton (117–22), and Dicaeopolis hints at similar
preferences in the soldiery (604) and the young prosecutors (716).
We come full circle in our description when we find sex and violence
linked in Cleon, whose prosecution of Dicaeopolis is presented in
terms of homosexual rape (379–82), in the ithyphallically dangerous
Odomantes (158ff.) and in the 'well-armed' Lamachus (592).[28]

Against this background of usurpation by the young and
foreign, suppression of the individual, and sexual violence, the
conventions of comedy naturally lead one to suppose that Dicaeopolis will produce a state of affairs that approximates more closely to
the Just City of Hesiod: this is, after all, what his name promises,[29]
and a plea for peace seems entirely natural. There are indeed obvious
beneficial changes in Dicaeopolis' new world, in just those areas
where Athens was most deficient. In the first part of the play we saw
the Athenian assembly easily bamboozled by the 'foreign words'
(634) of Pseudartabas, and the second part opens with another
foreigner speaking his own dialect, and bent on deception (736–9). In

---

[25] [Dem.] 25.24. Maltreatment of parents brought with it loss of citizen rights: cf. e.g. X. *Mem.*
2.2.1–14; Pl. *Legg.* 881D; D. L. 1.55 (a law of Solon); cf. Lacey 1968: 116f. and Rhodes 1981:
629.   [26] Euathlus' 'foreignness' spans three generations (*Wasps* 1221 with schol.).

[27] Henderson 1975: 57–62.   [28] Dover 1978: 204.

[29] Edmunds 1980: 1 n. 2 translates 'he of the Just City' (cf. Eupolis, Neopolis, Agathopolis), but
the name has perhaps a slightly more active sense: cf. Jebb on S. *Ant.* 370f. adducing Pi. *Ol.*
2.8 *orthopolis* of Theron 'raising up the city'. Given the ambivalent nature of Dicaeopolis and
his relationship with the city, the ambiguity in his name is at least appropriate. E. L. Bowie
1989 suggests Dicaeopolis hides Eupolis.

his case, however, and in that of the similarly foreign-speaking Boeotian who follows him, the tables are turned, as Dicaeopolis gets much the better of the bargain, acquiring the Megarian's two daughters for a string of garlic and a *choinix* of salt and the Boeotian's game for a sycophant trussed up as a pot: Megara pays once again for the two girls stolen from Aspasia.[30] On any rational calculation, neither foreigner gets a fair return for his wares, though the Megarian would still be happy to sell his wife and mother for the same price (816f.) and counts himself fortunate to have stolen a single fig: in comparison with the conditions supposedly caused by the earlier Athenian treatment of the Megarians,[31] Dicaeopolis' new trading arrangements are at least something of an improvement. Furthermore, they represent a return to the barter system of the countryside rather than the monetary economy that Dicaeopolis complained of in the city (32ff.).[32]

Both the Megarian and the Boeotian are beset by sycophants reminiscent of the over-zealous and litigious young men of the parabasis, but now these are rapidly worsted by Dicaeopolis: in his new world there is no place for the law-courts. He has already forbidden entry to any sycophant (725) and the Chorus celebrate his freedom from them, from Ctesias and from charges brought by Hyperbolus (839, 846f.). The threats posed earlier by Cleon and the perverted sons of Cleinias have faded away, so that Lamachus' catoptromantic warning of 1128f., that he sees an old man on a charge of desertion, is whistling in the dark: in Dicaeopolis' new world, old men will no longer serve where the young should, a point graphically made in the closing scenes.

Violence, so prevalent earlier, is excluded too, and order produced, represented in part by the dominance of the symposium over war. Dicaeopolis' insubordinate treatment of Lamachus' shield and helmet crest just before the parabasis prefigures this exclusion: the crest becomes a feather to cause vomiting into the shield which

---

[30] The figs, pigs, garlic and salt of this scene are reminiscent of the seizure of these things as 'Megarian' in the disagreeable world of Athens (520f.).

[31] It does not matter for our purposes what the precise historical cause was: on this topic see de Ste Croix 1972: 225–89, 381–400.

[32] 'Archaeology knows no markets in the whole territory of Athens outside Athens itself, the port of the Peiraieus, and Sounion. That there were other places where regular exchange was carried on is not unlikely, but it is significant that they have remained unknown' (Osborne 1987: 108).

serves as a bowl, and Lamachus is asked to hold his head in an image familiar from vases (585f.).[33] The world of pleasure's dominance over the world of war is confirmed when, at 979–87, the Chorus sing a song complementary to this scene, telling how they will in future refuse entry to their symposia to War, who used to turn them into drunken brawls, and towards the end, 'young' Lamachus goes off to a wounding in a wintry battle, while a triumphant Dicaeopolis prepares for a symposiastic feast. Vines, whose destruction in the war has been frequently mourned,[34] are now symbolically replanted (995–9). There are also echoes of the commonplaces of foundation-mythology's depiction of the creation of order out of chaos: Athens is in turmoil, but a conflict with the stone-throwing men of violence leads to boundary-markers for the agora and peaceful relations between men. The Chorus are never referred to as 'Acharnians' after the parabasis.

Furthermore, Henderson has argued that the disordered sexuality of Athens is replaced by one that would have been closer to the ideology of Athenian males.[35] Dicaeopolis hopes for a happy marriage for his daughter (253–6), sings lyrically of catching a pretty slave-girl stealing (271–6), looks forward to the maturing of the 'piglets' he has bought (781ff.) and gives some of his treaty-wine to the bride so that she may enjoy 'home comforts' even in wartime (1048ff.). The Chorus celebrate the absence of the perverts Prepis and Cleonymus (843f.), and of the adulterer Cratinus (849), and try to convince Diallage that they are not too old to give her a good time (989–99). The play ends with Dicaeopolis in the arms of the slave-girls, who escort him off to bed.

Dicaeopolis' first act on concluding his peace is to celebrate the Rural Dionysia,[36] which he can finally hold after a six-year hiatus, during which many in the audience will have been prevented from celebrating this festival as usual in their own demes (266). Dicaeopolis issues the call for holy silence and his daughter, as *kanephoros*, bears the basket with the sacrificial instruments in and pours the soup over the sacred cake; the slave Xanthias positions correctly the phallus which formed a central part of the procession (243, 259f.).

---

[33] Theopompus fr. 41 lists sympotic items, 'sponge, bowl, feather, *copious* drinking-cup'.

[34] 183, 232, 512.   [35] 1975: 57–62.

[36] Deubner 1932: 134–8; Simon 1983: 101–4; Whitehead 1986: 212–22, esp. 222; Pickard-Cambridge 1988: 42–56. *Ach.* is our main evidence; cf. Plut. *Mor.* 527D.

Dicaeopolis remarks how fine everything is, and tells his daughter to bear her basket 'attractively, as an attractive girl'; thieving by the bystanders is to be avoided. He tells his wife to watch from the roof as he himself sings the 'phallic song' in honour of Dionysus. The careful attention he pays to the proper organisation of the festival contrasts with the treatment of the 'Eleusinian' Amphitheus and the behaviour of the Acharnians who are in danger of smashing the pots used in the rite (284). The peaceful, religiously correct carrying of the erect phallus in the procession contrasts with its disordered and violent deployment by the likes of Cleon and the Odomantes.

As will be obvious, this account of the play has been created by the wholesale omission of anything that contradicts it, that is, much of the second half of the play. That Athens as depicted in the first half of the play needs peace is undeniable, and there are strong rhetorical pressures encouraging the idea that Dicaeopolis' peace is a good solution to the problems. Matters are not, however, so simple. What Dicaeopolis does is, I shall argue, highly ambiguous. The simple mythical opposition between the Just and Unjust Cities can be deconstructed first through the figure whose rags Dicaeopolis uses to win the sympathy of listeners to his discourse on war and peace, and then by other considerations in which reference to ritual plays a central role.

Telephus

Dicaeopolis turns to Euripides for a costume beggarly enough to create sympathy for his cause (383f.) and to dupe the Chorus (440–4): comedy turns to tragedy to make its 'serious' points. The rags of Telephus fit the bill best, and the costume that trod the boards thirteen years before steps forth again. Despite the existence of a number of papyrus fragments and ancient quotations, not least in *Acharnians* and *Thesmophoriazusae*, of fragments of Latin versions and summaries in the mythographers, it is not yet possible to give a certain account of the *Telephus* of Euripides, but the outline of the story is roughly as follows.[37] Mistaking it for Troy, the Greeks attacked Telephus' kingdom of Mysia and he was wounded by Achilles as he tried to defend it. When the wound failed to heal, a consultation of the oracle produced the reply 'the wounder will

[37] Handley & Rea 1957; Rau 1967: 19–42; Heath 1987b; Foley 1988.

heal', so that Telephus, in disguise as a beggar, went to Argos to seek healing from Achilles. While there he made a speech defending the Trojans and (in another?) himself, at one point perhaps saying that he would not remain silent even if threatened with an axe, which seems to be the source of Dicaeopolis' offer to speak with his head on the block. Odysseus announced the presence of a spy and Telephus was forced to seize the child Orestes in order to save himself, as Dicaeopolis seizes the Acharnians' coal-basket (325ff.). Somehow it was revealed that Telephus could help the Greeks to reach Troy. Achilles entered in haste and expressed anger at having to serve under a foreigner; he was however placated and, after initial perplexity that medical skill should be required of him, cured Telephus with rust from the spear that had wounded him.

As a device for generating sympathy, Telephus is well chosen. A king reduced to pain and beggary for defending his homeland, he is further threatened by his willingness to give a balanced view of the situation, despite being of great potential benefit to his opponents. He is thus emblematic of other such people throughout the play. Amphitheus tried to make peace for the city but was ejected;[38] Dicaeopolis tried to do the same, but despite his eloquent defence, he too was not listened to; Thucydides and the Marathonomachae were not rewarded for their pains. Aristophanes himself, though speaking 'justly' (645), was prosecuted by Cleon, as he says in a passage in the parabasis that appears to come from the *Telephus* itself (659–64).[39] As Edmunds says,[40] 'the nobleman disguised as beggar is the fitting image of comedy. Although comedy comes before the people with a just claim and with a didactic mission, it can only do so in disguise.'

The identification of Aristophanes and Telephus has been developed by Foley to show how it provides Aristophanes 'with opportunities to create multiple roles, audiences, and disguises, as well as to play off one style of dramaturgy against another'; Dicaeopolis becomes a complex figure 'simultaneously playing many incompatible roles: beggar man, nobleman, and comic hero, Greek and foreigner'.[41] In other words, however close the identification of playwright and hero in this play, the multi-layered nature of the figure of 'Dicaeopolis' means that his voice is fragmented into a number of different characters, which is another reason why it is a

---

[38] Amphitheus' ancestor Triptolemus (48, 55) suffered in a similar way (Hygin. *Fab.* 147).
[39] Fr. 918.   [40] 1980: 12.   [41] 1988: 40.

dangerous simplification to use the similarities between Aristophanes and Dicaeopolis to suggest that the hero 'speaks for' the poet.[42]

One of the positive roles that Telephus allows Dicaeopolis to play is that of providing a justification not only of a comic character making an unpopular speech but also of a comic poet presuming to lecture the city.[43]

> Aristophanes uses Euripides's tragedy first to defend comedy's social and political criticism (even during a war). By linking his comedy and Euripidean tragedy ... he claims for it the moral authority, literary prestige, and latitude that audiences have always given to more pretentious genres ... [Acharnians] manipulates tragedy to make the stronger claim that a comedy can offer justice to its discerning audience while allowing its outrageous hero openly to advocate and pursue treason ... The comic injustice of the hero ... reinforces the justice of comedy – above all, Aristophanes's exposure throughout the play of the dangerous effects of high style (political and tragic) rhetoric on a gullible and volatile audience.

All of this is true, but it should not lead us to neglect the negative side of Dicaeopolis and his private peace. The figure of Telephus also articulates these less agreeable aspects of Dicaeopolis. We have already noted that Telephus brought the Greeks victory in war, by showing them the way to Troy in return for the curing of his wound. A fragment of the exchange over this appears to be preserved in a papyrus, of which Lobel suggests the following interpretation: 'someone asks Telephus "What prevents you sailing with us to Troy?" He answers "Loyalty to my father-in-law, Priam."'[44] This scruple is obviously overcome in the end because, to effect his cure, Telephus is prepared to betray his wife's homeland; so too Dicaeopolis heals the pains described in the prologue by abandoning his city. Each thus puts himself before a community to which he might be felt to have strong obligations. At the end of the tragedy, the hero is recognised as a fellow-Greek and becomes their guide against his own relations, but the ending of the comedy is even more ambiguous: it is possible to take Dicaeopolis as a paradigm for peacemak-

---

[42] On 'fragmentation of the voice' in this passage, see Goldhill 1991: 167–201. On Aristophanes/Dicaeopolis, see the contrasting views of de Ste Croix 1972: 363 and Bowie 1982a: 29–32.   [43] Foley 1988: esp. 43–7 (quotations from 43, 46).

[44] P. Oxy. 2460 fr. 10.2f.

ing, but, as we shall see, despite the invitation to dine from the priest of Dionysus (1085–94), his refusal to share his good fortune, which is pursued to the end of the play, suggests a continued separation between Dicaeopolis and the rest of the city and casts doubt on his role as guide.

In the earlier part of the play, Telephus is used to generate sympathy for Dicaeopolis, but in many recent discussions of the comedy, it has been forgotten that reference to Euripides' play does not cease with the parabasis. When, at the end, the wounded Lamachus is borne on stage, the scene not only has obviously tragic affinities, but also relates closely to *Telephus*. The servant quotes from it in 1188, describing Lamachus as 'driving off the robbers and scattering them with his spear'.[45] As van Leeuwen says, this rather suggests that 'It is not, as in the earlier part of the play, Dicaeopolis who is now playing the part of Telephus, but Lamachus.'[46] This is supported by another fact, also noted by van Leeuwen, that Telephus and Lamachus are wounded in defence of their countries in similar ways. There appear to be two versions of Lamachus' misfortune in the comedy: according to the Servant (1178), 'he was wounded by a vine-prop as he leapt over a ditch'; but according to Lamachus (1194; cf. 1226), 'I die struck down by an enemy spear.' One might be tempted to explain this apparent discrepancy by seeing Lamachus' version as an attempt to preserve his dignity, were it not for the evidence about Telephus. According to a commentator on the *Iliad*, 'as he ran, he was entangled in a branch of a vine and wounded in the thigh; Dionysus was angry with him, because he had deprived him of honours.'[47] Lamachus too is the victim, not of a vine, but of a vine-prop, and also of an enemy's spear. There is an echo too of Dionysus' displeasure: in *Acharnians* the vines suffer at the hands of war and warriors (183 etc.), so they may, in wounding Lamachus, who stands in the play for war,[48] be said to have had their revenge on the warmongers.[49]

---

[45] Fr. 705a.

[46] Denied without discussion by Rau 1967: 139 n. 5, now accepted by Foley 1988: 39.

[47] Schol. *Il.* 1.59 (Dind.). Cf. *Ep. Adesp.* 3.1f. (*CA* 76); Lycophr. 200–15 with scholia; Dict. Cret. 2.3. Starkie 1909: 229 notes that 'by a pathetic coincidence the real death-scene of Lamachus resembled this; cp. Thuc. vi.101'.   [48] Cf. 269f., 566ff. and his name.

[49] It is worth noting that the Acharnians have Dionysus as ancestor through Oeneus, eponymous hero of their tribe Oeneis: cf. [Dem.] 60.30.

When the wounded Lamachus comes on, we have a reversal of the scene before the parabasis, in which a 'sick' Dicaeopolis confronted Lamachus with his gorgon and feather; gorgon and feather figure prominently once again, but now Lamachus is ailing and comes to Dicaeopolis for healing.[50] The scene is thus also a repetition of the *Telephus*, where the hero asks a cure of Achilles, who had earlier reacted to him with the same anger that Lamachus expressed to Dicaeopolis in disguise. In the tragedy, Achilles is slow to heal Telephus, but only because he claimed no knowledge of medicine;[51] Dicaeopolis by contrast shows no inclination at all to heal Lamachus; when he cries to Apollo Paean, Dicaeopolis dismisses him with the joke that it is not the Paeonia festival (1212f.), and Lamachus has to ask to be taken to another doctor (1222f.). This refusal is all the more shocking in the light of the *Telephus*. 'The wounder will heal': rust from the spear that wounded him cures Telephus; is not 'treaty-wine' the comparable cure for a wound from a vine-prop?

This reading of the play can throw some light on the problematic scene with Dercetes the farmer.[52] Like Lamachus he has suffered from a Boeotian raid (1023; cf. 1077) and finds himself in distress before Dicaeopolis. His request for some of the wine meets with the same reply as Achilles initially gave to Telephus, but it is expressed in a more dismissive tone:[53] 'I don't happen to be a Health Service doctor, you know' (1030). He too is packed off to Pittalus to whom Lamachus will turn. This scene is thus a precursor and doublet of the later one, repeating its message, and the two of them firmly establish the change that has come over Dicaeopolis: he is perfectly happy to rely on Euripides' help and to exploit the possibilities for sympathy that reside in the mythical tragic role of Telephus, but when it has served its purpose he as happily drops the mask.[54] When therefore Dicaeopolis doffs the rags during the parabasis, this is not merely

[50] The text of 1180ff. is problematic, but the dramatic roles given to the gorgon and feather in each case clearly link the two passages (note that 1181 almost = 574, and *kompolakuthos* in 1182 would pick up 589; but cf. Sommerstein 1980a: 212).

[51] Hygin. *Fab.* 101.3; cf. *P. Oxy.* 2460 fr. 13 with Handley & Rea 1957: 39.

[52] MacDowell 1983 and L. P. E. Parker 1983.

[53] For the public doctors, see Hdt. 3.131; X. *Mem.* 4.2.5; Pl. *Grg.* 514D–E.

[54] If Dercetes may be viewed as in some ways a sympathetic figure, it would demonstrate the dangers inherent in trying to posit actual historical events discreditable to a character behind passages whose meaning is not clear, as is done for Dercetes by MacDowell 1983: 159f.

done for practical reasons, but is also symbolic of his abandonment of that persona, which another will take on. His private treaty frees him from the constraints both of traditional politics and of traditional drama.

Another view of Dicaeopolis

The ambiguity inherent in the use of the myth of Telephus suggests the possibility of a revaluation of Dicaeopolis' activities. In the earlier section, we were essentially considering them from the point of view of the individual, Dicaeopolis; if we now change our viewpoint and look at them more from the perspective of the polis, they take on a rather different moral hue.

Dicaeopolis' first act after the parabasis is to set up the boundary-markers for his private market and announce the assumption of their powers by the officers elected by lot (719–24). These actions give graphic expression to the separation that now exists between himself and the rest of the *polis*: his market is instituted in a way that reminds one of the Athenian agora, but permission to trade (so long as it is with him) is given only to Athens' enemies from the Peloponnese, Megara and Boeotia, but not to the Athenian general Lamachus (719–22), and later he will mete out the same treatment to the Athenian farmer Dercetes. By excluding the Athenians in this way Dicaeopolis in effect reduces the status of his former fellow-citizens below that of *xenoi*, who were allowed to trade in the agora, on payment of the *xenika* tax;[55] they thus become like the Megarians under the Decrees, forbidden to use Athenian markets, or indeed the *atimoi* who were forbidden even to pass the *perirrhanteria* at the Agora's boundaries.[56] Furthermore, though the setting up in each city of *stelai* containing the texts of peace-treaties was a common practice,[57] it was sufficiently intolerable for an individual to make a separate peace for Plato to recommend the death-penalty for it.[58] From being taken in by the words of *xenoi*, the citizens of Athens have become *xenoi* themselves.

In his dealings with his visitors, Dicaeopolis is no paragon. The Megarian is allowed to trade, but on unfavourable terms. This is

---

[55] *Ach.* 896; Dem. 57.30–4; de Ste Croix 1972: 399.

[56] Aeschin. 3.176; de Ste Croix 1972: 397f.; Hansen 1976: 62.

[57] E.g. Rogers on 727.   [58] *Legg.* 955C; I owe this reference to R. J. Seager.

perhaps excusable, since Dicaeopolis is a peasant, but one might ask what sort of a world it is in which a man has to sell his daughters at all. It is true that enslavement of Greeks by Greeks was not exactly unknown in the fifth century, but Solon had long ago forbidden by law the sale of free children by their father.[59] So is it only twentieth-century squeamishness that wants to presume here at least a measure of negative reaction in some of the audience, especially when the manner of the sale is not altogether edifying? The pun on *choiros*, 'pig' / 'female genitals', is amusingly worked out, especially in the discussion as to whether 'pigs' are sacrificed to Aphrodite (793–6),[60] but the inspection, prodding and debate on the development of girls still five years from puberty (782f.) contrasts somewhat with Dicaeopolis' earthy but homely hopes for his own daughter at his Rural Dionysia (254–6). As if to provoke uncomfortable feelings in the audience, the girls are twice referred to as 'mystic pigs' (747, 764), the pigs with which the initiates first bathed in the sea and then killed as a purificatory sacrifice before going to the Eleusinian Mysteries.[61] The evocation of the Mysteries, a festival in which all Greeks could take part on an equal basis, is ironic in the context of this sale of children in an exclusive market. This reference to Eleusis to characterise an action in a negative manner is thus like the use of *spondophoros* of Amphitheus at the start of the play.

The refusal of the thrushes and eel to Lamachus is, given the state of relations between them, quite comprehensible,[62] but, as we have seen, the Dercetes scene is more worrying. In addition to the questions raised above, one would ask of Dicaeopolis here why he mistreats a countryman, especially when there are significant parallels between Dercetes and Dicaeopolis' helper, Amphitheus. Dercetes has lost his yoke of ploughing-oxen and Amphitheus traced an elaborate genealogy back to the patrons of ploughing and agriculture

---

[59] Plut. *Sol.* 13.4 (= fr. 31a, b Ruschenbusch); Sallares 1991: 209; cf. 151–7 on exposure of infants.

[60] Radermacher 1940; Delcourt 1959: 97. Pigs were not usually sacrificed to Aphrodite, though there were rare exceptions: cf. Frazer on Paus. 2.10.5; Sokolowski 1962: no. 39.23f.; R. C. T. Parker 1983: 30 n. 66.

[61] Schol. *Ach.* 747; *Peace* 374f. (and schol.); *Frogs* 337; Pl. *Rep.* 378A; Plut. *Phoc.* 28.6 etc.; Burkert 1983a: 256–64.

[62] The scene with the Boeotian is less morally problematic than that with the Megarian, though the stopping of the sycophant's mouth (926) and his manhandling are uncomfortably reminiscent of the similar treatment of Amphitheus.

(47–51). Both of these agricultural figures make a reasonable request
of the powers that be, and both are refused: where Dicaeopolis was
earlier the victim of arbitrary justice, he is now handing it out. Here
we can see the other side of the absence of legal activity which we
noted above as an apparent benefit of Dicaeopolis' new world: it
leaves those with a grievance against Dicaeopolis no method of
redress. In Athens, the impartial administration of the law was seen
as a guarantee of freedom from tyranny.[63]

Dicaeopolis does finally share some of his wine with the newly-
weds who send their bridesmaid, but the reason for so doing is
frivolous: 'Come, what are you saying? [She whispers]. What an
amusing request the bride is keen to make of me! She wants me to see
that her husband's cock is a stay-at-home' (1058–60). Amusing he
may find it, but from the city's point of view the war-effort would
not be much advanced if all young men behaved thus. The choice of
the verb *oikourein* is notable: this verb and its cognates are regularly
used of keeping women at home and, when used of men, carry
overtones of cowardice.[64] This scene immediately precedes the First
Messenger's summons to Lamachus to defend the passes against the
Boeotians, which acts as a reminder of the duties of citizens of
military age.[65] The phallus, which earlier stood for violence, now
features as an instrument of private indulgence, just as, when events
are considered from the viewpoint of the community, it had at
Dicaeopolis' Rural Dionysia and will again at the end of the play
(1216f.).

This act of sharing contrasts sharply with Dicaeopolis' treatment of the Chorus, who, since the parabasis, have all come over to
his side and sing his praises. It is to no avail: if they praise his success,
he asks what they will say when they see his thrushes (1008–11), and
he is unmoved when they complain he is killing them with hunger
(1044). Fundamental Greek notions of hospitality are being
ignored.[66] In fact, the language of the Chorus is sufficiently ambi-

63 [A.] *PV* 402–4 (complaint against Zeus's 'private laws'); *Wasps* 1102ff. (pride in the courts);
   Socrates in Pl. *Crito* and *passim* in the orators, e.g. [Dem.] 25.24.
64 Cf. Fraenkel 1950: 369, 770 on A. *Ag.* 809, 1625.
65 The scene where Dicaeopolis and Lamachus contrast their fates in the coming feast/battle
   (1071ff.) also splits up two aspects of Athenian life that were essentially connected:
   membership of the symposium and of the hoplite battle-line were parallel, as is shown by
   vases and cups which link them together: cf. e.g. Lissarrague 1990: 71, 115f.
66 Gernet 1981: 13–47; also Havelock 1978: 150–78; Nagy 1979: 127–41; [Dem.] 25.21 compares
   citizens to 'contributors' who must give to the 'common political feast (*eranos*)'.

guous to convey an implicit criticism in 'he's working on his own
behalf' (1017), 'it doesn't look as though he is going to share it with
anyone' (1038f.), and most strikingly in the choice of the phrase 'he is
thinking big thoughts indeed' (988), which is familiar as a fault in
tragic figures before their fall. When they remark that he has thrown
all the feathers into the street to show that he has dined on game
(989), one is reminded of Theophrastus' 'Man of Petty Ambition',
who puts the garlanded skull of an ox outside his front door as a sign
that he can afford to sacrifice one.[67] In 1150–61, the Chorus condemn
Antimachus to be robbed of a freshly-cooked squid which he has
been looking forward to, because he failed to give them the traditional dinner after a recent performance.[68] One could be forgiven
for thinking that this is an indirect way of making clear their feelings
about Dicaeopolis. The contrast with Trygaeus in *Peace*, who is also
praised by the Chorus and with greater justification, is instructive.[69]

The Anthesteria

We have already noticed the emotional force of Dicaeopolis'
Rural Dionysia as marking the end of the prohibition wrought by the
war on the celebration of that festival in the demes. The choice of this
festival can however also be given a more negative significance. This
was not a *polis* festival, but was celebrated by individual demes
under their demarch:[70] 'It is clear from the inscriptions that the
festivals ... afforded the demes an opportunity to mimic the city,
and to assert their identities as states within the state, by proclama-
tions of crowns for benefactors and a reflection in little of the
institutions of the city'.[71] The celebration of this local festival thus
marks the start of Dicaeopolis' independence of the city and his
separation from his fellow-citizens. The celebration of this Dionysia
by one family is highly anomalous, given that it was a public rite

---

[67] Thphr. *Char.* 25.7 Jebb (= 21.7), whose note should be consulted.

[68] *Peace* 1356f., *Eccl.* 1181; Pl. *Symp.* 173A.

[69] *Peace* 856–67 and the corresponding 910–21; also 1312–15.

[70] Only for the rather grander Rural Dionysia in the Peiraeus did the city choose the demarch:
[Arist.] *Ath. Pol.* 54.8; cf. Rhodes 1981: 256f. on ibid. 21.5 for the demarchs as local officials,
and Whitehead 1986: 121–39. On deme religion, cf. R. C. T. Parker 1987a.

[71] Pickard-Cambridge 1988: 51. Cf. Osborne 1985a: 80 on deme decrees: 'in their unchanging
expressions they reflect both one another and the central decrees, and there is little doubt
that the uniformity of language both annexes for the demes some of the prestige of central
government and limits the initiative of the deme'.

expressing the ideology and unity of the deme as a whole. For one family to arrogate the whole festival to itself (as opposed, say, to always supplying the main officials) was a denial of the nature of the festival and an act excluding all others from the rites. Dicaeopolis in effect moves back not just to his deme, but to a deme that has now become his own private kingdom: the Chorus are not invited in and there is no sign of his fellow demesmen. He is a kind of demarch, but one with sovereign powers somewhat wider than that office normally enjoyed.

The Rural Dionysia was held in the winter month of Poseideon, but by the end of the play we have moved forward two months to Anthesterion and the 'Choes', the second day of the Anthesteria festival, to which attention is repeatedly drawn.[72] Ending the play with this festival sets the seal upon the ambiguities of its protagonist and his actions. The Anthesteria was a festival of ambiguities,[73] in that it combined the celebration of the opening of the jars of new wine with the presence of ghostly figures in the city; it involved the competitive drinking of good quantities of wine with commemoration of the survival of the flood. Choes was an 'ill-omened (*miara*) day' on which doors were daubed with pitch and buckthorn leaves chewed; all temples were closed except that of Dionysus 'in the Marshes'; slaves were allowed a certain freedom and the city was full of *Kares*, foreigners or destructive spirits;[74] business involving oaths was forbidden. It was on this day that, in mythology, Orestes came to king Demophon to ask for purification from the murder of his mother. His arrival posed a problem for the king who wished neither to reject a suppliant nor to pollute the city by inviting him to join the celebrations. The solution to the dilemma was imitated ever after: Orestes was given his own table and wine-jug, and so, to avoid offence, was everyone else. At a trumpet-signal sounded on the orders of the Archon Basileus, there was a competition to see who could empty their wine-crater first.

Given the presence in this myth of the hero Orestes, it is interesting that the Chorus should end the lyrics preceding the arrival of the wounded Lamachus with curses upon Antimachus, expressing the hope that he might at night run into the notorious

---

[72] 961, 1000ff., 1068, 1076, 1086, 1133, 1203, 1211.
[73] Deubner 1932: 93–123; Burkert 1983a: 216–26; and further below on *Peace*.
[74] Burkert 1983a: 226–30.

Athenian mugger who went by the name Orestes,[75] and especially
significant that they refer to this Orestes as 'mad' (1164ff.), since the
mythical Orestes also went mad when pursued by the Furies after he
had killed his mother.[76] Aristophanes seems to be suggesting that
this myth is relevant to the scene on stage. It will be instructive
therefore to compare Dicaeopolis' treatment of Lamachus, who
arrives back during the Choes festival, with Demophon's of Orestes.
This comparison, like that of Dicaeopolis with Achilles discussed
above, works in two ways. First, it gives a negative view of Dicaeopolis in so far as he again falls short of the figure of authority in the
mythical exemplar. Demophon solved the problem of what to do
with a polluted matricide, but Dicaeopolis will have no truck with a
man wounded in the course of duty. It is worth remarking that when
Lamachus first appears it is in response to a call of the type used to
summon a hero from the ground:[77] he is twice described as a 'hero'
(575, 578) and arrives with the chthonic gorgon-device on his shield;
after the messenger calls him to battle he often uses the language of
tragic heroes (1072 etc.). In this guise as a heroic defender of the city,
he is not unlike Orestes, who in Aeschylus' version of the story
offered Athens protection from attack after his death.[78] This is the
man Dicaeopolis would exclude from his 'city'. Secondly, Dicaeopolis, as one who has separated himself from his community, has
affinities also with the outsider: like Orestes, he is invited to the table
by an important member of that society, the priest of Dionysus, not
the king, but the priest of the god of the theatrical competitions.[79] In
other words, the action of this scene can be read in two complementary ways through the comparison with the myth: if Dicaeopolis is
considered as Demophon, his treatment of Lamachus appears in a bad
light; if as Orestes, the apparently anomalous invitation from the city
he has abandoned not only becomes more comprehensible in terms of
the myth, but is also notable for a tolerance that has not been a
characteristic of Dicaeopolis' behaviour.[80] The Choes was a day when

---

[75] *Birds* 712, 1482–93 (with schol. on 1487); Eupolis, *Kolakes* fr. 179; Starkie 1909: 227f.;
Sommerstein 1980a: 211.   [76] A. *Cho.* 1021ff.; Jacoby, *FGH* 3b Suppl. 2.28f.

[77] Heracles functions in the same way in Euripides' *Heracles* (490ff.); Bond 1981: 191–3 for the
features of such addresses: e.g. short statement of the problem (571), imperatives (567, 570),
repetition (566–8), tricolon (569f.).   [78] *Eum.* 762–77.

[79] The 'King' Archon presided over the Lenaea: cf. [Arist.] *Ath. Pol.* 57.1.

[80] The city's apparent acceptance of Dicaeopolis here may also of course be taken as another
example of their blindness last shown when they invited the embassy to enter the
Prytaneum (124f.).

'outsiders', such as foreigners, slaves and ghosts, could take their part in the city's activities, and Dicaeopolis may thus be said to hover uneasily between *Kar* and king.

The day after this, the Chytroi, began the process of restoration: the *Kares* were expelled, and all (bar the priests) partook in a dish of grains cooked with honey, as had those who survived the Flood. The community re-establishes and redefines itself. It is interesting that Aristophanes stops the play at the ambivalent day of Choes: he thus leaves open the question of whether Dicaeopolis will play Orestes and allow himself to be reintegrated or will remain one of the *Kares*, who were expelled on the third day with the words 'Outside, *Kares*, it's no longer the Anthesteria.'

This ambivalence continues to the end. Dicaeopolis declares himself an Olympic victor with the cry *tenella kallinikos!* (1227, 1231), traditionally sung to mark an athletic victory.[81] The evocation of the Olympic games looks back to the poor, harassed *spondophoros*, Amphitheus, who made everything possible. Again there is irony, since this evocation of a major pan-Hellenic festival serves to high-light the difference between the athletic victor who is celebrated in a *komos* as the pride of his community and Dicaeopolis who triumphs in despite of his. Even his performance of the drinking competition is anomalous, since, instead of mixing his wine with water in a crater as was the convention, he claims that 'I poured it out neat and knocked it back in one gulp' (1229): drinking neat wine was characteristic of the Scythian[82] and the Thracian:[83] Dicaeopolis thus creates a gap between himself and his fellow Greeks by this aberrant act, which brings to mind the earlier abuses of ritual practices. Even the relationship between Dicaeopolis and the Chorus is uncertain. Dicaeopolis calls on them to sing the Olympic hymn to celebrate his victory, and they agree to do so 'if you really do invite us' (1228).[84] Whether he does or not is not clear. Chorus and protagonist go off together, perhaps singing Archilochus' hymn,[85] but this combined

---

[81] Scholia. Pi. *Ol.* 9.1.   [82] Anac. 356(b); Hdt. 6.84; Pl. *Legg.* 637E.

[83] Call. fr. 178.11f.; Hor. *C.* 1.36.14. Where earlier it was idle ambassadors who drank neat wine (73–5), it is now Dicaeopolis.

[84] This phrase is taken to mean 'since you do invite us' by for instance Starkie 1909: 237 in his translation, though in his note he says 'if it is true you *do* invite us'. On these two senses of *ge*, cf. Denniston 1966: 487f.

[85] Zielinski 1885a: 187 suggested that the exit-song was lost; cf. the end of *Frogs*, *Plutus* and perhaps *Knights*.

exit does nothing to answer the questions or allay the doubts that the last part of the play has raised. We appear to have the integration of Dicaeopolis into the city, but this is so hedged about with ambiguities through the references to the Anthesteria that one cannot be sure.

Dicaeopolis' private treaty and its consequences are thus presented through a number of filters; so that they appear in different ways depending on whether the viewpoint is that of the individual or the city. The actions of Dicaeopolis, which might, at first sight, appear to be laudable and an example to others, appear very differently when viewed through the mythical and ritual filters of Telephus, Rural Dionysia and Anthesteria, so that the characters take on a variety of different moral hues, depending on their conformity or otherwise to the stereotypes. The play does not convey any final judgements, but keeps in a careful balance the rhetorical and visual stimuli to one opinion or another. The first part of the play shows the effect on the individual of a corrupt and violent state, but this is set against a world in which the satisfaction of individual desires is pursued without regard for those of the state. The city's refusal to discuss peace is complemented by Dicaeopolis' refusal to share it.

Polis and deme

We may conclude this chapter with a broader consideration of the political issues raised by the play, especially in so far as they affect recent Athenian history. *Acharnians* does not look only at the relationships between individual and state in Dicaeopolis' relationship with the *polis*, but also at those between deme and *polis* and the demands each could make on the other.[86] We have so far spoken of the Chorus largely as if they stood, by synecdoche, for the Athenians as a whole. But if Dicaeopolis saw life back in his deme as symbolic of a peaceful existence, the Chorus come from another very important deme with a very different outlook. The question needs to be asked why Aristophanes chose the men of the deme of Acharnae, and the political and military events of the years before 425 provide an answer.[87]

---

[86] Note the emphasis on the idea of the deme in the first part of the play: 33, 267, 319, 328, 333, 349, 675. On the relationships of deme and city, cf. Osborne 1985a; Whitehead 1986: 253ff.; R. C. T. Parker 1987a; Wood 1988: 101–10.   [87] Cf. also Forrest 1963: 9–12.

In 431 the Spartan king Archidamus invaded Attica and, after
an abortive attempt on Oenoe camped in the deme of Acharnae and
conducted prolonged devastation of the land. Thucydides gives his
thinking:[88]

> His hope was that the Athenians, with a population of young men
> that had never been exceeded, and prepared for war as they never
> had been, might quite possibly come out to battle and not allow
> their land to be laid waste . . . Acharnae itself seemed to him a good
> position for a camp, and at the same time he thought it likely that
> the Acharnians, who, with their three thousand hoplites, were an
> important element in the state, would not allow their own property
> to be destroyed, but would force all the others as well to come out
> and fight for it. If, on the other hand, the Athenians did not come
> out and fight during this invasion, the Peloponnesians would in
> future invasions have all the more confidence in laying waste the
> plain and advancing right up to the walls of Athens. By that time
> the Acharnians would have lost their own property and would be
> much less willing to risk their lives for the property of other
> people; consequently there would be a lack of unity in the counsels
> of Athens.

The Acharnians therefore were not unjustified, at least in 431, in
demanding the chance to use war to protect their property. Furthermore, Acharnae was the largest of the demes,[89] so it is not surprising
that the Acharnians 'seeing that they formed an important part of the
whole state and considering that it was their land that was being laid
waste, brought particular pressure to bear in favour of marching
out'.[90] The young were especially keen to fight.[91]

The deme of Acharnae was about seven miles from the city. It
was unusual in several ways. It formed a whole *trittus*, which gave it
'more institutionalised power than simply a large deme'.[92] Its inhabitants had a reputation for toughness: Pindar, celebrating Timodemus
of Acharnae, says 'that the Acharnians are brave is proverbial';[93] we
have already quoted Amphitheus' description of them as being like

---

88 2.20 (tr. Warner).
89 2.19.2; they seem to have represented 4 per cent or more of the population of the citizens and
    their buleutic quota at 22 was the highest of all demes; Aphidna was next with 16, and
    Dicaeopolis' deme Cholleidae sent but two, close to the average of 3.7 (Traill 1975: map 2;
    Osborne 1985a: 43f.; Whitehead 1986: 397).
90 Thuc. 2.21.3 (tr. Warner). The Chorus state that destruction of their vines (183, 233) and of
    their lands (228) is the reason for their raising 'hate-filled' war (227).
91 Thuc. 2.21.2.   92 Osborne 1985a: 189.
93 *Ne.* 2.16f. The evidence for what follows is collected in Whitehead 1986: 397–400.

holm-oak and maple (180f.), and another, anonymous, comic poet called them 'oak-Acharnians';[94] their women too commanded respect.[95] The deme seems to have been unusual too in its cult of Ares: it had recently built a temple to him, which it had presumably seen in Spartan hands; in the fourth century, altars to Ares and Athena Areia were erected there.[96] Dover would seem to be right in suggesting that the Acharnians were exceptional in that 'few demes ... were felt to have martial traditions of their own'.[97] Again, Osborne suggests that 'Aristophanes' jokes about the Akharnians being charcoal-burners may further indicate that Akharnai did have something of a different economic base [from the rest of the city].'[98] Distinguished by size, ideology and perhaps economy, and removed from the city in their oak-forests, it would have been natural for them to have been conceived by members of other demes as in some ways exceptional and even marginal: Andocides speaks of the hope of not seeing 'charcoal-burners coming to the city from the mountains',[99] and there was a proverb about 'Acharnian asses'.[100]

In its depiction of the Acharnians and Dicaeopolis, therefore, the play gives us a deme hotly in favour of war and an individual who is equally committed to peace, to both of whom a number of different responses are possible. Thucydides says that in 431 'there were constant discussions with violent feelings on both sides, some demanding that they should be led out to battle, and a certain number resisting the demand';[101] it may be that things were slightly different in 425, but, if the problems were more acute earlier, they reflected continuing tensions within the various parts of Attica. Thus, it would have been possible for the audience to consider the Acharnians as a deme that had a right not only to want war because of the attacks on its land but also to expect the city to provide help in the defence of that land. On the other hand, the marginality of this deme would allow those from more 'central' areas or of more eirenic dispositions to feel a certain distance from a deme that was noted for

[94] *Com. Adesp.* 75 (*CAF* 3.413); cf. Hsch. s.v.; *EM* 288.15.

[95] *Lys.* 61f., *Thesm.* 562f.

[96] Boersma 1970: 77, 173f.; Osborne 1985a: 189 (temple); *SEG* 21.519 (c. 340) (altars); Pritchett 1979: 159f.; 'I know of no other Ares cult in a deme' (Whitehead 1986: 207 n. 185).

[97] Gomme–Andrewes–Dover 1970: 446. When [Dem.] 60.27–31 relates tales that encouraged men of the different tribes to die for the city, he looks to mythology rather than the martial exploits of recent history.　　　[98] 1985a: 189.　　　[99] Fr. 4.　　　[100] *CPG* 2.16 no. 90.

[101] 2.21.3.

its bellicosity. In other words, any suggestion that peace should be made would not have been an unproblematic one, because there were people in Attica who, in certain circumstances, had a justifiable right to demand that Spartan fire be met with fire: desire for war, therefore, need not result only from a bellicose nature that has spent too much time burning charcoal.

In the same way, many must have sympathised with Dicaeopolis' strongly expressed feelings about the wearisomeness of war, and with his desire to return from the cramped and crowded city to the familiar ways of his deme. It was membership of one's local deme that made one a citizen and, as Osborne writes, 'Kleisthenes' reforms politicised the Attic countryside and rooted political identity there. Those local political roots continue to be the basis for political activity throughout the classical period.'[102] Thucydides describes the reactions of the people forced to move into the city before the war as follows:[103] 'It was sadly and reluctantly that they now abandoned their homes and the temples time-honoured from their patriotic past, that they prepared to change their whole way of life, leaving behind them what each man regarded as his own city.'

If people envied Dicaeopolis' solution, they might at the same time naturally feel outrage at one who solved the problem in a way so profitable to himself but of no help to the generality. Dicaeopolis' peace may be attractive, but when he expresses his contempt for the city and retires to his country deme to celebrate his own Rural Dionysia, it might be argued that his actions are in danger of disturbing that balance between 'city' and 'deme', which was maintained remarkably well in Attica, but was not absolutely stable, as 431 showed.[104] Again, we would have a reflection of tensions within Attica between rural demes which aimed at self-sufficiency but still depended politically on the city, and the city areas whose close ties with the countryside were loosened by the import of foreign grain but never severed.[105] Dicaeopolis' agora 'where all good things come to him spontaneously' (976) and his trading with Athens' enemies from Megara and Boeotia demonstrate his separation from any need to rely on commerce with other parts of Attica.

What is striking, too, is the absence of any character who stands for a single *polis* viewpoint, whether that be deemed to be in

---

[102] 1985a: 189.   [103] 2.16.2.   [104] Osborne 1985a: 188f.
[105] Osborne 1987: 93–112.

favour of peace or of war.[106] It is possible to read the play with this viewpoint in mind, but nowhere does Aristophanes impose it upon the reader or audience. The views offered are of the contrasting extremes of peace at any price, in Dicaeopolis' determination that peace shall be discussed in the Assembly (38f.), and of war similarly, in the early feelings of the Acharnians, and in the vow to fight the Spartans on every front made by Lamachus (621–2), who figures the spirited reaction of the young men of Athens and Acharnae to the invasions. Indeed, although the city as a whole is bathed in an unalluring light in the first part, it is made plain that only certain elements are at fault: 'for some men amongst you – and I don't mean the *polis*, remember, I don't mean the *polis*, but rogues, ill-struck, worthless, counterfeit . . .' (515–18). Like Dicaeopolis disguised as Telephus, the city does not speak with one voice.

The attitudes of individual demes and men are displayed on stage: the citizens must decide what is best for the city. That Dicaeopolis comes from Cholleidae, a deme which seems to have been next door to Acharnae,[107] shows that geographical location need not determine attitude to the war. The confrontation at the end between the hedonism enjoyed by Dicaeopolis and the civic duty performed by Lamachus crystallises the problem: instinct may make one agree with Dicaeopolis, but mature deliberation with Lamachus – or vice versa. These differences of attitude may, as Thucydides and indeed Dicaeopolis say, depend not just on emotion but on age. Furthermore, the use of the figure of Telephus prompts further reflection: he, like the Acharnians, had his land ravaged by the enemy, and he, like them, fought back. Thoughts about his subsequent condition might deter some of the more lukewarm supporters of war; peacemakers could say that his curing by Achilles and the subsequent victory at Troy was an allegory of the way in which the wine of a treaty between Sparta and Athens would heal the wounds caused by the destruction of the vineyards of Acharnae and lead to joint hegemony over Greece.

This presentation of contrasting viewpoints is further carried out in the minor characters. Some may have believed, with Amphith-

---

[106] The Chorus's remark that it is 'in the city's interest' that Amphitheus should be caught (205f.) is merely their subjective opinion.

[107] Traill 1978: 99f. with n. 26 and map 2 in Traill 1975, reprinted in Whitehead 1986: xxiii and Osborne 1985a: 14 (adapted).

eus, that the gods themselves wanted peace. The farmer Dercetes is a blend of the Acharnians, who have suffered in raids, and Dicaeopolis, who wants peace. The newly-weds put forward a rather more personal reason for peace, which deserves sympathy – the death of a warrior soon after marriage or even before its consummation is a topos of Homeric battle-scenes[108] and it will have been a not uncommon experience; but such sympathy cannot be the basis of a general dispensation from military service for such young men. The use of these minor and major figures in the play is complicated by the comic distortions, in the form of exaggeration, bawdy, disguise, to which the scenes are subject.

Acharnians therefore offers its audiences a kaleidoscopic variety of ways of viewing not only the broad question of peace or war, but also the more complex problem of how to reconcile the competing claims of individual, deme and *polis*, young and old, countryman and city politician and so on. There is no paradigmatic narrative of what should happen, but a series of vignettes containing a range of more or less justifiable reactions to the political and military situation. The decision on what course of action to take is left to the spectators, who must check and evaluate their own strongly held opinions against the equally strongly propounded views of the characters. Such evaluations may not all have been possible during the course of the original production: they may have had to wait for discussions in agora, barber's shop, gymnasium or symposium, or for repeat performances in the deme theatres – perhaps at the Rural Dionysia.[109]

---

[108] Cf. Griffin 1980: 121f., 131–4; Lattimore 1962: 192–4; Alexiou 1974: index II s.v. 'marriage, death and'.

[109] For these theatres, cf. Whitehead 1986: 218–22; Pickard-Cambridge 1988: 52–4; for Acharnae, *IG* 2².1206.2ff. (end of fourth century). For enthusiastic attendance at such performances, cf. Pl. *Rep.* 475D; they are attested for Icarion in the second half of the fifth century (*IG* 1³.254). The only possible evidence we have for fifth-century productions of Aristophanes outside the city festivals is *IG* 2².3090 from Eleusis; if we interpret the use of the word *didasko* strictly, the presence here of Sophocles (and Aristophanes) would date the stone before 405 (cf. Pickard-Cambridge 1988: 47f. on the problems of this stone).

3

Knights

In *Acharnians*, we found that interpretation of the play involved consideration of the strong political and social element through mythological and ritual references to Telephus, Rural Dionysia and Anthesteria, which were explicitly drawn to our attention on the stage. In *Knights*, myths and rituals will play an equally important role but as elements which form the structure of the plot, without being introduced in so overt a manner as in *Acharnians*.

Rites of passage

Knights, and the two plays that follow, all make use of the myths and rituals concerned with passage from one status in life to another, the so-called 'rites of passage'.[1] Such rituals ease the movement from, for instance, birth to acceptance by the father, from immaturity to puberty, from adolescence to maturity, from single to married estate and from life to death. Our particular concern will be with the passage from youth to maturity, citizenship and political rights, and I shall devote the first section of this chapter to a general discussion of the institutions involved in this process in ancient Greece.[2] In addition, a number of other types of myth will also be encountered, which, though they deal with different ideas such as succession to power, the New Year and city-foundation, are none the

[1] The classic work is van Gennep 1909. For more recent literature, see Bianchi 1986; Ries & Limet 1986; Versnel 1990: 78 n. 88.

[2] The bibliography is now considerable. See in particular, Jeanmaire 1939; Brelich 1969; Bremmer 1978; Vidal-Naquet 1981b, c, 1986; Osborne 1987: 145–51; Versnel 1990: esp. 44–59 (useful bibliographies); Wilkins 1990; Winkler 1990. For women's rites, cf. Calame 1977; Dowden 1988; Sourvinou-Inwood 1988; for evidence of vases, Neils 1987.

less complementary to the myths of youth in their concern with the change from chaos to cosmos.

Myths and rituals of passage from youth to maturity articulate the transfer of the youth from the *oikos* or household, where he is in the sphere of influence of the women (especially his mother), has no political status and is often conceived of as 'uncivilised' or as an animal, to the *polis*, where he joins his father and the other male citizens, takes his civic responsibilities in the lawcourts, assembly and hoplite-phalanx, and marries a wife for the procreation of children. This change is dramatised in a wide variety of ways, but usually involves a period of withdrawal from the community to a 'marginal' world.[3] This may be expressed physically, in separation from the community followed perhaps by military training on the boundaries of the land, or symbolically by a change of clothing, life-style or sexual role. These marginal periods can be characterised by an inversion of normality or by a mixture of the normal and abnormal.

In mythology, the examples of Theseus, Jason and Perseus provide a clear illustration of the pattern.[4] A young man on the verge of manhood is displaced from his rightful position: Theseus is brought up not in Athens but in Troezen, Jason is sent to the country to the centaur Chiron and Perseus is expelled from Argos. Before they can attain their proper status, they must visit a land that is marked as marginal, either because it is far away on the edge of the world or because it combines the human or 'real' world with the non-human and monstrous: Theseus goes to Crete, Jason to Colchis and Perseus to Ethiopia. They undergo various trials which are manifestations of the marginality of these worlds: Theseus kills a minotaur, which is half man and half bull, in the Labyrinth, which is a house, but not one in which one can safely reside; Jason ploughs with fire-breathing bulls; and Perseus kills both a gorgon whose gaze turns men to stone, and a sea-monster. In these trials, the youths regularly make use of trickery to counteract the heavy odds against them: Theseus has a ball of thread, Jason a magic chrism and Perseus

---

[3] On the term 'marginal', cf. Versnel 1990: 44–59, esp. 50–9, and 81f. n. 110 for a bibliography on the concept.

[4] See especially, Jeanmaire 1939: 228–383; Pélékidis 1962: 225–39; Sourvinou 1971a on Theseus; on Perseus, J. E. M. Dillon 1989 who shows that though they share a basic pattern, these myths are not exactly parallel.

Table 3.1

hoplite	kruptos
1. heavily armed	1. light- or unarmed
2. member of phalanx	2. operates alone
3. fights on plain	3. lives, hunts in hills
4. fights in summer	4. operates in winter
5. fights openly	5. uses stealth
6. fights by day	6. associated with night
7. lives in *sussition*	7. eats what he can find
8. in peace stays near city	8. lives on boundaries

winged sandals and a helmet of invisibility. These bring victory, kingship and a wife, though there can be variations at this point.

In ritual, the neatest demonstration of the pattern is to be found in Sparta. That city divided its youths into groups described in terms like 'herd' appropriate to the beasts of the field, such as *agelai*, *bouai*, *bouagoi*, etc., and put an elite group through the *krupteia*, 'hidden period', at the age of about eighteen.[5] During this time, they lived in the countryside a life that was the symmetrical opposite or, in Levi-Strauss's words, 'logical inversion' of the hoplite life into which they were being initiated.[6] This inversion serves, not so much to prepare them for the next stage, as to dramatise the fact that they are changing status.

The relationship between *kruptos* and hoplite may best be expressed as a table: see table 3.1, from which it can be seen that 'With the hoplite order [*taxis*] reigns; in the *krypteia* there is nothing but cunning, deception, disorder, irrationality. To borrow Levi-Strauss's terms ... the hoplite is on the side of Culture, of what is "cooked", while the *krypteia* is on the side of Nature, of the "raw".'[7]

The ideology of these rites can be further exemplified from Cretan examples.[8] In the *harpage* ('seizure')[9] an older youth captured

[5] Jeanmaire 1913; Michell 1952: 162–4, 177–80; Brelich 1969: 113–207; Vidal-Naquet 1981b: 153–5.

[6] Aristotle quoted by Plutarch (*Lyc*. 28.4) said that war was declared on the helots; the *kruptoi* thus took part in a marginal type of warfare before becoming hoplites (the tradition is defended by Finley 1975: 165 n. 9).

[7] For this and the table, Vidal-Naquet 1981b: 154f.   [8] Willetts 1955, 1962.

[9] Ephorus, *FGH* 70 F 149; the analysis is that of Bremmer 1980a.

a younger with the aid of the latter's friends and took him to the *andreion* ('men's house'), whence, having given him gifts, he took him and his friends to the countryside. Here they hunted and dined together for two months in a kind of brief homosexual 'marriage', which reversed the heterosexual one for which the boy became eligible after the rite. The lover then released the boy and gave him a suit of armour (to mark his attainment of adulthood; a similar custom obtained in Thebes), a bull (an animal regularly connected with initiation, as shown by the Minotaur, Jason's ploughing, Hippolytus' death, ritual activity with bulls by Athenian ephebes etc.) and a cup (to mark his entry to the adult male symposium). For the rest of his life, the boy wore special garments and was known as a *parastatheis* (probably 'helper') and a *kleinos* ('famed one').[10]

The practice of changing garments at such a juncture is found in other Cretan rites.[11] At the Ekdysia in Phaestus, the title of the festival suggests that the *skotioi* ('dark ones'), presided over by Aphrodite Skotia, in some way laid aside their adolescent clothes, and there was also a myth about Leucippus who was changed from a girl to a boy.[12] At Dreros and Malla, we hear of the *egduomenoi*, *azostoi* and *panazostoi*.[13] Such changes of clothing are a feature of rites of passage generally, and we shall come across a number of examples of such practices in the comedies. The ephebes in Athens wore black cloaks, which they changed for white ones on becoming citizens, and which commemorated Theseus' failure to change his black sails to white.[14] Such changes of clothes are also found in other rites. In Sparta, brides had their hair cut off by a *numpheutria* ('bride's attendant'), were given men's clothes and shoes and made to sleep alone in the dark[15] and in Argos, women who had just married

---

[10] Compare also the Cretan myth of the birth of Zeus, in which the god is taken from his mother Rhea and hidden in a cave on Mt Aegaeum, where he is suckled by animals and attended by the Curetes or 'Youths' (cf. *Hymn to the Curetes* (*CA* pp. 160–2; *c.* 400) hailing Zeus as 'greatest *kouros*', and possibly celebrating at an initiation ceremony his return as a mature youth; and cf. Willetts 1962: 199ff.).

[11] Lloyd-Jones 1983: 94f. on clothes and initiation.

[12] Cf. Schol. E. *Alc.* 989; Ant. Lib. 17 ('Leucippus', from Nicander); Willetts 1962: 175–8, 285f.; Lamprinoudakis 1972; more sceptically of the importance of transvestism in Greek rites, Forbes Irving 1990: 149–70, esp. 153–5.

[13] Dreros: *IC* 1.IX.1.11f. (p. 84; 3rd/2nd cent.), 99f., 140f. Malla: *IC* 1.XIX.1.18 (p. 232; 3rd cent.); Vidal-Naquet 1981b: 158.

[14] Roussel 1941; Maxwell-Stuart 1970; Vidal-Naquet 1981b: 256 n. 16.

[15] Plut. *Lyc.* 15.3; Dümmler 1897; Nilsson 1906: 369–74; Halliday 1909–10; on clothes symbolism, Geddies 1987.

had to wear a beard to bed with their husbands.[16] Complementarily, in Cos, bridegrooms wore women's clothes to welcome their brides.[17]

Turning to Athens, we find that youths underwent two initiations, each with its distinctive myths and rituals, into phratry and into deme.[18] The older of the two, giving membership of the phratry, was conducted at the age of sixteen at the Apaturia in the month of Pyanopsion.[19] It occupied three days, *Dorpeia* ('Feast'), *Anarrhusis* ('Sacrifice') and *Koureotis* ('Cutting of the Hair' (of adolescence)). A myth was told of a border dispute between Athens and Boeotia over Melania ('the Black Land'), which was to be settled by a single combat between the two kings, Thymoetes of Athens and Xanthus of Boeotia. Thymoetes, too old to fight, offered his kingdom to the champion who would take his place. Melanthus, a descendent of Periclymenus, son of Neleus from Pylos, did so and defeated Xanthus ('the Fair Man') by a trick: he claimed that Xanthus had deceitfully brought a helper and killed him as he turned to look. In some versions, Dionysus Melanaegis appeared beside Xanthus. Ancient etymology derived the name Apaturia from this trick (*apate*). The fight thus reverses the face-to-face combat of the hoplite, in a manner reminiscent of the life-style of the *kruptos*. It also provides for the surprising victory of 'the Black Man' with chthonic connections over 'the Fair'.

Initiation into the deme and so citizenship became the more important after the reorganisation of Attica by Cleisthenes, which made the demes the most important division of the citizenry. When precisely the training of youths by the state was introduced we do not know, but it would not be surprising if Cleisthenes, having reduced the power of the traditional political groupings by redrawing the political geography of Attica, also introduced some sort of city-based military training and initiation into the new demes in order to lessen the importance of initiation into the phratries. It is unlikely that this introduction was a single process. Italian cities in the Renaissance similarly assumed the training of soldiers from the

[16] Plut. *Mor.* 245F.
[17] Plut. *Mor.* 304C–E; Halliday 1928: 212–19. Compare also the presentation of a new robe to Athena at the Great Panathenaea, and the new red cloaks for the Furies turned Semnai in A. *Eum.* 1028.   [18] Labarbe 1953; Golden 1979.
[19] The sources are collected in Vidal-Naquet 1981b: 255 n. 9; the earliest are Hellanicus, *FGH* 4 F 125 = 323a F 23; Ephorus, *FGH* 70 F 22; Conon, *FGH* 26 F 1 (xxxix). See also Deubner 1932: 232–4; Parke 1977: 88–92; Schmitt 1977; for the date, Mikalson 1975: 79, 197–204.

hands of the nobility, so that the armed forces owed allegiance to the state rather than to individual noblemen. Chapter 42 of the Aristotelian *Athenaion Politeia* describes the elaborate training given to Athenian youths as it was at the end of the fourth century; this was by then known as the *ephebeia* ('training of those on the verge of manhood').[20] At eighteen, the ephebes were entered onto their deme-register after satisfactorily proving their maturity and citizen parentage, which were then ratified at a *dokimasia* in the Boule. Grouped together under a *kosmetes* and ten *sophronistai* responsible for their discipline, they toured the sacred places of the city, having first sworn the Ephebic Oath in the sanctuary of Aglaurus on the Acropolis. They then spent their first year in the garrisons at Munychia and Acte being trained in military arts by the *paidotribai* and *didaskaloi*. They ate together in *sussitia*. At the start of the second year, they displayed their skills at an assembly in the theatre, and were presented with a spear and shield by the city. They then garrisoned the frontier posts as *peripoloi*. Their dress was a black *chlamus* ('cloak'). Lest they should be distracted from training, they were exempt from taxes and were permitted only exceptionally to take part in lawsuits. At the end of the second year, they joined the ranks of the citizens with full rights.

There is no evidence that such a highly-organised system existed in the fifth century, but one need not go so far as did Wilamowitz in denying the very existence of anything that might be called an *ephebeia* until the late fourth century.[21] It is true that the names *ephebos*, *ephebeia* do not appear in the fifth century, and that there is no single, conclusive piece of evidence for a fifth-century *ephebeia* of whatever form. However, there is a certain amount of evidence to suggest that we would not be wrong to talk of some kind of *ephebeia* in Aristophanes' time. One would after all expect *a priori* that there was some training for youths in hoplite tactics, which were by no means simple,[22] and some ceremonial marking of the membership of the deme and so accession to full political status of the next generation of Athenians; the *dokimasia* ('examination') of the youths is datable to the fifth century.[23] There is, of course, a problem of

[20] Jeanmaire 1939: 225–383; Reinmuth 1952; Pélékidis 1962; Brelich 1969: 216–28; Siewert 1977; Rhodes 1981: 493–510; Vidal-Naquet 1981b, c, 1986; Winkler 1990.
[21] 1893: 193f. Pélékidis 1962 is a full reply; see also works in Winkler 1990: 27 n. 13; Westlake 1954: 93. [22] Krentz 1985.
[23] MacDowell 1971: 210 on *Wasps* 578; Rhodes 1981: 497–503.

definition here: when does a series of different kinds of training, examinations and rites come to be seen as an entity and get a single name? Even if nothing like the *ephebeia* existed in the fifth century, the argument of these chapters would not be substantially affected: the Athenians were familiar enough with 'ephebic' rites of passage, as we have seen, in mythology and the Apaturia.

The main military training of the ephebes appears to have been in forts on the boundaries of Attica as *peripoloi* ('those who go round') and *neotatoi* ('the youngest').[24] Again, we have the idea of being on the margins.

Theseus appears to have been the hero *par excellence* for the ephebes, and the myth of his voyage to the 'margins', and his return to the city was probably the aetiological story that explained the rites undergone by the young Athenians. In the autumn, the traditional time for the 'return' of troops to the city, there were three festivals relating to Theseus, which would have provided a ritual movement of the ephebes from margins to centre. The Oschophoria[25] was held on 6 Pyanopsion, at the temple of Athena Sciras at Phalerum. Theseus had disguised two extra youths as girls when he took the tribute of (nominally) seven youths and seven girls to Minos. Having killed the Minotaur, he returned to Athens and sacrificed in thanksgiving at Phalerum, making a procession headed by the two disguised youths. The herald sent to Athens to announce his arrival returned with news of Aegeus' death, caused by Theseus' failure to change his sails. Grief was thus mixed with joy and the herald put his garlands on his staff, not his head. This was imitated in the Oschophoria, where a procession was led by two youths, dressed as girls

---

[24] Pélékidis 1962: 35–49. The former are first attested for 458/7 by Thucydides 1.105.4 (cf. 2.13.7). The latter are citizens in *Birds* 1177–9, and this is corroborated by Thuc. 8.92.2 (cf. Gomme–Andrewes–Dover 1981: 310). For the *peripoloi* on the frontiers compare Aeschin. 2.167; Eupolis fr. 340; [Arist.] *Ath. Pol.* 42.4. Gomme says that the *peripoloi* 'seem in Thucydides' time and later to be a special mobile force, in peace time at least probably already formed of epheboi who got their training partly ... by garrison-duty in the fortresses' (1956b: 529 on Thuc. 4.67.2). Cf. also the *phrouroi* of Epidaurus, 'die aus den Epheben rekruitierte epidaurische Miliz' (Graf 1985: 224), and the significantly named Spartan youths Phrurarchidas and Parthenius (Paus. 9.13.5; X. *HG* 6.4.7; Diod. 15.54; Plut. *Pelop.* 20–2).

[25] W. S. Ferguson 1938; Jacoby, *FGH* 3b (Suppl.) 1. 285–305; 3b (Suppl.) 2.193–223; Jeanmaire 1939: 338–62; Vidal-Naquet 1981b: 156–8; Parke 1977: 77–81. The festival's marginality is also shown not only by the transvestite youths (Plutarch describes them as subject to 'training in the shadows' (*Thes.* 23.2)), but also by the name 'Sciras'. Names from the *skir*-root are regularly used for marginal areas and activities, Jacoby, *FGH* 3b (Suppl.) 2.200–4 and Brumfield 1981: 156–81.

and carrying *oschoi* (vine branches with grapes on). It was accompanied by a herald with garlands on his staff, and cries of joy were mixed with those of grief. The black sails were reflected in the black cloaks of the ephebes. Next day, the Pyanopsia was held in honour of Apollo. A large pot of vegetables was cooked and eaten by the celebrants in imitation of a similar meal eaten by Theseus and his companions in fulfilment of a vow.[26] This was celebrated in the city, as was the Theseia, which Plutarch describes as 'the chief sacrifice which the Athenians make in his honour'.[27]

To sum up therefore, these myths and rituals of passage involve a youth on the verge of manhood, who experiences a time and a space whose marginality is expressed through changes of clothes, inversions of life-style and sexual role, darkness and death, isolation, trials and tribulations. The reward is integration into a new place in the community.

Knights and *ephebeia*

The Sausage-Seller conforms to the pattern of the various ephebic myths and rites that we have discussed. He is of an age with the ephebic heroes of mythology and the youths of Athens or Sparta, in that he is *neanikotatos* ('most youthful', 611) and on the verge of manhood (1241);[28] he doubts that he can become an *aner*, a full citizen (179), but after his victory the Chorus remind him that he has become one through them (1255). Like the heroes, this is his first exploit: his very lack of political expertise is his greatest asset and is manifest in 178–93, a scene parodying the *dokimasia* of youths of ephebic age.

He is also characterised in ways that tend to separate him from what for convenience one might call the 'ordinary citizen', in other words, marginal. He does not aspire to a reputation for *kalokagathia* ('excellence and virtue'), as a citizen might,[29] but prides himself on low birth (184–6). His reference to self-prostitution (1242) shows him to be sexually marginal: no citizen would admit to this, which would

---

[26] Deubner 1932: 198–201; Parke 1977: 75–7.

[27] *Thes.* 36.3; cf. *IG* 2².1006.77; Deubner 1932: 224f.; Pélékidis 1962: 228–35; Parke 1977: 81f.

[28] Cf. ἀπηνδρώθη of Ion, another youth about to discover his true identity and status (E. *Ion* 53). At 492, the Sausage-Seller is said to need a *paidotribes*.

[29] De Ste Croix 1972: 371–6; Dover 1974: 44f.

have brought the penalty of *atimia*.[30] This is reminiscent of the sexual role-reversal of the ephebic myths and rituals. He belongs furthermore to the class of small traders, amongst whom there certainly were citizens, but who were more often foreigners: not a few political thinkers argued for the exclusion of this class from citizenship.[31]

He is connected with the Ceramicus, which is itself highly marginal. It is literally on the edge of the city and the Sausage-Seller emphasises that he worked at the very gates (1247, 1398).[32] The Ceramicus was also the city's burial ground, the place where the worlds of the dead and living met. It was the home of the more 'marginal' elements of society, of prostitutes and sellers of dog- and ass-meat;[33] the first public baths, an institution of low status, were built outside the Dipylon gate.[34] The Sausage-Seller associates himself specifically with the sellers of salt-fish (1247), who were counted amongst the meanest of the traders.

The Sausage-Seller is therefore very different from the citizen at the centre of power in the Agora or on the Pnyx. Just as the ephebe undergoes a number of role-reversals, so the saviour of Athens lives through a period when he is the lowest of the low, the worst of a line of degraded politicians (128ff.).

The ephebic heroes of mythology receive divine help, as does, despite his villainy, the Sausage-Seller. A number of omens also portend his final success. He is the subject of the crucial oracle stolen from Paphlagon (143f., 177f., 193–210), and he arrives on stage 'by god's chance' (147).[35] There are vulgar omens of his greatness in the bystander's remark, on seeing him hide stolen meat in his buttocks, that he will undoubtedly run the city (425f.), and the flatulence of the *bouleutes* which he takes as a propitious sign when he steels himself to confront the Paphlagon before the Boule (638f.). Apollo, the god who regularly presides over ephebic rites of transition,[36] is

---

[30] Hansen 1976: 74 n. 20; Dover 1978: 19ff.; R. C. T. Parker 1983: 94f.

[31] E.g. X. *Oec.* 4.2f.; Andoc. fr. 5 Dalmeyda (*ap.* schol. *Wasps* 1007); Pl. *Legg.* 846Dff.; Arist. *Pol.* 1277b33ff., 1329a36, 1331a32–5 (cf. R. Martin 1951: 305f.); Newman 1902: III 173ff.; Burford 1972: 28–36.

[32] For gates as an important marginal area, cf. below on *Wasps* 869ff.

[33] *Kn.* 411–28, 1235–47, 1399f.; *Frogs* 1093–8; Lys. 24.20; Hsch. s.v.; Naber 1900: 134–8; Neil 1901: 164; Wycherley 1957: 221–4.   [34] Ginouvès 1962: 184, 212ff.

[35] Traditionally heroes appear at crucial moments: Brelich 1958: 90–4; Pritchett 1979: 11–46 (though see Mikalson 1983: 121 n. 11).   [36] Cf. Burkert 1975; Graf 1979.

with him (229), and Athena, who has ordered him to defeat Paphlagon (903), gives him the crucial idea of stealing the hare (1203). At
499f., the Chorus pray 'may Zeus Agoraeus preserve you',[37] and at
1253 he attributes his victory to Zeus Hellanius, and on his subsequent return with Demos (as on his first arrival), he is welcomed in
the language associated with divine epiphanies.[38] Finally the fact
that he can rejuvenate Demos by boiling betokens the more than
human powers of a Medea.

In addition to help from the gods, the heroes need to make use
of cunning. This is especially true in the case of the Sausage-Seller,
because Paphlagon excels in this area. To be precise, the play is more
than a series of contests in low deceit: all of *dolos* ('deceit', 'trickery'),
metis ('cunning intelligence') and *techne* ('skill') are involved.[39]
Panourgia, literally the ability to do anything, to meet any situation,
is applied to Paphlagon a dozen times and to the Sausage-Seller three
times;[40] *apatan* ('deceive') and its cognates are used five times and
once respectively;[41] both are *poikilos* (758; 459, 686). Paphlagon is
always on the *qui vive* and the Sausage-Seller is repeatedly warned to
emulate him, as he is very clever at escaping trouble (253f., 758f.).
They are both adept at theft and both merit comparison with the
arch-trickster Themistocles (812–19; 884f.).[42]

Both men are characterised by the possession of *techne*: Paphlagon 'has come up with a clever plan' (63) for dealing with slaves, and
the Sausage-Seller has a 'remarkable craft' (141, cf. 144); indeed, the
politicians in the play are largely identified by their *technai* (128ff.,
852–7). Furthermore, the imagery of the contests not infrequently
draws on various crafts, such as leather-working (369–72), navigation (429–41, 756–62), or wood- and metal-working (461–70). The
Sausage-Seller is also supreme in the art of oratory,[43] and Aristophanes sometimes groups together three or four examples of the same
rhetorical skill, as for instance in 847ff., where he reveals the *arrière-
pensées* of Paphlagon's supposed benefits to Demos, and at 997ff.,

---

[37] Cf. R. Martin 1951: 175–86 for this aspect of Zeus, 'la plus haute représentation du génie
civilisateur qui soit intervenue avec efficacité dans la formation de la *polis* grecque' (182).
Compare the way Athena attributes victory to Zeus Agoraeus in A. *Eum.* 973.

[38] Kleinknecht 1939.   [39] For this concept, see Detienne & Vernant 1978.

[40] Paphlagon: 45, 56, 247, 249 (bis), 250, 317, 450, 684, 803, 823, 950; Sausage-Seller: 331, 684,
902.   [41] Paphlagon: 48, 633, 809, 1103, 1224; Sausage-Seller: 418.

[42] Jameson 1960: 210 detects an echo of the opening of Themistocles' decree in 763f. Cf. Thuc.
1.138.3; Detienne & Vernant 1978: 313f.   [43] Cf. Littlefield 1968.

where he deals in similar fashion with his oracles. His final victory is won when, by a neat conceit, he turns the emptiness of his hamper to his own advantage: unlike Paphlagon, he has given Demos his all (1211ff.).

The mythical contests and the training of ephebes typically take place in a world which is characteristically topsy-turvy in one way or another. So, a house where the Athenian Demos is an old fool dominated by a slave and a foreigner, who prevents the attentions of the Athenian 'slaves', is obviously disordered.[44] The complex monster whom the Sausage-Seller combats also repeats those defeated by the mythical heroes: he is 'the first of Paphlagonians', a people from the eastern 'edge of the world', where there be monsters: Zeus' opponent Typhoeus came from Cilicia. We shall look more fully at the monster-killing aspect of the play in the next section of the chapter.

Especially noteworthy in the context of the ephebe are the two occasions on which the Sausage-Seller employs the same 'Look behind you' trick that brought Melanthus victory in the Apaturia myth. When stealing meat in the agora he tells how 'I used to fool the cooks by saying, "Look boys, there's a swallow, it's the new season." They'd look, and at that moment I'd steal some of the meat' (418–20). Just before his final victory, he uses it again to purloin the hare from Paphlagon (1195–9):

> SS. I'm not worried because, look, there are some ambassadors
>   coming to me with purses of silver.
> Paph. Where, where?
> SS. What's that to you? Won't you leave the foreigners alone? Dear
>   Demos, do you see the hare I've brought you?

The Sausage-Seller's victory over this chaos-monster brings him a new position, as he moves from the lowest status to be the *prostates* ('leading citizen') of the Demos,[45] operating no longer at the gates of the city but enjoying the *sitesis* in the Prytaneum, the 'ceremonial headquarters of the state' (1404),[46] wearing as the symbol of his office

---

[44] I see no reason not to name these slaves Nicias and Demosthenes, in inverted commas if necessary. References to Pylos (esp. 54ff.) point surely to the latter, and piety (30–5), timidity and abstemiousness to the former (cf. Sommerstein 1980b: 46f.) The slaves 'are' the two politicians as much and as little as Paphlagon with his tanning 'is' Cleon.

[45] Rhodes 1981: 344–7.

[46] Rhodes 1981: 105; cf. Wycherley 1957: 166–74; Miller 1978.

the garland of the usurper Paphlagon.[47] Like Theseus, he has moved
from the margins to the centre. In the myth, Theseus also becomes
king; in the play, it is Demos who assumes this role as *monarchos*
(1330) and *basileus* ('king', 1333).

There are two further marks of the Sausage-Seller's status.
First, there is the frog-green cloak (1406). The precise significance of
this garment and its colour is difficult to pin down, but we have
noted the importance of a change of clothing in expressing the
meaning of the myths and rituals: the ephebes ceased to wear black
cloaks on completing their training and the Sausage-Seller takes new
clothes to mark his new status. It is interesting to note that, as
Sommerstein says, the *batrachis* is sometimes found among the
garments dedicated to Artemis Brauronia, the goddess who presided
over transition rites for Athenian girls, but it is not necessarily the
case that these garments were actually dedicated at the end of the
Arcteia, and other garments are more frequent.[48] Why the Sausage-
Seller should have what seems to have been a woman's garment is not
obvious, unless, as Sommerstein suggests, it was 'associated in the
popular mind with the supposedly luxurious Athens of the early
fifth century': this would accord with the return of Demos to his state
in the days of Aristeides and Miltiades (1324).

Secondly, as he is hailed as victor (1254) he is finally given a
name, Agoracritus (1257), which he interprets as 'he who was tested
in the agora':[49] this would give an echo of the trials undergone in
training and mythology by the ephebes.[50] Hitherto he has acted as a
kind of No-Man, but is now revealed as the man of whom Paphlagon
was warned in his oracle. In the same way, Odysseus, whose exploit
with the Cyclops has a number of ephebic overtones, reveals his true
name only when his cunning has enabled him to escape from the
monster and Polyphemus realises he is the man of whom the oracle

---

[47] Cf. [Dem.] 26.5. In the fourth century and later, ephebes are given garlands at the end of
their training.

[48] Sommerstein 1981: 220; *IG* 2².1514.16f., 48; 1516.25; 1517.B.II.154; 1523.II.24; 1524.B.II.187
(the stones record dedications of the 340s and 330s). On the dress of the Bears, Sourvinou-
Inwood 1988: 119–35; for an analysis of the dedications, Osborne 1985a: 154–72.

[49] 'Der in der Volksversammlung erprobte' (Pohlenz 1952: 125f.); so Landfester 1967: 99f. on
the grounds that the -*kritos* element usually has a positive force. Compare the similarly
named Polycrite, who also saved her city: Andriscus, *FGH* 500 F 1; Plut. *Mor.* 254B–F (she
dies at the gate); Stadter 1965: 93–7.

[50] Cf. Pi. *Py.* 4.84f. γνώμας ... πειρώμενος ἐν ἀγορᾷ of the ephebic Jason on his way to
establishing his true status and identity.

had warned him.[51] In many cultures, the giving of a name is common in *rites d'agrégation*,[52] and Athenian children received their name when they were acknowledged by their fathers.[53]

In the light of the strong ephebic nature of the play, it is worth considering why it might be that Agoracritus should undertake his journey to power aided by the Knights.[54] There are two possible answers. The Chorus were presumably equipped with some kind of horse, if not other actors suitably attired, as on the famous black-figure amphora in Berlin.[55] As such, in a context of status transition, they might evoke the centaurs, compounded of men and animals; not only do these span the divide between nature and culture being crossed by the young, but the most famous of them, Chiron, oversaw the education of a number of ephebic heroes such as Jason and Achilles.[56]

Again, the Knights in Athens were not all of ephebic age,[57] but were a mixture of those of ephebic age and older men. The youthfulness of at least some of the Chorus is clear: we have a reference to the *neoteroi* ('younger') Knights in 604, and Paphlagon calls them *neaniskoi* in 731.[58] In 580, they ask indulgence for wearing their hair long and appearing, presumably from the gymnasia, neatly groomed with the strigil. Furthermore, Siewert detects a quotation from the Ephebic Oath in their words at 576f.: 'we claim the right to defend nobly the city and the gods of our land'; compare the phrase from the epigraphic version 'I shall defend the holy and sacred things.'[59] If we are right to think of the Knights as a mixed group, the combination of older and younger men can be paralleled from actual rites of passage, where those who have already completed the transition act as guides to those currently undergoing it.[60] One might also think of those deities and heroes who preside over rites of passage and partake of characteristics of both sides of the divide: Theseus is both an ephebe and king of Athens. The Knights would thus be doubly appropriate

[51] *Od.* 9.507ff.   [52] Van Gennep 1909: Index, s.v. 'dénomination'.
[53] Lacey 1968: 111f.; *Birds* 494, 922f.; Dem. 39.22, 40.28; Isaeus 3.30 etc.
[54] A. Martin 1887; Helbig 1902; Rhodes 1981: 303f., 564–8 (*Ath. Pol.* 24.3, 49.1f.); Bugh 1988.
[55] Beazley 1956: 297 no. 17: beardless young riders on 'horses' with beards, cf. Sifakis 1971: 99f.   [56] Dumézil 1929; Kirk 1970: 152–62.
[57] Dover 1968a: xxvii mentions the Knight Dexileos, born 414/13, died 394 (*IG* 2².6217).
[58] Cf. 'the *neaniskoi* of the *hippeis*' in Thuc. 8.92.6. Neil 1901: 105 quotes Thuc. 8.69.4 and X. *HG* 2.3.23 where he says the *neaniskoi* were Knights, but this is not stated.
[59] 1977: 108 n. 36; the similarity is a little tenuous.
[60] Calame 1977: I 92–143, II 98–104, 115–19.

to a transition myth, combining human and animal and spanning the
poles between which the Sausage-Seller is moving.

Knights and the succession

This rise of the Sausage-Seller from obscurity to prostates of
Demos is structured not only by the ephebic mythos but also by a
'succession myth', in which, by a kind of priamel, a list of rulers or
gods climaxes in and legitimates the power of the current lord: the
parallels with this type of myth thus give to the victory of the
Sausage-Seller a cosmic as well as a local significance.[61] That Knights
depicts a parody of a succession myth is early made clear, when the
purloined oracle places the Sausage-Seller at the end of a sequence of
four politicians of increasing awfulness (128–43, condensed):

> Dem. The oracle clearly says that first there is a hemp-seller, who
> will control the city's affairs ... After him, there will be a
> second ruler, a sheep-seller ... who must rule, until a more
> awful man than he comes. Then he's lost, for his successor is the
> leather-selling Paphlagon, a thief and shrieker with the voice of
> Cycloborus ... There is still one more man, with an amazing
> craft ..., a sausage-seller who will drive him out.

These myths, like the ephebic ones, regularly involve a battle
between the god or hero, who represents civilisation and cosmos,
and a monstrous figure representing chaos. Indications that the
audience is to think of *Knights* in terms of such gigantomachic
succession myths are to be found in the parabasis. At 510f., the
aristocratic Knights give their reasons for supporting a comic poet:
'because he hates the same people as we do, dares to tell the truth,
and nobly advances against the typhoon[62] and the hurricane'. There
are echoes of the Gigantomachy in the syzygy too, when the Knights
praise their ancestors as 'worthy of the peplos' (566), thus ranking
their deeds alongside the Gigantomachy which was depicted on
Athena's peplos at the Great Panathenaea. This battle was often

---

[61] See esp. Fontenrose 1959, but more for the material collected than the methodology: a good
critique Vian 1963: 94–113. See also Vian 1952; Trumpf 1958; Eliade 1965; West 1966: 18–
31, 106f.; Mondi 1990; specifically on *Knights*, Trencsényi-Waldapfel 1957; Bowie 1982b:
114f. For *Knights* and apocalyptic literature, Burkert 1983b: 248f. On the question of the
origins of such myths, Kinnier Wilson 1979.

[62] Identified by the scholia vetera with Cleon and Typhon; for Cleon as a monster, *Wasps*
1029–37, *Peace* 752–60.

accompanied on temple decoration by another cosmic struggle, between the Greeks and Persians, to which reference is made in the description of Agoracritus' deeds as 'worthy of the trophy at Marathon' (1334) and, in a more comic fashion, in the horses' eating 'crabs instead of Medic grass' (i.e. lucerne, 606) on their nautical campaign.[63]

The classic Greek myth of this kind, with roots in Near-Eastern traditions,[64] is Hesiod's account in *Theogony* of the sequence Uranus–Cronus–Zeus, which culminates in Zeus's two battles against the Titans and Typhoeus. The similarities between *Theogony* and *Knights* are striking and can best be seen in tabular form (see table 3.2). The parallels with Zeus thus justify the language of divine epiphany that accompanies the Sausage-Seller's return with the newly-boiled Demos.

Central to this type of myth is the battle, which we have seen is also a feature of our ephebic myths. There are many similarities between the play and the Hesiodic (and other) versions, and Paphlagon is a good substitute for Typhoeus. Indeed, the Paphlagonians are a suitable race to typify our villain. In ancient tradition, they form part of a group of peoples on the Euxine coast with characteristics that mark them as separate from the Greek world.[65] Apollonius of Rhodes includes them alongside the Cimmerians and Mariandyni: Homer describes the former as living at the 'limits' of Ocean, forever wrapped in night, mist and cloud,[66] and the latter are the neighbours of the Paphlagonians and named after a son of Cimmerius.[67] Apollonius describes their land as follows (2.353–5, 357f.): 'Here there is a path down to the house of Hades, and the promontory of Acherusia stretches up high; eddying Acheron cuts through it at the bottom . . . and near here you will sail by many hills of the Paphlagonians.' It is an area of great storms. Tradition placed the Cerberus story at this promontory, and Xenophon says the 'signs' of Heracles' descent are

---

[63] Lucerne was introduced into Greece during or just after the Persian Wars (Sallares 1991: 303 with n. 25).   [64] Burkert 1979: 18–22, 152 n. 10; 1987b.

[65] [A.] *PV* 707–35; Hdt. 4.99ff.; A. R. 2.311–407; also Arist. *NE* 1148b19–25, *Pol.* 1338b19ff.; Minns 1913: 101–14; Hartog 1988 *passim.* Why the Paphlagonians? Lewis 1977: 20f. suggests the choice may have been influenced by knowledge of the famous Paphlagonian eunuch Artoxares, king-maker for Darius II in 424.

[66] *Od.* 11.13ff.; cf. S. fr. 1060; Ephorus, *FGH* 70 F 134.

[67] Schol. A. R. 2.723; Eupolis, *Golden Race*, fr. 302. Theopompus, *FGH* 115 F 388 made Mariandynus leader of part of the Paphlagonians.

Table 3.2

Theog.	Knights
1. Zeus's Gigantomachies are the climax of a succession myth, Uranus–Cronus–Zeus.	1. The comic hero's battle is the climax of a succession, hemp-seller, sheep-seller, leather-seller, sausage-seller (128ff.).
2. Warned by an oracle from Uranus and Gaia that his son will replace him, Cronus keeps watch and swallows all his children at birth; he is given a stone in place of Zeus by Rhea; Zeus is brought up in Crete (453–506).	2. Warned by an oracle from Bacis that a sausage-seller will replace him, Paphlagon keeps watch and oppresses his fellow-slaves, letting none of them near Demos (40–80).
3. Zeus and the younger Olympians revolt and fight a ten-year war with the Titans; an oracle from Gaia says they must free the Hundred-Handers from Tartarus to be successful (617–38).	3. Nicias and Demosthenes decide to run away,[68] but the oracle from Bacis says they should find a sausage-seller (80–146).
4. Nectar, ambrosia and the excellence of Zeus' intelligence persuade the Hundred-Handers to help (639–63).	4. The prospects of great political power and the help of the *agathoi* and *dexioi* (the 'good' and 'intelligent') persuades the Sausage-Seller (147–233).
5. Battle begins between the Hundred-Handers and Titans; Zeus enters combat, which involves thunder, lightning, storms, and turbulence of land, sea and air (664–710).	5. Battle begins between Knights and Paphlagon (247ff.); Sausage-Seller enters combat, whose images are those of thunder and lightning (626, 696), storms and turbulence on land, sea and in politics.
6. The Titans are sent to Tartarus with its decay and storms, and sealed behind bronze doors (711–45).	6. Paphlagon is sent down to Ceramicus (cemetery) to be taunted by harlots and to drink bath-water (1395–1408; cf. 1039f. for iron towers restraining him).
7. Zeus inaugurates his reign with figures allegorising its peace and prosperity: Metis, Themis, Eunomia, Eirene, etc. (886–929).	7. The Sausage-Seller inaugurates Demos' reign with the allegorical figures of the Spondai.

[68] Fontenrose 1959: 582, theme 7c: panic on the part of gods other than the next champion.

still shown.[69] Again we have neighbours of the Paphlagonians with chthonic connections. There is a tradition too that the Mariandyni became the voluntary slaves of the people of Heraclea.[70] The first reference to the Paphlagonians themselves is in the Trojan Catalogue:[71] 'Leading the Paphlagonians was the shaggy heart of Pylaemenes, from among the Eneti, whence comes the race of wild mules.' 'Pylaemenes' recalls those names in 'Pyl-' which regularly have chthonic associations,[72] and the chthonic elements in Paphlagonia. The 'race of wild mules' also indicates the unusual nature of the Paphlagonians: abnormal occurrences like fertile mules are appropriately attributed to barbarian areas.[73]

Indeed, Paphlagon is a wholly appropriate denizen of such worlds. He is of monstrous appearance (75–9): 'he watches over everything, because he has one leg in Pylos and the other in the Assembly. So great is the area he spans that his arse is among the Chaonians, his hands in Aetolia and his mind in Clopidae.' Compare 626–8: 'Inside he broke off words that rolled like thunder, and full of bombast he hurled them at the Knights, piling up stupendous phrases.' In keeping with the blustery nature of his native region, Paphlagon is much associated with winds and floods, most strikingly in 430–41:

> *Paph.* I shall come out against you like a wind set fresh and mighty,
>   stirring up alike the earth and sea in confusion.
> *SS.* And I shall shorten my sausage-skins and sail before a favour-
>   able wave, as I tell you to go to hell.
> *Dem.* I'll look after the bilge, in case we spring a leak.
> *Paph.* By Demeter, you won't run off with all the talents you stole
>   from the Athenians.
> *Dem.* Look out and slacken your sheet; he's blowing a nor'easter of
>   indictments.
> *SS.* I know for a fact that you got ten talents from Potidaea.
> *Paph.* All right, will you take one to keep quiet about them?
> *Dem.* He'd gladly take it. Slacken the ropes; the wind's easing up.

---

[69] X. *Anab.* 6.2.2; cf. D. P. 784–92 (with Eustathius' commentary).

[70] Pl. *Legg.* 776C–D; Strabo 12.3.4; Athen. 263D–E. The Amazons live near by: A. R. 2.987f., 995.

[71] *Il.* 2.851f.; cf. in general, Ruge, *RE* 18.4.2497f. Pericles had led a force there perhaps in the early 430s (Plut. *Peric.* 20.1f.; Meiggs 1973: 197–9).

[72] *LGRM* III 2.3325ff.

[73] *Hemionoi* breed in Syria and Cappadocia, but they are not the same as the offspring of horse and ass (Arist. *HA* 577b23f., 580b1ff., *Mir.* 835b1). In Hdt. 3.151.2 and 7.57.2, asses giving birth are portents. *Equus hemionus onager* does in fact give birth.

At 692, he is 'rolling a wave', at 248 Carybdis and at 137 has a voice like the Athenian river Cycloborus; he is a 'mud-stirrer' (308; cf. 864ff.) who catches eels. His name not only puns on *paphlazein* but recalls the *kumata paphlazonta*, 'foaming waves', of Homer.[74]

Like the Minotaur, he combines the human and the animal. The play's imagery presents him in the guise of several beasts: for instance, a *bursaietos* ('leathern eagle', 197), a pig (375–81), an insect (403), 'a dog-headed one' (416), a cockerel (496), a cormorant (956), a lion (1037), and a hawk (1052). By contrast, this type of imagery is rarely found applied to the Sausage-Seller.

Paphlagon seems also to be able to change his shape at will.[75] There are two strikingly 'kaleidoscopic' images, at 258–65 and 305–13.[76] In the former, he is successively a greedy guest seizing food out of turn, a man informing on those under audit and squeezing them like figs to see if they are ripe, a wrestler, a fig-eater again, and finally a man seeking out the rich and weak-minded as victims. In the latter, he is a man filling the universe with his shouting, a stirrer of mud, a stormer of the city, again one who deafens all with his shouting and finally a watcher for revenues as if they were tunny.

Not surprisingly, such a figure acts like the Minotaur in its demand for tribute.[77] Demosthenes tells of his despotic ways and his habit of robbing fellow-slaves of gifts they had destined for Demos (40ff.; cf. 774–6). He has a voracious appetite not only for food (248, 353ff.) and the *sitesis* (573f., 709, 766), but also for his victims (e.g. 258ff.).

We have seen the chthonic connections of his country: he himself is called Cerberus at 1030. Twelve times in the play he is connected with Pylos. For this there are obviously good historical reasons in Cleon's recent military triumph, but Pylos, the 'gate' to Hades, was also the place where Heracles, the civilising hero, fought against the god of death:[78] history and mythology thus coincide. Paphlagon will eventually return to the gates of the Ceramicus with its cemetery.

---

[74] The verb is used elsewhere of Cerberus (*Peace* 313f.); cf. Eubulus, *Titans*, fr. 108; Timocles fr. 17.3; [A.] *PV* 370 (Taillardat 1962: 191–4).   [75] Fontenrose 1959: 580f., theme 3E.

[76] Brunck rearranged 258ff. to make them tidier, and this has been accepted by Sommerstein; however, the similarly kaleidoscopic passage in 305ff. might support the traditional order here.   [77] Cf. Paus. 6.6.7–11 on The Hero and the list in Frazer's note on 9.26.7f.

[78] *Il.* 5.395–404 ; Pi. *Ol.* 9.29–35. At *Il.* 11.690ff., he fights Neleus and his sons there and at [Hes.] *Aspis* 359ff., Ares: cf. Fontenrose 1959: 327–30.

The conventions of the Gigantomachy myths allow us to explain to some extent the paradox that one so degenerate as the Sausage-Seller (or so 'lowly' as a comic poet) could be of such importance to the safety of the city. As Fontenrose says of these myths, 'It is possible to run through the whole list of themes and show that the champion is the duplicate of his opponent.'[79] Thus, Zeus, like his opponents, is found changing shape and using weapons such as lightning; he is as tyrannical as they (compare his treatment of Prometheus), and as lecherous; he too is a usurper; he is helped by Ge, mother of his opponent Typhoeus; his storms are both fructifying and destructive; he began his exploits when young; he swallowed Metis to maintain his power, as Cronus did his children, and so on. The opponents must be defeated at their own game by a figure who combines elements of the vile and the divine. The Sausage-Seller and Paphlagon share several features: they are both tricksters, employing theft, violence and flattery to gain their ends (54–63: 744f.); they are both of low social standing and poor education (188ff.: 985ff.); they both have loud voices (218, 638: 137 etc.); Paphlagon was recently purchased (2), the Sausage-Seller is new to politics.

After their victories, both Zeus and the Sausage-Seller undergo transformation: Zeus moves immediately from being a thunder- and lightning-wielding battle-god to a god of peace and prosperity, who creates children symbolising the new-found stability of his reign; the Sausage-Seller becomes *prostates* of the people and introduces the Spondai. So Demos, allegory of the people,[80] is transformed like the cosmos in Hesiod. The degeneracy of the characters in the play is not just a farcical paradox but comparable to the periods of chaos dramatised in myth and ritual, and to the period of marginality of the ephebe soon to be a citizen of the centre.

The parabasis gave indications that the play should be read as a gigantomachic succession myth, and it also reinforces such a reading by the way that not just the Sausage-Seller's but also Aristophanes' own battle with the monster Cleon is set in the context of this kind of myth. Complaining of the fickle way the Athenians have treated their poets, Aristophanes has the Chorus say (520–40):[81]

[79] 1959: 470; cf. Cornford 1914: 148–53; Nagy 1979: 142ff.
[80] Newiger 1957: 11–49.   [81] Tr. Sommerstein 1981.

He knew what happened to Magnes, for one, as soon as the white hairs stole upon him: Magnes who had set up so many trophies of victory over his rivals' choruses, yet though he produced every kind of sound for you, twanging the lyre, flapping wings, speaking Lydian, buzzing like a gall-fly and dyeing himself frog-green, he did not stay the course, but in the end, in his old age (never in his youth!), he was driven from the stage in his declining days because he was found wanting in satirical power. Then our poet remembered Cratinus, who once, gushing with your lavish applause, used to flow through broad plains of artlessness, and uproot oak trees, plane trees and rivals, sweep them from their places and bear them downstream. At a party no song could be sung except 'Goddess of Bribery, fig-wood shod' and 'Artificers of dextrous songs': so greatly did he flourish. And now you take no pity on him, though you see him drivelling, with his pegs falling out, his tuning gone, and joints gaping; in his old age he wanders about, like Connas 'wearing a garland old and sere, and all but dead with thirst', when in honour of his former victories he ought to be drinking in the Prytaneum, and instead of spouting drivel, should be sitting sleek-faced in the audience by the side of Dionysus. And what rage and buffeting you made Crates endure, who used to send you home with a good lunch provided at small expense, preparing the most exquisite idea-cakes from his so-refined lips! Indeed he only just held his own, sometimes coming to grief, sometimes not.

The rough chronological sequence brings to mind the succession of four politicians in the oracle.[82] The details with which Aristophanes describes these poets have been taken, I think rightly, as evidence for the titles or styles of their comedies and as humorous banter against other rival poets,[83] but more importantly they also cast them in the role of the defeated figures of succession myths: they are similar to Paphlagon and to creatures like Typhoeus.

Thus, Magnes' very name, 'Magnesian', marks him out as a foreigner, as does his performance 'playing the Lydian'. He is a figure of violence, who set up many trophies over his enemies – the military metaphor is notable –[84] and the way in which he turned himself into a variety of animals etc. recalls the frequent animal imagery of

---

[82] The order is that of their debuts. Cratinus was still producing plays, but 'by sandwiching him between Magnes and Crates Aristophanes insinuates that he belongs to the past and his retirement is due' (Sommerstein 1981: 171). On Magnes, Meineke 1839–41: I 29–35; on Cratinus, Norwood 1931: 114–44; Pieters 1946; on Crates, Bonanno 1972.

[83] Against this view, Spyropoulos 1975.

[84] I have not found *tropaion* of poetic contests elsewhere.

Paphlagon and the shape-changing of the chaos-monsters: 'putting forth all sorts of voices' recalls Hesiod's description of Typhoeus as 'putting forth every sort of sound'.[85]

Cratinus' name is formed from the root *kret-, which signifies 'power', 'violence'; he is a mighty stream bearing all before it, including his enemies. His song to the Goddess of Bribery from the days before his lyre[86] fell apart echoes not only the frequent charges against Paphlagon of bribery and sycophancy,[87] but also Cleon's inability to play in any modes except 'the Bribery mode' (985–96). The references to Cratinus' not enjoying the *sitesis* and *proedria* recall the complaints at Paphlagon's possession of them (cf. 702–4).

Crates' name is formed from the same root as Cratinus'. His benefits to the city are expressed in culinary terms, one of the central metaphors of the play, and there may be more than a hint of Paphlagon's meanness in 538f.: the food is cheap and Crates offers an *ariston* not a *deipnon*, which would have been more substantial.[88] This is very different from Themistocles who 'when the city had lunched, kneaded for her the Peiraeus' (815). That Crates' mouth was very dry suggests an unbecoming frugality – a lunch without wine?

If this sequence is to parallel that of the four politicians, we need a fourth term, and it is immediately clear who this is: as a climax to the anapaests Aristophanes relates his own prudent conduct in rising slowly through the naval ranks. Fearing to suffer as the other poets had, he hesitated (541–50):

> What's more, he said one ought to be an oarsman before setting one's hand to the helm; then stand in the prow and watch for the winds and only then be a steersman for oneself. For all these reasons, therefore, because he was careful and did not jump in feet first to produce rubbish, raise a great shout for him and send him on his way with eleven oars and a jolly good Lenaean cheer, so that our poet can go on his way rejoicing, having achieved success, splendid with his shining pate.

---

[85] *Th.* 830; cf. Pl. *Legg.* 653D–E, 808D.

[86] A lyre, not a flute (van Leeuwen). For a broken lyre standing as a symbol of the end of a poetic career, compare the representations of Thamyris, after he became blind, in Paus. 9.30.2, 10.30.8; cf. 4.33.3. Furthermore, Connas, to whom Cratinus is compared, was a lyre-player and teacher (Pl. *Euthyd.* 272C).   [87] 66, 259, 403, 437, 802, 834 etc.

[88] Plut. *Mor.* 726C–D; *mattein* is normally used of the less luxurious barley-bread (Neil 1901: *ad loc.*).

Aristophanes thus becomes the poetic equivalent of Agoracritus on his re-entry to songs of praise with the rejuvenated Demos,[89] who is similarly *lampros* ('splendid', 1331). There are also elements in Aristophanes' self-praise that align him with the ephebe and Sausage-Seller. He emphasises his inexperience and youth to explain his unwillingness to ask for a chorus in his own name; he prefers to serve a long apprenticeship before aspiring to the office of helmsman. This choice of metaphor reminds one of the Sausage-Seller's skill in nautical matters (430ff., 756ff.) and points via the common image of the ship of state also to political power. The support of the Knights for a 'mere' comic poet and naval rating is of a kind with that for a Sausage-Seller. A Lenaean victory for Aristophanes therefore will have the same rejuvenating effect as that of Agoracritus over Paphlagon. In *Acharnians*, Aristophanes identified himself with a ragged king, now he takes the form of a vile sausage-seller whose victory in competition with his rivals and accession to the highest place in the state brings the city safety.

Knights and Athens

The Hesiodic myth of Zeus's succession is the foundation myth of the universe as at present constituted. It is also possible, however, to detect a purely Athenian strand in *Knights*, whereby the Sausage-Seller's victory is represented in terms reminiscent of the foundation myth of the city and the rituals, celebrated at the turn of the year, that were connected with it. The analysis of the Athenian New Year followed here is essentially that of Burkert.[90]

The myth told of the contest for the patronship of the city between Athena and Poseidon, who brought gifts to sway the Athenians. When Athena's olive-tree was preferred to Poseidon's salt-spring and war-horse, the god unleashed either a flood or his son Eumolpus with an army from Eleusis. Erechtheus, 'son' of Athena,

---

[89] The language of the Chorus' prayer for the Sausage-Seller's success in 498–502 is very similar to that of their request for Aristophanes' in 548–50.

[90] 1966, 1983a: 135–61 and 1985: 227–34; see also Schachermeyr 1950: 23, 157f.; Siewert 1979: 284f.; J. Binder 1984. Strictly speaking, there was no 'New Year festival' in Athens, but see Burkert 1985: 233 for a justification of speaking thus: 'this New Year festival is stretched into a long series ... Many elements have been drawn into this festal sequence in a contingent way.'

opposed and killed him at Sciron, but was rammed into the earth by Poseidon with his trident. This ended the conflict and Poseidon–Erechtheus was worshipped alongside Athena in the Erechtheum.[91] Another story, which cannot easily be reconciled with this in narrative terms, but is clearly related in ritual and conceptual ones, tells of the birth of Erichthonius after Athena had wiped Hephaestus' seed from her thigh with a piece of wool (*erion*) and cast it on the ground (*chthon*).[92] Athena put him in a chest (*kiste*), which she entrusted to the daughters of Cecrops, Aglaurus, Pandrosus and Herse, with instructions not to open it. They duly disobeyed and threw themselves off the Acropolis, when they discovered Erichthonius as half child, half snake, or, in some versions, guarded by snakes. Erechtheus and Erichthonius are clearly hypostases of the same figure: 'Erechtheus is dead, long live Erichthonius', as Burkert says.[93]

The victory of Athena over Poseidon is another way of expressing the victory of cosmos over chaos found in the myths we have examined. As Detienne and Vernant have shown, these two deities are both opposed and complementary to each other, the main difference being that Poseidon's power over the war-horse and the sea is more elemental, while Athena exercises her power through technical skill, controlling horses by the invention of the bit and the sea by the art of navigation.[94] Athena is patroness of the civilised skills of art and technology, and guardian of the city's hearth, but also a warrior-goddess whose arms terrify; Poseidon is lord of the chaotic sea, but also an Olympian who fought to defeat the Giants and is worshipped alongside Athena in the heart of Athens.

This period of conflict and the subsequent restoration of harmony was also reflected in the festivals that encircled the New Year at Athens. These were of two types: of 'dissolution' at the end of the old year, and of 'restoration' in the first month of the new. The first group began on 3 Scirophorion with the Arrhephoria, when the young girls who had helped weave the peplos ended their seclusion on the Acropolis with a night-time descent to the temple of Aphrodite *en Kepois* ('In the Gardens'), bearing down one set of sacred

[91] For other such pairings, Brelich 1958: 130f.   [92] Powell 1906.

[93] 1983a: 156; cf. Loraux 1981: 35–73.

[94] 1978: 187–213; for Athena and *techne* see also Herington 1955: 54 n. 1.

objects and bringing up another.[95] With this the birth of Erichthonius was associated. Next was the Scira, on the 12th.[96] Under a sunshade held by an Eteobutad, the priestess of Athena Polias, accompanied by the priest of Poseidon–Erechtheus left the Erechtheum and travelled out through the Sacred Gate in the Ceramicus to the temples of Athena and of Demeter and Core at Sciron near Eleusis. Sciron, like the Ceramicus, had a reputation as a place of licence. The women gathered together apart from the men so that family life was disrupted, and garlic was eaten in quantities as a ritual antaphrodisiac. During this ritual absence of the city's gods near Eleusis, the Ceryces, an important Eleusinian priestly clan, 'occupied' the Acropolis and performed the unusual Buphonia rite to Zeus at the Dipolieia two days later.[97] At this, oxen circled the altar on which were cakes, and the ox that first ate a cake was slain by a man with an axe, who then fled. The others then shared the guilt by eating the ox in the Prytaneum. A trial was held at which the blame was passed from person to person until it fell on the axe and flaying-knife. The latter (or both) of these was flung into the sea and the hide was stuffed and harnessed to a plough. The sacrifice to Zeus on Athena's Acropolis in her absence, the presence of 'Eleusinians' there and the anomalous Buphonia rite all mark this as an abnormal period. A month later, on 12 Hekatombaion, was the Cronia, the equivalent of the Roman Saturnalia, when the master–slave relationship was reversed to represent the age of Cronus before Zeus imposed order.[98]

Celebration of the re-creation of order began with the Synoecia on 16 Hekatombaion, which commemorated Theseus' unification of the villages of Attica into the city of Athens, but the great New Year festival was the Panathenaea, founded by Erichthonius.[99] The Pan-

---

[95] Paus. 1.27.3; Burkert 1966; Deubner 1932: 9–17; Parke 1977: 141–3; Calame 1977: I 236–40; against Burkert, Simon 1983: 39–46 and van Sichelen 1987.

[96] Deubner 1932: 40–50; Parke 1977: 156–62; Brumfield 1981: 156–81; Burkert 1983a: 143–9; Simon 1983: 22–4. The sources are in Jacoby, *FGH* 3b Suppl. I.286–9. For the absence of gods, see Frazer on Paus. 2.7.7f.

[97] The principal ancient sources are Paus. 1.24.4 and Porph. *De Abst.* 2.10, 29–31; cf. Deubner 1932: 158–74; Parke 1977: 162–7; Detienne 1977: 54f; Burkert 1983a: 136–43; Simon 1983: 8–12.

[98] Plut. *Comp. Lyc. et Numa* 1.5; Athen. 639Bff.; Mommsen 1898: 32–5; Deubner 1932: 152–5; Parke 1977: 29f.

[99] Deubner 1932: 22–35; Brelich 1969: 314–48; Thompson 1961: 225–31; Parke 1977: 33–50; Burkert 1983a: 154–8; Simon 1983: 55–72; and for the vases, Bérard 1989b: 109–14.

athenaic procession began at the Sacred Gate in the Ceramicus and mounted to the Acropolis via the Agora, thus reversing the direction of the Scira procession and representing the return of the gods to the city. There was a ship-cart with the *peplos* illustrating the Giganto-machy mounted on the mast;[100] on this the priests and priestesses rode crowned and garlanded; a choir sang.[101] The cart was drawn to the Eleusinium, where the mast was removed and carried to the temple of Athena Polias. Representatives of all ages and classes took part, including metics and slaves, with the young men on horse-back taking a significant role, as the Parthenon frieze shows. One hundred cows were sacrificed to Athena Polias and to Victory and, after butchering by the priests, the meat was taken back via the Agora to the Ceramicus for distribution to the people. At the Great Panathe-naea, there were horse-, ship- and chariot-races, including the spectacular *apobates*-race, where an armed warrior leapt on and off a moving chariot. This latter has been interpreted as the 'advent' of the new king to take possession of his land, and tradition has it that Erichthonius was the first victor.[102] After the Panathenaea some new officials took up their state posts.[103] By the end of this festival, therefore, unity and order are restored and Athena and Poseidon are again together in the Erechtheum: the opposition between them was no more than another sign of the dissolution at the year's end.

The play makes much use of the symbolism and ideology of both the myths and the rituals. We shall consider the myths first. The Sausage-Seller is, as it were, Athena's champion. He twice claims a connection with her: at 903, she orders him to defeat Paphlagon, and at 1203, she gives him the idea of stealing the hare. This theft comes at the end of a series of gifts from Athena which the two men present to Demos in competition: Athena gives the Sausage-Seller ultimate victory. Similarly, both have dreams from Athena

[100] The earliest reference appears to be Strattis fr. 31, from the *Macedonians or Pausanias* of *c.* 400 (Geissler 1925: 70 and xviii).

[101] There is an elaborate, but perhaps not substantially misleading picture of the event in Himerius, *Or.* 47.12–16 Colonna.

[102] Vian 1952: 247f.; Connor 1987: 45 n. 31 on Peisistratus' use of this device on returning to power, and for bibliography (esp. D. H. *AR* 7.73). See also R. Martin 1951: 219; Mikalson 1976; Plut. *Demetr.* 10. E. *Ion* 1528f. associates this practice with the Gigantomachy.

[103] Cf. Meiggs & Lewis 1988: no. 58a.27–9; [Arist.] *Ath. Pol.* 43.1, with Rhodes 1981: 517; also Vian 1952: 258f. on the Panathenaea and political power.

(1090ff.), but the Sausage-Seller's is deemed wiser by Demos. We
have already seen that the play represents a victory for the Sausage-
Seller in Athena's sphere of cunning and *techne*.

Furthermore, the Sausage-Seller has a number of attributes in
common with Athena's hero, Erichthonius. Associated with snakes
in his *kiste*, Erichthonius was identified with the *oikouros ophis*, the
snake in the temple of Athena Polias, which was fed with sacred
cakes: when, just before Salamis, the cake was uneaten, the Athenians left the city believing Athena herself to have abandoned it.[104]
He appeared with her in Gigantomachies, stood between the goddess
and her shield on Pheidias' statue, and was probably sculpted
twined around Athena's olive tree in the west pediment of the
Parthenon, between her and Poseidon.[105] The Sausage-Seller is also
connected with snakes. In the oracle, Paphlagon will perish 'when
the crooked-clawed leathern-eagle seizes in his talons the foolish
snake that drinks blood' (197f.). This snake is explained in 207f.:
'The snake, like the sausage, is long; and then the sausage, like the
snake, drinks blood.' Might one wonder whether a Sausage-Seller
with his sausage-skins (160) was chosen to be hero of the play as a
comic reflection of Athena's 'son'? Is it pure coincidence that he wins
his contest when Demos is asked to look into his *kiste* (1211ff.),
precisely the kind of box in which Erichthonius was given to the
Cecropidae and into which they were not to look?

By contrast, Paphlagon resembles Poseidon. Like the sea-god,
he is a raiser of storms (430ff. etc.), and at 247 he is a *taraxippostratos*,
which recalls Poseidon Taraxippos at Olympia, Nemea and the
Isthmus, who was said to terrify the race-horses.[106] His interest in
tunny is twice remarked on (313, 354), the first fruits of which were
offered to Poseidon, whose trident is a tunny-spear.[107] He is connected with Pylos, where Poseidon was a major deity from the
Mycenaean period onward and where he is the protecting god in
stories of Heracles' attacks.[108] Finally, when Demos dismisses Paphlagon, he does so with the words 'Wretch, have you then been
deceiving me with your thefts? And I garlanded you and gave you

104 Hdt. 8.41.2f.; Powell 1906: 18.
105 Paus. 1.24.7; Vian 1952: 131; Brommer 1963: 41, 96f., 101.
106 Paus. 6.20.15–19; Detienne & Vernant 1978: 200f.
107 Antigonus Carystius *ap.* Athen. 297E; Burkert 1983a: 208; 1985: 137; Shapiro 1989.
108 Chadwick 1976: 94–6; Fontenrose 1959: 327–30; on Poseidon and the Underworld,
      Schachermeyr 1950: index s.v. 'Poseidon', p. 216b.

gifts!' (1224f.). The scholiast's comment is noteworthy: 'He is imitating the Helots, when they garland Poseidon.' It is most likely that Demos' words are a quotation from a play, probably Eupolis' *Helots*, which contained passages in Doric; whatever the truth about this, the reference to Poseidon at this crucial moment is significant.

Just as Athena ultimately controls Poseidon, so the Sausage-Seller's boat overcomes the storms of Paphlagon (430ff.); he trumps Paphlagon's prodigious quantities of fish with larger quantities of meat (354ff.), and his slice of fish with animal offal (1177–9); when Paphlagon offers a cake to help the navy, he presents the more substantial 'belly-timber' of entrails (1184f.); he wins the debate in the Assembly through his control of the price of sprats;[109] and his knowledge of the oracles of Glanis, 'the Cat-fish',[110] gives him an insight into the future. Before it is revealed that he is the saviour of the city and not its next tormentor, the Chorus envisage him ending up as the master of the sea: 'You will rule the allies with a trident, with which you will make a fortune, by your shaking and turmoil' (839f.).

When we come to the festivals, the similarities with the play are also striking. At the start of the play, a slave and outsider is in control of Demos and his house in the absence of the proper protectors. This recalls the Cronia, with its inversion of the roles of master and servant. One of Paphlagon's crimes of which Demosthenes complains is the following theft: 'Only the other day, when I'd kneaded a Spartan barley-loaf, like the devil he is he ran round,[111] snatched it up and presented what *I* had kneaded as his own' (54–7). This theft has similarities with that of the ox who circled the Buphonia altar and stole the cake, which Porphyry, whose account seems to go back to Theophrastus, says was a *pelanos*, a cake made with barley;[112] Pausanias says that it was 'barley mixed with wheat'.[113]

Fittingly, after this 'Buphonia', not only is the ox Paphlagon punished, but the course of the Sausage-Seller's career follows the pattern of the Panathenaea. He begins, like the procession, in the Ceramicus, the antithesis of the normal centres of influence in the

---

[109] For the parody of the *euangelia* here, cf. Pritchett 1979: 189–92.

[110] Thompson 1947: 43–8.

[111] For a defence of the majority reading *peridramon*, Bowie 1982b: 114 (coll. *Wasps* 237 and 924).

[112] *De Abst.* 2.29; cf. Burkert 1983a: 137 n. 6 for bibliography on the origin of Porphyry's account.   [113] 1.24.4.

city;[114] the procession mounted to the Acropolis via the Agora, while the Sausage-Seller moves through the Agora to the two main political centres, the Pnyx and the Prytaneum.[115] The goddess returns to her land in a ship with a Gigantomachy on its mast, and the Sausage-Seller is depicted in naval imagery as he performs his deeds of Gigantomachy. He is supported in his struggle by the Knights, who played an important part in the festival. After butchery, the meat was taken via the Agora to the Ceramicus, rather as Paphlagon makes a similar descent after his 'butchery' by the Sausage-Seller (1397–1401).[116] After the Panathenaea, officials took up their posts, and Agoracritus assumes his garland, symbol of office and prize in some of the festival's competitions.[117] He and Paphlagon, both great villains, change places: 'Paphlagon is dead, long live Agoracritus!' A new order is created amongst gods and men at the festival, and so it is in the play. At sea, the navy will be properly funded (1366–8); on land, the lawcourts will be properly run (1358–64), the hoplite registers will not be tampered with (1369–72) and beardless young men, who now sit gossiping in the latest slang in the Agora or making decrees, will be sent off to a more appropriate (and indeed classic) ephebic activity, hunting (1373–83).[118] Over all, peace will reign, with the discovery of the Spondai whom Paphlagon has been hiding (1388–95).

Finally, the presence in the Panathenaic procession of people from all estates symbolised the unity of the *polis*.[119] This unity is celebrated in the play also, as the forces of order join together to oppose chaos and the 'outside': *Knights* therefore is like the *Oresteia* in invoking the Panathenaea as a symbol of the uniting of forces for

[114] R. Martin 1951: 258f.; Loraux 1981: 41–5.

[115] Around the beginning of the fifth century, the Agora gave way to the Pnyx as the focus of power and decision-making, but still retained much of its traditional prestige (R. Martin 1951: 280–3, 287–94). This may account for the contradiction between the suggestion that the Sausage-Seller worked in the Agora (181 etc. and the name Agoracritus) and his claim to have worked in the Ceramicus, not the Agora (1245–7): the mythical pattern demands that he work in a place far removed from the 'centre' of the city, but the Agora is still the natural place for business.

[116] The Panathenaic sacrifice of one hundred cows to Athena Polias and Nike is mentioned at 654–6 by Paphlagon (he is doubled by the Sausage-Seller). For the distribution, cf. *IG* 2².334 (335/4, but indicating that earlier practices are to be followed). Neil 1901: 156 on 1168f. suggests the scene of giving food to Demos has its origin in the Panathenaic banquet.

[117] Schol. Pl. *Parm.* 127A; Photius, Suidas s.v. *Panathenaia*; Deubner 1932: 34.

[118] E.g. Vidal-Naquet 1981b, 1986; Durand & Schnapp 1989: 61–5; Schnapp 1989.

[119] Bérard 1989b: 109–14.

the good of the city.[120] In the parabasis, the recent campaign against Corinth led by Nicias in 425, when cavalry were shipped out on horse-transports, is described as maritime activity by the horses themselves (598–602):[121]

> We do not so much admire what they did on land as the time they leapt manfully into the horse-transports, after buying their water-bottles – others brought garlic and onions; then, grasping their oars, like we mortals, they struck out and cried 'Yo-neigh-ho! Who will row?'

By undertaking these naval manoeuvres and performing the concomitant menial tasks, the aristocratic Knights unite themselves with tʰ common sailors, just as they have lent their support to a Sausage-Seller and a comic poet (each of whom is presented in naval terms, to reinforce the parallel). They mediate the oppositions rich and poor, land and sea. Furthermore, though young, they represent the old aristocracy, which is presumed to have lost its power to the new demagogues.[122] In this they resemble Zeus' helpers, the Hundred-Handers, who belong to the generation of gods that is being superseded, but whose help is still required for the seizure of power: 'Zeus' accession to power involves the intervention in his favour of divinities who belong to another generation than his own, that of the ancient gods related to those primordial powers which the new king is going to subordinate to himself.'[123]

In recreating in Athens the former golden age of Aristeides and Miltiades with the help of these creatures, the Sausage-Seller himself achieves true heroic status. 'The hero stands at the point where the divine and human spheres intersect', as Segal says, and the hero is often a man who, like Odysseus or Heracles, experiences contact with the Olympians and the underworld powers.[124] So it is with the Sausage-Seller: at 156 both Olympian and Chthonian deities approve

---

[120] Headlam 1906; The evidence is collected in Sommerstein 1989: 34, 281f.; cf. 275–8; Bowie 1993.

[121] Thuc. 4.42–5; cf. 2.56. The antepirrhema of the second parabasis (1300–15) presents the complementary scene where sea transport moves onto the land, as triremes speak like humans and threaten to seek refuge in the Theseum, a place of refuge for the oppressed (Plut. *Thes.* 36.4; Ar. fr. 577).

[122] Neil 1901: on 551. We may contrast the role of the 'young' in *Acharnians*: groups and classes do not necessarily have the same role in all plays.

[123] Detienne & Vernant 1978: 73.　　　[124] Segal 1981: 8; for Odysseus, Vidal-Naquet 1981a.

of his coming to power; like Erechtheus/Erichthonius, the Sausage-Seller/Agoracritus spans a period of dissolution and restoration.

In the lyrics of the parabasis, Athens is described as mighty 'in war and poets and power' (583f.), and her patron goddess is asked to bring 'Victory, who is friend of choral song and contends with us against our enemies' (589f.). Rich Knights and poor Sausage-Seller, the deities of city and sea, and Victory herself all unite with the poet in the struggle for order in Athens. The whole is bound together by the ideology and symbolism of ephebic and succession myths and of the Panathenaea. Aristophanes standing, pate gleaming, in the prow of his ship, accompanied by the cheers of the crowd, recalls the Panathenaic ship with its priests and priestesses setting off to the sound of choruses to bring the goddess home from Eleusis.

Sausage-Seller and salvation

All of this is very splendid, but the reading of the Sausage-Seller as a figure of heroic stature has been achieved, as in the case of our first look at Dicaeopolis, largely by the constant suppression of the facts not only that he is worse than Paphlagon, but that he is also the culmination of the series of awful politicians. Aristophanes makes no attempt to play down the repellent qualities of the Sausage-Seller, which are his title to political dominion.

There are, it is true, ways in which an Athenian audience could have 'made sense' of the domination of Paphlagon and the triumph of a sausage-seller: we have seen in myth how deities can undergo marginal periods before rising to high status. At 1405, Demos calls Paphlagon a '*pharmakos* in the Prytaneum'. Every year at the Thargelia, a man and a woman, chosen for particular physical loathsomeness and poverty, were maintained at state expense, and then, wearing a garland of figs were driven out of the city to purify it.[125] Paphlagon/Cleon has many qualities that would make him an admirable *pharmakos*, not least his physical appearance: a fragment of Cratinus describes him as 'dreadful of aspect, especially in his eyebrows',[126] and Aristophanes has horrific descriptions of him repeated in *Wasps* 1031–5 and *Peace* 753–8. In 230–2, Demosthenes reassures the Sausage-Seller as Paphlagon arrives:[127] 'Don't be afraid;

---

[125] Burkert 1979: 59–77, esp. 72–7; Bremmer 1983b, esp. 318 n. 97 on the festival.
[126] Fr. 228.   [127] Dover 1968b: 16–24 = 1987: 267–74; Welsh 1979.

they've not made a likeness of him: none of the mask-makers wanted
to do it, because they were scared.' It seems that the mask-makers
were too horrified by Cleon's appearance to be able to reproduce it,
but have none the less come up with something suitable and, no
doubt, suitably horrific. This role of *pharmakos* throws some light on
the problematic lyrics at 1111ff., where Demos replies to criticisms of
his behaviour by claiming (somewhat implausibly, on the evidence
of the play so far) that he knows what he is doing: he likes to watch
one of his *prostatai* waxing fat on theft and fraud, and then to dash
him to the ground. Like the *pharmakoi*, therefore, Cleon has been
entertained by the Demos but is duly expelled at the end of the
play.[128] That one of the first things Demos says as he comes out is that
the contestants will damage his *eiresione* with their violence perhaps
looks forward to Cleon's status as *pharmakos*: this branch of offerings
was hung on house doors either at the Pyanopsia in autumn or the
Thargelia in summer.[129]

This may give some account of the role of Paphlagon, but not
that of the Sausage-Seller. His villainy can be mitigated by another
group of myths in which the founders or re-founders of a city come
from marginal areas of society, in two of the cases after they have
been forced to withdraw there by usurpers.[130] As a result of the
battle of Sepeia, the Argives lost all their men.[131] The slaves (the
gumnetai, 'the naked, unarmed ones') took over all affairs of state,
until the young Argives grew up and threw them out by force. This
was carried out against a background of an oracle about the domination of the female over the male. Similarly, at Cumae in Magna
Graecia, Aristodemus made himself tyrant in 505/4 by getting the
slaves to murder their masters, the reward being their wives,
daughters and property.[132] The male children were spared and sent
into the countryside to work, where they were brought up as girls,
with long hair in nets, dresses, parasols, baths and perfume. When
they came of age, they rose up and drove out the tyrant with the help
of other exiles: the initiatory schema is obvious. Finally, the founders
of Taras were the Partheniae, 'Maidenly Ones', expelled from Sparta

---

[128] There are echoes also of how Zeus allowed Prometheus to trick him in the division of meats
at Mecone before punishing him and mankind (Hes. *Th.* 535–60). Brock 1986 argues that
the play has two alternative endings.   [129] Burkert 1985: 101.

[130] Pembroke 1970; Sourvinou-Inwood 1974; Vidal-Naquet 1981d.

[131] Hdt. 6.77–83; Plut. *Mor.* 245C–F; Paus. 2.20.8–10.

[132] D. H. *AR* 7.2–12, esp. 9.1–11.4; Plut. *Mor.* 261E–2D.

either because they had not fought in the Messenian War, or because they were born of indiscriminate intercourse between the women and young men or slaves.[133] Such tales of foundation by those marked as the opposite of the male, legitimate hoplite did not necessarily carry any stigma with them:

> because these three reversed world situations were placed inside the Greek world, integrated in tradition in a rational way into the context of a historical Greek city, they inevitably have an anti-establishment character at the historical and political level. But at the same time, another value of the three stories emerges, a positive quality. In the case of Taras and Locri, a new city was created as a result of the reversed world situation, a new 'order' out of the chaos and nothingness preceding the foundation.[134]

Political mythology may be happy with these ideas, but the insistence in the play upon the Sausage-Seller's negative qualities constantly reminds us that salvation is coming through a very unpromising figure indeed. One could react to this in a number of ways. It could be simply amusing: 'So bad are the politicians available to Athens today that the only way things will improve is if we get some worse ones'; or it could convey despair: 'nine-tenths of the play is deeply pessimistic.'[135] But both of these would be too extreme in their one-sidedness, because they fail to take account of the way in which Aristophanes so juxtaposes myth and reality that each deconstructs the other: the myth offers a hopeful reading of a political situation that is so disagreeable as to admit only of mythical solutions. This is tacitly acknowledged in the final boiling of Demos, which takes us away from the world of achievable realities, at least in the human sphere: boiling to rejuvenate is fine in mythology,[136] or in the case of refreshing statues of the gods, but mortals are not so susceptible.[137] The manner in which the vile Sausage-Seller changes

---

[133] Heraclid. Pont. 26 = Arist. fr. 611.57; scholia on Hor. *C.* 2.6.12; Serv. on Virg. *Aen.* 3.551. Compare also Rhacius, 'the Man of Rags', founder of Colophon (Schol. A. R. 1.308). Richard Seaford draws my attention to the tyrant of Corinth, Cypselus, another man whose rise to power from unpromising beginnings was foretold by oracles (Hdt. 5.92b–e).

[134] Sourvinou-Inwood 1974: 193.   [135] Sommerstein 1981: 2.

[136] For this motif, Frazer 1921: I 121–3, II 359–62; A. B. Cook 1914–40: II 210ff.; Burkert 1983a: 83ff. That Demos is rejuvenated is rightly argued by Olson 1990 against Edmunds 1987b: 256.

[137] Compare the bathing of the statue of Athena at the Plynteria, Simon 1983: 48 n. 28. Such radical changes of nature are also met with in more 'historical' traditions, e.g. in Herodotus 1.155–157.2 the sudden change in the Lydians from warriors to proverbial sybarites was the result of no more than a decree from Cyrus after his defeat of Croesus (cf. Pembroke 1970: 1243 n. 4).

miraculously to Agoracritus on his defeat of Paphlagon, without any 'realistic' explanation being given, points up the fact that the change from youth to man does not involve any real change in the youth's nature, but is deemed to take place at a certain moment chosen by ritual and social rather than psychological criteria. The ephebic mythos is ultimately not one that offers a practical solution to the problem of politicians whose nature one does not approve of. The citizen youth is ritually marginalised to mark his transition to being a citizen, but has, as a member of the next generation of the *polis*, really been central all the while: the marginality of a base sausage-seller does not change in reality. Similarly, the *pharmakos* who feeds himself at the city's expense is easily removed at the Thargelia, but removing politicians with their snouts in the trough is not so easy. In any case, another *pharmakos* takes his place and so the references to the Thargelia make more problematic the splendid ideas conveyed by the evocation of the Panathenaea, as was the case with the references to Choes in *Acharnians*. Gigantomachies depict the victory of cosmos over chaos, but the victors, be they Zeus or a Sausage-Seller, have a tendency to win because they outstrip their opponents in their own monstrosity: the Sausage-Seller is, in his earlier manifestations, potentially a much better *pharmakos* than Paphlagon. New-Year festivals may swap the roles of master and slave and dramatise the renewal of the city, but they are essentially dramas, unless a wise choice of new officials is made. Mythology happily proposes *kakoi* as founders or re-founders of cities, but these mythological patterns are not necessarily consistent, since the *kakos* can as easily found a city as be expelled from it in the role of *pharmakos*.

Amidst all the humour, burlesque, shouting, obscenity, celebrations of unity and so on, there is a strong thread of realism about the nature and possibility of political change.[138] Where in *Acharnians* contrasting pictures of excess were set before the audience without there being any exemplary narrative of what ought to be done, in *Knights* they are shown an apparent solution, but at the same time how little help are the artificial ideologies of political myths in such a situation. But then, Athens could console itself that it was not in the grip of a Paphlagonian slave.

---

[138] Loraux 1986: 304–12 for the ambiguities inherent in Aristophanes' use of the standard *topoi* of eulogies of Athens.

4

Wasps

Wasps and transition

In *Knights*, one of the codes that structured the rise of the Sausage-Seller was that of the *ephebeia*. *Wasps* too employs the pattern of the *ephebeia*, but does so in reverse. That such a cultural pattern can, for comic purposes, be presented in reverse may be some small confirmation of the method of this book: that patterns could be so played with suggests they were familiar enough in their usual form for a playwright to rely on his audience recognising the reversal.[1] Here therefore we have, instead of a young man undergoing trials to become a citizen with political power, an old man who is (at least by his own account) possessed of such power and whose trials literally make him young again. The ephebe stands on the boundary between two stages of life, and it is in just such a position that we find Philocleon at the start of the play: he is an old juror on the verge of retirement, whose son wishes him to make the transition; but a rather different transition takes place.

Wasps begins with two drowsy slaves, who recount troubling dreams. Xanthias begins:[2] 'I thought I saw a huge eagle fly down to the agora, seize a bronze shieldtail and bear it heavenwards. But then it was Cleonymus, dropping a bronze shield' (15–19). Sosias' is rather more complex (31–6, 39f., 42f.):

> when I fell asleep, I thought I saw an Assembly of sheep gathered together on the Pnyx, with sticks and cloaks; they were being

---

[1] Segal 1982: 158–214 detects a similar reversal in Euripides' *Bacchae*. This chapter reworks material from Bowie 1987.

[2] The 'shieldtail' is Sommerstein's. For an interpretation of the whole play in terms of dreams, Reckford 1987: 217–81; on the opening most recently, Borthwick 1992.

harangued by an omnivorous whale with the voice of singed sow
... which, with a pair of scales, was weighing beef fat ... Then
there was Theorus sitting near her with a crow's head.

When Sosias asks whether it is not somewhat ominous that Theorus
should have become a crow, Xanthias says that, on the contrary, it is
an excellent sign, because: 'he was a man and suddenly became a
crow. Isn't it obvious we should interpret this to mean he will fly
away from us to birdition?' (49–51). The puns in this passage, on
aspis 'shield'/'snake', *demos* 'fat'/'people' and, with the help of
Alcibiades' lisp, *korax/kolax* 'crow'/'flatterer', are almost impossible
to render satisfactorily in English, but they serve to underline the
idea of the shifts in these dreams between animal and man and vice
versa, which not only give an indication of the importance that
animal imagery is to have, but also announce the theme of status-
transition that is to be a major code in the play. The dropping of the
shield by the eagle–Cleonymus is a parodic reference to *rhipsaspia*,
abandoning one's shield in battle, one of those offences which
resulted in the loss of citizen rights,[3] so that this dream also highlights the theme of loss of mature, citizen status, which is to be the
fate of Philocleon at the end of his 'reversed *ephebeia*'.

In *Knights*, the parabasis provided corroboration for reading
the play and the poet's self-presentation in terms of the *ephebeia*, and
the same is true for *Wasps*. In the anapaests, Aristophanes again
reviews his career and benefits to the city: he began (1018–22)

> not openly, but hidden away helping other poets, pouring out
> many comedies by entering the bellies of others, in imitation of the
> oracular device of Eurycles. After this, he acted openly and took
> risks on his own responsibility, guiding with his reins the mouths
> of his own Muses not those of others.

The use of *krubda* ('hidden away'), with its echo of the *krupteia*, is
noteworthy. He then goes on to boast of how he behaved when he
became *megas* (1023). In the context of poetic competitions, this
word means 'raised to greatness', but it is also regularly used to mean
'mature', 'adult' as opposed to young. The slightly unusual choice of

[3] MacDowell 1962: 107 and 112 on Andoc. 1.74; Hansen 1976: 54–98, esp. 72 n. 3, comparing
Lys. 10.1; Isoc. 8.143; Aeschin. 1.29 for throwing away of the shield (cf. also Pl. *Rep.* 468A,
Legg. 943f.), and 55–74 for definition and privileges lost: 'we may conclude that *atimia* was
the penalty *par excellence* which an Athenian might incur in his capacity of a citizen, but not
for offences he had committed as a private individual' (74).

ektelesai (1024) may be explained by the use of the simple verb *telein* not only of rituals but of the birth and maturation of children.[4]

In 1029ff., the Chorus tells how, when he began to write, he did not attack men, but like the hero Heracles immediately took on (1031–5)

> the jagged-toothed dog, from whose eyes flashed the most dreadful rays of the Bitch-star; around his head there licked the heads of a hundred cursed flatterers; he had the voice of a death-dealing torrent, the stench of a seal, the unwashed balls of Lamia and the arse of a camel.

The monster is again Cleon, and the passage has affinities with Hesiod's description of Typhoeus, especially 'From his shoulders there came a hundred dread snake-heads, licking with black tongues; from his eyes in his terrifying head the fire blazed under his brows . . . all of his dread heads had a voice.'[5] These voices were of a bull, a lion, dogs and snakes. Further monsters follow in Aristophanes' catalogue, which clearly places him among the monster-defeating heroes. The parabasis thus characterises Aristophanes as a youthful monster-fighter akin to the Sausage-Seller.

The play's protagonist Philocleon is also, as we shall see, represented by a variety of different animal images, and this imagery, combined with the fact that Philocleon is first described as a 'monster' (4), the names of the main characters which both have 'Cleon' as an element, and Aristophanes' claims for himself, might all lead one to suppose that his son Bdelycleon's attempts to persuade his father away from ferocious jury-service is to be the play's ephebic struggle, just as *Knights* depicted the young Agoracritus' struggle against the powerful Paphlagon. The ephebic mythos is however to be used in *Wasps* in a manner more complex than that found in *Knights*. Bdelycleon, the younger man, does have physically and intellectually to combat his violent father, the fiercest of the Wasps (277), who tries many means to escape; and he apparently achieves his aim, as his father is reduced to nothing (997), abandons his position of apparent influence in the courts and accepts a new status. On the other hand, he is a much less colourful figure than the Sausage-Seller, and our attention is drawn much more to Philocleon, so that the son's combat is very much a sub-plot to the major plot of

---

[4] Van Leeuwen *ad loc.*; Pi. *Is.* 6.46; E. *Ba.* 99f.

[5] *Th.* 821–35: 824–7, 829 are quoted. Smell is a monstrous characteristic: Mastromarco 1988.

the shift in the character of Philocleon. One may argue too that
Bdelycleon's triumph is very much a pyrrhic one, since the essential
nature of his father is to remain unchanged. The play does not
celebrate the victory of common sense.

This shift employs the ephebic mythos in two ways. First, there
is the reversal of the normal process of the *ephebeia*, which takes
Philocleon from age to youth: just as the ephebe is subjected to trials,
so in *Wasps* the liminal Philocleon is put through three *agones*
('contests') with his son. In mythology, the world in which the trials
occur is marked by abnormality, and in each *agon* the text makes it
clear that an inversion or perversion of the 'natural' order has taken
place. Philocleon fails in each contest and, after Bdelycleon's final
victory at the end of the trial, he cries out significantly 'I am nothing
now' (997). Entry into the house with the parabasis then marks the
end of Philocleon's 'reverse *ephebeia*', after which he is found with a
new and frequently emphasised status as a 'young man', richly
characterised by such symbols of chaos and marginality as the sea
and animals. Second, in the first part of the play down to the
parabasis, there is also a complementary code in that the *agones*
themselves follow the normal sequence of the stages of human life,
from youth to age: the first surrounds Philocleon with the imagery of
youth and the *ephebeia*, the second sees him as a mature hoplite and
the third as a juror, a job much associated with the older generation.
As the *agones* proceed to the parabasis, however, they at the same
time strip him of all his existing identity and status as an old citizen.[6]

Philocleon's *agones*

Philocleon the ephebe

A variety of social, moral and physical characteristics marked
the marginal status of the Sausage-Seller, and that of Philocleon is
similarly indicated by the double portrayal of him, both as a figure
who fulfils the requirements for being an active Athenian citizen,
and as one who is either about to retire from so active a participation

---

[6] There are similar complementary and contradictory movements in the status of Odysseus in
the *Odyssey*. In Books 5–12, he moves from the 'omphalos of the sea' (1.50), where he has no
companions, ships or any other symbols of status, through various stages which culminate
in his recognition as Odysseus, king of Ithaca. The narrative of the wanderings seals this
achievement of high status, but at the same time, in the course of that narrative, he is
gradually stripped of all the marks of that status.

in the state or who is no longer qualified, for various reasons, so to participate.

Of citizenship Aristotle said: 'We call a citizen one who has the right to office in the Boule or lawcourts.'[7] At the start of the *Politics*, he defined the household as consisting of four elements: the relationships of master and slave, husband and wife, parents and children and *chrematistike*, the art of acquisition.[8] Philocleon fulfils all these criteria: he has slaves (1ff.), a wife (610–2), a daughter (607) and a son; the play takes place in his house and the family are clearly not destitute. He possesses *patrooi theoi*, the gods of the family (388): in the *dokimasia* of officials one question was 'Have you an Apollo Patroos?', meaning 'Are you an Athenian citizen?'[9] An important function of a citizen was to fight for his city, and we learn of Philocleon's and his fellow-jurors' service in the Persian Wars and other campaigns (235ff., 354ff.). As juror, paterfamilias and hoplite, then, Philocleon is marked as an Athenian citizen.

At the same time, he has ceased to be master of his household, having given way to his son as was customary when the father could no longer cope: he is 'the old master' (442), his son now 'master' (67).[10] In 'normal' circumstances, his insane behaviour at the beginning of the play would have rendered any act of his legally invalid on grounds of senility:[11] Philocleon may be a juror, but he is a crazed one suffering from a disease (114) which neither Corybantic rites nor Asclepius can cure. In mythology, disease is regularly a sign that the world is out of joint.[12] His desire to conduct trials by night (91–124) also turns the world upside down, by confusing the daytime which was normal for trials with the darkness which we have seen to be associated with the ephebe and *kruptos*.[13] He is also emotionally

[7] *Pol.* 1275b18; cf. 1275a22ff.; Pl. *Legg.* 768B.   [8] 1253b5ff.; cf. Lacey 1968: 237 n. 4.
[9] [Arist.] *Ath. Pol.* 55.3; W. S. Ferguson 1938: 31f.; Rhodes 1981: 617f.; de Schutter 1987; Hedrick 1988.   [10] Lacey 1968: 116–18.   [11] Ibid. 116 with n. 111.
[12] Hp. *MS* 1ff.; Rohde 1925: 294–7, and 320 n. 81; Segal 1981: 35–8.
[13] Philocleon's condition shares symptoms with the melancholic disease 'lycanthropia' (Roscher 1896: esp. 79–81): it appears in spring; the sufferers abandon their homes to spend the night amongst tombs; they are weak, dry and cannot weep; their legs are covered with wounds; the cure is blood-letting to fainting, then good nourishment and baths. *Wasps* is set in early summer (264f.:MacDowell 1971: *ad loc.*); for tombs read lawcourts; Philocleon is weak and surprised to feel tears (973f., 982–4); he will miss his chilblains (1167); the cure involves fainting (756, 995ff.) and the good life with Bdelycleon. Lycanthropes were believed to eat human flesh (Pl. *Legg.* 565D; Paus. 8.2.3, 6; Euanthes *ap.* Plin., *NH* 8.34.81): Philocleon consumes his victims (289). Philocleon is not a lycanthrope, but shares symptoms with sufferers from this disease which isolated them from society.

disordered: an Athenian male might legitimately find Demos, son of Pyrilampes, attractive, but to prefer the *kemos* ('voting-pebble', 97–9) is to take enthusiasm for jury-service a little far. Finally, hoplite he may have been, but his behaviour as one, especially his predilection for running away (357–9), would have earned him the loss of citizen rights consequent upon *lipostratia*.

Alongside these characteristics there are also a number of animal images, as was the case with Paphlagon. First and foremost, he is a wasp and the most fearsome of them all (278; cf. 88, 268). At the very start, the slaves refer to him as a monster (4); in Xanthias' speech to the audience he is successively a limpet (105), a bee (107; cf. 366), a crow (129), a mouse (140); later, he is a sparrow (207) and a weasel (363).[14]

In Philocleon, therefore, the civilised and the natural, *nomos* and *phusis*, co-exist, the latter barely restrained by the former. He contains within himself man and animal, the latter symbolising the youth into which, as we shall see, he will turn.[15] This duality in Philocleon is further symbolised in two ways. First, by the beach which he keeps in the house in order not to run out of voting-pebbles (109f.): this odd conjunction mirrors the way the animal is contained within the citizen, and the sea-imagery will be important at the end of the play. Secondly, there is his status as a wasp: this insect, in Greek natural history, was described both as a *politikon zoon* and as a fierce fighter.[16]

I have said that each of the three contests between father and son take place in a context of disorder, and disorders of various kinds surround the start of the play. We have already noted those in Philocleon's life-style, and further reversals may be detected in the fact that a son is trying to educate his father rather than the reverse, and that slaves are engaged in attempts to control their master. The situation is not too dissimilar from that in Demos' household, even if the causes are at first sight different: Paphlagon usurped control for his own ends, but Bdelycleon has done so for the benefit of his father, even if the Chorus of Wasps see his restraint of his father from civic

[14] Whitman 1964: 162–5.

[15] For the equation of youth with the wild, cf. e.g. the Spartan *agelai*, the 'herd' of ephebes at Drerus (*SIG*³ 527; Osborne 1987: 147); Pl. *Tim.* 44A–B, *Legg.* 653D–E, 666A–C; for education and marriage as 'taming', Calame 1977: I 372–81, 411–20; Vidal-Naquet 1981c: 174.

[16] Keller 1909–13: II 431–5; Davies & Kathirithamby 1986: 47–83; on wasps in the play generally, Weber 1908: 145–64; Newiger 1957: 74–80.

duties as tantamount to setting up a tyranny in a democratic state (464, 470).

The scene is set with suitably ephebic imagery. Xanthias draws attention to the nets Bdelycleon is using to imprison his father: 'We're on guard in a circle, having covered the whole court-yard with nets' (131f.). Nets do not belong in the *oikos*, but in the wild, so that, in symbolic terms, he has turned the civilised space of the house into a hunting-ground, the classic *locus* of the ephebe and *kruptos*. Guard-duty, movement in a circle and the fact that it is night (the slaves are on 'night guard-duty', 2), all repeat features of the marginal world of the ephebe found in *Knights*. This confusion of opposed areas recalls similar blends of the normal and abnormal, that are found in the ephebic myths; one might compare that other anomalous house, the Labyrinth, where Theseus had to evade entrapment.

The first *agon* is the 'jack-in-the box' scene (144ff.). This is essentially a contest in cunning or *techne*, in which Philocleon has already given evidence of his skills, as Bdelycleon remarks: 'you're a devil, well advanced in cunning, and deceitful' (192; cf. 176). Philocleon makes various attempts to escape, but can do so neither as smoke, nor as Odysseus nor as a bird. Smoke is a common metaphor for nothingness,[17] and to call himself 'Son of Capnias (Smoky)' is the equivalent of his later claim to be *Outis* ('No-Man', 184–6). We have seen that absence of a name and identity is characteristic of ephebes and men like Agoracritus in his struggle for a meaningful position. This trick with names is part of an elaborate parody of the scene in the *Odyssey*,[18] where Odysseus tries to escape from the Cyclops' cave by suspending himself and his men under the flocks of the monster. Philocleon wishes to have the donkey brought out so that he can take it to market, and hangs under it. Bdelycleon, mindful of his Homer, urges the slaves to be on the look-out, and when the donkey moves suspiciously slowly, addresses it: 'Neddy, why are you weeping? Because you are to be sold today? Get a move on! Why do you groan – unless you're carrying some Odysseus?' (179–81). Polyphemus too addresses his ram:[19] 'Poor ram, why are you the last of the flock to leave the cave? You were never before left behind by the others like this.' Reversing the order of the original, Philocleon now tries the trick of the false name, calling himself 'No-Man, of Ithaca, son of

---

[17] Blaydes on *Clouds* 320.   [18] 9.364–7.   [19] Ibid. 447f.

Abscondippides' (185, Sommerstein), but it is of no avail.[20] Odysseus is, of course, not an actual ephebe, but he is in a transitional stage in a marginal world, and the story of his encounter with the Cyclops has an 'ephebic' structure, in that a combat with a monster, in a dark cave, where cunning alone brings safety, closely parallels the exploits of, say, a Theseus. Unlike his mythical or ritual counterparts, however, Philocleon fails to escape from the house.

The subsequent scene with the Chorus and their sons maintains the ephebic tone, but at the same time confirms that the old jurors are not ephebes nor much endowed with physical vigour. The picture of the old men stumbling through the mud with their way lit by their sons, who could at any moment abandon them, is not only comic and pathetic but also emblematic of the play's action, in which a son tries to lead his father out of the juridical mire. The Chorus may, like Philocleon, boast of their prowess, but they are ultimately wholly dependent upon their sons. None the less, their lament for their youth is noteworthy for the concentration in it of elements that are identified with the ephebe: 'Alas, we are all that is left of that youthful band from the time we were together in Byzantium, you and I, on guard-duty. Then, creeping round at night we fooled the bread-lady and stole her mortar, before chopping it up to cook pimpernel' (235–9). They regret the loss of their youth and the exploit took place in foreign lands at the 'edge' of the Greek world, where they were on guard-duty, moving in circles, like *peripoloi*, by night. Their theft of the bowl to cook the coarse pimpernel,[21] recalls the *kruptoi* who lived in the country as best they could.

This ephebic language is picked up when the Chorus and Philocleon finally make contact. They suggest that he find a 'new, clever, plan' (346), to escape 'in secrecy' (347), 'hidden in rags like resourceful Odysseus' (351). Odysseus appears again and this time the reference is to his entries into Troy in disguise or via a drain.[22] Then, in language which echoes that of the passage just discussed, they recall an exploit of Philocleon's youth as an example to him, but to no avail (354–64):

---

[20] Philocleon says he wants to sell the donkey with its panniers (170), which is slightly unusual, but the donkey and two panniers would imitate in comic fashion the way Odysseus lashed together three sheep to carry each of his men (cf. *Od.* 9.424–30).

[21] For this as a poor food, compare the proverb quoted in the scholia 'pimpernel amongst the vegetables'.   [22] *Od.* 4.244–50; E. *Hec.* 239–41; S. fr. 367; Starkie 1897: 187.

Cho. Do you remember when you were on campaign once, how you stole the skewers and let yourself quickly down the wall, when Naxos was captured?

Ph. Yes, but what of it? This problem's not like that at all. I was young then and could steal; I was fit and no-one was guarding me, so that I could run away without fear. But now hoplites with weapons have drawn themselves up in battle order and are guarding the passes; there are two of them at the door keeping an eye on me with skewers, as if I were a cat that had stolen the meat.

The ephebic elements in this passage will be familiar now, and the mixture of ephebic and hoplite language here creates a bridge to the next *agon*.

Philocleon the hoplite

Once again, the inverted nature of the world Philocleon now inhabits is stressed. The hoplite no longer holds the weapons, which have passed to his son and, most irregularly, to his slaves: on Naxos, Philocleon held the skewers, now others do. The elaborate nature of the sentence in 359–61 seems to draw attention to the hoplite metaphor. Line 361 brings wild mountain-passes into the house where they are as anomalous as Bdelycleon's nets, somewhat laboured and punning reference to which immediately recurs in 367f.: 'The best thing for me to do is to gnaw through the net: may Dictynna forgive me for what I shall do to the net (*diktuon*).' It is furthermore unusual to find hoplites guarding mountain-passes.[23] This topsy-turvy blend of the domestic, the wild and the world of the hoplite is completed by Philocleon's calling himself a 'cat' (363), and the fact that 'weapons' are confused with 'skewers'.[24]

Undaunted by the inauspicious nature of this symbolism, Philocleon and the Wasps prepare to fight as the hoplites they once were. The Chorus have been summoned by Cleon in words reminiscent of the orders given to hoplites when they mustered for a campaign: they are to come 'with three days' rations of anger' (243). Dawn has broken just before (366): the hoplite fights by day.[25] The

---

[23] On the need for flat ground for the hoplite phalanx, cf. Polybius 18.31.5; Osborne 1987: 144; on guarding mountain-passes, de Ste Croix 1972: 190–5.

[24] Lissarrague 1989: 44–8 discusses vases depicting scenes which similarly mix hoplite and ephebic elements to represent status transition.

[25] For this change from night to day and ephebe to hoplite, cf. Vidal-Naquet 1986: 130, quoting Bravo 1980 (esp. 954–7).

Chorus summon up their anger (403ff.) and the leader bids them line up in hoplite fashion 'in good order' (424);[26] 'shoulder to shoulder' points to the importance of closed ranks in the hoplite phalanx, and 'wheel round' (422), 'raise your stings' (423) and 'attack' (423) are all appropriate to military contexts.

The ensuing battle takes the form of a repetition of the Persian Wars, in which the Wasps served, as their reference to the capture of Byzantium shows. Bdelycleon calls out foreign slaves with eastern, barbaric names, Midas, Phryx, Masintyas (433), and is himself called a *barbaros* (439). Philocleon invokes Cecrops, first king and culture-hero of Athens, who like the Wasps (1076) is an autochthonous being (438).[27] The Athenian Wasps are defeated, when Xanthias gets the slaves to attack them with smoke (457, 459). The parabasis provides a commentary on this battle. The language of the two passages is closely similar in its depiction of the jurors as wasps and autochthonous, and also in the description of the battle between the Athenians and Persians as an attack on wasps with smoke: the same verb, *tuphein*, is used in both. With 457–9, compare 1078f.: 'when the barbarian came filling the whole city with smoke and setting it ablaze'. There is, however, a significant difference. In the parabasis, the Athenians recall defeating the Persians, but here the barbarians rout the Athenian Wasps and their Cecrops. The roles are reversed and Philocleon is no longer the successful Marathon-fighter. At 522, he arms himself with a sword before his debate with his son, but it is now only in order to kill himself should he lose; earlier he had called for one with the more aggressive purpose of killing his son (166f.).

Philocleon the old juror

Having defeated the 'hoplite' Wasps, Bdelycleon is able to persuade them to listen, and, in the contest that follows, confronts them in their current guise as jurors. This third 'stage of life' is in two parts: first, there is the debate between father and son before the Chorus, and then the domestic lawcourt. In the course of the first part, Bdelycleon exposes as delusions several things on which his father prides himself, showing that as a juror he has no more real power or influence than as an ephebe or a hoplite.

---

[26] For *eutaktos* of hoplites, cf. LSJ s.v. I.2; also e.g. X. *Anab.* 1.2.15–18, *Oec.* 8.6f. For this use of hoplite imagery, see below on *Birds* 343ff.

[27] E.g. schol. *Pl.* 773; Philochorus, *FGH* 328 F 93–8. For Cecrops as typical of Athens, E. *Hipp.* 34; *Clouds* 300 (with Dover's note); see also Parker 1987b: 193–8.

Philocleon's principal claim is that his power is absolute:[28] it is second to none (549) and the jurors exercise it uniquely *anupeuthunoi*, free of the scrutiny undergone by Athenian magistrates and officers (587).[29] He sees himself deified by its possession, since defendants beseech him like a god (571), and he finishes his case with what amounts to a hymn to himself as Zeus (620–7).[30] The rest of his case depends on the influence he thinks he has over the rich and the domestic pleasures he gets when he returns with his jury-pay (605ff.). These fantasies of power do not long survive Bdelycleon's reply, in which he insinuates that Philocleon, far from being a divine king, is subject to a barbarian despotism: he 'almost bows down' to his masters and does not realise he is a slave (515–17).[31] He goes on to show that the real people of influence are not the poor jurors who have fought to make the city prosperous, but the politicians and their boy-friends (686ff.). He confronts Philocleon's simple-minded pleasure at receiving the three obols with a calculation of how small a percentage this is of the total income of the city. It is made clear to Philocleon that he does not possess power at all and that he is the dupe of those who do.

The effect of all this on Philocleon is deep: 'how you stir up my beach!' (696) is a striking expression recalling his 'beach' of 110. He drops his sword (714), giving a further sign that he is no longer a warrior. He has now been defeated in cunning, and hoplite warfare; his delusions about his power in the city and his wealth have been laid bare; and his son and slaves are in virtual control of his livelihood. He is all but finished: 'Where is my soul?' (756). Yet his passion for the lawcourts remains, from which death alone will separate him (750–63). It is to the cooling of that ardour that Bdelycleon now turns, with the ploy of the domestic trial.

This trial begins with a sacrifice (86off.). MacDowell points out that such a sacrifice is anomalous: no such rite appears to have taken place at this stage in Athenian courts.[32] One may explain it as follows. At 876, Bdelycleon refers to the proceedings as a *telete* or 'rite';[33] it is

---

[28] This point is heavily emphasised: 518, 520, 546, 549, 571, 575, 577, 587, 604, 620, 622ff. 635f.   [29] [Arist.] *Ath. Pol.* 48.4f.

[30] For a similarly misguided 'self-*makarismos*' in *Clouds*, Macleod 1981.

[31] *Proskunein* of oriental submission, Neil 1901 on *Kn.* 156.

[32] 1971 on 860–90. Prayers do appear to have been said: Stengel 1920: 79; Kleinknecht 1937: 52.

[33] 'A telete of this kind was a form of ritual whose chief function was not worship of gods but the direct benefit of the participant . . . Those who resorted to the teletae sought relief from

thus parallel to the other rites of purification, called by the same word in 121, which he tried earlier: we have the call for silence and the appeal to Apollo of Delphi and as *Paian*, the healer (868f., 874).[34] So we have a sacrifice which inaugurates the next stage of the rite of passage transferring Philocleon from the civic world of the courts to the domestic world of the house (cf. 873). Rites take place at similar junctures in *Clouds* 254ff. and 497ff., as Strepsiades is progressively initiated into the Phrontisterion.[35]

The location of the sacrifice and trial at the doors of the house is significant. Much emphasis is placed on the fact that they take place at this junction of the two areas between which Philocleon is being moved in his reverse *ephebeia*, the city and house: the court is truly 'liminal'.[36] Philocleon recalls the prophecy that the Athenians would have their own domestic lawcourts as they have shrines of Hecate built 'in their very doorways' (802)[37] and the Chorus refer to the rite as taking place 'before the doors' (871); Bdelycleon calls on Apollo in a guise that stresses the locality four times: 'neighbour, god of the street, gateman of my forecourt' (875).[38]

Again, the unusual nature of the circumstances is marked, as the three main 'worlds' of *Wasps*, the lawcourts, the house and the animal kingdom, are mixed together. To begin with, the household objects are introduced simply for Philocleon's comfort (805ff.), as Bdelycleon provides potty, fire, soup and cockerel alarm-clock. Later however they become parts of the court (829ff.):[39] Hestia's pig-

---

some anxiety with which they were afflicted and assurance of future happiness' (Linforth 1944–50: 155). Cf. Zijderveld 1934; Burkert 1985: 276; Seaford 1984: 8f.

[34] The ritual aspects of this scene are well discussed by Sidwell 1989 and 1990 in terms of practices such as those of the Corybantes. He suggests, unnecessarily (1990: 9 n. 1), that my initiatory and his medical readings may be 'incompatible': the two codes cross here, so that the rite attempts to remove both his disease and the status of 'old citizen' which is in part its cause.

[35] Sidwell 1989: 272 notes how frequent such rites are at crucial moments in the plays; he quotes *Ach.* 237ff., *Kn.* 105–8, *Peace* 431–58, 837–1126, *Birds* 848–1047, *Lys.* 185ff., *Thesm.* 36–62, 284ff., *Frogs* 871–94.

[36] For another court at a liminal point, Paus. 1.28.11: 'In Piraeus, beside the sea, is a court called Phreattys. Here exiles, against whom in their absence another charge has been brought, make their defence from a ship, the judges listening on the shore' (tr. Frazer); cf. also 2.29.10. For a court of ephebes, *SIG*³ 525 (Gortyn; Osborne 1987: 147).

[37] Sommerstein 1983: 206 on 804; Graf 1985: 258.

[38] For bibliography on Agyieus, Boegehold 1967: 116 n.21 and esp. Graf 1985: 173f. There might also be a reflection of Apollo's role in the rites of passage of ephebes, but this was not one of his functions as Agyieus.

[39] For ancient evidence on the accoutrements of the lawcourts, cf. Richter 1858: 119–44.

pen becomes the bar, jugs (amusingly, the scholiast on 855 reveals
that another name for these *arustichoi* was 'ephebes')[40] become the
voting-jars, and the chamber-pot the clepsydra. In the trial itself,
other household objects are summoned as witnesses: cup, pestle,
cheese-grater, hearth and water-jug, followed by 'the blackened
utensils' (936–9);[41] the cheese-grater gives evidence through
Bdelycleon.

The animal world is represented first of all by the cockerel
(815), who plays his part in the trial when his opinion is requested by
Philocleon (933f.). The prosecutor and defendant are both dogs, the
one who 'never stays in the same place' (969), the other merely an
oikouros ('stay-at-home', 970); they too thus represent the inside and
outside worlds between which Philocleon is making his transition.[42]
Dogs are regularly markers of margins:[43] Cerberus stands at the gates
of Hell and Hecate has her shrines at crossroads on the edge of towns;
a bitch might be sacrificed to Eileithuia for a successful birth,[44] and
armies passed between the halves of a dog to be purified;[45] in the
Phoebaeum in Sparta, puppies were sacrificed by night in a Spartan
rite with initiatory overtones.[46]

The language of the charge against Labes recalls the ephebic
imagery of the exploits of Philocleon and the Wasps discussed above.
He is 'of all dogs the man most given to eating alone.[47] He sailed
round the mortar in a circle and ate the rind of the cities' (923–5).
Furthermore, Philocleon's feeble joke on *skiron* 'plaster'/'cheese-
rind' in 926 draws attention to this word from the *skir*- root, which
is regularly used of marginal areas. The crime of stealing a cheese is
fitting for an animal, but it too also has an 'ephebic' flavour. Burkert
describes thus the whipping of Spartan youths at the altar during the
festival of Artemis Ortheia:[48]

> First there is an interim period in the country, the fox time,
> *phouaxir*; what follows is, to judge from the allusions in Xenophon

---

[40] Cf. Athen. 469A.

[41] If these actually appeared on stage, might one be tempted to see in them the black-cloaked
ephebes?

[42] For the actual trial of animals in Athens, cf. Dem. 23.76; MacDowell 1963: 85–9; Rhodes
1981: 649f. on *Ath. Pol.* 57.4.   [43] Mainoldi 1981.   [44] Plut. *Mor.* 277B (Argos).

[45] Plut. *Mor.* 290D (Boeotia); Polybius 23.10.7 (Macedon).   [46] Paus. 3.14.9.

[47] For this as a sign of anti-social behaviour, cf. Ameipsias fr. 24 K.

[48] 1985: 262. *Phouaxir*: Hsch. s.v.; robbing Ortheia: X. *Lac. Pol.* 2.9; robes: Plut. *Aristeid.* 17.
Cf. also Pl. *Legg.* 633B–C; Graf 1985: 82–90.

and Plato, a kind of cult game. The goal is 'to rob as much cheese as possible from Ortheia', while others, who, as it seems stand around the altar defending it, lash out with their whips . . . A procession in long Lydian robes follows.

In a purely Athenian context, one might note also that Pausanias ascribes the origin of the Prytaneum court, where lifeless things and animals were tried, to the first of the Buphonia sacrifices, when the ox that 'stole' the cake was slaughtered.[49] Here too we have theft at a transitional festival.

That the hero Lycus ('Wolf') presides over this court requires some discussion. Philocleon has already prayed to him for help when he was confined in the house (389) and he makes a special plea that his *heroon* be brought into the court (819).[50] There is a great deal of uncertainty surrounding this hero: it is not clear whether he was connected with the law as a 'Gerichtsdämon' or because his shrine was near a lawcourt; whether he was connected with one court or all of them; whether he was the same person as Lycus, son of Pandion and so on.[51] The precise relationship with the courts may not now be recoverable, but for our purposes the existence of some sort of connection is sufficient, and 389ff. provides the evidence. Aristophanes draws out the scene involving him in a manner that suggests he is of more than passing significance. Indeed, he is a further important indication that the domestic trial is a rite of passage.

The wolf is a classic symbol for men who have, temporarily or otherwise, withdrawn from society and thus of those undergoing initiation or change of status. Of many examples, I will look only at certain Greek ones.[52] Perhaps the most famous are the myth and ritual connected with the precinct of Zeus Lycaeus on Mt Lycaeus in Arcadia.[53] In the myth, first found in Hesiod fr. 163, Lycaon served a

---

[49] 1.28.10.

[50] For this type of prayer to a neighbouring hero, Rusten 1983.

[51] Boegehold 1967: 111–15 (though I cannot accept his suggestions as to why he is here) and Kearns 1989: 182.

[52] Jeanmaire 1939: 540ff.; G. Binder 1964: Index s.v. 'Wolf'; Piccaluga 1968; Detienne & Svenbro 1979; Gernet 1981: 125–39; Buxton 1987. Many names in Greek tradition from the *luk-* root appear at transitional points in narratives or indicate the marginal status of a character, as e.g. the youthful Achilles disguised as a girl among the daughters of Lycomedes of Scyrus; Orestes is sent to live by the shrine of Lycaeus after murdering his mother (E. *El.* 1273f.); Dolon wore a wolf-skin (*Il.* 10.334); there are many other examples.

[53] Immerwahr 1891: 1–24; and esp. Pl. *Rep.* 565D; Paus. 8.2.3, 6; Burkert 1983a: 83–93; Buxton 1987: 67–74.

boy (in some versions his own son) to Zeus and was turned into a wolf. In the ritual, one of the participants became a wolf for nine years. It was said of Damarchus, Olympic victor in boxing in 400 BC, that he had undergone this transformation before his victory. The historian Euanthes tells of an Arcadian rite which may be a later development of an earlier one.[54] In this, a youth removed his clothes, which he hung on an oak tree, swam across a lake and lived as a wolf for eight years before returning across the lake to his clothes. Another story, of status transition rather than initiation, is told of Athamas, who slew and sacrificed his children.[55] He was ordered to wander until given hospitality by wild animals. He came upon some wolves dividing up a sheep, who fled at his approach leaving the carcass, so he founded his city there. Athamas is not actually transformed into a wolf, but his return to human society is mediated via these animals.[56] In the same way, Philocleon makes his transition presided over by the wolf-hero.[57]

There is one further point to be made about Lycus: he is compared to Cleonymus, a man famed for having thrown away his shield (822). This episode is referred to twice in the play, in Xanthias' dream of the eagle–Cleonymus (15ff.) and in Philocleon's scornful 'Flatteronymus, the shield-thrower' (592). It is this act which makes him, like Lycus, a suitable figure to preside over the trial. By casting aside his shield, Cleonymus ceased symbolically to be a hoplite and legally to be a citizen: such acts as we have seen were punished by *atimia*, one of the penalties of which was not being permitted to be a juror or to speak in the lawcourts. The absence of 'tackle' also marks Cleonymus as a 'non-man' (823): he is again mocked for his effeminacy in *Clouds* 673–80. The gods who preside over rites of passage regularly possess characteristics which bridge the gap over which the transition is being made: Artemis is a virgin goddess concerned with childbirth, who presided over many rites for young girls;[58] in Laconia, Helen is tutelary goddess of two stages of initiation, at

---

[54] *FGH* 320 F 1.   [55] Apollod. 1.9.2; Detienne & Svenbro 1979: 226f.

[56] Compare too the story of the founding of Lycorea by those saved from the flood by wolves (Paus. 10.6.2; Immerwahr 1891: 22–4).

[57] Eratosthenes, writing on Old Comedy, describes Lycus as 'the hero with the form of the beast' (*ap.* Harpocration, s.v. *dekazon*; cf. Suda s.v. *dekazesthai*, Hsch. s.v. *he Lukou dekas* and Pollux 8.121).

[58] Calame 1977: I 252–304; Sourvinou-Inwood 1991: 100–4; 1988.

Platanistas as an unmarried, adolescent girl and at Therapne as wife of Menelaus;[59] and Theseus is ephebe and king of Athens.[60] The deities who watch over the final transformation of the savage Athenian juror into a youth through a defeat in hoplite-warfare, the dropping of his sword and loss of adult-male status are, appropriately enough, a wolf with legal connections, and an effeminate who threw away his shield and thus spans citizenship and non-citizenship, hoplite and non-hoplite, masculinity and non-masculinity.

The scene proceeds as a parody of a real trial and the 'end' of the old Philocleon follows shortly afterwards. In ephebic style, he is tricked by Bdelycleon (992); the mightiest juror has 'unexpectedly' met his match, as did the 'fair' Xanthus when tricked in his fight with 'black' Melanthus at the Apaturia. The oracle that he will perish if he ever acquits is fulfilled (158–60). He collapses (995) and exclaims that he is 'nothing' (997): unlike his earlier claim to be 'No-Man' (184), this is true. The process of stripping him of his characteristics is complete: the man who began the play by thinking he was Zeus is now nothing, not even a juror, and the scene is set for his re-education by Bdelycleon in the ways of social not political life (1005). The parabasis follows, late, but marking the end of the first part of the play.

Philocleon redivivus

We have already seen that in initiation ritual a change of clothes frequently accompanies a change in status: the ephebe doffs his black cloak to become a citizen. The first thing that Bdelycleon has to do is to fit his father out with appropriate garb, and his attempt to get him out of his old *tribon* may parody this aspect of the rituals: the father would have brought his son new clothes. In this scene, he removes the *tribon* (a cheap, short cloak) and shoes which have served throughout the play as symbols of jury-service: Bdelycleon tried to persuade Philocleon 'not to wear the *tribonion*', that is, not to go to the courts; Philocleon calls for his shoes when he wishes to go (103) and the Chorus fears that loss of shoes may be the reason for his

---

[59] Calame 1977: I 333–50.
[60] There is a similar idea in Aristotles' zoology: cf. Lloyd 1983: 44–53, esp. 45–8 on 'animals that were popularly thought of as boundary-crossers'.

lateness (274f.).[61] But the *tribon* has another symbolic value. Philocleon gives the following reason for not wishing to shed it: 'It alone saved me when I was drawn up in the battle-line, as the great north wind campaigned against us' (1123f.). The *tribon* was thus also his *hoplite* garb,[62] and its removal signifies the end of his condition both as jury-man and as hoplite.

This point is then developed by the foreign nature of the garments he puts on: a Persian cloak and Spartan shoes. When Bdelycleon shows him the cloak he calls it both a *Persis* and, using a Persian word, a *kaunake* (1137);[63] Philocleon makes an explicit contrast between it and a good old Attic garment (1138). Bdelycleon then refers to Sardis and Ecbatana and the fact that it was woven by 'barbarians' (1145f.). Similarly, the shoes are twice called *Lakonikai* (1158, 1162); Philocleon expresses horror at putting on 'the wretched leather-clippings of the enemy' (1160) and at Bdelycleon's insistence that he put his foot 'into enemy territory' (1163); as a last gesture of resistance, he claims that one of his toes is particularly 'anti-Spartan' (1165). The former Attic jury-man in his *tribon* who once defeated the Persians is now, in manner reminiscent of the symmetrical opposition of *kruptos* and hoplite, dressed in the clothes of barbarians and of Athens' bitterest enemies.[64] Like any youth undergoing initiation he is now to be educated in how to behave in polite society.

Freshly clad, Philocleon is characterised more and more as the antithesis of the crusty old juror that he was. Emphasis is much laid on his youth, with the frequent repetition of words like *neos* ('young'). He learns to walk in the manner of affected young men: *schema* ('posture', 1170) and *sauloproktian* ('wiggling the hips', 1173) echo the *schema* and *euruproktia* ('sodomy', 1069f.) of youth scorned by the Wasps in the parabasis. His 'bravest deed in youth' (1199) is another petty theft, this time of vine-poles, and when asked to think of something *neanikotaton* ('particularly appropriate to young men', 1204f.), he comes up with an athletic exploit (even if it has a legal sting in the tale). Xanthias, explaining Philocleon's behaviour at the

---

[61] The sheep in the Assembly of Sosias' dream also have *tribonia* (33). Cf. Suidas s.v. *bakteria kai schema kai tribonion*: 'used for mocking jurors at Athens'; Richter 1858: 144–7. On *tribonia* and *embades* as typical Athenian wear, Vaio 1971: 336 n. 4.

[62] For *paratassein* of hoplites, LSJ s.v. I 1.

[63] Chantraine 1968–80: 212 s.v. *gaunakes*: cf. Pers. **gaunaka*, 'hairy'.

[64] Compare the series of vases on which youths wait in ambush with barbarian shields and Scythian caps, signs that these are ephebes (Lissarrague 1989: 41–3).

symposium, says he beat him 'like a young man' (1307; cf. 1362), and an offended man threatens to prosecute him 'even if you are a very young fellow' (1333). His youthfulness is seen most strikingly in his speech to the flute-girl. His interest in her accords with his new-found youthfulness, but more importantly, the father–son relationship is turned completely upon its head (1351–9):

> If you're not a bad girl now, when my son dies I'll set you free and make you my concubine, my little pussy. As it is, I don't have control of my own money, because I'm very young and kept under close watch. It's my little son who keeps his eye on me, and he's a miserable cummin-splitting cress-parer: he's afraid I might lose it all – you see he's got no other father but me.

This joke about his rejuvenation, so often repeated, cannot be merely farcical. We are dealing with a true rolling back of the years for Philocleon. He is once again embarking on an ephebic career of theft and trickery: he gives the flute-girl the torch, 'to trick him as a young man would' (1362) and prides himself on the theft (1345). These thefts recall his earlier exploits at Byzantium and Naxos, and, as if to confirm this, a bread-woman, like the one who suffered at Byzantium, appears to accuse him (1388). The change in Philocleon is also indicated by his attitude to the lawcourts; he cannot bear to hear the word (1335–41), taunts Bdelycleon for his interest therein (1367) and shows little concern for the cases that are being stored up against him (1392ff., 1421ff.). This is a shocking rejection of his once beloved social responsibilities and liabilities, on the performance of which depended one's standing in the city.

The final scene has caused difficulties,[65] but it is in fact the culmination of Philocleon's removal from age to youth. We have seen him established as a young man; now the imagery of the wild that characterised him at the start of the play reasserts itself and images of animals and the sea, the element that stands for chaos, dominate the language. Philocleon dances against the sons of Carcinus, 'The Crab', who themselves are characterised in a variety of animal images as owls, moles, pea-crabs, brothers of shrimps and wrens (1509ff.);[66]

[65] A summary of views in Vaio 1971: 344–51; cf. also MacCarey 1979; Sidwell 1990. On the dancing, see Roos 1951; Lawler 1964: 135; Whitman 1964: 160–2; Rau 1967: 155–7; Borthwick 1968.

[66] On the problematic 1509, see Sommerstein 1983: 247 and Borthwick 1968.

the crab itself is a marginal animal.[67] The maritime nature of their father is made much of in 1518–22: 'Come, famed children of the sea-god, leap along the shore and the strand of the unharvested sea, brothers of shrimps'; compare 1531 'the sea-ruling lord'. Effectively, we have a hymn to Carcinus as the sea-god Poseidon. Philocleon has thus made a transition that is the opposite of his earlier model Odysseus, who was finally freed from the sea.

This picture of Philocleon returned to youth, the wild time of life, whirling uncontrollably by night (1478), despising the *nomoi* of the city, unchecked by son, slaves, fellow citizens, bread-sellers or witnesses and accompanied by the animal-sons of a 'sea-god', is surely the very antithesis of the adult Philocleon, serving in courts and phalanx, with his violence checked (nominally, at least) by convention and law, and enjoying the pleasures of family life due to an old man. He has the freedom to steal and immunity from prosecution of the ephebe and *kruptos*. We may well wonder whether MacDowell is not being too sanguine in viewing his 'probable development in years to come' with optimism,[68] or Henderson right to claim that 'we realize that beyond the wild, reeling dance of life with which Philocleon ends the play, await a hangover, court appearances, and fines for damages'.[69] These views take insufficient account of the imagery of the end of the play. Bdelycleon will pay the fines (1419f.), but Philocleon seems beyond such procedures.

Implications

It is time to say something about the implications of this analysis for the reading of the play. That Philocleon is cured of his mania for jury-service and that the jurors are shown to have little real power has regularly been interpreted as a comment on the jury-system, which, allowing for the comic *décalage* between play and strict reality, is not unreasonable. The Athenian courts, like any courts, were open to abuse and to exploitation for political ends, and Aristophanes draws the audience's attention to these problems in ways both comic and serious. Not the least of these problems is the almost tyrannical nature which Philocleon gives to the exercise of his

[67] Detienne & Vernant 1978: 269–73; Aristotle includes the *karkinion*, the hermit-crab, amongst his 'dualisers', animals that cross the boundaries between different groups of creature (*HA* 521b9 ff.; Lloyd 1983: 47f.).   [68] 1971: 319.   [69] 1975: 82.

powers. His power is 'second to no kingship' (549) and 'no less than Zeus's' (620), the greatest in the state kow-tow to jurors (551ff.), they are not bothered about the laws concerning *epikleroi* (583–7), they are not subject to the *euthuna* (587), and so on. Philocleon thus stands as a representative of the worst of the jury system, excessively zealous, easily fooled and irresponsible.

At the same time, there are passages which present a different view of the courts. Most strikingly, the parabasis suggests that his waspish manner is characteristic of all true Athenians: the Chorus proudly describe themselves in an echo of Cecrops as 'the only truly native, Attic, aboriginals' (1076),[70] and in the epirrhema and ante-pirrhema respectively depict first their martial and then their legal activities in terms both of men and of wasps, concluding with the words (1117–21):[71]

> this is what hurts us most, that someone who has not served in the army should gulp down our revenues, though he's never taken oar, spear or blister on our land's behalf. I propose that in future anyone who hasn't got a sting should simply not get the three obols.

To be Attic therefore is to fight for the city, to serve it in the courts and to do this in a spirited fashion, a statement that few Athenians would have quarrelled with: the Laws say to Socrates that a man must carry out whatever the city demands 'in war and in the courts'[72] and in *Plutus* 561, Penia praises her citizens as 'tough, wasp-like and hostile to their enemies'. As with the wasp, there is a tension in man between wildness, which helps him defend his society, and civilisation, which lets him do this in an ordered and rational way. Bdelycleon may describe the Athenian passion for the courts as 'an old disease, endemic to the city' (651), but this is simply a negative way of saying the same thing.[73]

What is more, Philocleon, the autochthonous Attic juror, with his stick and his *tribon* for phalanx and lawcourt, and his fiercely protective attitude to justice and the democracy, will not have been

---

[70] Cf. Hdt. 7.161; Thuc. 1.2.5; Pl. *Menex.* 245D; Chantraine 1968–80: 136 ('le nom du citoyen d'Athènes est *Athenaios. Attikos* est employé avec une intuition expressive ou plaisante'); Loraux 1981: 36 n. 2.

[71] For the union of military and legal, cf. the linking of sword and penalty-tablet in 166f.

[72] Pl. *Crito* 51B8–C1.

[73] For ancient estimates of the Athenian jury-system, cf. Bonner & Smith 1930: II 288–306; Meder 1938: 89–92.

an entirely unsympathetic figure, especially beside the somewhat colourless Bdelycleon, pedantically writing things down (529f., 538), with the long hair, fringed cloak and untrimmed beard that pointed to moral turpitude and pro-Spartan sympathies (474–6), combined perhaps with the monarchical tendencies of which the Chorus accuse him.[74] As with the Sausage-Seller, it is important not to react one-sidedly to the two men: one can sympathise with the satisfaction of the 'little man' at seeing in the sycophantic fawning of the powerful an index of his power (and his ironic realisation that the man gets off anyway (548–58)), as well as appreciate the threat of his extremism to the whole fabric of the legal system.

For a democrat, however, what Bdelycleon produces by his attempts to reform his father is, in one way at least, troubling. The Chorus, in a number of places, sense monarchical tendencies in Bdelycleon's behaviour: when he detects his father's escape, they call him 'city-hater' (411), and, when he refuses to let him go, it is 'manifest tyranny' (417). When they have been subdued by the smoke, they make their case as follows (463–70):

> Is it not now manifest to the poor that this tyranny has crept up secretly and tried to seize me, when you, wretched wretch and long-haired Amynias, keep us from the laws the city has made, without any justification or subtle argument, just as if you alone were in power?

Faced with a request for negotiations, they call him 'hater of the people and lover of monarchy' (474), and they will continue in this vein against one who has 'set his sights on tyranny' (484f.). Bdelycleon may complain at the wearisome repetitiousness with which such charges are bandied about (488–507), but there is substance in the Chorus' complaints, as becomes clear, not in any tyranny of Bdelycleon, but in what happens to Philocleon.

We have analysed in detail the change from age to youth in Philocleon, but there is another change that merits attention in this context. He also ceases to be a member of a democratic jury, and consorts with leading politicians at symposia, an institution long associated especially with the aristocracy and political elites. Two sets of symposiasts are listed in the play, one hypothetical, consisting of Theorus, Aeschines, Phanos, Cleon, Acestor and a foreigner

[74] Cf. *Lys.* 1072; *Frogs* 1281f.; Pl. Com. fr. 132. For the moral significance of long hair, see *Clouds* 545, 1101; Agathon fr. 3 K.; Starkie 1897: 322; W. A. Becker 1880: 453–61.

(1220f.), the other 'actual', including Hippyllus, Antiphon, Lycon, Lysistratus and Thuphrastus, 'Phrynichus' set' (1301f.). Unfortunately, difficulties of identification and lack of knowledge of these men's careers make confident interpretation of the nature of these groups problematic. On the second group, MacDowell well sets out the problems:[75]

> There are ... indications that some of them were men of an undemocratic turn of mind ...: Antiphon and Phrynikhos were leaders of the oligarchic revolution in 411; Lysistratos seems to have been associated with Andokides and the mutilators of the Hermai ..., who had oligarchic tendencies ... But to conclude ... that Phrynikhos' set was an oligarchic *hetaireia* is to go too far. It is not clear that any oligarchic revolution was being planned as early as 422, nor that the members of the group held oligarchic views at this time: ... Phrynikhos himself is said to have opposed oligarchy as late as 412/11.

He prefers to see the group as 'men with similar tastes and interests, whose purpose in meeting was more social than political'. This is possible (though one might wonder a little whether opposing 'social' and 'political' thus is entirely appropriate for the upper echelons of fifth-century Athens), but the change from being a poor member of a large public jury to being one of a private, wealthy group is striking in a play concerned with the question of the manipulation of the courts by the likes of Cleon. One is therefore loath to abandon all hints of undemocratic ideology in these men. The groups look to be formed from a mixture of types of politician, and so are perhaps not related to any actual contemporary political symposia, but there still remains a suggestion that Philocleon has left the democratic sphere for something if not more sinister at least more private.

Whatever the truth about these symposia, the picture we get of Philocleon, from the moment that debate is finally allowed on the position of jurors in Athens, is increasingly autocratic. This debate takes the form of competing arguments by father and son, with the Chorus as judges: both men agree to 'turn the matter over to them' (521). The competition is thus a kind of trial. When Philocleon has been defeated, however, and we have the domestic trial, we enter a very different legal world. Gone are the jury, to be replaced by a

[75] 1971: 302f. Storey 1985 disagrees with some of MacDowell's identifications here, but accepts his idea that politics is not the main determining factor: the men are mocked for their style of living and arrogant behaviour.

single judge. What is more, Philocleon thus laying down the law in his own household is uncomfortably reminiscent of Homer's Cyclopes, amongst whom 'Each man lays down the law to his children and wife, and they have no regard for each other.'[76] This is a passage which Aristotle chose to illustrate the most primitive form of social organisation: villages and cities grew from individual families, and 'were formed of persons who were already monarchically governed, [and] households are always monarchically governed by the eldest of the kin'.[77] Has Bdelycleon, in trying to keep his father in the 'Cyclops' cave' (a scene which now takes on a political as well as a comic hue), really improved matters by providing a precedent for the replacement of the (however flawed) democratic legal system of Athens by a series of 'monarchically governed' domestic courts in which an old fool can, at his whim, condemn, despite legitimate defence, anyone he wishes? The justice of this court is scarcely recommended by the way that this judge can be easily tricked into giving a verdict that is the opposite of what he intended, something that was guarded against in Athens by the large size of the juries. Bdelycleon's domestic court thus gives the Athenians an insight into one of the possible alternatives that might ensue from tampering with the legal system they have, which gives many citizens the possibility of taking part in the administration of the law and all of them the chance to be judged by a wide range of different peers. If the present system can be presented, as Philocleon effectively presents it, as a kind of mass tyranny, one has to ask oneself whether this is not in fact better than Bdelycleon's alternative. Once again, there is no overt protreptic from Aristophanes: the vices of democratic and tyrannical justice at opposite ends of the judicial spectrum are set before the audience, who may do with them what they will. Bdelycleon offers no constructive proposals, and his criticisms have a highly rhetorical tone to them, so that his warnings about the power of rhetoric to pervert the course of justice are cast, like Dicaeopolis', in an admirable example of the genre.

Philocleon is a caricature of what can go wrong when jurors become officious and set too great a store by their ability to protect the city; but the value of such zeal is not nil and he has other characteristics of a more endearing sort. After all, when they look at Philocleon, a large section of the audience who had served and

[76] *Od.* 9.114f.   [77] *Pol.* 1252b21f.; tr. Barker.

continued to serve on the juries were looking, not just at a comic buffoon, but at themselves, albeit in a distorted and burlesqued form. Aristophanes demands a complex series of reactions from them, including acknowledgement of their own tendency to excess, analysis of the benefits of the system, perception of the dangers of manipulation even of such large bodies, and the ability to see where the boundary between defence of the state and abuse of the individual lies.

All in all, it is striking how little in some ways Bdelycleon's efforts actually achieve in the end. At the start of the play, Philocleon was a mixture of human and animal, mature juror and cunning ephebe, and so he remains at the end:[78] his youthful disregard for the courts is as disordered, from the city's point of view, as his earlier senile obsession with them. The reversed rite of passage may have changed external features, but his basic nature appears to be unaffected. May it be that the play is about some aspect of the Athenians even more fundamental than the lawcourts that are so often said to be their defining characteristic?[79] The Chorus seem to think that Bdelycleon has changed his father (1449), but the evidence is against this view, and their own words highlight the problem: 'to depart from the nature one has been given is difficult' (1457f.). It has happened before, through persuasion, they say, but it is not clear that Philocleon bears out this dictum. The Athenian character appears to be remarkably resistant to the kind of changes that can be wrought by rituals like the rite of passage,[80] just as it is resistant to the restraints of legal and social *nomoi* which fail to bring Philocleon to heel. There should be no surprise therefore that the lawcourts are an ambiguous good, since they are the product of the Athenian *phusis*, which is itself as ambiguous as that of the wasp. On such a *phusis*, Thucydides' Diodotus may have the last word:[81]

> it is quite impossible (and it is foolish to think otherwise) that any restraint through force of law or any other deterrent will stop the human *phusis* when it is desirous of doing something.

---

[78] Compare the way this 'youth' wants to prove the old dances superior to the new.

[79] E.g. Strepsiades in *Clouds* 207f. will deny that a place shown him on a map is Athens, because he cannot see the dicasts.

[80] N. J. Lowe points out to me that Aristophanes, who here tacitly acknowledges the artificiality of rites of passage, had recently been through the pomp of such ceremonies as the fifth century used for its ephebes.   [81] 3.45.7.

5

Clouds

Clouds is structurally similar to *Wasps*, in that once again an old man
is subjected to various trials in an attempt to remedy an unsatisfactory circumstance, and in the process experiences a form of rejuvenation. At the same time, there are a number of important differences: in *Wasps*, the old man is apparently freed by this from all
moral and political restraints; whereas in *Clouds* the folly of his
attempts is borne in upon him with some force. Both plays use the
ephebic mythos, but in *Clouds* there is woven into the text a series of
commentaries on Strepsiades' actions which constantly suggest that
he is not only reversing the natural pattern of the *ephebeia* but also
contravening moral and religious rules that are fundamental to the
well-being of the city. The moral disapproval implied by these
commentaries can however be prevented from dominating the reading of the play by a consideration of the outcome from two perspec-
tives and by attention to what Aristophanes has to say about himself
in the parabasis. This chapter will begin with a discussion of
Strepsiades' ephebic odyssey, before looking at the treatments of
Socrates and the Cloud-Chorus, which together provide the frame-
works through which Strepsiades' errors of choice are to be enjoyed.

Strepsiades' *ephebeia*

The prologue of the play can be analysed in terms similar to
those found at the start of *Wasps*. Strepsiades' adult, citizen status is
clear from the ill-tempered complaints about his slaves, son and wife
with which he opens the play. Where Philocleon was bound to the
city by his participation in the lawcourts, Strepsiades is so bound by
his debts to other citizens. If Philocleon tells us little of his wife,

Strepsiades is eloquent on the subject of his. The account he gives of his marriage has often been read as a nostalgic longing for the countryside, much like Dicaeopolis', and is taken to be typical of Old Comedy's supposed preference for rural over city life.[1] No doubt Greek peasants did feel affection for their lands, especially when comparisons with the city were being made as in Strepsiades' case, but one must none the less beware of imposing on the Greeks views about the countryside that are more characteristic of the Romantic Age: such nostalgic views tend to be found when men have freed themselves from close dependence on the land for their survival. Greek ideology allows us to consider the relationship between city and country in more than one way.

Strepsiades describes his marriage as follows (43–52):

> I had a pleasant rustic life, mouldy, unkempt, lying about as one pleased, full of bees and sheep and pressed olives. Then I married the niece of Megacles, son of Megacles, I a rustic, she from town, classy, luxurious, very much the *grande dame*. When I married her, I lay down with her, smelling of wine-lees, fig-crates, fleeces, and bountiful creation, while she smelled of myrrh, saffron, tongued kisses, expense, gourmandising, Colias and Genetyllis.[2]

Strepsiades' contrast between himself and his wife is all the more arresting because his wife is portrayed not simply as a city girl, but as a sophisticated woman with high-up connections, both in 'Megacles son of Megacles', who has the name of a man of the Alcmaeonid clan who was Secretary to the Treasurers of Athena in 428/7,[3] and in his mother, Coesura (48), noted for her haughty ways and evident wealth.[4] Strepsiades has therefore moved from a life and smells clearly expressive of 'nature',[5] not just into the life and smells of the *polis* and 'culture', but into the very heart of Athenian political life. Reduced to its simplest terms, it is the move of the ephebe. The emphasis on this contrast is suggestive of more than just nostalgia and seems designed to draw attention to that opposition between city and country which is one code of status-transition rites.

The aged Philocleon occupied a position of ambiguous status,

---

[1] E.g. Segal 1969.   [2] On the last two, see Paus. 1.1.5; Henderson 1987a: 67.

[3] On the importance of this office, cf. [Arist.] *Ath. Pol.* 8.1.

[4] Dover 1968a: 99 on 46; Davies 1971: 380f.; Sommerstein 1980a: 187f. on *Ach.* 614.

[5] Strepsiades wishes to return to a life lived lying about εἰκῇ (44, 'at random'), a word used by Prometheus to describe the primitive state of man, before he gave them civilisation ([A.] *PV* 450).

and Strepsiades is a similarly ambiguous figure, though in a somewhat different way. He unites some of the key oppositions of the play
and articulates Greek attitudes to country and city by being characterised by aspects of each. He may be viewed in a variety of lights. A
countryman might warm to his praise of the country against the
sophistication of the city, to his blunt, common-sense approach to
intellectual matters and even to his desire to free himself from debt
(unless he were a creditor himself), but might find his description of
the countryside in 44f. (quoted above) somewhat uncritical, and
would not have had much sympathy for a man who had made a
match with a rich and sexy woman and was *still* able to complain
about debts. A townsman might take a similar view, except that he
would see a gap between himself and Strepsiades in the latter's
agroikia, in the sense both of rusticity and of buffoonery. Only the
aristocracy might not feel great affinity with him, though his marriage does presumably come close to making him one of them.

Strepsiades is thus not an easy man to categorise.[6] We cannot
take him simply as a peasant, for the reasons just given, and also
because the text manages to make problematic exactly where he
lives. The Athenian custom whereby wives went to live in their
husband's house, and Strepsiades' claim at 138 that 'I live far away in
the fields'[7] might suggest his stage-house was in the country. He
belongs to the deme Cicynna (134), the position of which is uncertain, though Traill places it east of Hymettus.[8] In 1322, he summons
the help of his demesmen, which might again support such a country
setting for the house.[9] On the other hand, the fact that he can see the
Phrontisterion from his house (91f.) would suggest that he lives in
the city: it is hardly likely that Socrates would have set up a school
for rich young aristocrats in Cicynna. Comedy can tolerate considerable jumps of place and time, but this 'contradiction' seems to have a
significance beyond mere dramatic convenience: town and country
are juxtaposed not only in the text but also in the theatrical space.[10]

[6] On character in Aristophanes, Silk 1990.

[7] On the analogy of the use of *porro* + genitive, though *telou* + genitive elsewhere always
means 'far away *from*' (cf. *KG* I 402f.). The scholia say the phrase is a parody of Euripides'
Telephus fr. 884 (Page 1962: 130–3) but the two are not so very close.   [8] 1975: map 2.

[9] Although it is equally possible to imagine him calling on other men from the same deme
living near by in the city.

[10] For the juxtaposition of two doors that are not to be conceived as 'actually' next to each
other, compare vases depicting erotic pursuit between the doors of the houses of the
bridegroom and the bride, which doors mark the transfer of the girl, not a case of marrying
the boy next door: Sourvinou-Inwood 1991: 85–7.

The marginal nature of Strepsiades is complemented by the similar characterisation of his son Pheidippides and Strepsiades' attitude to him. Because he is still living at home and a member of the cavalry (120), one might well conceive of Pheidippides as being of about ephebic age. That his name is also significant is shown by Strepsiades' account of his dispute with his wife over what the boy should be called: 'she wanted to add 'hippus' to his name – Xanthippus or Chaerippus or Callippides – but I wanted give him his grandfather's name, Pheidonides' (63–7). They ended up with a compromise that combined elements signifying the thrift of his rural father (*Pheid-*) and the horse-riding, aristocratic background of his mother (*-hipp-*). His name thus situates him ephebe-like on the margins of their two spheres of influence. Furthermore, names with the *hipp-* element are not uncommon in myths of transition.[11] There was a further dispute over the child's career. Strepsiades wanted him to follow in his father's footsteps, as was appropriate for an ephebe about to leave the *oikos*, but curiously desired him to tend goats, not just in the country but on the poorest sort of land,[12] wearing a peasant's cloak: by contrast, his wife wished her son to ride in the Panathenaic procession wearing the saffron-coloured cloak (*xustis*), one of the highest honours which the city could offer an ephebe.[13] Garments and names are again important symbols of status. In his ambition to return himself and his son to a fantasy world of the country, Strepsiades thus goes against the expected movement of men from nature to culture, against, that is, the ideology of the *ephebeia*. Several myths provide a commentary on such reversals or refusals to take the next initiatory step, such as those of Hippolytus, whose rejection of sexuality and attempt to hide from it in his sacred grove in the country[14] led to death in a chariot crash, or Atalanta, who, though she married, refused to leave the countryside for normal married life and was eventually, with her husband, turned into an animal.[15]

Like Philocleon, therefore, the hero is represented as both central and yet in some ways marginal and desirous of becoming

[11] E.g. Hippolytus. Young unmarried girls are regularly referred to in the imagery of horses: Calame 1977: I 411–20.

[12] On *phelleus*, cf. Harpocration and LSJ s.v.; Pollux 1.227; Dover 1968a: 103; Osborne 1985a: 20, with reference to X. *Cyn.* 5.18; Arr. *Cyn.* 17.4; *SEG* 24.152.2.

[13] The *xustis* (70) is worn by the riders on the north frieze of the Parthenon; cf. scholia *ad loc.*

[14] E. *Hipp.* 73–87.

[15] Sourvinou-Inwood 1991: 73 and Calame 1977: I 77–9 on the daughters of Eumelus.

more so in his wish for a return to the country. His son is no more willing to undergo the initiations of the Phrontisterion than he was to tend goats on barren land, so that Strepsiades is forced to free himself from his unsatisfactory life in the city by turning to another marginal world, the Phrontisterion, which stands in a similar relationship to the city as does the country, but as it were further up a scale of 'civilisation'. If the country is 'insufficiently civilised', the Phrontisterion is 'excessively civilised' as is shown by the extreme forms that things familiar from 'normal' existence take there. It will correspond to the topsy-turvy world of Philocleon's house and domestic lawcourt.[16]

The Phrontisterion is characterised as abnormal or marginal in ways similar to those used in *Wasps*. It is strongly characterised as chthonic: it is the haunt of 'souls', like Hades (94); their pallid complexions are quite unlike those of normal healthy young men such as the Hippeis (103, 119f.),[17] and recall the half-dead Spartan prisoners from Sphacteria (186); their concerns are with the things beneath the earth (188, 192), whence they are said to have sprung, as *gegeneis* (853). The fact that they live permanently inside the school and cannot stay long in the open air (198) contrasts with the daily journey to school and gymnastic training of normal boys (964f.).[18] One remembers the darkness and hiding of the ephebe. As beasts (184), they differ from normal people: they do not wash, shave (835–7) or wear shoes (103). Their interests and beliefs, and the instruments with which they investigate them, are far from the experience of the ordinary man (200–17). There are admirable emblems of the inverted nature of the school not only in Socrates, a mortal, swinging up in the air in a basket and concerning himself with the heavenly bodies (225–34), but more particularly in the students of 191–4:

> *Str.* What are these doing so bent over like that?
> *Student.* They are searching in the nether darkness
> below Tartarus.
> *Str.* Then why are their arses looking at the sky?
> *Student.* They are learning astronomy on their own account.

[16] The attempt to change Philocleon was prompted by a 'disease', and Strepsiades is similarly driven to the Phrontisterion by the 'disease' of his son's love for horses (74, 243; for an actual 'horsy' disease, cf. Hp. *MS* 4.23f. (I owe this reference to Mr E. L. Hussey)).

[17] For pale skin as a sign of effeminacy beside the virile sun-tan, *Frogs* 1092, *Thesm.* 191, *Eccl.* 62–4, 699.

[18] Starkie 1911: 53 contrasts Solon's description of Athenian training in Lucian, *Anachar.* 24.

It was a topos of ancient thought that man is distinguished from the animals by the fact that his eyes look up to the heavens, whilst theirs look at the ground.[19]

Philocleon's domestic trial was described as a rite, and Strepsiades' entry into the Phrontisterion is cadenced by 'rituals' marking the stages. The Student, who first broaches the secrets of the school, calls them 'mysteries' (143). When Socrates accepts him as a pupil, he undergoes the enthronement, garlanding and sprinkling that was associated with initiation into mystery cults (255ff.). After this he is introduced to the new gods of the Phrontisterion and prepares for a severely austere life-style: just as the marginal existence prepares the ephebe for becoming part of the centre, so this austerity serves to dramatise his transition, in a reversal of the life of untroubled ease into which he thinks he is being initiated. A second rite is performed when Strepsiades moves into the inner recesses of the Phrontisterion: he asks for a honey-cake as if he were entering the cave of the oracle of Trophonius (508), for which elaborate rituals were prescribed. It is after this that he discovers himself in a new world where everyday things are not as they were outside: *metra*, 'measures', refer not to measures of corn but to poetic metres (639–46); *rhuthmoi*, 'rhythms', not to sex but to prose (647–54); and the names of everyday objects are changed according to new rules of gender (658–91).

It is thus wholly appropriate that the ruler of this topsy-turvy world should be Dinos, the celestial Whirl (380):[20] the key verbs for 'turning', *strephein* and *kamptein*, appear regularly, in connection with rhetoric (317, 884, 901), poetry (331–7, 969–71) and philosophy (700–4).

Like Philocleon, Strepsiades has made a transition from the *nomoi* of normal life to the natural world of *phusis*, which is here signified not so much by reference to animals, but rather in the more appropriate philosophical terms of the *nomos/phusis* debate, which

---

[19] First in X. *Mem*. 1.4.11; cf. Pease 1955–8: 914; Bömer 1969: 46; Lloyd 1983: 30–2, 40f., where note especially Arist. *HA* 502b20f. and *PA* 695a3ff. On man as a standard against which animals are measured, Lloyd 1983: 26–43. Compare the two satyrs on Beazley 1963: 317 n. 15 'walking on their hands, with their rear ends in the air, symbolizing their upside-down world' (Lissarrague 1990: 39f.).

[20] J. Ferguson 1978–9 (1972–3 is remarkably similar) and 1971; on 'turning' in the play, see Marzullo 1953.

was central to so many discussions in the fifth century.[21] The more reprobate denizens of the Phrontisterion delight in the overthrow of the *nomoi*. The Worse Argument boasts that 'I was the very first to conceive of speaking against accepted morality and just pleas in court' (1039f.), and Pheidippides exclaims 'How agreeable it is to spend one's time on new and clever things, and to be able to flout the established laws!' (1399f.). He will later show no respect for the laws covering debts (1178ff.). In the *agon*, the Worse Argument offers Pheidippides the chance to do as he pleases: 'if you consort with me, indulge your nature, leap about, laugh, think nothing shameful' (1077f.). Pheidippides learns his lesson well and is soon proving to his father the mere conventionality of the laws: 'Was it not a man, like you or I, who first made this law, who persuaded the ancients by argument? Do I have any less right to make for the future a new law that sons should beat their fathers?' (1421–4). Strepsiades is thus inducted into a world where the *nomoi* that mark Athenian civilisation are abrogated in favour of the kind of self-indulgence and lack of restraint seen at the end of *Wasps*: abandonment of *nomoi* leads to a similar kind of chaos to that enjoyed by the rejuvenated Philocleon.

Sadly, the instruction offered by the Phrontisterion is too much for the addled brain of Strepsiades and the attempted initiation fails, so that he turns once again, this time with more success, to his son. Curiously, this pupillage of Pheidippides brings about the change which his elderly father had earlier sought by himself: it enables him to deploy sophistic arguments before his creditors and turns the clock back for him so that he becomes young again. This produces, in realist terms, the comic incongruity whereby Strepsiades is at one moment a stupid old man and the next able, albeit farcically, to use the logic of a Socrates, simply because his son has been to the school. To explain this, one might have recourse to comedy's flexibility in such matters or to the possible incompleteness of the revision of the play, but these are somewhat desperate expedients. There is however a mythical story-type in which a young person, often a relative, is in some way sacrificed so that another may achieve his end.[22] For instance, Elpenor, 'youngest' of Odysseus' Companions, dies as his leader sets off for Hades and has been interpreted as a kind of 'ritual

[21] Heinimann 1945; Guthrie 1969: 55–134; Nussbaum 1980: 52–67. *Nomizein* is frequent in the play.　　[22] See also Vian 1963: 214f.; Bremmer 1983b; J. E. M. Dillon 1989: 32–52.

substitute' whose death permits another's return from Hades.[23] Iphigeneia and Creusa, daughter of Erechtheus, are examples of children actually sacrificed so that their fathers may succeed. In Euripides' *Alcestis*, her death keeps her husband Admetus on earth,[24] so that it is appropriate that, when his career as a Knight has been abandoned for the Phrontisterion, Pheidippides should echo a line from that play: compare *Clouds* 1415, 'Children weep, do you think the father should not?', and *Alc.* 691, 'You delight to look on the sun; do you think your father does not?' Can one see Pheidippides, therefore, as a child sacrificed for his father's success?[25] Further support for this idea may be found in the fact that Strepsiades summons him from the school with the words of Euripides' Hecuba summoning her daughter Polyxena to tell her she must be sacrificed at Achilles' tomb, though there the sacrifice of the child is not on behalf of a parent.[26]

Whether or not this be accepted, the scene between the two Logoi continues the theme of transition set out at the start of the play, with Pheidippides now the figure undergoing the transition. As Ernesti was the first to point out, Pheidippides' choice between the Better and Worse Arguments recalls Prodicus' parable of Heracles at the Cross-Roads, where the hero was faced with a choice of two life-styles offered by the allegorical figures of Virtue and Vice.[27] The parallels are close, and, since they have not been spelled out before, I shall do so briefly here. The date of Prodicus' allegory is not known, so we do not know whether Aristophanes was imitating it directly, but it and the Judgement of Paris, with its demonstration of what can happen when a young man chooses bodily pleasures instead of political and military power, provide parallel stories of youths making their transition to manhood: when the wrong choice is made, disaster follows.

[23] *Od.* 10.552–60; van Brock 1959; Nagy 1979: 292f. Perithous remained there to allow Theseus to return (Frazer 1921: II 234–7).   [24] Lesky 1925.

[25] Strepsiades' requests to Pheidippides to suffer on his behalf also parallel Admetus' requests to his parents to die for him (*Alc.* 614ff.).

[26] Cf. 1165f. and E. *Hec.* 173f. (for the possible corruption of the text, Diggle 1984: 347).

[27] X. *Mem.* 2.1.21–34; cf. Schultz 1909 (who notes the ephebic element in the story). For the 'roads of life' cf. M. L. West 1978 on *Op.* 287–92. If Aristophanes is writing after Prodicus, for those who spot the parallel with Prodicus' tale, there is a mischievous reference to Heracles in 1048–52.

Heracles faced this choice, which concerned his education (30, 34), 'when he came to maturity from childhood' (21); Pheidippides, as we have seen, is of ephebic age and character. Prodicus depicted the character of his figures by means of their dress (22), and the Better Argument describes the effects of the two kinds of education on Pheidippides' dress and physique (1002–23; cf. 1112, 1171). Virtue is dressed in white, is attractive and adorned with *sophrosune* (22); Pheidippides will be garlanded with white reeds and white poplar (1006f.), his body will be 'shining and blooming' (1002) and his companion will be *sophron* (1006), a virtue shared by the Better Argument (961 etc.). Virtue's eyes are full of *aidos*, whose statue Pheidippides will learn to revere (995). Vice offers indulgence in boys, food and drink (23, 24f., 30), as does the Worse Argument (1071–82). Virtue tells Heracles that training, toil and sweat are needed for bodily strength (28) and that Vice makes the young feeble (31); Better says that Pheidippides will shine in the gymnasia (1002) and complains that, since the young ignore the wrestling schools (1054), they are too feeble to hold their shield properly (987–9). Finally, under Virtue, young and old stand in a proper relationship: the young rejoice in the praise of the old and the old in the respect of the young; Better claims he will teach Pheidippides not to snatch food from his elders (982), to give up his seat to them, and to avoid being mischievous towards them (994), answering them back or calling them names (998f.). Virtue claims Heracles, but the victor in the ephebic *agon* in *Clouds*, as in the Apaturia myth and in *Wasps*, is the 'unexpected' one, the Worse Argument.

When Pheidippides returns, however, Strepsiades is unaware of the moral warning carried in such tales, and sings an encomium to himself (1206–12). The use of songs in these metres before a calamity in tragedy bodes ill for Strepsiades,[28] but he proceeds to deploy his sophistic skills. It is here that he appears to have achieved his desire to be a Sophist and even to have been rejuvenated. Earlier in the play, two things characterised the young, the competing interests of philosophy and horses; Strepsiades now displays his control of both. To 'Pasias' he denies the gods and plays with language just as Socrates taught him (1233–51), and with 'Amynias' he uses a neatly spurious set of analogies from meteorology and geography to argue that, just as the sea does not get any bigger as the rivers flow into it,

---

[28] On the metres, Rau 1967: 148–50; also Macleod 1981 on 'self-*makarismos*'.

so debts ought not to increase as time flows on (1278–96). He then calls for a goad and drives him off as a horse and chariot (1298–1302):

> *Str.* Go on! What are you waiting for? Won't you get a move on,
> you thoroughbred?
> *Cred.* What is this but violent assault?
> *Str.* On you go! I'll lay into you and poke your thoroughbred arse!
> On your way, are you? I knew I'd make you move, wheels,
> chariot, pair and all!

Then, in their subsequent song, the Chorus declare him a *sophistes* (1309), albeit one about to come to grief. Strepsiades thus possesses the two youthful qualities of philosopher and horse-driver , but their sharp opposition earlier suggests that this combination is not to be stable.

Indeed, Pheidippides demonstrates its superficial quality immediately, by taking it quite literally, through the proverb 'old men are in their second childhood' (1417), and uses this as a justification for beating his father. Strepsiades' new 'childhood' is then confirmed, when he contrasts his own past treatment of Pheidippides with what Pheidippides has done to him (1380–90):

> I brought you up, and understood everything you meant by your
> lisping. If you said 'bru', I'd understand and bring you a drink; if
> you asked for 'mamma', I'd bring bread; you'd scarcely said
> 'kakka' before I'd carry you outside and hold you out. But now,
> when you were strangling me, as I cried and shouted that I wanted
> to go, you didn't think to carry me outside, you villain, but you
> choked me until I did my 'kakka' where I was.

As at the end of *Wasps*, the roles of father and son are reversed: Strepsiades now behaves like, and is beaten as, a child.[29]

Strepsiades' reversed rite of passage has thus ended, as both comparable myths and the perverse direction and intent of the rite always portended, in disaster: all his twisting has left him with his debts still to pay (1463f.), but without his cloak and shoes (856–9); his son has abandoned the *cursus honorum* of the rich and, where he was earlier willing to obey, in some things at least, his father and mother, will now beat them both (1443). Strepsiades appears as an

---

[29] For the use of the imagery or memory of childhood at a point of transition, compare the story of Odysseus' scar, related when his nurse Eurycleia realises who he is (*Od.* 19.392ff.), and the sad reminiscences of a similarly incontinent if less vocal Orestes by his nurse Cilissa (A. *Cho.* 734ff., esp. 755–60).

agroikos, 'a rustic', in the fullest sense of the word. By replacing the upbringing of his son (*trephein*) with twisting (*strephein*) in an attempt to escape his 'debts' (*tokoi*), he has only succeeded in losing his son (*tokos*) and maintaining those debts.[30]

Some lines of Pheidippides highlight the futility of Strepsiades' attempts to become a young man and a sophist. Explaining why his father need not fear the 'Old and New' day, on which debt-settlements had to be made,[31] he says (1181–4):

> *Pheidippides.* Those who make their deposits will lose them,
>   because there's no way that one day could become two days.
> *Strepsiades.* It couldn't?
> *Pheidippides.* No, how could it, unless a woman could be both aged
>   and young at the same time?

For 'old woman' read 'old man'. The immortal Clouds may be able to change their nature in order to deceive wrongdoers (348–50), but this is denied to the mortal Strepsiades: his desire to mock at the Old and New day by becoming at once old and young is not permitted to succeed.

Socrates *goes*

It is to this philosopher that Strepsiades turns for help in his escape from normal Athenian life. There have been many attempts to decide how close to the historical Socrates the figure in *Clouds* is, but I shall not be concerned here with that question so much as with how the Athenian audience would have read and reacted to the character on the stage. Sophistic features are obviously an important aspect of the characterisation,[32] but there is another side which has not received the attention it deserves. Basing himself on evidence from Aristophanes and Plato, A. E. Taylor argued that:[33]

---

[30] For this pun, cf. *Clouds* 1156–9; *Thesm.* 839–45; Pl. *Rep.* 507A, 555E; Arist. *Pol.* 1258b4–5.
[31] Kassel 1981.
[32] Dover 1968a: xxxii–lvii is still the best introduction, to whose view I incline: 'it will be apparent . . . that most of the elements in Ar.'s portrayal of Socrates can be identified either as general characteristics of the sophists or as conspicuous characteristics of some contemporary intellectuals' (xl). See more generally Guthrie 1969: pt 2, Nussbaum 1980, and most recently Brickhouse & Smith 1989.
[33] 1911: 30; cf. esp. 1–39, 129–77 (I owe knowledge of this article to M. J. Edwards). On the question of Socrates' political affiliations, Rankin 1987.

one chief reason for the prosecution of Socrates was that he was
suspected of having been the centre of an anti-democratic *hetairia*,
and that the suspicion was supported by the belief that he was
addicted to the 'foreign' cult of the Pythagoreans.

The indictment was that 'Socrates is charged with not believing in
the gods the city believes in and introducing new deities; he is also
charged with corrupting the young', in other words, Socrates was
isolated from the city both politically and religiously.[34] The main
points of the argument are that Socrates was at the centre of a group
of men who were interested in a number of areas especially connected with Pythagoreanism, such as the immortality of the soul, the
afterlife, mathematics, biological and medical studies, and who lived
an ascetic life style, as the Pythagoreans were famed for doing:
Socrates is regularly depicted by Plato as using the language of
initiation rites.[35] When we add the stories of Socrates' periodic
trances, as at Potidaea or before Agathon's party,[36] and of the
daimonion semeion, which was said to have warned him off certain
courses of action throughout his life,[37] Taylor's view becomes all the
more natural: 'Whether Socrates was an actual member of a religious
thiasos or not, it is clear to me that Aristophanes thought he was, and
assumed that his audience would think so too.'[38] What Aristophanes
thought we do not of course know, but I think that Taylor is on the
right lines in seeing Socrates in *Clouds* as a cult-leader of a Pythagorean colour, with traits that characterise him as unusual. I would
however prefer to discuss him in the more general terms of that class
of wandering miracle-workers, healers and purifiers who went
under the names of *goetes, agurtai, magoi, kathartai* and the like. In
Rep. 364, Plato is keen to distinguish between Socrates and these
men, but Aristophanes has drawn a picture with so many of the
features of this class that I think that many in the audience, perhaps
less *au fait* with the niceties of the distinctions between the philosophical groups, would have thought in terms of even less complimen-
tary models than the Pythagoreans. Plato's desire to maintain the

---

[34] For the different versions of the indictment, cf. Taylor 1911: 5f.

[35] Riedweg 1987; Adkins 1970; Hawtrey 1976; Nussbaum 1980: 73 n. 58.

[36] *Symp.* 174Dff., 220C–D.

[37] *Apol.* 31C–D, 40A–C; X. *Mem.* 1.1.2ff. etc. (Guthrie 1969: 402–5).   [38] 1911: 169.

distinction may be a response to a tendency to view Socrates in the light of these men.

These wandering priests, whom I shall designate with the collective name of *goetes*, seem to have become much less respectable in fifth-century Athens than in the Greece of the preceding centuries.[39] In fifth-century and later sources, Burkert can find only three non-pejorative uses of the word *goes*, one of which is textually uncertain.[40] By contrast, many of those whom we now call 'pre-Socratic philosophers', such as Pythagoras,[41] Empedocles[42] and Parmenides,[43] and other figures of comparable status, such as Orpheus,[44] Abaris,[45] Aristeas,[46] and Epimenides, all appear in the tradition with characteristics which would qualify them for the title of *goes*.[47] The change in estimation suffered by this class seems to have resulted from the desire of the *polis* or the demes to control all important forms of religious worship: state- and deme-cults were to be the focus of religious activity, and initiation and hopes for the afterlife were offered at the official mysteries at Eleusis. The *goes* was difficult to assimilate into such an official religion, but operated his own secret cults and initiations, and thus placed himself outside the city's control.[48] Since the city's safety depended upon the correct worship of and relationships with the gods, the *goes* with his private religion was naturally suspect; his privacy also left him open to charges of politically damaging activities. The increasing importance of oracles as sources of knowledge of the divine will and the growth in technical subjects like medicine would also have made inroads into the influence of the *goes*. It was an easy step to see the Sophists or

---

[39] See esp. Burkert 1962. For the differences between these men and the Orphics and Pythagoreans, Detienne 1979a: 53–94 (also 17f.). I refer to them by a Greek term to avoid the question of possible historical connections with shamanism. In favour of a historical connection between shamanism and Greece is M. L. West 1983: 146–50; against, Dowden 1979 (he posits an Indian origin) and 1980a, and Bremmer 1983a: 25–48. Shamanistic practices do, however, shed light on the Greek figures: see esp. Meuli 1935; Dodds 1951: 135–78; Eliade 1964; Burkert 1972: 120–65.

[40] Grg. *ap.* Satyrus *ap.* D. L. 8.59; Pl. *Symp.* 203A; and possibly A. *Cho.* 823. For ancient views on enthusiasm, Delatte 1932.   [41] Burkert 1972.

[42] Dodds 1951: 145–7; Burkert 1972: 153f.   [43] Burkert 1972: 136f.

[44] M. L. West 1983.   [45] Ibid.: 54 with n. 62.   [46] Bolton 1962.

[47] Clement, *Strom.* 1.133.2 (= Heracl. Pont. fr. 90 Wehrli) includes Socrates in a list of those who could tell the future alongside Pythagoras, Abaris, Aristeas, Epimenides etc. C. H. Kahn 1960: 30–5 argues for a distinction between shamans and mystics (though this distinction perhaps belongs more to the history of philosophy than to popular perceptions).

[48] On the concept of '*polis* religion', Sourvinou-Inwood 1990.

Socrates in terms of the *goes*:[49] we find this in Plato, where the Eleatic Stranger says of the Sophist 'is it not clear that he is one of the *goetes*, because he is an imitator of reality?',[50] and in the description of Eros as 'a dread *goes*, sorcerer and sophist'.[51] Burkert puts this equation in colourful terms:[52]

> Is not the Sophist actually the successor to the wandering wonder-worker? Homeless, relying on his own talents, he comes before the people in a purple cloak and attempts to put them under his spell by his performance. To be sure, in place of a magic *goos* he has a *logos epitaphios*, in place of magic formulas he uses figures of speech, and *psychagogia* is now a matter not of 'conjuring up spirits' but of affecting his audience, and entertainment.

That the *goes* could be perceived as standing for what was non-Athenian is well brought out by a swashbuckling attack on Aeschines by Demosthenes.[53] In this, he contrasts his own life and politics, which are represented as exactly what a wealthy Athenian should do, with those of Aeschines, which belong to the slave, the mystery-cult practitioner and the traitor. Demosthenes had a proper education; became choregus, trierarch and a payer of the property tax; was of benefit to city and friends and pursued a political line that was distinguished by numerous crowns. Aeschines by contrast worked in his father's school, grinding the ink and sweeping the floor in the manner of a slave rather than a free man; even his inscription as a citizen was irregular. He helped his mother in initiation and orgiastic rites of a disreputable kind; he was a mere clerk and assistant to minor magistrates; he was an actor; his politics were those of a traitor whose interests were not the same as those of his city. As well as suggesting that the devotees of mystery cults were aliens and a threat to the city, the passage provides colourful evidence for the activities they involved themselves in:[54]

> When you were grown up, you assisted at your mother's initiations. You read from the books and helped with the rest of the ceremony: at night, you wrapped the initiates in fawn-skins, drenched them with wine, purified them, rubbed them clean with clay and the bran, raised them up after the purification and told them to say 'I have escaped evil and have found better' ... By day,

---

[49] Burkert 1962: 55 with n. 87.   [50] *Soph.* 235A.
[51] *Symp.* 203D; cf. also *Euthyd.* 288B 'You are imitating the Egyptian Sophist Proteus and acting like *goetes*.'   [52] 1962: 55.   [53] 18.257ff.   [54] Ibid. 259f.; cf. Brown 1991: 44–6.

you led your noble *thiasoi*, crowned with fennel and poplar, through the streets, squeezing the big-cheeked snakes, lifting them above your head, shouting 'euoi saboi', dancing to the words 'hyes attes attes hyes', hailed by the old women as 'Leader', 'Conductor', 'Ivy-Bearer', 'Fan-Bearer' and such like, getting as your reward cakes and rolls and buns. For this any man would justly bless himself and his good fortune!

In the *Republic*, Adeimantus is scarcely less uncomplimentary about such cults. Of Musaeus and Eumolpus, supposed authors of Orphic texts, he says that 'they take [the just] to the other world and provide them with a banquet of the Blest, where they sit for all time carousing with garlands on their heads, as if virtue could not be more nobly recompensed than by an eternity of intoxication'.[55] Furthermore,

mendicant priests (*agurtai*) and soothsayers (*manteis*) come to the rich man's door with a story of a power they possess by the gift of heaven to atone for any offence that he or his ancestors have committed with incantations and sacrifice, agreeably accompanied by feasting. If he wishes to injure an enemy, he can, at a trifling expense . . . by means of certain invocations (*epagogai*) and spells (*katadesmoi*) which, as they profess, prevail upon the gods to do their bidding . . . Others . . . produce a whole farrago of books in which Musaeus and Orpheus . . . prescribe their ritual; and they persuade entire communities . . . that . . . wrongdoing may be absolved and purged away by means of sacrifices and agreeable performances which they are pleased to call rites of initiation (*teletai*).[56]

That this is the world of the Phrontisterion is not difficult to prove: we shall follow the initiate on his journey to enlightenment.

Entry to the rites of the *goes* was by initiation. This sharply separates the Aristophanic Socrates from the Sophists, who required no such ritual before people were permitted to learn their secrets.[57] We have already heard the evidence of Demosthenes and Plato, and Ephorus, writing of the Idaean Dactyls, says that as *goetes* they made use of initiation rites (*teletai*) and mysteries (*musteria*).[58] In *Clouds*, the Student refers to the teachings of Socrates as 'mysteries' (143) which only he and the other students may learn. We have noted that

[55] *Rep.* 363C–D (tr. Cornford). For ancient opinions on these practices, Foucart 1873: 153–77.
[56] *Rep.* 364B–5A.
[57] 'There is nothing in our evidence for the sophists to suggest that they used the language or procedures of mysteries and initiation' (Dover 1968a: xli).
[58] *FGH* 70 F 104 = Diod. 5.64.4; cf. Hemberg 1952.

Strepsiades undergoes two rites of initiation into the Phrontisterion. The first marks his initial acceptance into the school. It resembles the rites of the Corybantic cult and has to be endured by all those being initiated (*teloumenous*, 258). In *Euthydemus*, Socrates consoles Cleinias, who has been confused by Dionysiadorus' and Euthydemus' arguments:[59]

> These two are doing to you what they do in the rite of the Corybantes, when they perform the Enthronement (*thronosis*) about the one to whom they are about to administer the rite: there too there is dancing and fooling about . . . Just consider that you are hearing the preliminaries of the holy rites of the sophists.

The second rite, which takes him into the interior of the school is compared to the entry to the oracular cave of Trophonius.[60] This was a famous oracle, which was consulted, according to Herodotus, by Croesus and Mardonius,[61] but it may be that its reputation did not stand so high in the later fifth century: Cephisodorus and Cratinus wrote comedies on Trophonius and the latter's contained a fragment apparently about Sophists who made fraudulent gains by their oratorical skills.[62] Trophonius was not himself a *goes*, but the tradition associated him with such men.[63]

After initiation, there was an ascetic life-style to be endured.[64]

[59] 277D–E; cf. *Legg.* 790D–1A; Kern 1922: 298.

[60] Paus. 9.39.4ff., with Frazer; Philostr. *VA* 8.19; Bouché-Leclerq 1880: 321–32; Guthrie 1950: 223–31; Brelich 1958: 46–59; Clark 1968; Hani 1975; Bremmer 1983a: 88; Burkert 1985: 115, who quotes also the oracle at Clarus where initiation was required.

[61] 1.46, 8.134. The earliest references are in the *Telegonia* of Eugammon (Allen, Homer OCT vol. v: 109); *H. Ap.* 295ff.; Pi. frr. 2–3; cf. also Paus. 4.16.7. Given the presence of the Clouds in the play, it is interesting to note that not only did the original discovery of the oracle bring about the end of a drought (cf. Paus. 9.40.1; schol. *Clouds* 508), but that Lebadea can be a very wet place: today the town has an average yearly rainfall more than 50 per cent in excess of Thebes thirty kilometres away (Osborne 1987: 33; cf. Frazer on Paus. 9.39.4).

[62] Fr. 239; cf. Meineke 1839–41: I 143. There was a proverb 'he has consulted Trophonius' oracle', used of the sullen, which sprang from the belief that the power of laughter was lost by those who consulted the oracle (cf. Frazer on Paus. 9.39.13). On the initiatory aspects of this passage, Petersen 1848: 25, 41 n. 124; Dieterich 1893; Taylor 1911: 168 n. 3; Rohde 1925: 307 n. 19; Guthrie 1935: 210–13; Méautis 1938; Adkins 1970; Graf 1974: 107 n. 63; Hawtrey 1976; M. L. West 1983: 166–8. Is there, in Strepsiades' fear that he is to be sacrificed like Athamas, a parody of the supposed 'sacrifice' of the initiand in such ceremonies (cf. Eliade 1964: 36ff., 53ff.; M. L. West 1983: 140–6, 147–9)?

[63] Hani 1975 notes the parallels between this oracle and shamanism; Strabo 16.2.39 links Trophonius with Orpheus, Musaeus, Amphion and Zalmoxis; Gregory of Nazianzus (*Or.* 4.59) with Empedocles and Aristaeus.

[64] Cf. the *Orphikos bios*, Lobeck 1829: II 244–55; Rohde 1925: 341–5.

Of Abaris,[65] Epimenides[66] and Pythagoras[67] it is said that they went for long periods without food, and Plato's Diotima, in her description of Eros as a young vagabond, notes the toughness wrought in him by his life-style.[68] In fourth-century comedy, the famous Pythagorean rules of abstinence led to the stock jibe that they did not eat properly, as in the following fragment of Alexis:[69]

> A. They feed on Pythagorisms, clever arguments and chiselled
>   thoughts. This is what they get each day: one loaf of pure bread
>   each and a glass of water – that's all.
> B. It sounds like a prison regime.

The life of the Phrontisterion is similar: the students have no shoes (103, 363) and are often short of food (175–9, 186).[70] The Chorus promise Strepsiades success (414–17):

> if you have a good memory and ability to think, and have
> toughness in your soul; if you don't grow tired when standing or
> walking, don't complain too much if you are cold and don't
> constantly want your breakfast, but keep away from wine and
> gymnasia and other follies.

He himself expresses a willingness to endure beatings, hunger, thirst, even flaying, so long as he can escape his debts (437ff.). During his time in the Phrontisterion, he also suffers from flea-ridden beds (723ff.) and the loss of his cloak and shoes. Once again, this ascetic life-style distances the Aristophanic Socrates from the wealthy and aristocratic Sophists.

The purpose of the initiation and asceticism of the *goes* was to enable him to contact and have power over 'the other', the worlds of heaven and hell from which human beings are normally separated, as we saw in the passage of Plato quoted above: the summoning of souls from Hades, *psuchagogia*, was one of his classic activities.[71] Empedocles promised his adherents that they would be able to bring back from Hades the *menos* of a dead man and claimed to have become a god himself.[72] When the Spartans had trouble with the ghost of the

---

[65] Hdt. 4.36.   [66] Burkert 1972: 151 n. 174.   [67] Ibid. 159, 177f.

[68] *Symp.* 203C–D.

[69] 222 K. References to Pythagoreans in comedy: Diels & Kranz 1951: I 478–80. For the Pythagorean rules of abstinence, Arist. fr. 195.

[70] Cf. 834–7 (the wisdom of the students shown by their unhygenic habits), 1015ff. The priests of Dodona mentioned by Achilles, who 'with unwashed feet slept on the ground' (*Il.* 16.235), presumably drew no such stigma in their time.

[71] Rohde 1925: 326 nn. 106–7.   [72] Frr. 111.9, 112.3f.

murdered king Pausanias, they summoned Thracian *goetes* to exorcise it.[73] The *goes* is also famous for undertaking supernatural journeys, either in person or, more strikingly, by releasing his soul from his body; on these journeys he gained his knowledge of the other worlds. Orpheus,[74] Pythagoras and Epimenides[75] all went to Hades, and Parmenides to the Gates of Night and Day, where Justice promised to teach him all things;[76] after his disappearance, Aristeas went on a seven-year journey to the north.[77] Socrates describes the freedom of the philosophic mind in terms of a soul-journey:[78]

> It is really only his body that sojourns in his city, while his thought, disdaining all such things [politics, pleasures etc.] as worthless, takes wings, as Pindar says, 'beyond the sea, beneath the earth', searching the heavens and measuring the plains, everywhere seeking the true nature of everything as a whole, never sinking to what lies close at hand.

Plutarch recounts the tale of Timarchus, a young admirer of Socrates, who consulted the oracle of Trophonius about his hero's *daimonion*:[79] he felt his skull part to free his soul, which then wandered, attached to his body by a thread, through fantastic scenery, where it learnt of the celestial bodies and the punishments of the dead. The same author tells a similar tale of Aridaeus–Thespesius at the oracle of Amphilochus in Cilicia.[80]

The Phrontisterion, as we have seen, also has its links with Hades and the heavens. It is the home of 'wise souls' (94), and men half dead (504; cf. 186); its studies include 'things under the earth' (188) and the emblematically reversed students study both things below Tartarus and astronomy (192–4). Complementarily, Socrates spends his time studying the orbits of the moon and the sun (171–3) and swinging in a basket (225ff.), and Strepsiades will learn a new meteorology. As the *goes* can summon souls, so Socrates can summon the divine Clouds. If there are no actual soul-journeys in *Clouds*, there may well be a parody of them in Socrates' remark: 'Don't always wind your ideas about yourself, but let your thought go into

[73] Plut. *Hom. Mel.* fr. 1 (VII.99 Bernadakis = schol. E. *Alc.* 1128); cf. *Mor.* 560F and also Pi. *Py.* 4.159f.   [74] M. L. West 1983: 10, 12f.   [75] Burkert 1972: 121–65.   [76] Fr. 1.

[77] Hdt. 4.15.4f. In general, Rohde 1925: 329–31 nn. 110–12; Eliade 1964: 205ff., 308ff.

[78] Pl. *Tht.* 173E. Cf. perhaps *Ach.* 396–400.

[79] *Mor.* 590Aff. That those who consulted the oracle went into the opening feet first and returned head first may imply some kind of journey.

[80] *Mor.* 563Bff.; for such stories, Bolton 1962: 146ff.

the air like a cockchafer with a string round its leg' (762–4). That the
soul was attached to the body by some kind of cord is an idea found
as early as Plato's *Timaeus*, where the *desmoi* of the soul are described
as 'anchors' and 'hausers'.[81] We have already referred to Plutarch's
account of Timarchus' soul, and may mention too the sad tale of
Hermodorus of Clazomenae, whose soul, whilst he slept in bed,
journeyed attached to his body, until his wife betrayed him to his
enemies, who burnt his body while he was away:[82] it is noteworthy
that Socrates makes Strepsiades do his thinking when lying in bed.[83]

The *goes* has other magical powers, not least over things in the
air and the weather.[84] Empedocles offered wide powers in this area:[85]

> you will stop the force of the tireless winds, which rise up over the
> earth and destroy the fields of crops with their blasts; and again, if
> you wish, you will bring back in requital the breezes; from a black
> storm you will make a timely drought for men.

Socrates too believes that he can control the Clouds. Strepsiades
catches the tone of the Phrontisterion, when he suggests as a means of
escaping his debts the procuring of a Thessalian witch to bring down
the moon (749–56) and buying a burning-glass from the merchants of
pharmaka to concentrate the rays of the sun on the charge-sheet
(765–74).

The *goes* can change shape: Herodotus calls the Neuri *goetes*
because each year they change into wolves for a few days;[86] Plato's
Socrates asks Adeimantus whether he thinks god is a *goes* who
changes his shape at will.[87] Socrates does not change shape, but the
Clouds themselves are said to do this. Explaining the shapes of the
Cloud-Chorus, Socrates says (346–50):

> have you ever looked up and seen a cloud that resembled a centaur
> or leopard or wolf or bull? . . . Well, they become whatever they
> like; so, when they see a long-haired wild man, one of those shaggy
> characters like the son of Xenophantus, they make fun of his
> madness by turning themselves into centaurs.[88]

---

[81] 73D, 85E; also esp. Plut. *Mor.* 592A for the metaphor of the bridle.
[82] Plut. *Mor.* 592C–D. In general, Frazer 1927: 32f., 43f., 51; Eliade 1961: 95ff., 99ff.; for a
      different view of the *Clouds* passage, Killeen 1986: 32.
[83] For beds in initiatory rites, Paradiso 1987: 261–4.
[84] Hp. *MS* 4.21ff. J.; Rohde 1925: 326f. n. 107.   [85] Fr. 111.3–7.   [86] 4.105.2.
[87] *Rep.* 380D; cf. also Hes. fr. 33.12f. (Periclymenus).
[88] For 'centaur' = 'paederast', Hsch. s.v. and schol. Aeschin. 1.52.

They similarly become wolves, bears, women etc. in order to mock other follies of mankind, such as embezzlement of public moneys, effeminacy and so on: shape-changing is central to their mode of operation.

Healing, as the passage from *Rep.* 364 showed, was another important activity of the *goes*:[89] Epimenides purified Athens and Thaletas Sparta.[90] Empedocles wrote a book of *Purifications*, and Abaris was a healer.[91] Trophonius' cave was associated with cures, as is shown by the statue of the hero in the form of Asclepius and the tale of Phormio's cure in Cratinus' *Trophonius*.[92] Professional doctors felt it worthwhile to criticise such practitioners, which suggests they were a common place of resort of the afflicted.[93] So in *Clouds*, Strepsiades seeks healing for his 'horsy disease' (243) and *hipperos* (74), a word coined on the analogy of *ikteros*, 'jaundice', *huderos*, 'dropsy'.

Many aspects of the Phrontisterion therefore have their counterpart in the world of the *goes*. That Socrates could be referred to in such terms is shown from a passage of Plato. Meno complains to him that 'you act on me like a *goes* and you bewitch me and completely enchant me, so that I am full of confusion', and there follows the famous simile of the sting-ray and the warning that 'If you were a stranger in another city and did this sort of thing, you might well be carried off to prison as a *goes*.'[94] This idea is clinched by the description by the chorus of Birds of one of the strange worlds they have visited:[95]

> Near the Sciapodes there is a lake, where the unwashed Socrates summons up souls (*psuchagogei*). There went Peisander when he wished to see the soul which had left him when he was still alive, bringing as an offering a camel-lamb, whose throat he cut like Odysseus – but then left. To him there came up from below to the slaughter of the camel – Chaerephon the Bat.

Initiation into the cult of this *goes* implies the rejection of the city's religion, and as Strepsiades moves deeper into the mire of the Phrontisterion, the text of the play reminds us, often in significant

---

[89] Rohde 1925: 106 n. 13, 114 n. 56, 317 n. 69, 331 n. 113; R. C. T. Parker 1983: 207–34.

[90] Pl. *Legg.* 642D.   [91] Pl. *Charm.* 158C–D.

[92] Cratin. fr. 238; Rohde 1925: 327 n. 108, 333 nn. 118–20.

[93] Esp. Hp. *MS* ch. 1 and *Virg.* 8.466.4ff., 468.17ff. L. (Lloyd 1979: 10–58; 1983: 69f.).

[94] *Meno* 80A–B; cf. *Charm.* 155E; X. *Mem.* 3.11.16–18 for Socrates and 'spells'.

[95] 1553–64; cf. also Timo, *SH* 799.2.

places, of the normal social and religious traditions of the *polis* that he is abandoning. Athens is early established as a holy city when the Chorus sing of its elaborate religious observance (302–11):

> the solemn rites whereof none may speak, where the temple that receives the initiates is opened in the holy festival; offerings to the heavenly gods, high-roofed temples and statues, most holy processions for the Blessed Ones, garlanded sacrifices and feasts for the gods at all seasons, and, when spring comes, the Dionysian delight
> . . .

The special emphasis at the start on the Eleusinian Mysteries, open to all unpolluted Greek-speakers, regardless of status, and at the end on the City Dionysia, one of the most spectacular city festivals, is significant. By contrast, we later find Socrates mocking the Cronia (398) and the Worse Argument the Dipolieia and Buphonia, ancient festivals of Athens (984f.). One of the complaints of the Clouds in the parabasis (relayed from the Moon) is that mortals are tampering with the calendar (617–23):

> she says the gods threaten her whenever they are cheated of their dinner and leave the festival without getting what they ought according to the calendar. And then, when you should be sacrificing, you're torturing and sitting in the courts; but often, when we gods are observing a fast as we mourn Memnon or Sarpedon, you're pouring libations and laughing.

The Sophists and their science are clearly already affecting the idealised picture of the city given by the Clouds in their parodos.

There are also references either to festivals concerned with the city as a unity and with the importance of family life, or to festivals of Zeus, who is supposed to have been overthrown by Dinos. The great city New Year festival, the Panathenaea, is mentioned three times in the course of the play, twice as being adversely affected by the activities of the likes of Socrates. We have noted Strepsiades' desire that his son should tend goats rather than ride in the Panathenaic procession, which was an early indication of his decision to abandon traditional values (68–72), and the Stronger Argument's complaint that the new education has so enfeebled the youths who dance at the festival that they cannot hold their shields up properly (987–9). The third reference comes in Socrates' explanation of thunder, not in terms of Zeus but of the collision of water-laden clouds. He uses the analogy of soup in Strepsiades' stomach at that festival: 'Have you ever been filled with soup at the Panathenaea and then suffered an upset stomach, when a sudden agitation set it rumbling?' (386f.).

This juxtaposition of the removal of Zeus from one of his traditional functions with a reference to an important festival is repeated with reference to lightning, which is explained by analogy with the flash of a haggis that burst when Strepsiades was celebrating the Diasia (398–411).[96] This was Zeus's most important festival,[97] dedicated to him as Zeus Meilichius, in which guise he was associated with the weather: the 'Fleece of Zeus' was paraded[98] and Zeus Meilichius was also known as 'Maimactes', 'the Blusterer'.[99] The other important aspects of this festival are that it was celebrated *pandemei* ('by the people as a whole') and that it was customary to give presents. In a second reference to it, Strepsiades reminds Pheidippides of his gift to him of a little waggon bought with his first jury-pay (861–4);[100] he does this at the very moment he is persuading his son to abandon his successful career for the Phrontisterion, where he too will lose his belief in Zeus. Thus, just as Zeus is being deprived of aspects of his role as a weather-god and Strepsiades is turning his son from traditional law, morality and religion, our attention is drawn to a festival celebrated by the whole city in families or local groupings, at which gifts expressed and confirmed the bonds that bound people together.[101] The new and old religions are significantly juxtaposed as an indication of the nature of Strepsiades' attempts to escape his debts. Furthermore, the references that Byl detects to the Eleusinian Mysteries would stand in similar contrast to the unofficial and misguided mysteries purveyed in the Phrontisterion.[102]

[96] For the Diasia, Deubner 1932: 155–7; Parke 1977: 120–2; Simon 1983: 12–15.

[97] Thuc. 1.126.6: Cylon is told to seize power at the 'greatest festival of Zeus', and wrongly chooses the Olympic Games rather than the Diasia.

[98] Nilsson 1955: I 110–13. Fleeces have a regular connection with weather-magic.

[99] Jameson 1965: 159–65; Plut. *Mor.* 458B; *LGRM* II 2242f., 2558–63 (esp. 2560).

[100] Such waggons are often depicted on the pots given to children and there may be some connection between the Anthesteria and the Diasia held ten days later: Deubner 1932: 157; Burkert 1983a: 221 n. 28, 242 n. 16.

[101] Zeus in his chthonic guise of Meilichius may have had a particular tutelary function with regard to children: Simon 1983: 15.

[102] See especially Byl 1980 and 1988. Not all his claimed allusions are convincing, but there are enough that are for this point to stand (it is notable that several of them are also given by the scholia). I would select the reference to the Mysteries at 302–4, the use of Eleusinian epithets for the Clouds, the use of the thunder-machine (*bronteion*, schol. 292) as the Clouds appear, which recalls the use of the gong when Persephone was invoked (Apollodorus, *FGH* 224 F 110), and the name Phrontisterion echoing the Telesterion.

A further commentary on his actions is provided by an incident in Xenophon's *Anabasis*. When chronically short of funds himself, Xenophon did not resort to *goeteia* but took a very different, pious and ultimately more successful attitude. A friend explained that Zeus Meilichius was the cause of his problems:[103]

> He asked whether Xenophon had ever sacrificed to this Zeus, as he said he himself was accustomed to sacrifice and make holocausts at home on his behalf. Xenophon said he had not done so since he left home. His friend advised him to sacrifice as he used to and said that things would turn out for the better. Next day, Xenophon ... sacrificed ... and on the same day Bion and Ameusicleides arrived with money to give to the army.

The Cloud-Chorus

That the Clouds, who have earlier acted as the sophistic deities of Socrates, should at the end reveal themselves as agents of divine justice has sometimes been felt to be a problem in the play. In fact, as Segal 1969 has shown, the Clouds give ample indication of their true nature throughout the play from their very first entry. Their delight in the open air (275–90) contrasts strongly with the enclosed nature of the Phrontisterion (198f.). Their father is Ocean (277), who is hardly a sophistic deity, and they hymn Athens for the richness of its celebrations of the Olympians (299–313, quoted above). Socrates thinks they support the idle (331–4), but they praise hard work (414–19); they praise too the Stronger Argument but not the Weaker (1024–30; cf. 959f.). They give warnings of the consequences of Strepsiades' actions on three occasions (810–12, 1114, 1303–20). In the parabasis, they relay the complaints of the Sun and Moon and the other Olympians, whom they hymn as rulers of the universe (563–74) and as protectors of cities (595–606).[104] In all of this there is little to encourage Socrates in his belief that they are on his side.

Furthermore, their change of character is of a piece with their normal method of operation. We have quoted Socrates' explanation of their shape-changing and how they 'become whatever they want' to mock men's folly (348–50): if they have turned themselves into appropriate animals to deride the infamous, they have now become goetic, sophistic deities in order to mock at and punish a goetic

---

[103] 7.8.4–6.   [104] Scodel 1987.

Sophist. That the 'wise' Socrates is unable to see what is happening is not only comic in itself, but also in the tradition of seers who can see the future for others but not for themselves.[105] One might even say they have twisted their nature to mock at Strepsiades, 'the son of Twister'.

It has not I think been noticed that alongside these indications of their true role there are in the early part of the play several warnings given to Strepsiades in the form of weather signs which in traditional weather-lore portended a storm. Strepsiades has this very morning conceived his plan (75f.) and immediately there are 'portents' which, as a self-proclaimed *agroikos*, he really ought to recognise as telling him that a stormy encounter with clouds is ahead.[106]

The first sign comes at 56, when the oil runs out in the lamp and Strepsiades threatens to beat the slave for having put in a 'thirsty' wick. This might be a comic demonstration of Strepsiades' meanness, but lamps at all times in antiquity were held to give indications about the weather.[107] According to the pseudo-Theophrastan *De Signis*, 'If a lamp does not wish to light, it is a sign of a storm.'[108] It might be objected that this is not a precise parallel to the *Clouds* passage, because the lamp goes out simply because of the lack of oil, but a passage in the parabasis suggests that the lamp's behaviour is significant. When the Athenians were electing Cleon as general, the Clouds thundered and 'the Moon left its orbit, and the Sun, immediately drawing its wick into itself, said it would not shine for you if you elected Cleon general' (584–6). In each case, the extinguishing of wick gives a warning which the mortals will ignore at their peril:[109] the election of Cleon was a 'mindless expedition (*exodos*)' (579f.), just like the 'path' (*atrapos*) pursued by Strepsiades (76).[110]

The frequent biting of insects was another rain-sign: 'The

---

[105] X. *Symp.* 4.5. Plato makes much of the ignorance of *manteis* concerning the things they talk of: *Apol.* 22B–C, *Meno* 99C–D, *Ion* 534B–E; Otto 1890: s.v. *sapere*.

[106] For a collection of ancient weather-lore, see McCartney's sequence of articles in *CW* from 1921 onwards (cf. 1929: 2 n. 1), and 1929 on clouds.

[107] Ganszyniec, *RE* 13.2115–19, s.v. *luchnomanteia*.

[108] 42. On this work, see Heeger 1889. Cf. also Aratus 976–81, 1033–6; Virg. *Geo.* 1.390–2; Plin. *NH* 18.357f.

[109] On eclipses as portents, Pritchett 1979: 108–13. For a link between bad politicians and bad weather in comedy, Philippides fr. 25 (R. C. T. Parker 1983: 269).

[110] See Harry 1910 on this latter word, and the proverb 'When the road (*hodos*) is there, why do you take the side-track (*atrapos*)?' (Apostol. 12.34); cf. also Ar. fr. 47.

popular saying about flies is true: when they bite a good deal it is a sign of rain.'[111] Aratus combines the two signs we have looked at: 'If flies bite and desire blood more than before, or snuff gathers around the wicks of lamps on a damp night, [it is a sign of rain].'[112] There are several references to the biting of various sorts of insect in *Clouds*, some of them of a surprising kind. Strepsiades complains from his bed that he is 'being bitten by expense and fodder and debts' (12f.), and later (37f.) that the demarch, responsible for the regulation of debts,[113] is biting him. In the Phrontisterion, the bed-bugs will not let him bring his bed out and he begs Socrates to allow him to sleep on the ground to avoid them (699); at 709–26 he describes their merciless torture. At 146, a flea-bite is the starting point for some research into mosquitoes.

Not unnaturally, clouds played an important role in weather-lore. Their very gathering pointed to rain,[114] and Strepsiades curses himself for not having brought a hat when Socrates announces their arrival (267f.). The shapes assumed by clouds were also significant. To Strepsiades some of the Clouds resemble 'fleeces of wool stretched out' (343), which was a bad sign: 'When the clouds are like fleeces of wool, it signifies rain.'[115] Aristotle warns of the times when clouds are to be seen moving about on the earth:[116] 'Again, clouds have often been seen borne over the earth itself with a great noise, in a way that is terrifying to those who see and hear them, because they seem to portend some great event.' In the same way, when Strepsiades hears the voice of the Clouds, he too is struck with awe (293) and finds it 'holy and august and ominous' (364). Clouds on mountain-tops were an especially bad sign: 'When Athos and Olympus and mountain-tops generally are covered in clouds, it is a sign of a storm';[117] and it is over mountain-tops (279–81) that the Cloud-Chorus arrives. More significantly, *De Signis* says: 'If the parts of Mount Parnes towards the west and Phyle are covered with clouds, when the north wind is blowing, it is the sign of a storm.'[118] Our Clouds too first appear over Mount Parnes, as Socrates says: 'look towards Parnes; I can already see them coming down in silence'

---

[111] *De Sign.* 23.   [112] 974–7.   [113] Whitehead 1986: 124–7.

[114] Aratus 1018–20; *De Sign.* 45; Plin., *NH* 18.355; McCartney 1929: 3.

[115] *De Sign.* 13; also Aratus 938f.; Lucr. 6.502–4; Virg. *Geo.* 1.397; Plin. *NH* 18.356; Lydus, *De Ostentis* 9D (p. 27 Wachsmuth).   [116] *Meteor.* 348a24–8.

[117] *De Sign.* 43; McCartney 1929: 4–7; Frazer on Paus. 1.32.2.   [118] 47; cf. 43.

(323f.). The commentators note that Parnes is not visible from the theatre of Dionysus because the Acropolis is in the way, and Dover has suggested that there may be a 'compromise with theatrical conditions',[119] but Aristophanes could easily have chosen another mountain to avoid that problem: did he not choose Parnes because of its popular connection with stormy weather?[120]

There is a final sign to complete this section. At 169–74, the Student tells of the gecko that deprived Socrates of a thought by excreting on him. This animal was generally thought to be ill-omened, although there seems to be no connection between the gecko itself and rain. On the other hand, we find 'When the lizard they call the salamander appears, it signifies rain.'[121] Perhaps one should not be too particular about which lizard is involved.[122]

A knowledge of Greek mythology would also have helped Strepsiades, since clouds regularly feature in myth as the agents of divine retribution, not least in cases where a mortal has received some boon from the gods and has misused it. Parallels between *Clouds* and cloud mythology have been noted before,[123] but further scrutiny will be profitable. Clouds are often used by gods in their commerce with mortals, as when they save their favourites in battle.[124] In Hesiod, the thirty thousand guardians of justice cloak themselves in mist to watch over mankind's misdoings.[125]

More specifically, there is a group of myths in which a 'cloud' plays a prominent role in the punishment of transgressors. The most revealing example is that of Ixion, which has a structure with striking similarities to that of *Clouds*.[126] Ixion married Dia, daughter

---

[119] 1968a: 143.

[120] The point about Parnes is also made by Lalonde 1982: 80f.; see too Böker, *RE* Supplbd. 9.1645f. The fact that *De Signis* has this piece of obviously Attic lore suggests that other pieces may have been current in Attica too.   [121] *De Sign.* 15.

[122] On the gecko, cf. Gossen-Steier, *RE* 11.1966.60ff.; Keller 1909–13: 278–81; Douglas 1928: 132–4; Nock 1972: I 271–6; Waegeman 1984; Davies & Kathirithamby 1986: 173. For the gecko's connection with divination, cf. Frazer on Paus. 6.2.4. For a similar tale told about Gorgias, cf. Arist. *Rhet.* 1406b15–19.

[123] By Dover 1968a: lxviii and Köhnken 1980 (esp. 163).

[124] Wagner, *LGRM* III 179f.; e.g. *Il.* 3.373–82; see also *Od.* 13.187ff.

[125] *Op.* 252–5. West 1966: 155 (on *Th.* 9) says that it is misleading to translate *aer* as 'mist' in such contexts: 'mist is something visible, and *aer* is the very stuff of invisibility.' However, see *Od.* 8.562 and 11.5 (of the Phaeacian ships and cities of the Cimmerians) and *Il.* 17.649, which suggest the distinction is not so rigorous; see in general Roeger 1924: esp. 26–49.

[126] For the stories about Ixion, *LGRM* II 766–72; Pi. *Py.* 2.21ff. (with scholia); Pherecydes, *FGH* 3 F 51; S. *Phil.* 676ff.; Diod. 4.69; schol. E. *Phoen.* 1185; Detienne 1977: 86–9.

of Eioneus but refused to pay the debt generated by this marriage, the bride price; in revenge, Eioneus stole his mares. Strepsiades has married the niece of Megacles, son of Megacles, who may not have the exalted name of Eioneus' daughter but is still a major catch; he is reluctant to pay the debts, arising from his son's horse-racing, which have been made the result of this marriage into affluent society. Ixion invited Eioneus to collect the debt but murdered him in a fiery pit; Strepsiades' creditors also come for their money and are maltreated. Ixion went mad as a result of the subsequent pollution, and Strepsiades' attempts to escape his debts are referred to as madness (844–6, 1476–80). Zeus alone was willing to purify Ixion and invited him to heaven, but he abused this divine kindness by attempting to seduce Hera. Strepsiades too has the divine help of the Clouds and makes illegitimate use of it. Both men are eventually punished by clouds. Zeus created one to look like Hera to test the truth of her claim that Ixion had made advances to her; when the truth was established, Ixion was punished by being tied to a blazing wheel by Hermes and whirled through the universe as a warning to others not to maltreat their benefactors.[127] *Clouds* ends in a slightly different way, although the 'mythemes' of the Ixion story do appear: Strepsiades punishes Socrates and his confrères by burning the Phrontisterion down to teach them not to believe in the divine 'whirl' but to revere the gods (1472ff.); Hermes prompts him to this (1478–85). The fruit of Ixion's union with the cloud was the violent and uncivilised race of the centaurs; the fruits of Strepsiades' meeting with the Cloud-Chorus are an alienated son who beats father and mother, continued debts and impending lawsuits; in short, a life in tatters.

The two stories convey the same message: the failure to maintain a relationship involving mutual responsibility results in disaster.[128] In *Clouds* this point is underlined by the two complaints in the parabasis by the Clouds and the Sun and Moon that, though they are the city's greatest benefactors, the Athenians do not make offerings to them (575ff., 607ff.). This is also the substance of Aristophanes' complaint, again in the parabasis, that the Athenians maltreated him despite the many benefits conferred on them by his

---

[127] As on the Ixion Vase (*LGRM* II 769f., 3.183f., but see Simon 1955: 19f.). Hermes appears regularly in the punishment scenes.

[128] See Simon 1975 for an interpretation of the Ixion myth depicted in the Parthenon's southern metopes as showing the unfortunate results of the failure of *charis*-relationships.

comedies (518ff.). Such relationships form a central topic of play and parabasis.

The second myth, that of Athamas, though it differs rather more from *Clouds*, carries a not dissimilar set of messages. Many and varied are the stories about this man and his wives, but I shall confine myself here to the version given in the scholia to 257 where Athamas is explicitly mentioned, since this appears to be a summary of one of Sophocles' versions.[129] Athamas sired Phrixus and Helle on his divine wife Nephele, but then transferred his affections to the mortal Ino. Nephele retired to heaven in dudgeon and blighted Athamas' land with infertility. He sent ambassadors to Delphi, who were bribed by Ino to say that Apollo demanded the sacrifice of Nephele's children. They were saved by the ram with the golden fleece, and Nephele forced Athamas to repay her by being sacrificed himself; Heracles saved him at the last moment. Here we have a man who, like Strepsiades, is dissatisfied by a marriage which he might have been expected to find great satisfaction in, and suffers at the hands of a 'cloud'.

The most famous cloud-myth is that version of the Helen story, first attested in Stesichorus, in which an *eidolon* ('phantom') took her place at Troy.[130] The details of Stesichorus' version are now lost, but the story was revived in Euripides' *Helen*, where the *eidolon* is regularly referred to as a *nephele*.[131] Paris is another man who, as a result of his judgement of the goddesses, is given an exceptional wife by the gods, but is subsequently destroyed by the agency of a cloud. Paris, like Pheidippides, is faced with a choice between the world of pleasure and sensuality offered to him by Aphrodite and that of power and dominion offered by Hera and Athena, and we have already seen that the message of such myths is that young men should not choose the life of luxuriousness but, like Heracles in Prodicus' parable, the more arduous road to fame and virtue. Strepsiades is pleased to see Pheidippides educated by the Worse Argument, another wrong decision, and as a result his *oikos* is also turned upside down.

---

[129] *LGRM* I 669–75; schol. Lycophr. 22; Apollod. 1.9.1 (with Frazer 1926–9: 74f.); Pearson 1917: I 1ff.; Dover 1968 on 257; *TGF* 4.99–102. The details of the earlier part of the story come principally from Tzetzes' and the Thoman–Triclinian scholia to Aristophanes, but the older ones also seem to presuppose a similar sequence of events.

[130] Stes. 192; Kannicht 1969: I 21–77; S. R. West 1982.   [131] 705, 707, 750, 1219.

The other two myths are less well attested but have similarities to these main parallels. Hesiod tells how Endymion was given the gift of dying when he wished. He was taken to heaven by Zeus, but fell in love with Hera, was deceived like Ixion by a cloud, and was cast into hell.[132] Iasion (or, in Hesiod, Eëtion) made a similar attempt on a *phasma* or *agalma* of Demeter, which Kannicht plausibly suggests may also have been a cloud.[133]

That the Clouds should turn out to be agents of divine justice should therefore be no surprise, given what they themselves say, the weather-portents, and the traditional significance and function of clouds in Greek mythology. Strepsiades may be thankful that, though he has broken the oaths of the gods in refusing to pay his debts (1227), his family has suffered less disruption than that of Ixion or Athamas, or indeed of Glaucus, the man of legendary honesty, who asked the Delphic oracle if it was right for him to break his oath. The oracle replied that asking to break an oath was tantamount to breaking it and that 'Oath has a son, nameless, without hands or feet, who moves swiftly until he captures and destroys a whole race and house.' Of Glaucus and his house nothing remains.[134]

Morality and humour

Strepsiades' refusal to pay his debts, the unnaturalness of his reversed *ephebeia*, his involvement with a *goes* and the example of the typical cloud-myth all serve to characterise his activities in a negative fashion, but it would be wrong to conclude that all of this endows *Clouds* with an unrelieved moral seriousness that is absent from, for instance, *Wasps*.[135]

The discovery of the contrasting comic aspect may begin from the parabasis. In the epirrhema, the Chorus refer to a divine blessing conferred on Athens:[136] 'they say that bad planning is endemic to this city, but that the gods turn to the better any mistake you make' (587–9). Strictly interpreted, this means that it is impossible for the

---

[132] Fr. 260; also in Peisander, *FGH* 16 F 7, Acusilaus, *FGH* 2 F 36, and Pherecydes, *FGH* 3 F 121; cf. scholia A. R. 4.57 and Theoc. 3.49b.

[133] 1969: I 36. For completeness, cf. the sad tale of Cephalus and Procris (Pherecydes, *FGH* 3 F 34).   [134] Hdt. 6.86a.2–d; R. C. T. Parker 1983: 186–8.

[135] Kopff 1977 and Nussbaum 1980: 78f. take a particularly gloomy view of the end of the play, and are opposed by Harvey 1981.

[136] Also *Eccl.* 473–5 (with scholia); Dem. 19.255f. (quoting Solon, fr. 4).

Athenians to go wrong: unlike the divine boons granted to Ixion or
Athamas, this one can hardly be abused. Such a strict interpretation
is not mere pedantry, but is borne out by the play. It is precisely
Strepsiades' 'bad planning' in trying to escape his debts which leads
to the destruction of the Phrontisterion, the expulsion of Socrates
and his minions, and the restoration of belief in Zeus and the
Olympians. The cost to Strepsiades may indeed be relatively high,
not least in the philosophically justified maltreatment he will suffer
at the hands of his son,[137] but it is greatly to the advantage of the *city*,
which is of greater importance than the individual. The play thus
turns upon a paradox: the Sophists and their ways are presented as
something that no true Athenian should have anything to do with,
but at the same time, the way to destroy them appears to be to
involve oneself with them.

At the same time, one should not underestimate Strepsiades'
blame for what befalls him nor forget the mitigating factors in the
case of Socrates. He may be worthy of a smoky end because of his
dethroning of Zeus (though the changing of the vowel-stem of
kardopos, and worrying about the obliteration of the distinction
between the genders in words like *alektruon* or in the vocative of
names like 'Amynias', might seem to be less of a threat to Athenian
integrity), but it is notable that he is less keen to teach Strepsiades
'the argument that does not repay' (244f.), despite 'a thousand
requests' (738f.; cf. 655f.), than Strepsiades is to force him to do it.
After all, the Phrontisterion is the home not just of the Weaker or
Unjust Argument, but of the Stronger or Just, and it is Strepsiades
who insists: 'See that he learns both of those arguments, the stronger,
whatever that is, and also the weaker, which overturns the stronger
by its corrupt arguments – and if that isn't possible, at least teach him
the unjust one, come what may' (882–6).

There is another point, too. If, *prima facie*, the destruction of
the Phrontisterion is a 'good thing' for the city, on reflection one
might argue that to bring violence (*bia*) against those who use
argument and persuasion (*logos, peitho*) is not unproblematic, in that
it goes against the value the Athenians placed on discussion as the

---

[137] On the seriousness of this, cf. X. *Mem.* 2.2; [Arist.] *Ath. Pol.* 56.6; Lacey 1968: 290 n. 113;
Rhodes 1981: 629. The relationship between Pheidippides and Strepsiades could also be
analysed in terms of myths of conflict between father and son, on which see for instance
Sourvinou-Inwood 1979.

basis of the settling of disputes, and recalls the many cases in tragedy and elsewhere where persuasion is presented as a more civilised device than violence.[138] Aristophanes can be said to have replied to the Sophists with words, but they are words in which an act of violence is inscribed. Indeed, violence is notably prevalent at the end of the play, in Strepsiades' attacks on creditors and Phrontisterion, and in Pheidippides' attacks on him (all of which are, ironically, the response to involvement with philosophical discourse): if we are shocked by Pheidippides' maltreatment of his father, should we not also be shocked by Strepsiades' treatment of Socrates? Should violence be the response to the challenges of philosophy?

Here it is instructive to consider Aristophanes' position. In the 'parabasis proper', he complains tactfully but clearly, that the audience whom he had supposed to be *sophos* ('wise') and *dexios* ('clever'), did not appreciate the excellence of the original version of the *Clouds*, composed by one who was himself possessed of the same qualities: 'I don't seek to deceive you by bringing on the same thing two or three times, but I play the *sophos* and put on ideas that are always new and clever and not like each other at all' (546–8). In the light of these claims it is striking that in the body of the play these qualities of wisdom, cleverness and novelty are characteristics of the villains. *Kainos* ('new') is used once of Socrates, three times of Pheidippides after his conversion and four times of the Worse Argument.[139] *Sophos* ('wise') and its cognates are used seven times of Socrates and the Phrontisterion, six times and twice of Strepsiades and Pheidippides when they have become involved with the Phrontisterion and three times of the Worse Argument.[140] *Dexios* ('clever') shows a similar distribution.[141] The qualities that bring about the downfalls of Socrates and Strepsiades are thus exactly the ones arrogated to himself (and applied, with greater irony, to the audience) by the poet.

It is clear too that Aristophanes himself has become acquainted with a wide range of philosophical and scientific doctrines on religion, meteorology, grammar, rhetoric etc. in order to write

---

[138] Buxton 1982.

[139] Socrates: 479f.; Pheidippides: 1397, 1399, 1423; Worse Argument: 896, 936, 943, 1031.

[140] Socrates: 94, 205, 331, 412, 489, 491, 517, 841, 1370; Strepsiades: 517, 765, 773, 1202, 1207, 1309; Pheidippides: 1111, 1370; Worse Argument: 895, 899, 1057. At 1378 it is applied to Euripides; 955 is neutral and only at 1024 is it used of a 'good' character.

[141] Of the Sophists and their learning: 148, 418, 428, 757, 834, 852; of Pheidippides: 1111, 1399.

Clouds,[142] so that he, like his Cloud-Chorus, turns into a figure of sophistic *goeteia* in order to make fun of contemporary philosophy. Had he not done so, *Clouds* could never have been written, nor the Phrontisterion burnt: it is, after all, he who has 'made the weaker argument the stronger' and sent a young man down the primrose path of philosophy. 'Aristophanes' is therefore an ambiguous figure in the text, who both displays and ridicules philosophical activity, and we have already seen that that ambivalence is enshrined in his self-presentation in the parabasis as the possessor of precisely those qualities which are said to make the Sophist so dangerous.

Any apparently uncomplicated 'message' that Socrates and his ilk represent a threat to Athens and its religion, which threat is condignly punished by divine agents, is thus deconstructed not just in the way in which characters who bear the names of real Athenians differ from the 'reality', so that 'Socrates' is a major distortion of the original, but more particularly in the way the moral status of all the characters is ambivalent and the author himself is characterised as closer to the Sophists than to 'ordinary' men in the audience.

Furthermore, these men have shown, by their failure to appreciate the first *Clouds*, that they are perhaps not best placed to make judgements about the place of philosophic argument in a state. Indeed, one could say they were little better than Strepsiades, their representative: their attitude to *Clouds* (first version) and Strepsiades' to Socratic teaching were of a piece, and Aristophanes' defeat by 'buffoons' (523–5) looks not unlike Socrates' at the hands of the *agroikos*.

---

[142] This range can be seen from Dover 1968a: xxxi-lvii: the breadth of his knowledge combined with the mockery to which he subjects it may account for the competing claims that Aristophanes was for and against intellectual endeavour.

6

Peace

Dung-Beetle

Peace, being essentially celebratory, is in some ways a simple play, but not without its distinctive features. It looks forward to the Peace of Nicias that was soon to be instituted, and, as was not the case with Dicaeopolis' peace, constantly emphasises the fact that all the Greeks are to benefit from Trygaeus' actions:[1] Trygaeus may be an *autokrator* (359), but he is a benevolent one. The basic plot is closely similar to those of *Acharnians*[2] and *Ecclesiazusae*: an initial representation of a world in poor case gives way to an idealised world which is at many points a symmetrical opposite of the former, and the remarkable actions of the hero effect the inauguration of a new era. *Peace* also shares with these plays themes and images through which this amelioration is demonstrated.[3] The distinctive nature of *Peace* lies in the scope it gives to the Chorus and other characters such as Hermes as executors of the action, thus reducing the concentration on the protagonist, and in the way it draws the audience into the action more than do the other extant plays.[4]

It begins with the jolly idea of journeying on a dung-beetle to complain to Zeus about the war, ladders having failed to provide a means of reaching the gods (69–71).[5] The obvious mythic parallel for

---

[1] 93, 105f., 292–8 etc.   [2] Moulton 1981: 81–92.

[3] Henderson 1975: 62–6 for some of what follows (not all of what he says is strictly accurate).

[4] The best treatment of the play is Cassio 1985: see esp. 43–5, 51–7, 59–67 on the above points.

[5] Polyaenus 7.22 quotes with disapproval the story of a Thracian general and priest of Hera, who had difficulty in getting his troops to obey him, and so joined a large number of ladders together to go to complain to Hera.

this is the story of Bellerophon, and parody of Euripides' play of that name informs the opening scenes.[6] This story is explicitly evoked at 76, when Trygaeus calls the Dung-Beetle 'Pegasus, O noble wing': the Beetle is preferred to Pegasus himself, because only one set of provisions will be needed for him and Trygaeus (135–9). Euripides' play dealt with the later stages of Bellerophon's life, when he lost his children and decided to ride up to heaven on his trusty Pegasus to complain. This gained him the wrath of the gods, and he fell from his horse and lamed himself, of which danger Trygaeus' Child warns him (146–8). In tragedy, the complaints and attempt to fly to heaven are hybristic;[7] in comedy, which, as we shall see in the next chapter, is happy to let its heroes triumph in such hybristic behaviour towards the gods, they are the prelude to peace.

This Dung-Beetle acts as an emblem of the world as it is at the start of the play, that is, heavily characterised by excrement.[8] Bad smells are a sign that all is not well in the world: they stand in opposition to spices and perfumes that are a means of communication with the gods,[9] and altars are naturally polluted by such as excrement.[10] Trygaeus' daughter is therefore reasonably sceptical of Aesop's tale that a dung-beetle once flew up to heaven: 'That's an unlikely story, that so foul-smelling a beast should reach the gods!' (131f.). This tale told of the conflict between the eagle and the dung-beetle. The eagle ate the young of the beetle, which retaliated by rolling the eagle's young out of its nest. The eagle complained to Zeus, who told it to make its nest on his lap, but the beetle flew round Zeus's head and forced him to stand up sharply and spill the eggs.[11] This conflict between the two creatures reflects an opposition between them in mythological terms.[12] The dung-beetle usually flies close to the earth and buries its eggs in excrement, and was believed either to be killed by or at least to hate sweet smells (which is why

[6] Rau 1967: 89–97. In 124ff. there are quotations apparently from Euripides' *Stheneboea* (fr. 669), which dealt with her attempted seduction of Bellerophon earlier in his life. The point of the parody of the *Aeolus* in 114ff. is not clear.

[7] So in Pi. *Is.* 7.43–8 he is an example of human *hubris* (cf. Alcm. 1.16); a more exalted treatment of him is *Ol.* 13.6off.

[8] On scatological humour in comedy, Henderson 1975: 187–203; Lilja 1972: 138–41.

[9] X. *Oec.* 5.3; Hp. *MS* 14.14–18 etc.

[10] R. C. T. Parker 1983: 162 n. 101, 293, referring to *Wasps* 394 and *Frogs* 366 in comedy.

[11] Aesop, *fab.* 3 H.–H.   [12] Detienne 1977: 5–36.

Trygaeus gives instructions for the hiding of dung under myrrh (166–9));[13] the eagle flies and nests high, and was believed to be restored by spices.[14] Trygaeus, by bringing about a reversal in the position of the dung-beetle, which will soon be pulling Zeus' chariot and thunderbolt and eating the 'ambrosia' of Ganymede (722–4),[15] also effects a reversal in the state of the world dominated by war.

The play opens with an uncompromising emphasis on the details of feeding-time for the Dung-Beetle, who devours with uncommon relish cakes of various grades of dung, which he orders from the two slaves kneading for him on stage. This is a world where no slave will eat what he is kneading (13f.) and where a nose without holes would be useful (19–21). The Beetle's fastidiousness makes matters all the worse: 'your pig or dog eats it any old way, just as it comes. But this creature puts on airs and, as if he were a lady, disdains to eat unless I give him a round cake that I've kneaded all day' (24–8). In this creature an Ionian is supposed to see a metaphor for Cleon who is 'a shameless eater of dung' (48). The war which characterises the old world is specifically associated with excrement. Polemos is described as 'him down the legs' (241), a slightly obscure expression which presumably does not refer to epic sweat. War brings 'Phoenician evils' (303), which appear to have the same meaning as the jokes in 1172–6 about the officer whose elegant scarlet cloak undergoes a change of dye when he is compelled to fight. In the new world, in an appropriate reversal, an excremental punishment is handed out to the one who benefits from war: the Arms-Dealer's breastplate is to form a convenient commode, until Trygaeus finds it chafes his bottom (1224–39).

Pleasant odours surround the return of Peace as the stench of dung is replaced by the fragrance of flowers and perfumes. Immediately after Peace has been drawn forth, Theoria appears, to be addressed by Trygaeus in the words:[16] 'How sweet you smell! A sweetness that goes to the heart. The sweetest smell as of freedom from military service, and of myrrh' (525f.). Trygaeus himself is subsequently addressed as 'young once again and anointed with

---

[13] Davies & Kathirithamby 1986: 85 (83ff. on the insect generally); cf. Detienne 1977: 26f.; Beavis 1988: 160.   [14] Aesop, *Fab.* 6 Ch.

[15] It will still eat the dung of catamites (cf. 11f.), but now malodorous human excrement is replaced by a sweet-smelling divine variety.   [16] With 525f. contrast 175f.

myrrh' (861f.). Later in the play, the cakes cease to be of dung and become sweet ones for weddings (1195, 1357).

The grisly picture of the dung-eating beetle introduces the fact that in the first part of the play food and eating provide little pleasure to mankind. The scarab may take a gourmet's delight in its pâtés (24ff.), but the slaves are sorely pressed. When War is about to come on stage, Trygaeus hears the sound not of a martial trumpet but of a 'martial mortar' (235). War's salad of the Greek cities will provide nothing but woe and only the fortuitous loss of the 'pestles' Cleon and Brasidas prevent its construction (236ff.); their deaths are a solitary indication that things may change.[17] We have a sorry picture of the city forced to be happy with the scraps of slander that are thrown to her (642f.). War means the provision of the dreaded 'three days' rations', carried in the soldier's wallet that thus 'smells of war' (527–38). When Hermes tells Trygaeus that he will die for freeing Peace, he complains that he has not brought his rations 'as one about to die' (368), which the Scholiast explains as 'as one about to campaign': war and death are synonymous. The Chorus express their delight that Trygaeus' call to them was not 'Come with three days' rations' (312) and rejoice in being freed from 'helmets, cheese and onions' (1128f.). They look forward to pleasant sympotic eating and drinking (e.g. 1127ff.). In fact, in the future, 'three days' takes on the new meaning of portending pleasure, especially for the Boule in their activities with Theoria in the three-day festival announced by Trygaeus (894ff.), where wrestling, pancration, horse- and chariot-racing are all described in terms of sex (894–905). One may compare also the 'three-day soup' (715f.) which the Boule will lap up. The enthusiastic devouring of food by the farmers (1305–10) replaces the horrible grinding of its food by the Dung-Beetle (33–7).

In fact, as Henderson shows, the pleasures of eating become synonymous with those of sex in many passages, and, as in *Acharnians*, a more normal sexuality and so fertility takes over from the earlier abnormal.[18] The Dung-Beetle is said to have nothing to do with Aphrodite or the Graces (40f.), and Zeus is described as *Zeus Kataibates* ('Zeus of the Thunder-crap', as McLeish renders it, 42),

---

[17] The descent to Hades of these two warmongers will balance the return of Peace from the ground.

[18] Henderson 1975: 65. See 706ff., 868–70, 965–7, 1338, 1345–52; also Whitman 1964: 112–4.

where the phonetic liaison produces a word of obscene (if obscure) connotations; some of the gods are even said to live off immoral earnings (847–50). The new era is instituted by the marriage of Trygaeus and Opora (706–8), and joyful procreative intercourse will be the order of the day (727f.).[19] The character of the protagonists will also undergo a suitable change: old age will be shaken off by Trygaeus and the Chorus,[20] and the traditional activity of the old, jury-service, will be abandoned (349–52; cf. 533f.). Military language becomes agricultural: the farmers form 'bright[21] serried ranks' (564f.), the mattock is 'shining and well armed' (566) and the pitchforks are 'sparkling in the sun' (567). The Chorus pray to the gods 'to be free of the shining iron' (1328). Military hardware is put to more agreeable uses: helmet-crests could sweep tables (1218); corslets could be commodes (1228); trumpets cottabos-targets or scales for weighing figs (1242–4, 1246–9); and helmets cups for emetics (1253f.). The pitchforks, which were earlier used to drive Peace away (637), will be put to their proper use (546f., 567).

The slave may accuse Trygaeus of being in the grip of madness (e.g. 54), but this turns out to be a beneficial one, unlike that of Philocleon. In sum, Trygaeus is an ideal emblematic figure to introduce the 'old way of life' (572), the world of Peace 'the lover of vines' (308; cf. 520), where vines and figs flourish[22] and love reigns (cf. 988): he is 'a skilled vineyard-worker, not a sycophant nor a lover of trouble-making' (191f.), and his name, derived from *truge*, points to the grape-harvest and perhaps also comedy's comic name for itself, *trugodia*.[23]

Hermes

On landing on Olympus, Trygaeus is met by Hermes, whose characteristics make him a particularly suitable god to participate in

[19] 863–8, 894ff., 964–6 etc.
[20] 336, 351, 861, 898; cf. 558. See Auger 1979.
[21] On *lampros* and other expressions of military 'brightness', Detienne & Vernant 1978: 177–86; Dillon 1989: 86–93.   [22] So very frequently: 308, 520–70 *passim*.
[23] For the last, cf. Sommerstein 1985: 138. Why is Athmonon Trygaeus' deme? It is said to have been known for its vines, but the only evidence is this passage and the existence of vines around modern Marusi. Its most famous cults were those of Amarysian Artemis (*IG* I².865, 2².1203.17; Paus. 1.31.4f.) and Aphrodite Urania (Paus. 1.14.7).

the raising of Peace.[24] He has been left behind to look after the pots and pans of the gods. There is here a comic twist to the idea of Hermes as the guardian of the household: a herm stood outside private homes and at Athens he was worshipped as Propylaeus and Strophius; elsewhere he has names such as Pylaeus, Pylius, Thyraeus, Pronaus and Puledokos. Generally, Hermes represents the *oikos* in its external relations with the *polis*, whilst it is the female Hestia who looks after the interior.[25] In the *Prometheus Vinctus*, Prometheus makes contemptuous reference to Hermes as Zeus' 'slave' and 'lackey',[26] and comedy here similarly gives a demeaning twist to the idea of Hermes as the gods' messenger. Cassio discusses the way that the characterisation of Hermes as a herald not only refers to one of his main aspects but also picks up negative feelings towards heralds in the fifth century.[27]

This role of Hermes as the god of the household is merely one aspect of his role as god of boundaries or margins. As well as mediating between *oikos* and *polis*, he also links men and gods, life and death, adolescence and maturity and so on. Orestes calls on him at the start of *Choephori* for aid in his attempt to regain his true status at Argos, and he speaks the prologue to and presides over Ion's recognition of his true nature in Euripides' play. Hermes regularly acts as the go-between in the relationships between men and gods: it is he who guides Priam to Achilles' tent[28] and who would have stolen Hector's body away if the gods had so decreed it;[29] he also guides Odysseus to Circe's cave[30] and is sent to warn Aegisthus of the consequences of the seduction of Clytaemestra.[31] He brings help to heroes such as Perseus and led the goddesses to Paris for judgement. In *Peace*, he is referred to as 'most philanthropic', 'greatest giver of gifts' (394) and 'most kindly' (602), which echoes Zeus's address to him in the *Iliad*: 'Hermes, you take the greatest pleasure in consorting with men, and listen to those you like.'[32]

His mediating role between men and gods is also found in the cult of Hermes Psithyrus at Lindos, where he had a shrine next to the

---

[24] Eitrem 1909; Farnell 1896–1909: v 1–84; N. O. Brown 1947; L. Kahn 1978; Vernant 1983: 127–75; Burkert 1984, 1985: 156–9; Osborne 1985b; Stockmeyer 1988.
[25] Vernant 1983: 127–75. [26] 941ff.; *Od.* 5.99ff; E. *Ion* 4. [27] 1985: 59–67.
[28] *Il.* 24.107ff. [29] Ibid. 334ff. [30] *Od.* 10.275ff. [31] Ibid. 1.35ff.
[32] *Il.* 24.334f.

temple of Athena and passed on the whispered prayers of her suppliants.[33] May we presume a similar function for Hermes Psithyristes, who had at Athens a shrine near those of Aphrodite and Eros Psithyrus?[34] It is presumably in a whisper that the 'mute' Peace makes known to Hermes her feelings about the mortals (657ff.) and that the equally mute herm counsels Strepsiades in *Clouds* (1478ff.).

As Psychagogus and Chthonius, Hermes is also connected with the boundary between life and death. There are jokes about this in 364–75 and 648–56. More specifically, he is a god concerned with binding and loosing. He brings back Persephone from Hades[35] and also Heracles,[36] and just in time frees Ares from the bronze jar into which Otus and Ephialtes had put him.[37] Conversely, he is present at the binding of Prometheus and Ixion.[38] This makes him an appropriate deity to preside over the imprisonment of Peace and her eventual release from under the rocks.[39] He is appropriate in other ways too. An Orphic hymn refers to his staff as 'blameless weapon of peace',[40] in an oxymoron that reflects the generally unwarlike nature of the god.[41] He is regularly associated with Aphrodite, Eros, the Graces and other such deities:[42] and at 456, Trygaeus invokes him along with the Graces, the Hours, Aphrodite and Desire (but not Ares or Enyalius) before the pulling up of Peace.[43]

Another central aspect of Hermes is his craftiness and trickery: he is *dolios* and a thaumaturge.[44] In the *Homeric Hymn*, he is able not only to spirit away the cattle of Apollo but also to escape from any

---

[33] Usener 1904; N. O. Brown 1947: 15 n. 22.

[34] Cratin. fr. 386 (with bibliography); [Dem.] 59.39; Plut. *Mor.* 138c.

[35] *H. Dem.* 377f. 'Hermes is almost a fixture in anodos scenes' (Cassio 1981: 17, quoting Zanker 1965: 81ff. and Raingeard 1935: 509ff.).   [36] *Od.* 11.626.   [37] *Il.* 5.385–91.

[38] L. Kahn 1978: 75–117.

[39] There is perhaps a mild joke here, because Hermes' name means 'the god of the stone-heap': Benveniste 1932.   [40] 28.7.

[41] Eitrem 1909: 355f.; *Peace* 395. That he is called Promachos at Tanagra is an exception which proves the rule, since he won that title by routing the Eretrians at the head of the ephebes, armed only with a strigil (Paus. 9.22.2).

[42] Hermes was concerned with human fertility: cf. his epithet Auxidemus *ap.* Hsch. s.v.; he is Epikarpios on Amorgos (*IG* 12.7.252; Roman period); cf. also the fertilising Hermesias and Hermoupoa (Plin. *NH* 24.166, 25.38–40); he promises crop fertility to the old man in *H. Herm.* 90–3 (L. Kahn 1978: 180).

[43] Trygaeus is endowed with three females through Hermes, who is often represented with three such figures, be they the goddesses to be judged by Paris, the Graces or other nameless figures: Farnell 1896–1909: V 35–7; Harrison 1908: 292–300; in *H. Herm.* 552ff., Apollo presents him with the three prophetic Thriae.

[44] L. Kahn 1978: 127–31 (and in general, 75ff.).

penalty for having done so. At crucial moments in his dispute with Apollo, he succeeds in producing some significant or wondrous ruse which turns the elder god's wrath from him. When Apollo picks him up, a fart and a sneeze cause him to drop him; when Apollo binds him with *Vitex*, the plant takes root and embraces the cows; when he tries the lyre, Apollo is quite enchanted and instantly proposes a settlement to their dispute, which accords Hermes high status among the gods. This aspect of the god is parodied in *Peace*, where it is Trygaeus who treats Hermes in a way that resembles Hermes' own treatment of Apollo: once again, the apparently less powerful figure gets his way by a judicious use of the resources available to him, but this time it is Hermes who is won over against his better judgement. Thus Trygaeus quickly changes the god's angry manner to an agreeable one by proffering a gift of meats (192f.); in the *Hymn*, Hermes' first act is to respond to his desire for meat and in *Plutus* it is hunger that prompts him to defect from the Olympians.[45] When Hermes attempts to fulfil his duty as divine watch-dog by calling on Zeus, Trygaeus uses a number of ploys to dissuade him. He has the Chorus supplicate the god in flattering terms (382ff.) and then he reveals the plot of the Sun and Moon to arrogate to themselves all sacrifice by humans (403–16). Next he informs Hermes that all the major city festivals and some more private ones will be celebrated in his honour alone (416–22). This is a powerful argument because, although his herm stood outside the houses and although he was offered sacrifice at important festivals, Hermes was not the main deity, in Athens at least, of any of the major festivals.[46] It is, however, not this which wins Hermes over, but rather another bribe, when Trygaeus offers him a golden libation bowl, to Hermes' great delight (425). As in the *Homeric Hymn* therefore, well-timed interventions and appropriate gifts lead the more powerful god to yield to his antagonist.

Despite this somewhat disrespectful treatment of the god on Trygaeus' arrival in heaven, Hermes does regain his proper status after he has agreed to help.[47] He conducts the rite that precedes the raising of Peace, pouring the libation after Trygaeus, who performs

---

[45] *H. Herm.* 64, cf. 287; *Plutus* 1120ff.

[46] The Hermaea was celebrated by young men and boys in the palaestra, a marginal rite, therefore (Pl. *Lys.* 206D–E; Aeschin. 1.10; Deubner 1932: 217). He receives sacrifice at a number of important festivals dedicated to other deities (Eitrem, *RE* 8.741f.).

[47] For this and the textual problems here, Cassio 1985: 59–67; he gives, with most MSS, Hermes not Trygaeus a dominant role during the raising of Peace.

the supporting task, has filled the bowl.[48] The importance of this rite
is increased by the fact that the audience are in effect included in it
by virtue not only of their very presence as it takes place, but also of
the prayer that 'this day may be the start of many good things for all
the Greeks' (435ff.): this being the Dionysia, representatives of many
parts of Greece would have been present in fact. It is then Hermes
who goes on to explain how it was that Peace left the world,[49] gives
instructions to Trygaeus about what to do with the newly raised
divinities and tells him how to get back to earth.[50] Hermes' actions
here thus set something of a divine seal on Trygaeus' liberation of
Peace: what Zeus and the other Olympians thought about this, we are
not told, as the action unfolds with blithe lack of interest in their
feelings.

The return of Peace[51]

The story of the recovery of Peace can be related to a number of
different kinds of tale. The initial state of affairs in *Peace* is so bad
that the gods themselves have been forced to withdraw to the *kuttaros*
of heaven, the highest point of its dome and as far from mortals as
possible (198f., 207–9), in order to spare themselves the sight of the
Greeks constantly warring against each other; only the destructive
deities War and Riot are left. There appear to be no parallels in Greek
mythology for this mass exodus of the Olympians. Individual divine
apodemiai, such as Demeter's in anger at the loss of Persephone, are

---

[48] Cassio 1985: 64.

[49] For a discussion of Hermes' speech and a justification of it as more than 'un ammasso di
assurdità', Cassio 1985: 87–103.

[50] Nevertheless, the only reference to him after the parabasis is the Slave's rejection of the
suggested inauguration of Peace's worship with pots of pulses: 'with pots? Like some
grumbling little Hermes?' (924).

[51] Personification of abstractions such as Peace appears in the earliest literary texts: e.g. Hes.
Th. 902, where she is child of Zeus and Themis, along with other signs of the new order, such
as the Horae, Eunomie, and Dike, with whom she is later regularly associated (Arnould 1981:
83ff., 106ff.). Only towards the end of the fifth century do cults of these abstractions become
common (Nilsson 1952; Hamdorf 1964; Burkert 1985: 182–9). In Attica, there were earlier
the temples of Nemesis and Themis (sixth century) at Rhamnus, and of Eucleia (early fifth) in
Athens. In the fifth century, Athena was given the attribute Nike, and a cult of Pheme was
instituted after 465 (Aeschin. 1.128, 2.145); in the 420s came the cult of Athena Hygieia.
Peace herself does not receive a cult until 374 (Isoc. 15.109f.; Nilsson 1952: 37 n. 2.; Pritchett
1979: 161). Aristophanes' representation of a cult of Peace would have been somewhat
novel, therefore, but it did not start a fashion.

not uncommon, as we shall see, but they are not always the result of anger.[52] We may however draw a parallel with those rituals in which the gods are presumed to abandon the city. The most obvious Athenian example of this is the Scira, where the withdrawal of Athena's priestess and Poseidon's priest marks the year-end, and is a symbolic representation of Poseidon's rage at losing to Athena the contest to be patron of the city, which led to a period of conflict with her and her representatives. The way in which War and Riot are left in the gods' places (205) would parallel the conflict between the deities, and also perhaps the 'take-over' of the Acropolis by the Ceryces who sacrifice not to the citadel's main deity Athena but to Zeus.

More directly relevant are the various kinds of 'return' of deities who in one way or another abandon their usual place.[53] We have already mentioned the Scira–Panathenaea cycle in Athens, but there are other more pertinent types of myth and ritual, which may usefully be termed 'anodos' ('coming up') and have analogues in the ancient Near East and elsewhere. The most famous example from Greece is that of Persephone, whose loss and return were celebrated in Athens at the Eleusinian Mysteries and Thesmophoria. When Persephone disappears into Hades, her mother Demeter stops all fertility on earth, and this situation is only remedied when the daughter is returned. The story is widespread, and also appears for instance, at Syracuse, where was celebrated the 'Return of the Maid',[54] with statues depicting the goddesses covered with symbols of fertility and fecundity.[55] Persephone raped by Pluto and kept in Hades is an obvious analogue to Peace who has been put into her 'deep pit' covered over with mighty stones by War (223–5), who, as we have seen, has his analogue in Death. The idea of the return of fertility and prosperity runs through myths of this sort,[56] and

---

[52] Richardson 1974: 158.

[53] Burkert 1979: 123–42; also Bérard 1974; Burkert 1985: 42, 115, 160, 161, 163, 242. The motif is found in other plays of Aristophanes, e.g. *Frogs* and *Poesis*, where the abject state of current writing is represented by the disappearance of Poetry, who is also brought back to remedy matters (frr. 466f.); see also fr. 591.84–6; Cassio 1981; and Adrados 1972 for the use of the rope in such tales.

[54] Cf. the *koragoi* at Mantinea (*IG* 5.2.265f.); Burkert 1979: 210 n. 9.

[55] Diod. 5.4.6; Nilsson 1906: 356f. Compare too the story of the statue of Hera on Samos (Menodotus, *FGH* 541 F 1; Burkert 1979: 129f.).

[56] Burkert 1979: 135; cf. 134f. on the *eiresione* as a similar symbol.

Peace's absence in the play has a frequently stressed deleterious effect on the corn, vines and figs: it is emphasised that it is the farmers who finally get her out (508, 511). There is no hint in *Peace* as to when in the year the action takes place, so that, given the extra immediacy generated by the way the play involves the audience, one may imagine it taking place at the same time as the Dionysia at which it was performed, at the end of winter. Peace, like Persephone, would thus naturally bring back fertility at the start of spring.[57]

In the myth of the rites of Black Demeter at Phigaleia in Arcadia, Demeter hid herself in a cave, either because of her anger at the loss of Persephone or because she had been raped by Poseidon.[58] Fertility failed and men began to starve. None of the gods could find Demeter until Pan happened across her. He told Zeus, who sent the Fates to persuade her, and her acceptance 'means that an orderly segmentation of the world, of space and time, will assure life of perpetuity'.[59] The Phigalians set up a wooden image in the grotto. At the altar no animal sacrifice was permitted, but grapes, fruits, honeycombs and unspun wool were laid on it and oil was poured on top. Demeter's recession to her cave carries the same message as the disappearance of Persephone and Peace. As Zeus sends the Fates to mark Persephone's return, so, when Peace is about to be hauled up, alongside Aphrodite and Desire, the Hours and the Graces are appealed to for help in a paean (456); Opora, who with Theoria rises beside Peace, is one of the Hours.[60] In *Peace* too the regularity of the seasons is restored. The special sacrifice for Demeter recalls the decision made concerning the sacrifice to Peace on her return: although a vegetable sacrifice is rejected as insufficiently grand (924) and a sheep is selected, its sacrifice (on stage at least) is forbidden, on the grounds that 'Peace does not like blood-sacrifice and her altar is not bloodied' (1019f.). Such 'bloodless' sacrifices were seen as characteristic of earlier, morally better eras before slaughter of animals was needed to placate the gods; they are therefore, as it were, pre-Olympian.[61]

---

[57] Her return is explicitly timed for the spring by *H. Dem.* 401–3; on the problems of relating myth and seasons, cf. Richardson 1974: 284f.

[58] Paus. 8.42. Cf. the story connected with Thelpusa at 8.25.4–10.

[59] Burkert 1979: 126.

[60] Hes. *Th.* 901f.; Pi. *Ol.* 13.6f.; M. L. West 1966: 406f.; Mullen 1982: 217–20.

[61] Graf 1981; Bowie 1993a.

Some versions of the Pandora myth are not dissimilar to that of Persephone. There are a number of fifth-century vase-paintings, which depict figures with mallets surrounding another figure who rises from the ground.[62] On a volute crater of c. 440 in Oxford,[63] on one side Zeus instructs Hermes, and on the other Epimetheus, holding a mallet, receives Pandora who is rising from the ground; on another crater of similar date, satyrs carrying mallets surround the figure who rises from the earth;[64] a white-ground cup shows Athena and Hephaestus attending a girl called Anesidora ('She who sends up gifts'), an epithet found elsewhere of Ge and Demeter.[65] With these representations we may compare Sophocles' satyric drama *Pandora or Hammerers*, on which Tzetzes' commentary mentions 'satyrs and banging', reminiscent of the hammering of the satyrs on the vases, employed to summon Pandora.[66] This suggests that Pandora was a chthonic deity whose *anodos* from the Underworld, like that of Peace, Demeter and Persephone, restored the fertility of the fields.[67]

Dionysus, the god of wine, has stories told of him and his descent to Hades to fetch his mother Semele. These are close to those of Demeter and Persephone, except that now the child searches for the mother.[68] At Lerna, he was said to have descended via the bottomless Alcyonian Lake and to have taken Semele to the market-place of Troezen, to the temple of Artemis Saviour;[69] yearly secret rites were conducted in his honour.[70] According to Plutarch, the god was summoned from the waters by trumpets.[71] Semele was also sought at Delphi, at the Herois festival: 'the explanation of the Herois is mainly a secret story, which the Thyiads know; but from the ritual one might clearly guess it to be a bringing up (*anagoge*) of Semele.'[72] There are many other rites in which Dionysus 'returns' to his worshippers after a period of absence, as at Smyrna, where he came in a ship into the agora at the very start of spring.[73] The bringing of

[62] Bérard 1974; M. L. West 1978: 164–6.   [63] Beazley 1963: 1562 no. 4.

[64] Beazley 1963: 612 no. 1.   [65] Beazley 1963: 869 no. 55.

[66] That this is what the mallets are for is argued by Bérard 1974.

[67] It is unnecessary to posit two Pandoras: Vernant 1979: esp. 114–32.

[68] Diod. 4.25; Plut. *Mor.* 566A; Apollod. 3.5.3; in general, Detienne 1986.   [69] Paus. 2.31.1f.

[70] Ibid. 2.37.5f.   [71] *Mor.* 364F.   [72] Ibid. 293C; Halliday 1928: 71f.

[73] Philostr. *VS* 1.25.1; Aristeid. 1.373, 440 (Dind.); also Hdt. 1.150; Deubner 1932: 103f.; Burkert 1985: 413 nn. 38f. Cf. *Katagogia* of Dionysus at Priene (*Inscr. Priene* 174.19f. (2nd. cent.)). For other divine returns, cf. e.g. Athen. 394F–5A; Ael. *NA* 4.2 (Aphrodite at Eryx); Paus. 9.2.7–3 (Zeus, Hera and the *daedala*); Hephaestus' 'return' was a feature of a major festival on Lemnos.

the god into the agora,[74] a ceremonial centre of a *polis*, in two of these festivals has its parallel in the sending of Theoria to an important section of the city, the Council (868ff.), which is a prelude to the installation of Peace in the city for all. These scenes are a counterpart to the general exodos to the fields with which the play ends. As Whitman says, Peace's two attendants 'prefigure respectively the immanent aspects of private and public peace, or, more accurately, peace in the country and peace in the city'.[75] The life-style much celebrated in the play may be georgic, but the city is not forgotten.

The statue is installed in the city in the course of a lengthy scene of sacrifice known technically as an *hidrusis*, the rite properly used to establish the cult of a deity. We are not very well informed on this rite,[76] but one of the clearest statements on it is found in the scholia to line 923: 'Every time that there were altars to be set up or statues of a god, they boiled peas and gave some of the porridge as a first-fruit offering to the altar or the image, assigning it as a thank-offering for their primitive food, as Aristophanes himself says in the *Danaides* [fr. 256]. At times, however, they were set up with a more expensive sacrifice.' Such a more expensive rite is appropriately used for a goddess of the importance of Peace. Her installation after a war may have reminded Athenians of the altar set up for Zeus Eleutherius after the victory over the Persians.[77]

Finally, there is a major Dionysiac festival of Athens, which though not strictly an *anodos*,[78] represents essentially the return of the god at springtime after an absence in an enclosed place and can also be structurally compared with *Peace* in more detail than those discussed above – the Anthesteria.[79] This festival occupied three days in Anthesterion, roughly February–March, a month before the Great Dionysia. The first day was the 'Pithoigia', when the jars containing the wine, which had been sealed since the vintage, were opened and tasted. Though this opening of jars was to lead to the consumption of not inconsiderable amounts of wine, Burkert has

---

[74] Pi. *Dithyramb* fr. 75 sings of celebrations of Dionysus and Semele in the spring, to which the Olympians 'who open the famed, decorated agora' are invited.

[75] 1964: 111; cf. Cassio 1985: 147.   [76] Burkert 1985: 89, with n. 59.

[77] Suda, s.v. *Eleutherios*; Harp. s.v. *Eleutherios Zeus*; Simon. 107B Diehl.

[78] Unless those are right who believe that Dionysus was brought into the city at this festival on a ship-cart: cf. e.g. Deubner 1932: 102–6; Simon 1983: 93; Burkert 1983a: 201 n. 26.

[79] Cf. Harrison 1908: 32–76; Deubner 1932: 93–123; Parke 1977: 107–20; Burkert 1983a: 213–47, 1985: 237–42; Simon 1983: 92–9; Pickard-Cambridge 1988: 1–25.

shown that the festival had many darker aspects. Plutarch says of it that 'at Athens ... since long ago they have apparently poured a libation of the wine before drinking and prayed that the use of this draught (*pharmakon*) would not harm but rather be good for them':[80] the consumption of the god is a potentially dangerous act. Indeed, in the concomitant myth, Icarius was taught viticulture by Dionysus and gave the first wine to his fellow-citizens, who fell over, unaccustomed to the beverage; Icarius was subsequently stoned for having poisoned them. As with Pandora's *pithos*, therefore, the opening of these *pithoi* contains a potential mixture of good and bad.[81]

The second day of the festival, the 'Choes', was a *miara* ('ill-omened') day.[82] All the temples were closed except that of Dionysus 'in the Marshes',[83] and 'Kares', spirits of the dead, wandered abroad. On this day, the famous drinking competition which appears at the end of *Acharnians* took place, as each person drank alone and in silence in memory of king Demophon's similar entertainment of the polluted Orestes. In the evening and on the following day, the 'Chytroi' ('Pots'), the restoration of the god was celebrated. At night, the priests sacrificed to Hermes Chthonius and the people cooked a *panspermia* in pots, which the priests were forbidden to eat. There was a myth to explain these pulse-dishes, in which 'those who survived the flood tried to appease Hermes on behalf of the dead' with such a dish, their first meal on dry land.[84] Also during the night between Choes and Chytroi, there took place the *hieros gamos* between the wife of the Archon Basileus, the 'Queen', and Dionysus.[85] Thus the god who had been hidden in the jars in the autumn returns to life and vigour in the spring amid general rejoicing; Hermes plays a crucial role in this release and return, and the god is wedded to the 'Queen' of the land. Summing up the Anthesteria, Burkert writes that it 'sets the whole city in motion: starting from the family unit, the house, the festival extends to embrace the higher orders of "king" and "queen" and the lower orders of small child-

---

[80] *Mor.* 655E.

[81] Compare also Zeus' jars at *Il.* 24.527f., in his comments on which Eustathius 1363.25 compares the opening of the jar of evils to the *Pithoigia*.

[82] Hsch., Photius s.v. *miara hemera*; Pritchett 1979: 209–29.

[83] Theopompus, *FGH* 115 F 347. The title of this temple, which did not stand in marshy ground, reminds one of the marshy margins of the Alcyonian lake at Lerna discussed above.

[84] Schol. *Frogs* 218, *Ach.* 1076 (from Theopompus).

[85] [Dem.] 59.73–8; [Arist.] *Ath. Pol.* 3.5.

ren, girls, and slaves ... the gods of the city are excluded, only
Dionysus and Hermes are present'.[86]

There are many possible echoes of this festival in the play. The
only Olympians who are operative in the festival are Hermes and
Dionysus: the latter's is the only temple open. In the play, all the gods
except Hermes have retired so that access to them is impossible, and
the freedom of the deity from its place of seclusion is achieved at a
festival of Dionysus, by Hermes and a man whose name associates
him with the vintage and its god: the name 'Protrugaia' is given of a
'festival of Dionysus and Poseidon' by Hesychius, and Pollux talks of
the *theoi protrugaioi*, but we do not know whether these names were
used at our period.[87] In the play, the deity beneficially affects wine
production: *opora* is especially used of grapes and figs,[88] and, as in
the festival, we have the advent of new wine (916).[89] Despite the
slave's dismissive remarks about inaugurating Peace's cult with
chutrai ('pots') in 922–4, it is possible that the audience would have
heard here a verbal echo of the name of the 'Chytroi' and the meal of
pulses. This meal was consumed in celebration of the survival of the
flood,[90] and the sacrifice in the play comes after a similar catastrophe
which the Greeks have just survived. The priests were forbidden to
eat the festival meal, and in *Peace* the *chresmologos* Hierocles is
refused a share in the sacrifice:[91] Smith points out that Trygaeus
renders the priest Stilbides unnecessary in 1031, when he shows
that he can build a fire as swiftly as a professional, ensuring the
offering will be burnt quickly.[92] After Choes, the 'Kares' were
expelled with the proverbial 'Outside, Kares, it's no longer the
Anthesteria', so that 'the dead lose their rights';[93] in *Peace*, it is the
agents of death in Athens who lose out with the coming of the
goddess, and no doubt War was made to yield up his place in the

---

[86] 1985: 241; cf. Detienne 1986: 80.

[87] Hsch., Pollux, s.vv.; Achilles Tatius 2.2 speaks of a Tyrian festival of Dionysus Protrygaeus,
associated with a story like that of Icarius in Athens; cf. Kany 1988.

[88] Pl. *Legg.* 844Dff.; Galen, *Alim. Fac.* 1 (Cassio 1985: 139f.).

[89] *Peace* blends in its celebrations events in the vegetable world that belong both in the spring
and the autumn in a way that is mirrored in the myths of the returns of the likes of
Persephone.

[90] Note the eightfold repetition of words for death in 364–75 (cf. 188f.) when Trygaeus reveals
to Hermes his plan to free Peace.

[91] Sommerstein 1985: 147 notes the absence of priests (and politicians and generals) from
Trygaeus' invitation in 296–8.

[92] 1989: 143.   [93] Burkert 1985: 240.

Olympian household. In the context of these other parallels, the ninefold repetition of the word *miaros* in 182–7 (cf. also 194, 362) might stand as a reflection of the ill-omened nature of the Choes.[94] Finally, we have the marriage between Trygaeus, the man of the vintage and second only to the gods (917), and Peace's lady-in-waiting Opora, almost therefore a *hieros gamos*?[95]

It might be objected that the play does not make explicit mention of some of the more striking aspects of the Anthesteria, such as the drinking competition, daubing of doors with pitch or the myth of Orestes. But the claim is not that the play is structured closely on the festival, as other plays are on their festivals, or that the Anthesteria is the dominant schema, merely that there are a series of features in the play which could have evoked the schema of that festival in the minds of the audience. Naturally enough, the comedy distorts many of the features that have a serious role in the festival, and it is in this that the humour presumably lay. The gloomy aspects are comically watered down: the *miaros* nature of Choes is debased in the insults flung at Trygaeus; the closure of the temples of the other Olympians becomes the retiring of the gods in disgust at the antics of the warring Greeks; the solemn *hieros gamos* between the god and the 'Queen' is represented by the lasciviously celebrated unions of Trygaeus and Opora and the Boule and Theoria, and so on.

One may ask what the point of an allusion to the Anthesteria might be. Cassio has shown how Aristophanes balances in the play criticisms of Athens' conduct in the war, of her attitudes to peace negotiations and of her treatment of the allies, with staging which gives Athens as the city where Peace is actually situated. Amongst the allies the Ionians are especially picked out, and Cassio detects elements of propaganda presenting Athens as the mother-city of the Ionians.[96] There is a strong pan-Hellenic flavour to the celebrations, but the leader of the action is for the most part either an Athenian or the city as a whole. It was around this time that all the allied cities were urged to send first-fruit offerings (*aparchai*) to Eleusis and its

---

[94] Though *miaros* is regularly used as a term of comic abuse, it also belongs to the vocabulary of pollution: R. C. T. Parker 1983: 3f.

[95] Simon 1983: 97 argues that a mid-fifth-century column-crater in Bologna shows the *Basilinna* being led to her marriage by Hermes (Beazley 1963 no. 532.44): it is he who orders Trygaeus to take Opora as his bride. We hear of *agones* at the Anthesteria, and Trygaeus describes in sexual terms a series of athletic competitions in 894ff.

[96] 1985: 105–18.

goddess: sacrifice was to be made in Attica therefore on behalf of all those who contributed.[97]

The Anthesteria was a festival common to Athenians and Ionians, which therefore went back to before the migrations: Thucydides says of it that 'It is still today celebrated by the Ionians from Athens.'[98] To evoke this festival would thus at once stress Athenian control of the restitution of Peace and also compliment the Ionians in the audience by stressing their connections with the chief city. There is evidence too to suggest that 'The Athenian becomes conscious of his Athenian-ness by the fact that he participates in the Anthesteria celebrations.'[99] Callimachus tells of an Athenian in Egypt who always celebrated the Anthesteria,[100] and Themistocles introduced the Choes into Magnesia during his banishment.[101] The play would thus appeal to a festival that was both characteristically Athenian but also shared by a wider group in the audience and in Greece. As the whole of Greece is called on to move 'to the fields', the call must have meant to many Athenians (and others) not Old Comedy's supposed romantic preference for the countryside, but the prospect of repairing the ravages inflicted on the Attic countryside by the previous decade of war. This peace is instituted through one marginal deity and the human representative of another, who was also deity of the dramatic festival. This pairing and many other echoes evoke the Anthesteria, a festival that marked a new start with indulgence, but also gave due weight to the more sinister aspects of life and death. For the time being, *Peace*'s 'Anthesteria' offers safety from the flood.

[97] Sokolowski 1962: no. 5; Burkert 1985: 67f.   [98] 2.15.4.   [99] Burkert 1985: 241.
[100] Fr. 178.1–5.   [101] Possis, *FGH* 480 F 1; and the similar sentiment in Alciphr. 4.18.10f.

7

Birds

Recent criticism of *Birds* has tended either to represent the play as an allegory, positive or negative, of the state of politics in Athens, or, where the play's ambiguities are felt to be too great, to speak of it as a play from which political commentary has been excluded.[1] In attempting to reconcile these competing readings of the play, I will argue that it not only provides a radical deconstruction of the fantastic notion that a 'place without trouble' (44) could ever exist,[2] but is also intensely political in its examination of the nature of Athenian democracy in general and of the specific political situation at the time of its composition.

Like *Peace*, *Birds* presents a new start. Since it recounts the creation of a new city, it is not surprising to find it structured in the manner of myths of city-foundation, designed to legitimate a city and to celebrate its foundation as something divinely inspired. But the city in *Birds* is to be unusual, not least because it is founded in despite of the gods, and the play prepares the audience for this abnormality by using the traditional elements of the foundation-myth, but persistently distorting them. Legitimated yet anomalous, like the new world of Dicaeopolis, Nephelococcygia will possess demerits in proportion to its merits, so that by the end it will have revealed itself to be far from a mere *Pays de Cocagne*; and the mythical notion of a paradise existing in some remote area will be shown to be, precisely, mythical.

---

[1] The fantastic has been emphasised most recently by Sommerstein 1987: 1f.: *Birds* has 'no strong and obvious connection with a topical question ... whether political ... literary-theatrical ... or intellectual-educational ... satire is kept firmly subordinate to fantasy'. For an account of the paradoxical interplay of social, political and utopian discourses, Konstan 1990.   [2] For a different deconstructive reading, cf. Dobrov 1990.

Birds and foundation-mythology

The wide diversity of foundation-myths precludes the drawing up of any simple pattern that covers them all. Analysis of *Birds* therefore must consist in the isolation of elements of the play that are regularly encountered in the myths.[3]

The opening scene gives no reason for thinking that a new foundation is in the offing, let alone a city of the cosmic significance of Nephelococcygia. Peisetaerus[4] and Euelpides are discovered bearing a basket, pot and garlands, and seeking a 'place without troubles (*pragmata*), where we could establish ourselves and live out our lives' (45). That they are seeking an already-existing city is suggested both by their language here and by their rejection of the places that Tereus proposes in 144ff., not because they wish to found a completely new city, but because these places are inherently unsuitable. From the ancient commentators onwards, two explanations have been offered of the basket, myrtle wreaths and pot which the men carry: either they are for a foundation-sacrifice or for a defence against the Birds. Hamilton 1985 has pointed out that these explanations involve reading back into the prologue subsequent events, of which neither we nor the two men can have any inkling at this point. He argues that the items are used in sacrifices of all kinds, and are not associated specifically with foundations; he prefers to see them as sympotic paraphernalia, appropriate to the kind of city they have in mind (128ff.). It may however be better to regard the items as ambiguous. They could be used at a symposium, but are not so obviously or exclusively sympotic that the possibility of a sacrifice would not have occurred to the audience. Indeed, the pot and the use of the verb *kathidruein* in 45 might well conjure up the possibility of a foundation-sacrifice, since they could point to the rite of *hidrusis*. Strictly speaking, this rite was used, not for the foundation of a city, but for the establishment of a god in a city, as in *Peace*, but in the light of the outcome of the play, line 45 will take on a prophetic quality. At the moment, however, the utensils are of uncertain purpose.

---

[3] Schmid 1947; Storetzki 1954; Vian 1963; Cornell 1983; Cairns 1979: 64–86; Leschhorn 1984. For the popularity of *ktisis*-myths at this time, Pl. *Hipp. Maj.* 285Dff. The mythical affiliations of *Birds* have been studied also by Hofmann 1976, Auger 1979 and Zannini-Quirini 1987 (which I have not seen).

[4] For bibliography on the spelling of this name, Gelzer, *RE* Supplbd. 12.1461.22ff.; also Marzullo 1970: 181–4.

If the idea of a city-foundation has not yet been evoked, in leaving Athens because they find the conditions there intolerable, Peisetaerus and Euelpides are none the less conforming to a common topos of foundation-myths. Future founders are often impelled to seek a new home by force of circumstance, which may manifest itself as a natural disaster, such as plague or civil strife, or in the scattered condition of those who will constitute the new colony. The Therans acceded to Delphi's command to colonise Libya when oppressed by a drought that destroyed all but one tree,[5] and Heracleia Pontica was founded after a plague in Boeotia;[6] plague also figures in the legends about Syracuse[7] and the Aeolic migrations,[8] and famine in that of Rhegium.[9] Vian characterises such events as 'le départ à zéro': 'l'acte de fondation tire du néant un nouvel organisme politique et social; il faut donc qu'il soit symboliquement précédé d'une période de chaos où les forces vitales sont plongées dans la léthargie'.[10] If Peisetaerus and Euelpides are spared plagues and famines, the chaos of Athens is manifest: fines are intolerable (38), activity in the courts is incessant (39–41), private life is interfered with (145–7) and there is a general *polupragmosune* ('officiousness', 'meddlesomeness') of which they wish to be rid (27–48; cf. 114–61). Indeed, Euelpides describes their problem as a 'disease' (31). Clear too is the distressed condition of Peisetaerus and Euelpides themselves as they wander at the mercy of their bird-guides, which either contradict each other (1f.) or themselves (23f.), whilst leading their masters into pathless ways (20–2). The men have wandered for a long time (5–8) and are lost: 'I've no idea where on earth we are now', says Euelpides (9). This is not simply an expression of frustration: 'It is not entirely clear, amid the jokes ... at what moment we cease to be on earth and cross the boundaries of the unreal and the au-delà.'[11] It is only at 49–52 that the two birds finally concur in their indications, and the quest draws to an end. Such wanderings are also a regular fate of colonists, as in the case of the Therans who had to find Libya before they could found Cyrene.

It will become clear later that Peisetaerus' and Euelpides' fellow 'colonists', the Birds, are also dispersed and in disarray. They have become a byword for flightiness and instability (164–70) and an easy

[5] Hdt. 4.150–3.   [6] Justin 16.3.4–8.   [7] Plut. *Narr. Am.* 773A–B.
[8] Demon, *FGH* 327 F 17.   [9] Arist. fr. 611.55.   [10] 1963: 80.
[11] Duchemin 1957: 277.

prey for men (522–38), so that they are much in need of Peisetaerus' *sunoikismos* (172) into a single city which will restore them to their former power, just as Theseus' made Attica strong and united. Tereus puts his somewhat dishevelled appearance down to his winter moult (103–6), but that he should be so run-down is of a piece with the general condition of the Birds: Tereus moulting will be reincarnated as Peisetaerus in his glory at the end of the play. The general decrepitude that reigns is manifested in the first encounter between Peisetaerus and Euelpides and the Servant of Tereus, when both sides, in a manner reminiscent of Papageno and Monostatos, display a lamentable cowardly fear (6off.).

As a prelude to the foundation of their city, colonists regularly consult an oracle (often on a topic that has nothing to do with foundation) and receive the command to create a new home.[12] Aristophanes reverses the normal order whereby the consultation of the oracle precedes the provision of the animal-guide. The role of the oracle is taken by Tereus, because he has been both man and bird (114–20) and so is in a position to be authoritative; he is like Teiresias to whom, because he had been both man and woman, Zeus and Hera referred the question of which partner gained the most pleasure from the sexual act.[13] There is a surprising further twist to the normal pattern, however, in the way that it is not the oracular figure who suggests the solution to the enquirers' problems (indeed all his advice is rejected), but the enquirer himself. More than merely comic, this is an indication both that the typology of the foundation-myth is not to be slavishly followed and that the order of things is about to be overturned: nothing has prepared us for Peisetaerus' sudden brain-wave.

An animal-guide is often indicated by the oracle, which the men will either hit upon by chance or learn the whereabouts of from the god.[14] The movements or behaviour of the guide are then the indications of where the new foundation is to be. Bulls and cows are common, as in the case for instance of Thebes and Bouthoe in Epirus;[15] Athamas, as we saw when discussing *Clouds*, was told to found a city where he was entertained by wolves;[16] and bees led to

---

[12] Schmid 1947: 94–133, 148–53; Vian 1963: 76–93. For the involvement of Delphi in colonisation, cf. Pease 1917; Parke & Wormell 1956: I 49–81; Murray 1980: 100–19 (esp. 113–17); Malkin 1987.   [13] Hes. fr. 275.

[14] Vian 1963: 76–93, with bibliography on p. 77 n. 3.   [15] Vian 1963: 78f.

[16] Apollod. 1.9.2, and above p. 92.

the oracle of Trophonius.[17] Physcus had to make his city where he was bitten by a 'wooden dog', a rose-bush.[18] There is a nice Hellenistic variation on this motif, in the story of the founders of Hamaxitus in the Troad, who were told to settle wherever they were attacked by the *gegeneis*, 'the earth-born ones', which turned out to mean not indigenous giants but the field-mice who ate the leather of their equipment.[19] Birds also are frequently employed. Ravens led the settlers of Cyrene, Magnesia, Coraces, Mallus, Lyon and Cardia; a crested lark those of Colonides in Messenia; and doves those of Cumae and Naples (they figure too in the legends of the oracles at Dodona and in Libya).[20] In a number of Hellenistic myths, an eagle took a piece of sacrificial meat to the place of foundation, as at Alexandria, where beforehand birds had come down and eaten up the meal that had been used, in the absence of chalk, to mark out the boundaries: this was interpreted as meaning that Alexandria would nourish the world, 'because birds travel over the whole earth'.[21] It is precisely the ubiquity of the Birds that Peisetaerus relies upon for the success of his plan (175ff.; cf. 423–6).

In taking birds as their guides therefore Peisetaerus and Euelpides are following good precedents, even if they have rather more difficulty with them than is usual in the more serious myths. On the other hand, crows and jackdaws do not figure very often as guides.[22] Indeed, the jackdaw and, to a lesser extent, the crow do not occupy a particularly elevated position in Greek tradition generally: the ill-tempered Philocrates would appear to have done the two men no favours (13). Neither bird seems to have been much used in augury (except in weather-prophecy):[23] there is a fable of Aesop in which the crow, jealous of the raven's reputation among men as a bird of augury, tried to imitate it by croaking loudly when some travellers passed; this merely provoked the remark, 'Let's go friends, it's a

[17] Paus. 9.40.1.   [18] Arist. frr. 560–1; Plut. *Mor.* 294E.

[19] Callinus fr. 7 (*ap.* Strabo 13.1.48); Ael. *NA* 12.5; (Schmid 1947: 8–11).

[20] Schmid 1947: 159–65; Vian 1963: 78; Frazer on Paus. 10.6.2.

[21] Ps.-Callisthenes 1.32; Plut. *Alex.* 26; Curtius Rufus 4.8.6 (possibly from Apollonius' *Foundation of Alexandria*).

[22] The bronze crow found at Corone when the foundations were being dug (Paus. 4.34.5), and the crow which showed the way to Hesiod's grave when his bones were sought to stop a plague (ibid. 9.38.3; Lucian, *Mort. Pereg.* 41) are not true contrary examples.

[23] D'A. W. Thompson 1936: 155–8 and 168–72. He says that jackdaws were frequently used in augury (156), but quotes for Greek as opposed to Latin beliefs only *Birds* 50. The crow's connection with augury is 'seldom mentioned in Greek, save in Ar. Aves' (172; a single crow is an evil omen in Ael. *HA* 3.9). Cf. West 1978: 341.

crow, and when he croaks it's not an omen.'[24] If the crow is not infrequently used in fables to convey wise words to more foolish animals, the jackdaw is regularly a figure of fun: most famously, he presented himself, at a competition to find the king of the birds, in the cast-off feathers of all the others, who, angered at the theft, each removed his own feathers and left the jackdaw bald.[25] There is thus a comic inappropriateness in the use of these birds by Peisetaerus and Euelpides: Alexander was better served by the ravens which led him to the oracle of Zeus Ammon when his human guides lost the track.[26]

Once the animal-guides have performed their function, the arrival of the would-be colonists can lead not unnaturally to a conflict with indigenous inhabitants, whose claim to the land will often reside in their autochthonous nature, as in the case of dragons or Athenians. The Birds, of course, being older than the earth (469f.), have an even greater claim to their 'lands'. We have discussed on *Knights* the foremost foundation-myth of all, Zeus' battle with the monstrous Titans and Typhoeus; Cadmus killed the dragon that guarded the spring at Thebes, as did Apollo at Delphi and later Alexander at Alexandria.[27] The conflict motif is repeated in the Theban myth in the subsequent struggle either between Cadmus and the Spartoi or amongst the Spartoi themselves. The story of the *gegeneis* field-mice at Hamaxitus is a parody of this motif, which is again repeated, as Scamander, the colonists' leader, subsequently fought the Bebryces, won the battle, but then disappeared in the Xanthus river, which took his name.[28] This is reminiscent of the Athenian myth in which conflict again appears twice, once in the peaceful competition of gifts between Athena and Poseidon and then in the battle between Eumolpus and Erechtheus. The various *agones*, musical and athletic, *lithoboliae*[29] etc. associated with foundation-festivals are also representations of this motif. *Birds* replicates it in the preliminary skirmish between the men and the Birds and in struggle with the gods who are to be deposed.

These mythical conflicts can stand for more than the inevitable hostility between newcomers and residents; they often have a

[24] *Fab.* 127 H.–H.

[25] Ibid 103; there are similar stories in ibid. 125 and 131.

[26] Plut. *Alex.* 27.3; Arrian, *Anab.* 3.3.5f. Ravens were able to distinguish fertile and barren lands (Arist. *HA* 618b9; Ael. *HA* 2.49).

[27] Vian 1963: 94–113, 158–76.; for Alexander, Ps.-Callisthenes 1.32; Schmid 1947: 64–70.

[28] Servius on Virg. *Aen.* 3.108.   [29] Eitrem 1915: 280–94.

symbolic value, conveyed by unusual elements in them, which mark the episode as taking place at a liminal time. This is true of the stand-off between Peisetaerus and Euelpides and the Birds. The two humans are 'old men' (320, 337), and so too old for active campaigning. They fight not with normal weapons, but with the implements they have brought: the pot acts as a wall to hide behind (357, 390f.), a spit is mounted as a pike in front of them (359f.), saucers are used to protect their eyes (360f.); and they resort to trickery (363).[30] By contrast, the Birds are characterised as regular hoplite troops. They are addressed as 'hoplites' (402, 448) and have a taxiarch who is to lead forward their right wing (353). They follow correct practice in using the battle-cry as they set their beaks (364),[31] and when, still in ranks, they deposit on the ground their 'spirit' and 'anger' as the soldier would his arms (401f.).[32] When the combat is called off, they are instructed to watch the notice-boards on which campaign instructions were posted (450).[33] Earlier, as the various birds ran on with their crests, some of them reminded Peisetaerus of runners in the *diaulos*, also called the *hoplites dromos* when run by armed men.[34]

The reversals in this conflict are reminiscent of those in the fight in *Wasps*, where the former hoplite Philocleon is guarded by slaves who are now 'hoplites' armed with spits, and the Athenian Wasps who once routed the Persians with fire and smoke are themselves driven off by slaves in the same way. In each case, the reversals serve to mark the battle as a period of chaos and transition: here birds become hoplites and men fight with sacrificial

[30] Cadmus, though involved in conflicts, is always depicted in early representations as a traveller not a warrior. This marks him as marginal before his foundation of a city. He often carries a vase to collect water from the spring (Vian 1963: 45f.). For trickery in military matters, Wheeler 1988.

[31] Blaydes *ad loc.* compares X. *Anab.* 6.3 [*leg.* 5].27 and 25. For the cry, cf. X. *Anab.* 1.8.18; Achaeus, *TGF* 20 F 37; Demetrius, *De Eloc.* 98; Plut. *Thes.* 22.3; schol. *Birds ad loc.* (Rogers on 364).

[32] Rogers (on 401) quotes X. *Hell.* 7.5.22, add *Anab.* 1.5.13; on hoplite practice, J. K. Anderson 1970: 111–64; Krentz 1985; Pritchett 1985: 44–93; Hanson 1991.

[33] Who gives the instructions? A herald is an uneconomical solution, and Tereus 'never utters pseudo-military orders' (Sommerstein 1987: 225). This leaves the coryphaeus and Peisetaerus. Sommerstein inclines to the idea that Peisetaerus is addressing Euelpides, but, as he shows, there are problems with this (Euelpides is singular not plural, the arms are to be given up not 'taken up' (449) and no-one is going home). Since the Chorus were 'hoplites' in 402, and the hoplite language has been used of them not the men, it seems more likely that they are addressed here. I prefer the coryphaeus therefore as speaker, since Peisetaerus has not yet assumed command of the Birds.   [34] Pl. *Legg.* 833A–B; Pollux 3.151; *RE* 8.2297f.

implements, before the new order is embarked upon. This motif of unusual conflict in transitional times is common: it occurs, for instance, in the Thesmophoria myths recounting the use of sacrificial implements by the women who attack Battus and Aristomenes, who infiltrated this festival which ritualised the temporary control of affairs by women in place of men, before the end of the festival reintroduced male power. Comparable too are the tales of women taking up arms to defend their city, which are exclusively connected with festivals held at marginal times of the year.[35] The foundation-story of the ritual beating of ephebic warriors at the altar of Artemis Ortheia told how Pausanias was surprised in the act of sacrificing by the Lydians, who scattered the elements of the sacrifice; Pausanias and his men were then forced to fight with sticks and goads because their weapons were not to hand: the initiatory rite continued the practice.[36] Finally, in the rite of the kings of Atlantis, which was a periodic reaffirmation of the precepts of Poseidon, Plato has them sacrifice the bull 'without iron weapons but with clubs and nets'.[37] If in *Wasps* the battle is just one stage in the development of Philocleon, in *Birds* the resolution of the conflict comes with the revelation of Peisetaerus' startling plan to the other Birds.

Peisetaerus' arguments in favour of this plan – that the birds once ruled the world, still have remnants of that power and can defeat Zeus and benefit mankind – lead to a ready acceptance. Tereus is persuaded to call Procne and she is welcomed as harbinger of a spring that contrasts with the winter of Tereus' moult (105f.). The scholiast says that in Attica the nightingale appeared in spring, and part of the parabasis (676–84) has echoes of the 'chelidonisma' songs that welcomed the swallow's return after winter.[38]

In the anapaests that follow, the Birds sing their version of the cosmogony.[39] City foundations were seen as repetitions of the original cosmogonic act, when Zeus defeated Typhoeus: Pindar uses this

---

[35] Graf 1984.   [36] Plut. *Arist.* 17.8.

[37] *Critias* 119C–20D (quotation in 119E). The 'hunting' of bulls that roam free is itself anomalous: compare the Buphonia and the festival of Demeter Chthonia at Hermione (Paus. 2.35.5–8); Herter 1966.

[38] Note the 'spring songs' of 683; cf. *PMG* 848. For spring marking a new beginning after disorder, Austin 1975: 239–53 on the *Odyssey*.

[39] Cf. Schwabel, *RE* Supplbd. 9.1472f. (Aristophanes), and 1501f. (wind and eggs); Kirk–Raven–Schofield 1983: 21–33; Hofmann 1976: 177–96. For eggs and cosmogony, Baumgarten 1981: 94–139; M. L. West 1983: Index s.v. 'egg'.

myth to give significance to the foundation of Aetnaea in *Pythian* 1.[40] Nephelococcygia occupies a special position in this framework of ideas, because its foundation will take the world away from the 'chaos' of Athens and the current state of the Birds back to its primordial state, not just in a mythical or ritual sense, but in 'reality'. Peisetaerus refers to Nephelococcygia as 'the plain of Phlegra, where the Gods outshot the giants at the game of brag' (824),[41] so that it becomes the site of a repetition of that earlier conflict, but a repetition in which, as in the *Wasps* example quoted above, the earlier result is reversed and the defeat of the gods leads to the supersession of Zeus' dominion. The cosmos is returned to an even earlier stage before his usurpation of the Birds' power.[42]

Once they have convinced the Birds of their good intentions, Peisetaerus and Euelpides undergo 'metamorphosis' into birds,[43] the comic banter between them serving to recall the banter over Tereus' moult (95ff.) and thus to mark this change of plumage as a new starting-point in the drama.[44] Here too they gain an identity contrasting with their earlier anonymity (or pseudonymity, 65–8), by being properly named (644f.). As in the case of Agoracritus in *Knights*, this occurs at a significant moment. Metamorphosis is a feature of foundation-mythology: in the Theban myth, Cadmus fought men who sprang from the dragon's teeth, and the subsequent Thebans continued to be called 'Spartoi' ('Sown Men'). The men and women who repeopled the world after the Flood grew from the stones cast by Deucalion and Pyrrha,[45] and the original inhabitants of Cyprus were the 'Wasps'.[46] Most famously, the Myrmidons were created from ants by Zeus to repopulate Aegina, which Hera, in anger at the

---

[40] Trumpf 1958; NB 'founder of Aetna' (*Birds* 926), a reference to Hieron, the dedicatee of *Olympian* 1. In *Olympian* 7 Rhodes' birth is glorified by its coincidence with the moment the gods divided the world amongst themselves.

[41] Tr. Rogers. The text and meaning are corrupt, but, given the motif of the Gigantomachy in the play, it is likely that Aristophanes means Nephelococcygia could be well called 'the plain of Phlegra', not that he is referring still to the wealth of Theogenes and Aeschines.

[42] The period after the foundation of the cosmos was often seen as a Golden Age, to two aspects of which the Birds promise a return: the presence of the gods on earth (726–9: the new gods will not hide on Olympus but come amongst men) and good things will be given in abundance (726–36).

[43] Forbes Irving 1990: 96–127, 223–60 on metamorphosis into birds.

[44] The change is effected by a root (654f.). For the hoopoe's use of herbs, cf. Ael. *NA* 1.35, 3.26; Horap. 2.93 (D'A. W. Thompson 1936: 98). For herbs that change men's shapes, cf. Paus. 9.22.7 (with Frazer's note); Athen. 296ff.   [45] Hes. fr. 234.

[46] Philostephanus, *FHG* 3.30 fr. 10 = Alex. Polyh. *FGH* 273 F 144.

inhabitants, had smitten with a plague.[47] Again, the strangeness of
the foundation story in *Birds* is marked by a variation in the topos: in
the myths just quoted the movement is from stones or animals to men
and women, that is, from nature to culture, as befits the foundation
of a city. In *Birds*, however, the movement is the other way: in the
mythology of metamorphosis, change into animals and lifeless
objects is often a punishment for the failure to live up to the norms of
human society or the ordinances of the gods,[48] and Nephelococcygia
will indeed be a place where such transgressions can flourish, but
apparently unchecked.

It only remains now to choose the name of the city and its
presiding deities.[49] Its difference from the Athens that has been left
behind is clearly marked. Sparta is suggested as a name, but rejected
in favour of Nephelococcygia (812–26). In the choice of gods, Athena
is rejected and in her place the cockerel, the 'Persian bird', is
preferred (826–36). When sacrifice is made on behalf of the city,
Athena is not mentioned at all, but the hawk, whose description as
Sounierakos ('Sounion-hawk', 868) points to her rival Poseidon, is
among the first addressed.[50] The suggestion of the name Sparta, the
Persian bird and Poseidon, god of the chaotic sea and opponent of
Athena, all function like the Persian cloak and Spartan shoes in the
transformation of Philocleon in *Wasps* to show that a new stage has
been achieved. In the *Odyssey*, it is Poseidon's temple that presides
over the agora of the seafaring Phaeacians, whose marginal land,
mixing the human and superhuman, is Odysseus' last port of call: it
stands between the worlds of his wanderings and the 'real' world of
Ithaca, where he consorts once more with Athena.[51] So too, Nephelococcygia, situated in the air, is a world similar to but different in
significant ways from the 'real' Athens.

As is traditional in foundation-myths and rituals, a sacrifice to
the gods is now begun by Peisetaerus, whilst Euelpides is sent to
supervise the building of the walls. The array of greater and lesser

---

[47] Hes. fr. 205; Pherecrates, *Murmekanthropoi* (frr. 113–31); Strabo 375; schol. Pi. *Ne.* 3.21 etc.
(Vian 1963: 170). Aeschylus' *Myrmidons*, quoted by Peisetaerus and Euelpides when they
return as birds (807f.), concerned Achilles and Patroclus, not the original Myrmidons.

[48] Calame 1977: I 77–9; Sourvinou-Inwood 1991: 85–7.

[49] The establishment of cult is naturally an important aspect of foundation-mythology: Vian
1963: 134–57.

[50] Cf. *Knights* 560. On the textual problems here, see most recently Sommerstein 1987: 255f.

[51] *Od.* 6.266f.; Segal 1962; Detienne 1981a: 34; Vidal-Naquet 1981a.

alazones who arrive to obstruct the sacrifice is what one would expect at the inception of a new city: priests, poets, oracle-mongers, surveyors, overseers and law-vendors. In serious foundation-myths, such sacrifices are often to be interpreted as expiatory ones, which recompense the previous owners and sometimes take the form of a human sacrifice.[52] In *Birds* the motif is quite perverted, as the sacrifice is made by the new possessors to themselves not to the old, and, to make matters worse, it marks the beginning of a ban on the old gods receiving any offerings at all.

As the Second Argument hints and has been amply demonstrated by Hofmann, the part of the play after the parabasis is reminiscent of the Gigantomachy, although, despite the Chorus's belligerent 'war is let loose, unspeakable war' (1189), actual physical combat is not involved in this version.[53] Instead, the Birds use against the gods the unpleasant 'Melian hunger' (186), which the Athenians employed to reduce the island of Melos, and prevent the sacrificial smoke from reaching heaven. There are various indications that a Gigantomachy is being enacted. When Peisetaerus says they should build a city with baked-brick walls like Babylon, Tereus swears by Porphyrion and Cebriones, two Giants, and at 1246–52, Peisetaerus warns Iris that, if he has any trouble from Zeus, he will send six hundred 'Porphyrions' ('rails') against him, and reminds her how much trouble a single Porphyrion had caused Zeus in his struggle with the Giants. Again, when Nephelococcygia is selected as the name, Peisetaerus makes an explicit connection with the Gigantomachy by calling it 'the plain of Phlegra' (824); at 926, the Poet hails Peisetaerus as 'founder of Aetna', the mountain placed on top of the defeated Typhoeus.

The arrival of Prometheus points in the same direction: he was a Titan who abandoned his fellows because, according to the *Prometheus Vinctus* 197ff., they would not listen to his advice. He was earlier able to help Zeus first gain power, because, as the arch trickster, he knew that victory in the struggle with the Titans would go not to force but to cunning,[54] and then keep it by revealing (somewhat reluctantly) the secret of the threat posed by any son of Thetis. He

---

[52] Vian 1963: 172f., and compare the similar tradition about the foundation of athletic games as compensation: Nagy 1986.

[53] Hofmann 1976: 79–90; *Hypoth.* 2.21–4. There is the regular confusion of elements from the Gigantomachy and Titanomachy.   [54] Hofmann 1976: 209–15.

was later mistreated by Zeus and is now once again changing sides
out of dissatisfaction; he comes to Peisetaerus with another secret of
how Zeus may be deposed. His arrival under a sun-shade (1508f.) is
puzzling. The obvious reason for this is the one he gives himself, that
he does not want Zeus to see him, but one wonders whether there is a
gesture here to the sun-shade under which the priestess of Athena
abandoned her temple on the Acropolis at the Scira, or, if the parasol
was also used in the Panathenaic procession, to the return of the gods
to the city.[55] This passage (and its scholion) are the only evidence in
favour of the idea that the parasol was used in the Panathenaea
procession, but the 'Chair-Bearers', to which Peisetaerus makes
reference in telling Prometheus to 'carry a chair' (1552), are particularly characteristic of this festival.[56] If this nexus of ideas is present,
then Prometheus' desertion of the gods under a parasol would recall
this New Year festival of renewal and return of the rightful gods and
accompany a similar 'cosmic' change, in which new rightful owners
take possession of the heavens.

The presence of Prometheus at the moment of a distribution of
powers allows one to consider this scene also in terms of the events at
Mecone, as described by Hesiod. There the Titan tricked a knowing
Zeus into taking the less edible portion of the sacrificial animal, thus
providing the reason why men now eat the palatable sections of the
animal and give the gods the rest, and why men and gods no longer
consume their portions side by side. From then on, men had to
scratch a living from the soil, aided by the fire Prometheus stole for
them, and were given the mixed blessing of the first woman,
Pandora. This event therefore established the nature of the world as
it is.[57] Events in *Birds* have the same function, and themes from the
Mecone myth recur.[58] Sacrifice plays an important role in each case
as the *locus* for the distribution of power:[59] the transformation of the
world into the fiefdom of Peisetaerus takes place at a sacrifice,

---

[55] Cf. discussion in Deubner 1932: 31 n. 14.

[56] The *diphrophoros*, as opposed to the *kanephoros*, is not quoted for any other festival by
Deubner 1932.

[57] Hes. *Th.* 535–57, and *Op.* 47–105; for an analysis, Vernant 1979: 37–132. The verb used in
Hesiod, *krinesthai* (*Th.* 535), 'denotes a "settlement" in the legal sense, though not
necessarily in a legal context; a definitive division between two parties, however arrived at'
(M. L. West 1966: 317), and has an echo in the *diallagai* of *Birds* 1532. Call. fr. 119 refers to a
settlement at Mecone after the Battle of the Giants.

[58] Cf. also Auger 1979: 85f.   [59] On this function of the *dais*, Nagy 1979: 127–41.

performed by him to the new gods, and Zeus is this time deprived not simply of the edible pieces but of all ritual meats. At 1546, Peisetaerus refers to the gift of fire, gratefully admitting that it is because of Prometheus that 'we can broil our food' (1546). Prometheus' cunning is used in *Birds* not simply to deceive the gods at a crucial moment, but to defeat them completely, as Peisetaerus and Euelpides resort not to open conflict but to Prometheus' informed tip of demanding the woman Basileia (1536): again, he has the secret to Zeus's overthrow. Finally, the transfer of a woman from gods to men marks the change in the nature of the world in both stories. Pandora was so called because 'all (*pantes*) those who live on Olympus gave her gifts (*dora*)',[60] and there is a similar emphasis on 'all' in *Birds*: Prometheus says that Basileia looks after 'absolutely everything' (1539) for Zeus, and that 'if you get her from Zeus, you've got everything' (1542f.). There is obviously an obscene undertone to this exchange, but the emphasis on the *pan-* element is perhaps an echo of the highly significant woman in Hesiod's myth. In Hesiod, Pandora is the 'lovely evil', 'better suited to riches than to poverty'[61] and cause of pain to men. Peisetaerus is more fortunate in that Basileia is a woman of 'unspeakable beauty' (1713) and a conveyor of power.[62]

In taking as his bride this former servant of Zeus, Peisetaerus conforms to another foundation-myth topos. Marriage to the women of the new country is sometimes an end to foundation-myths, as in the marriage of the Argonauts to the women in the 'refoundation' of Lemnos, to be discussed in the next chapter. In a similar fashion, Zeus' first bride is Metis, a daughter of Oceanus and Tethys and thus a representative of the pre-Olympian gods; because of the threat to Zeus from any child of hers, he swallows her 'so that no-one else but he should hold the kingly power'.[63] Peisetaerus resembles also e.g. Cadmus, who received from Athena *basileia* ('kingship') and from Zeus Harmonia as wife,[64] when he gets a sceptre from the Birds and a divine bride from (an unwilling) Zeus (1535f.). Thus a *hieros gamos* concludes the foundation, inaugurating a period of political and domestic order. This marriage of Peisetaerus has been compared, not unjustly, to the *hieros gamos* between the wife of the Archon Basileus (the 'Basilinna') and Dionysus at the Anthesteria, which marked the

---

[60] Hes. *Op.* 81f.   [61] *Th.* 585, 593.
[62] A sacrifice to Pandora is recommended by the Oracle-monger at 971.
[63] Hes. *Th.* 358, 886–900.   [64] Apollod. 3.4.2.

acceptance of the god into the city in the spring.[65] Once aged, Peisetaerus is now hailed in terms appropriate to a young bridegroom (1709ff.), and the man whose first sight of the Birds caused him to give himself an excremental name, *Epikechodos* (68), is now wafted on sweet perfumes.

There has been much debate about Peisetaerus' question 'Who is Basileia?' (1537),[66] even though Prometheus appears to make her identity quite clear: 'a very pretty girl, who is stewardess of Zeus' thunderbolt – and everything else: planning, law and order, wisdom, docks, slander, paymasters, three-obol allowances' (1537–41).[67] Accentuation differentiates *basíleia*, 'queen', from *basileía*, 'kingship', so that strictly speaking she is not a personification like the Spondai of *Knights*; but it is none the less clear that she is essential to kingship in this context,[68] since at 1535f. and 1631–4, she and Zeus' sceptre are said to be interdependent, and at 478, the sceptre and kingship are linked. She is thus like those objects in myth, possession of which ensures royal power, such as the golden ram disputed over by Atreus and Thyestes.[69] Comparable in naming and effect are Crateia, 'Might', mother of the tyrant Periander, who is said to have slept with her,[70] and Basile, ancestress of the royal Codridae family (also known as the Basilidae).[71] Finally, the fact that

---

[65] Sheppard 1909. Craik 1987 would see a good deal more of this festival in *Birds*. For the *hieros gamos*, Klinz 1933.

[66] A review of the theories is found in Hofmann 1976: 147–60; cf. also Pascal 1911: 97–110; Kearns 1989: 151.

[67] I see no reason to take her to be anyone else than this servant of Zeus. That she is not the same as Basile, who had shrines near the gymnasium of Taureas and at Erchia, is suggested by an Attic red-figure pyxis of the 410s, where Basile attends the birth of Erichthonius in one scene, and Basileia the punishment of the daughters of Cecrops in another (cf. Shapiro 1986). Nor is the homely Basileia, who was worshipped as protectress of the Bouleuterion and won herself the title *Megale Meter* ('Great Mother') for her sisterly affection, a likely candidate as model for the stunning, divine beauty of *Birds* (cf. Diod. 3.57.3).

[68] Furthermore, strict distinctions between nouns in *-eia* and *-eía*, *-oia* and *-oía* were breaking down in the fifth century (*GG* I 469; Palmer 1980: 251, 253): as early as Aeschylus, we find *eukleia* and *eukleía*. Aristophanes has the later *hugieía* in *Birds* 604 (also in the textually problematic 731?). *plouthugieia* is usually printed as an original proparoxytone in *Wasps* 677 and *Kn.* 1091; both instances stand at the line-end, but Sommerstein 1987: 245 is over-bold in saying 'for Ar. the final vowel of *hugieiá . . .* was long'. Though *basíleia* and *basileía* are formed from a different stem, uncertainty about accentuation and lack of difference in the oblique cases may have blurred the distinction. See also fr. 238.

[69] Gernet 1981: 73–111.   [70] D. L. 1.96.

[71] Wilamowitz 1893: 2.130: '*basíle* ist der göttliche exponent für die *basíleia*, die ihre enkel auf erden üben'.

Peisetaerus must marry her to assume power accords with a number of tales in which the accession to power takes place through a woman related to the one who relinquishes it.[72] Thus, Gyges became king of Lydia after killing Candaules and marrying his wife.[73] More importantly, in an Athenian context, Peisistratus married Megacles' daughter, when the latter fell out with his allies and relinquished control.[74] Peisistratus entered Athens in a chariot attended by the tall girl Phye, who was dressed as Athena and subsequently became the object of cult. Writing of this episode, Gernet says:[75]

> in myth the chariot is a chariot of triumph and marriage; Pelops figures in such a situation as charioteer at the side of Hippodameia. Pisistratus ... is the king who is pleasing to the country's goddess, and his kingship is proclaimed on the occasion of his marriage and by virtue of it. In mythical thought the two are connected; the woman a man marries confers the kingship on him.

It is not explicitly stated that Peisetaerus and Basileia come on stage in a chariot, but a number of things are in favour of the idea. The wedding is compared to that of Zeus and Hera, at which Eros was their *parochos* (1740), the 'best man' who drove the bridegroom to fetch his bride and rode back with them.[76] It is somewhat unlikely that the queen of the universe was forced to walk to her wedding, as a mere *chamaipous*, the bride who was too poor to ride.[77] Vases show that the vehicle did not have to be grand, but was a normal feature of the procession.[78] Connor, discussing Peisistratus' entry into Athens, notes the restraint and humility implied by the fact that the tyrant rode as the charioteer to Phye/Athena, who was the *parabates*, the one who was to make the ritual descent from the car to assume power.[79] There is no such modesty on the part of Peisetaerus, 'highest of the gods' (1765), whose name interestingly echoes that of the Athenian tyrant. We shall return to this point later.

So Peisetaerus has established his new city, secured a wife and possession of the power of Zeus. It is noteworthy that twice reference is made to his possession both of the 'thunders of Zeus' and of the

[72] Gernet 1981: 289–302.   [73] Hdt. 1.8ff.   [74] Hdt. 1.6of.; [Arist.] *Ath. Pol.* 14.4.
[75] 1981: 300; cf. Connor 1987: 42–7.   [76] Pollux 3.40, 10.33.
[77] Ibid. 2.195. For the bridal car, Daremberg & Saglio 1904: III 1651–3; Simon 1983: 97 n. 38; Bérard 1989a: 97–103.
[78] Cf. for instance the cheerful group on a New York black-figure lecythus illustrated in Bérard 1989a: 100, fig. 137.   [79] 1987: 45f.

'chthonian thunders' (1745f., cf. 1749–51). His power thus extends
to the upper and lower worlds, as did Zeus' in his guise as Chthonius.[80] This conclusion is glorious, the staging spectacular, but is this
new foundation as desirable as we are being led to believe? This is the
next question.

Fantasy and utopia?

Peisetaerus has been presented in terms of a city-founder and of
a victor in a Gigantomachy, but also with echoes of the tyrant
Peisistratus. That all is not as ideal as it seems may be suggested by
the presence of the figure of Tereus, who presides over the earlier
stages of Peisetaerus' rise. His myth is a particularly gruesome one.
What significance does he have?

Tereus' story is briefly as follows.[81] King of Daulis or Thrace, he
married Procne, daughter of Pandion of Athens, but then raped her
sister Philomela, whose tongue was cut out to keep her quiet. She
however worked her troubles into a *peplos*, and, with Procne, served
Itys, the son of Procne and Tereus, to his father. Tereus, realising
what had happened, chased them with an axe. Zeus then changed
them into a hoopoe or hawk (Tereus), a nightingale (Procne) and a
swallow (Philomela).

It is true that Aristophanes does not emphasise the gruesome
elements in Tereus' career: Itys is referred to briefly only in 210–12,
and relations between Tereus and Procne seem to be nothing if not
harmonious (207ff.). On the other hand, Itys is described as 'of many
tears' (212) and Procne is here referred to not by name but as 'the
nightingale', the bird she became after the dreadful events (208;
contrast however 665). Furthermore, the story was sufficiently well
known to support the idea that the unpleasant aspects of the tale
could have been one of the filters through which the audience would
have viewed the play's actions. Aristophanes may suppress the
unpleasantness, but Tereus is connected essentially with this one
story,[82] whose events act as a troubling 'sous-texte' to the more

---

[80] 'Zeus Chthonios . . . can be conceived as an extension of Zeus, or as a chthonic counterpart of
Zeus' (M. L. West 1978: 276); cf. *Il.* 9.457; Paus. 2.24.3f.

[81] Oder 1888; Mihailov 1955; Zaganiaris 1973; Hofmann 1976: 72–8, esp. 73 n. 1 for further
bibliography; Burkert 1983a: 179–85. On the hoopoe in antiquity, D'A. W. Thompson 1936:
95–100; Pollard 1977: 45f.; Forbes Irving 1990: 99–107, 248f.

[82] Not entirely true: he also murdered his own brother (Hygin. *Fab.* 45.3).

cheerful aspects of the play.[83] Metamorphosis takes place only in traumatic circumstances.

Part of the significance of this figure lies, obviously, in the fact that he underwent transition from man to bird,[84] so that he is emblematic of the change that is at the heart of the play. It is further notable that, as his servant points out, Tereus has maintained his human characteristics and desires after his metamorphosis (71ff.):

> *Serv.* When my master became a hoopoe, he begged me to become a bird, so that he should have a servant and attendant.
> *Eu.* Does a bird need a servant too?
> *Serv.* This one does, at any rate, probably because he was once a man. Sometimes he wants to eat sprats from Phalerum, so I grab the bowl and run to get sprats. If he wants soup, we need a bowl and spoon, and I run after the spoon.

He has too 'all the thoughts of a bird and a man' (119). That becoming a bird has not greatly changed his nature will be of importance for an understanding of the play.

What significance we should give him is made problematic by our uncertainty about his place in fifth-century Athenian tradition. Many versions of his myth exist, but their contexts are uncertain. At Athens, Sophocles had produced a version of the myth in which Tereus was changed into a hoopoe (cf. 101f.)[85] and the fact that Tereus married the daughter of a king of Athens may suggest that he was known in the city and had a role in cult: Pausanias saw a statue of Procne in Athens, which may well be that discovered on the Acropolis and attributed to Alcamenes, of the third or last quarter of the fifth century.[86] There is more evidence for Tereus in cult at Megara, where stood the shrine of Pandion and Tereus. At the latter's tomb, where it was said the hoopoe had first appeared, there was a yearly sacrifice, at which small stones were used in place of the usual barley-meal.[87] The abnormality of this sacrifice is consonant with the nature of the myth.

Tereus' story of cannibalism and metamorphosis belongs to a

---

[83] C. Spencer, reviewing T. Wertenbacker's version of the story, *The Love of the Nightingale*, complains that she suppresses the cannibalism caused by the women (*The Daily Telegraph*, 25 August 1989): if modern audiences can feel this absence of a crucial element of the story, would not ancient ones have been at least equally aware of it?

[84] Emphasised early in the play: 71f., 75, 97f., 114, 117.   [85] Kiso 1984: 75.

[86] Paus. 1.24.3; on the statue, C. M. Robertson 1975: 286–8, with pl. 94c.

[87] Paus. 1.41.8f.; for Pandion, ibid. 5.3, 39.4.

group of such stories.[88] For instance, Burkert discusses Tereus in conjunction with two myths connected with the Agrionia festivals of Orchomenus and Argos. In the first, the daughters of Minyas angered Dionysus by refusing to join his rites, because they wished to marry. When they were weaving, the loom was covered with vines and ivy; driven mad, they drew lots for who should destroy her child. The Maenads chased them and they were turned into a crow, a bat and an owl. In the second, the Proetids angered Hera or Dionysus and, driven mad, believed they were cows; they devoured their own children. They were chased by the ephebes under Melampus, who married one of them when they returned to their senses.

The Tereus myth differs in story-line from these tales, but carries a similar message about the shift to the wilds that accompanies the cannibalism: 'The basic framework of a large number of bird stories . . . depends on the opposition between the family order and the outside or animal world.'[89] Tereus is, therefore, an ambiguous forerunner of the new world of the Birds, and after its inception, traces of his sinister story remain. Tereus the cannibal is reborn in the Peisetaerus who will be discovered roasting birds guilty of instigating a revolt (1583–5). On this Auger writes: 'The logic of the comedy corresponds to that of the myth: Tereus, on becoming a cannibal, was transformed into a bird; the hero of the comedy, transformed into a bird, becomes a cannibal.'[90]

The consumption of enemies as a means of preserving power is a not uncommon motif in myths of sovereignty: Cronus devoured the children presented to him by Rhea,[91] and Zeus devoured Metis to possess himself of her powers.[92] In these stories, however, there is, as Detienne has pointed out,[93] no real cannibalism, since Cronus is able to regurgitate his children when given a drug by Metis, and Metis herself continues to function inside Zeus. By contrast, Peisetaerus' cooking of the revolutionaries has more in common with the activities of monsters and tyrants, who were represented as cannibalistic in order to mark them as outsiders from normal society. In Plato's *Republic*, the tyrant is said to 'abstain from no sort of food'.[94] As in

---

[88] Burkert 1983a: 168–90 for fuller argumentation and evidence on what follows; also Forbes Irving 1990: 99–107, 248f.   [89] Forbes Irving 1990: 111.   [90] 1979: 84.
[91] Hes. *Th.* 459–62.   [92] Ibid. 886–900.   [93] 1981b: 215f.
[94] 571D; cf. 619C and A. *Supp.* 226 'How could a bird that eats another bird be clean?'

other versions of the Golden Age story, utopian novelty and cannibalism go hand in hand.[95]

In fact, despite the structuring of the play in terms of foundation-mythology, the city of Nephelococcygia turns out to be far from
the idyllic place originally envisaged by its founders. As in other
comedies, the message of the myths is both repeated (Nephelococcygia is founded in the usual apparently well-omened way) and
undermined (it is not the paradise expected).[96] Peisetaerus has earlier
spoken of the benefits that birds give to men (588–610), and in the
new world there are many causes for satisfaction, such as Peisetaerus' persuasion of the father-beater to take up another career, his
treatment of the officious, the bureaucratic and the meddling who
come to the new city, and the decent treatment meted out to
Prometheus. Not to be scorned is the promise of the proximity of the
new gods, in contrast to the remoteness of the Olympians caused by
the sacrifice at Mecone (723–31). There is here a hint of the Golden
Age, when gods and men mingled together.

Beside the general rejoicing however there are signs that some
things may be much the same as they were before the coup. Looked
at with some scrutiny, the benefits which the birds offer the humans
in return for their worship are either striking by their triviality or
dangerous in their implications. The main passages are in the epirr-
hematic parts of the parabases. The first parabasis (753ff., 785ff.)
offers a typically Aristophanic mixture of things that provide wish-
fulfilment and yet threaten the fabric of society: sons will have the
right to beat fathers, slaves and *atimoi* the rights of citizenship, and
members of the audience the ability to take sustenance, relieve
themselves or commit adultery during the festivals. The second
(1071ff., 1101ff.) promises rewards for destroying bird-sellers and
for giving the play the prize.

Apart from the roasting revolutionaries (who form the actual
wedding feast (1688f.)), violence is remarkably prevalent, not only in
Peisetaerus' reactions to the vexatious officials, to the divine messenger Iris,[97] and to the slave Manes beaten for sluggishness as he (no

---

[95] Vidal-Naquet 1981a.
[96] See the varied discussions of Newiger 1957: 80–103; Whitman 1964: 167–99; Arrowsmith
1973; Paduano 1973; Hofmann 1976; Auger 1979.
[97] On the treatment of heralds and envoys in antiquity, Adcock & Mosley 1975: 152ff., 201ff.

doubt) works frantically to collect the wings (1317ff.), but also in the Birds' calls for the death of Philocrates (1071ff.) and their description of their treatment of insects (1062–70): in both cases the repetition of words for 'kill' is instructive, even if insects are no friends of farmers and the Birds are prepared to pay four times as much for Philocrates alive – what have they in mind for him? Furthermore, the military forces of Nephelococcygia are not inconsiderable.

The superiority of Nephelococcygia to Athens may indeed be displayed in the way in which disagreeable figures like the Oracle-monger, the Decree-monger and the Sycophant are sent packing, and in the way the two poets are reasonably treated; but the treatment of the other visitors is more ambivalent. The priest is dismissed simply for an inappropriate prayer (889–94) and Meton because Peisetaerus thinks him an *alazon* (1016); the Father-Beater is persuaded to abandon his desire to harm his father but is freed from the obligation, firmly believed in by the Athenians, of looking after him. Further-more, though in fantasy freedom from priests, town-planners and political agents may be much to be desired, in reality such people can be seen to have a legitimate role in a god-fearing democracy with an empire to control: even the Sycophant, never the most popular class of citizen,[98] is a feature, however disagreeable, of the democracy, as an embodiment of the Solonian principle that 'he who wished' could bring a prosecution. The Episcopus may come inopportunely early to Nephelococcygia (1033f.), but men of his position were appointed to oversee the smooth running of the empire; they may have been more unpopular with the allies they oversaw than with the people of Athens, but they clearly constituted a crucial aspect of Athens' control of its empire.

Significantly, as the Episcopus is driven off, Peisetaerus tells him to 'take your voting-jars away!' (1032), and when he returns, Peisetaerus refers to them again: 'I'll scatter your voting-urns' (1053). These urns symbolise the democratic system, and there is apparently no place for them in Nephelococcygia. As Sommerstein says, jury-courts are 'the very element of Athenian life that Peise-taerus and Euelpides most detested',[99] but their absence removes the possibility of recourse to the courts that was the defence of any citizen in a democracy. This absence is indicative of the kind of state that Peisetaerus is creating: it is a tyranny. Poseidon refers to Zeus's

[98] Lofberg 1914.   [99] 1987: 269.

power which it is proposed to transfer to the Birds as a 'tyranny' (1643), and at 1708 the Birds are called on to welcome their *turannos*: Peisetaerus has spoken of the 'democratic Birds' (1584), but his monarchical control of this 'democracy' seems stronger than that of Zeus over the democracy of the gods (1570f.), which is at least capable of electing ambassadors who can and do vote for his overthrow. As in *Acharnians* and *Wasps* therefore, Aristophanes begins by representing Athens as a place full of disagreeable, even intolerable aspects, but then goes on to portray a world with other features which, especially from a democratic viewpoint, are even more worrying. Democracy is again displayed both in a critical light and in contrast to a different world which shows that, bad though democracy may be in some or many respects, there are far worse systems available: 'always keep a-hold of Nurse'. Nephelococcygia may be free of some of the more irksome features of Athens, but it has other, graver faults, in part precisely because of the lack of these features, such as a range of officials with divers powers that prevents power from falling into the hands of one man.

Given the political situation in Athens at the time and the events of the immediately succeeding years, including the oligarchic coup of 411[100] this was a timely warning and suggests that the idea, so often propounded, that *Birds* has no topical political reference, may need some revision. We have noted that Peisetaerus' name contains an echo of that of the tyrant Peisistratus, and that Peisetaerus is a tyrant in his own right. One may add that the earlier tyrant was at least a 'Persuader of the *stratos*', a word which in poets at least could stand for 'demos'; Peisetaerus, by contrast, is the 'Persuader of his companion or companions', which carries overtones of the oligarchic political clubs, the *hetaireia*, which were becoming increasingly active at this time. The play can then be read as giving a clear demonstration of the dangers of wishfully thinking of a better world in the sky and exaggerating the problems of the democracy: such dissatisfaction with the present state of affairs might lead to support for changes that would usher in a political system even less tolerable. It may not be insignificant that, once the construction of the city is

---

[100] On the political situation in general, Aurenche 1974. If Peisetaerus' name also evokes that of the opportunist Peisander (mocked in 1556–64), he takes on further levels of ambivalence: in 414 a champion of the democracy, he was one of the leaders of the oligarchic coup of 411 (Thuc. 8.67.1; cf. Rhodes 1981: 407f. for his career).

completed, the character Euelpides ('Mr Good-Hope') disappears: is this simply a matter of theatrical convenience or another case of 'lasciate ogni speranza voi ch' entrate'?[101]

The world of the Birds is often presented as one opposed to that of mankind from which Peisetaerus and Euelpides wish to escape (e.g. 753–68, 1347ff.), but this opposition is also frequently called into question, so that men and Birds, though obviously different in many ways, come to seem close in nature. The possibility therefore of a world free of human *pragmata* ('affairs') becomes less and less credible. The play makes this point in three ways: first, it shows comically that, as the figure of Tereus has shown, the differences between men and birds are less than might appear, which suggests that a move to a world of birds will make little difference to the quality and type of life men lead; then, it deconstructs its own fantasy by implicitly showing how it is put together; and thirdly, it reinforces this by a series of concrete demonstrations that one can never get away from the *pragmata* that afflict Peisetaerus and Euelpides, no matter how far one travels.

The similarities between birds and men are demonstrated again by two principal devices, by the complementarities in their lives and institutions, and through the language used by and of birds and men. We have already noted that Tereus, on becoming a bird, did not substantially change his inner nature and maintained a diet of human and bird food (71–9); the Birds adopt hoplite tactics in their confrontation with Peisetaerus and Euelpides (344ff.), and have their own cosmogony (685ff.). Furthermore, they share with mortals such institutions as laws (1345f.), oaths (331ff.) and slaves, and even follow the Athenian practice whereby the person swearing an oath set the penalty he was to pay if he broke it (444–6). They employ human moral terms such as 'unholy' (328, 334) and show a proper concern for burial (471–5).

This same point is made more subtly by the use the play makes of linguistic matters.[102] Again, there are two aspects. When Peisetaerus asks Tereus who will reveal his plan to the Birds, Tereus tells him that he can do it himself, since the Birds have learned Greek

---

[101] Comparable perhaps to Odysseus' and his companions' abandonment of Elpenor before their descent into Hades (*Od.* 10.552–60)?

[102] On language in the play, Newiger 1957: 8off. and Whitman 1964: 167–99, though the latter is wrong to suggest that 'nothingness' is at the heart of the play.

(198–200). This apparently simple comic device is in fact of some importance: not only does the very act of giving the Birds Greek speech immediately bring them closer to men, because they will inevitably use the same words, concepts, value-judgements etc., but in this device there is too a tacit admission that even in comedy it is not 'really' possible to create a bird-state without such concessions to dramatic illusion: a chorus saying nothing but 'tiotinx' and 'kikka-bau' would scarcely be tolerable or a credible world force.[103]

The likeness of birds and men is also established by reference to men who either are so like birds as to be almost indistinguishable from them or, because of some characteristic, could easily become birds. Two passages particularly bear this out, 275–300 and 760–8. In the first, the Birds are arriving in answer to Tereus' call and, as each arrives, it is identified by Tereus in ornithological terms and by Euelpides in human ones. The jokes are many and laboured, but this is one of Aristophanes' techniques for drawing attention to a passage. In the second sequence, the Birds are showing that what is morally wrong amongst men is acceptable amongst the Birds, so that, in a manner complementary to the last passage, various men could easily become birds. The Chorus's case is later proved by Dieitrephes who, with his wicker *ptera* ('wings' or 'jar-handles'), has risen to high rank from lowly origins: 'Look at Dieitrephes, who with nothing but wicker "wings" was made phylarch, then hipparch and now, having started from nothing, does great things and has become a tawny hippocock' (798–800). It is no surprise after this to discover that, when the bird-kingdom is set up, many humans took on bird names that suited their characteristics (1290–9).

All of this shows that there are similarities in character, language and names between the worlds of birds and men. The large number of avian metaphors points in the same direction. These similarities can be said to do two things: from the point of view of the play, they make the idea of the metamorphosis from man to bird seem all the more acceptable and easy; but, given the impossibility of such a metamorphosis actually taking place, they also draw attention to the fact that they themselves are the product of games with language. In a play, one can put wings on a man and say he 'is' a bird, but in reality one cannot: however like a bird a man may be, he cannot

---

[103] If birds can speak Greek, the opposite can also happen: in 57ff., as Peisetaerus and Euelpides knock on the rock, they introduce a highly alliterative, bird-like passage.

become one. The importance of this protean nature of language is pointed up in the scene between Peisetaerus and the Sycophant (1410ff.). On stage are the wings with which Peisetaerus could literally *pteroun* ('give wings to') the Sycophant, and it is in this literal sense that the latter has put his request. When the wings do not appear to be forthcoming, he complains, but this exchange ensues (1437–46):

> Peis. But by speaking I'm giving you wings.
> Syc. And how could you give a man wings by speaking?
> Peis. Everyone is given wings by words.
> Syc. Everyone?
> Peis. Haven't you heard fathers talking about their sons in the barbers' shops? 'It's amazing how Dieitrephes with his talking has sent my son flying off to be a charioteer.' Another says that his son has taken wing for tragedy and his mind is all of a flutter.
> Syc. So it's with words that they're given wings?
> Peis. That's right.[104]

When the Sycophant still insists upon wings, Peisetaerus gives him 'excellent Corcyrean wings' (1463), a double goad, and chases him off with the words 'Won't you fly off?' (1466), thus bringing in another metaphorical meaning of 'take wing'. By juxtaposing the concrete and metaphorical in this way, the scene draws attention to what the play is saying and the message it conveys: a tragedy (or comedy) can *pteroun* a man in the sense of 'excite' him, but it cannot do so in the sense of 'make into a bird'. This demonstration is important because it undermines the whole of Peisetaerus' scheme: Nephelococcygia is seen indeed to exist where the wealth of the poor is, that is either nowhere or in wishful thinking, and flight to it is thus an impossibility.[105]

Metaphorical wings therefore provide little hope of the escape from Athenian *pragmata* into the kind envisaged by Peisetaerus and Euelpides in their fantasy worlds (128–42). But the play's realistic view of the world does not rely merely on linguistic matters; it brings reality before the eyes and ears of the spectators. As soon as the city has been founded, a whole host of characters from the normal Athenian professions hurry on. Many, we have seen, are driven off, but some gain what they want, and the scenes generally show that

---

[104] *Birds* may be similarly affected: 433f.
[105] There is another important scene with a Sycophant in *Wealth* 850ff.

such people will appear even in a city in the air run by birds: escape from things Athenian is not possible, even in fantasy.[106]

This point about escape is reinforced by the four fantastic sights which the Chorus recall seeing on their flights.[107] In each of the four stanzas, we have a place which, though far away, none the less feels the malign effect of Athens and its denizens. In the first place mentioned , 'there is a strange tree that grows beyond Cardia, the Cleonymus, which is good for nothing though it is large and cow-ardly. In spring, it always grows and bears indictments; but in winter on the other hand it sheds its leaves as shields' (1473–81). The second is apparently even farther away, 'far off towards the darkness itself, . . . in the desert where there are no lamps' (1482–4),[108] in a land of a golden-age type where men and heroes feast together. But there too, the lamps point to the Athenian politician Hyperbolus, and a notorious Athenian footpad with the heroic name Orestes plies his murderous trade. The Sciapodes (1553ff.), variously located by tradition in Ethiopia, Nubia, Libya and India, are beset by the soul-conjuring Socrates, his client Peisander and familiar Chaerephon. Finally, Phanae (1694ff.), though a real town on Chios, is here mysteriously located beside the Athenian clepsydra and peopled with the dread barbarian *Englottogasteres* ('Tongue-to-Belly Men'[109]), Gorgias and Philippus, prominent rhetoricians in Athens at the time. Well might one say of Athens with the Psalmist:[110] 'Whither shall I go from thy spirit? Or whither shall I flee from thy presence? If I ascend up into heaven, thou art there: if I make my bed in hell, behold, thou art there. If I take the wings of the morning, and dwell in the uttermost parts of the sea . . .'

Complementary to this idea that escape from specifically Athe-nian meddling is impossible is the play's other major implication that the desire to escape *pragmata* is, in general, an impossibility. Peise-taerus makes the point explicitly when the Birds express amazement that they are amongst the oldest gods. He tells them they are 'stupid and not busy-bodies' (*apragmones*, 471). In other words, *pragmata*

---

106 This confirms the fears of Peisetaerus and Euelpides that Athenians will surface in the far-away places on the Red Sea mentioned by Tereus (144–7).

107 These vignettes are closely related to their contexts: the Cleonymus-tree which *sukophantei* follows the Sycophant; the Sciapodes follow the parasol (*skiadeion*) carried by Prometheus and the 'Tongue-to-Belly Men' follow the gluttony of Heracles.

108 On this 'desert' and its echoes of 'the Scythian desert' of *Ach.* 704, see scholia [A.] *PV* 2, with M. Griffith 1983: 81 *ad loc.*   109 Sommerstein 1987: 308.   110 Ps. 139.7–9.

are required if one is to be master of one's fate: it is precisely by becoming *apragmones* ('uninvolved in affairs') that the Birds have lost their kingdom to the Olympians. The *apragmon* city is thus not an answer to the problems that have driven Peisetaerus and Euelpides from Athens, since such a city would immediately fall prey to one which is *polupragmon*, like Athens, or to the equally active Olympians. This point recurs, with reference to the Athenian empire, in the words of Thucydides' Pericles, Cleon and Alcibiades. Pericles tells the Athenians 'Your empire is a tyranny, which it seems unjust to have created, and yet dangerous to give up.'[111] The Athenians may have qualms about their empire and the methods needed to preserve it, such as the siege and massacre of Melos, *episkopoi*, tribute and so on, but the uncomfortable truth is that someone is going to be the strongest and there are many compensations for these qualms in being that strongest. To avoid domination by those more eagerly engaged in *pragmata*, the Athenians must shoulder the burdens and themselves remain *polupragmones*. They face the choice of accepting things as they are or running the risks of entertaining dreams about other political systems, which may contain unpleasant surprises. After all, one of the losers in the power struggle in *Birds* is Athens, overcome by another even more *polupragmon* than herself. As in *Wasps*, therefore, dissatisfaction with democratic Athens leads to a tyranny of a worse kind, because it is that of one man, but Philocleon's pales into insignificance beside Peisetaerus'.

Thus, in Nephelococcygia as in Athens, there is ruler and ruled, coercion by *pragmata* and *nomoi*: only thus are the gods overcome and power seized. Perhaps the time will come when the cycle will be repeated, but the repetition will be as fruitless as when Peisetaerus and Euelpides left one 'bird'-dominated city to found another. Peisetaerus is now king, but as the play shows, succession myths are not only reversible, they are also extendible.

Birds was, like *Peace*, produced at the Great Dionysia, and so before the assembled Greeks of many cities. It has significances for them too. The city of Athens, its officers and imperialism, which had shortly before been paraded in glory in the theatre, are now dis-

---

[111] Thuc. 2.63.2f.; also 3.37.2, 6.18.3 and 1.70ff. On *polupragmosune* etc., Nestle 1925–6; Ehrenberg 1947 and the bibliography in Edmunds 1987b: 250 n. 57, to which add Carter 1986.

played in comedy in a disagreeable light with which not a few no doubt felt some sympathy. At the same time, however, there is an implicit justification of that imperialism and its methods, and a demonstration of what is essentially a necessity under which the imperialists labour, to preserve their power in order to avoid subjugation by others. On the other hand, the play also suggests that dissatisfaction with Athenian rule could lead to another form of tyranny more wilful and violent even than Athens at its worst. For Athenians and allies, therefore, the play can be read as recommending the devil you know, as well as making plain his cloven hoof.

Birds, then, bases itself on myth-types that promise regeneration and new beginnings: foundation-myths, cosmogony and even Gigantomachy and Zeus' succession. But, as in plays like *Acharnians*, the basic message of the myths is subverted and their artificial nature laid bare. The foundation of Nephelococcygia is not only a fantastic impossibility for reasons physiological and physical,[112] but it is also not a solution to the problems it is supposed to resolve; rather, it becomes a restatement of the problems in a different form. In *Birds* therefore we have echoes of the debates on empire and its problems which are to be heard at greater length in Thucydides. Despite Peisetaerus' dramatic success, *Birds* should not be read as an escapist fantasy: Nephelococcygia is no Schlaraffenland, and if *Birds* is Aristophanes' greatest exercise in fantasy, it is also his best deconstruction of it. Even as we enjoy the spectacle of Peisetaerus' victory, the play is implying that such an attempt at escape is not open to anyone, but a mere *logos* which may cause a flutter but cannot happen. Will the Birds, faced with their new *turannos* (1708) who has displayed little patience with opposition from birds, gods, or men, have cause to remember Aeschylus' eagle, which, shot with an arrow, recognised the feathers: he had been struck down 'not with another's but with his own'?[113]

---

[112] Virtually admitted by Peisetaerus on hearing of the stupendous wall: 'Seems just like a lie to me!' (1167). That Iris is immediately announced as having breached these defences without difficulty also raises doubts.

[113] Quoted at 807f. = A. fr. 139.4.

8

Lysistrata

Women in Athens

Lysistrata portrays the temporary imposition of a gynaecocracy on the city of Athens.[1] Impossible as this was in practical terms, it was a concept frequently found in mythology and ritual. For the Athenians, the story of the Amazons was the best known local example, but they were also well acquainted with other famous versions, such as that of the Lemnian Women. Elements from these tales, along with others from a further, more historical example of the seizure of control by one who has no legitimate claim, are used in *Lysistrata* to present the women's actions in a negative light, but at the same time, there is a counterbalance of other, more positive models, such as the Thesmophoria, of times when women acted alone to the benefit of the city. This is a double presentation of events which we have seen in other plays.

This ambivalence in the play's representation of women reflects a similar ambivalence in their place in Greek ideology.[2] In law, they were defined as 'incapable of a self-determined act, as almost . . . an un-person, outside the limits of those who constitute society's responsible and representative agents'.[3] They had no formal political representation and were for a great part of the time confined to the *gunaikeion*, the women's quarters of the house. Marriage was conceived as the 'taming' of the wild young woman, as

---

[1] An outline version of this chapter appeared as Bowie 1984. R. P. Martin 1987 arrived independently at similar ideas, and should be consulted for others that are not here.

[2] The bibliography on this is enormous and growing. For a general orientation see Gould 1980; also e.g. Foley 1981; Cameron & Kuhrt 1983; Just 1989; for the evidence of vases, Bérard 1989a. A distinction often needs to be made between older and younger women: Bremmer 1985 and Henderson 1987b.   [3] Gould 1980: 44f.

can be seen from the language used of it[4] and the representations on vases of young, ephebic males 'hunting' the fleeing girl.[5] Summarising his discussion of women in myth, Gould writes that[6]

> male attitudes to women, and to themselves in relation to women, are marked by tension, anxiety and fear. Women are not part of, do not belong easily in, the male ordered world of the 'civilised' community; they have to be accounted for in other terms, and they threaten continually to overturn its stability or subvert its continuity, to break out of the place assigned to them by their partial incorporation within it. Yet they are essential to it: they are the producers and bestowers of wealth and children, the guarantors of due succession, the guardians of the *oikos* and its hearth. Men are their sons, and are brought up, as children, by them and among them. Like the earth and once-wild animals, they must be tamed and cultivated by men, but their wildness will out.

The idea of women in power is clearly marked in Greek ideology as abnormal, in that it occurs in mythology at times of crisis and in ritual at periods of the year which are themselves marked as abnormal.[7] There is thus a similarity to the way 'slaves in power' is represented, which we discussed in connection with *Knights*. In the case of Argos after its defeat by Sparta,[8] an oracle was fulfilled promising female domination over men; the women married the slaves, and the poetess Telesilla organised the defence of the city by the women. The myth was connected with the Hybristica festival in Argos, which commemorated the act of bravery by the women through the exchange of clothes between males and females. Similarly in Cumae, it was a woman, Xenocrite, who persuaded the young men, whom the tyrant Aristodemus had sent to a girlish existence in the country after murdering their fathers, to rise up and restore the city to normality.[9] Women play comparable roles in the foundation-legends of Tarentum and Epizephyrian Locri.[10] The case of the Lemnian Women will be discussed below.

The importance of women to the community was openly acknowledged in matters of religion: many priesthoods were held by women. The Thesmophoria, to be discussed in the next chapter,

[4] Calame 1977: I 411–20, II 82–6.
[5] Cf. Sourvinou-Inwood 1991: 25–143. Many of the motifs that are found on these vases are to be encountered in Pi. *Py.* 9 with its account of Apollo's marriage to the wild girl Cyrene.
[6] 1980: 57.   [7] Vidal-Naquet 1981d; Graf 1984.
[8] Hdt. 6.77, 83; Paus. 2.20.8–10; Plut. *Mor.* 245F.
[9] D. H. *AR.* 7.2–12; Plut. *Mor.* 261E–2D.   [10] Sourvinou-Inwood 1974.

dramatised the ritual assumption by women of roles normally taken by men, in such areas as politics, sacrifice on behalf of the city, death and corruption. The whole festival celebrated women's role in the fertility of mankind and field.

In the parabasis of *Lysistrata*, the women claim the right to speak 'useful words' to the city on the grounds that the city brought them up and that they have demonstrated their importance to the city by filling a number of important religious offices:[11] 'at seven years I was straightway an Arrhephoros, then I was a Grinder; when I was ten I was a Bear at the Brauronia, shedding the saffron dress for the Leader; and in my time as Basket-Bearer I was a pretty girl with a necklace of figs' (641–7). This distinguished career of Arrhephoros, connected with the weaving of Athena's *peplos* and the secret rites of the Arrhephoria, Grinder of corn for Demeter,[12] Bear at the initiation-rites of Artemis Brauronia,[13] and Basket-Bearer, an office found at several festivals, such as the Panathenaea, represents a sequence of gradual acculturation of young girls from immaturity to the status of marriageable *parthenos*, which was attained at the Arcteia and continued through her time as a Basket-Bearer. It also acts as a means of 'rebutting the accusation of animality and wild behaviour made against the women by the men'.[14] These services to the major female deities of Athens, along with the Thesmophoria in which they participated as citizens' wives, signify the women's importance to the city.

The play also makes reference to another form of ritual activity involving women, which stands at the opposite pole to the decorous picture given in this chorus and to their traditional duties as defined by the religion of the city. When the Proboulos appears to investigate what the women are doing, without any preamble he breaks into a complaint about female behaviour during the debate on the Sicilian expedition (387–98):

> so female lasciviousness has broken out again, and tambourine-banging and endless rites of Sabazios! That song for Adonis, too, from the roof-tops, which I once heard in the Assembly. Demostratus, whom god rot, was saying we should sail to Sicily, and some

---

[11] A much-discussed passage. I follow Sourvinou 1971b and Sourvinou-Inwood 1988: 136–48, with bibliography at 68 n. 1.   [12] Not Athena: Sourvinou-Inwood 1988: 142–6.

[13] Lloyd-Jones 1983 and Sourvinou-Inwood 1988 for full treatment and bibliography.

[14] Sourvinou-Inwood 1988: 137.

woman was dancing about and singing 'Alas, Adonis!' Demostra-
tus said we should muster Zacynthian hoplites: the drunken
woman on the roof said 'Lament for Adonis!' Still, that enemy of
the gods and villainous madman forced his proposal through.
That's the sort of lubricious songs you get from them.

The Adonia was an unofficial festival, imported from the East, which
celebrated the love of Aphrodite for the sexually precocious Adonis,
who inspired love at a preternaturally early age, and died on the
tusks of a boar before reaching manhood.[15] This rite, as is suggested
by those with which the Proboulos associates it, had a reputation for
lasciviousness: though it was a festival for women, men do not seem
to have been entirely excluded.[16] The rites involved the placing by
women of the 'Gardens of Adonis', potsherds with earth planted
with seeds, on the roofs of houses, where they sprang up because
they had no depth of earth, and because they had no root, they
withered away. Detienne has argued that this rite was an inversion of
normal agricultural practice, where men plant seed in good soil, on
the ground, where it grows slowly to maturity; a reversal, therefore,
of the rites of Demeter with which the Thesmophoria is concerned.
The festival is also opposed to normal marriage, in the way it
commemorates the love of a goddess for a young child which comes
to nothing, a reversal of those aspects of life behind the Arrhephoria
or Arcteia.[17]

The plot of Lysistrata will be inscribed within these contradictions in the male views of women and their role in society, and will
clearly expose those contradictions, which are constructed between
Thesmophoria and Adonia.

Preliminaries

The play opens with Lysistrata, early in the morning, waiting
for the women to assemble. Such a gathering, clearly taking place
without the knowledge of the men, would immediately have suggested to the audience that something untoward was about to
happen. This would not appear to be one of those occasions when the

---

[15] Deubner 1932: 220–2; Atallah 1966; Detienne 1977; Burkert 1979: 105–11, 1985: 176f.;
    Adonis (cf. Servais 1984); below on Ecclesiazusae. For its unofficial nature, schol. Lys. 390.

[16] Men. Samia 39–45.

[17] Bérard 1989a: 96f., with fig 132, where this opposition is symbolised by the painting of the
    Adonia on a wedding lebes.

women were permitted to assemble for religious reasons of importance to the city. It is more reminiscent of tragedies in which women
on stage is a sign of the disorder within the palace.[18] These suspicions
are reinforced by remarks early in the play. Lysistrata's first words
are: 'If they'd been summoned into the shrine of Bacchus, or of Pan or
Colias or Genetyllis, you wouldn't have been able to move for
tambourines!'(1–3). There is some small consolation here for the
husbands, in that, though this is obviously not a religious occasion, it
is at least not one of those orgiastic festivals like the rites of Sabazios.
Calonice, however, shows that no permission has been given on this
occasion: 'It's difficult for a woman to get out of the house: one will
be busying herself over her husband, another waking the slave, or
putting the child to bed, or washing him or feeding him' (16–19).

We are eventually told that Lysistrata has summoned them to
discuss the saving of Greece (29f.), and that this is to be achieved by a
refusal of sexual relations with their husbands and by a seizure of the
Acropolis. The gathering can thus be read in two ways: it is not a
festival sanctioned by the men, and is, therefore, of a disordered
nature; at the same time, its aim is an entirely laudable one which
everyone would wish to see, and so it is potentially beneficial. As we
have seen, the women can justify their actions by the fact that they
have in the past carried out a number of central religious offices on
behalf of the *polis* (638–47). Here we see for the first time the
ambiguity that will characterise the presentation of the women's
actions throughout the play.

This ambiguity is clearly articulated in the scene of oath-
swearing (181–239).[19] Here appear features both of the *sphagia*,
blood sacrifice, associated with oaths and the opening of hostilities,
and of the *spondai* that closed them:[20] their actions are both a
declaration of war and an attempt to make peace. The *sphagia* appear
in Lysistrata's proposal that they sacrifice a sheep over a shield (185)
and in the revised idea that they do the same into a wine-bowl (194f.);
in 204 this sacrifice is called *sphagia*. Calonice suggests cutting up a
white horse (192): dismemberment of the victim and standing on or

---

[18] Padel 1983: 15 on tragedy: 'When they emerge, they often indicate a sense of something
wrong within; within not only themselves, but society.'

[19] Henderson 1987a: 90–6 provides some elements for this discussion, but I cannot agree with
him that the rite is 'entirely farcical' (90).

[20] Burkert 1985: 71 (*sphagia* and *spondai*), 250–4 (oaths).

touching the pieces (*tomia*) were a standard element of oath-swearing. Also standard was the self-curse (cf. 235f.). The verb *enagizein* (cf. 238) was used of *sphagia*, as opposed to *hiereuein* of sacrifices to the Olympians.[21] Aristophanes gives these *sphagia* a negative quality in two ways. First, there is the reference to and visual representation of the oath taken by the Seven in Aeschylus' *Septem* (188f.);[22] this oath was sworn when Polynices, like the women, was about to attack his own city. Secondly, Calonice's proposal to sacrifice a white horse is unusual for Greece, but characteristic of the Scythians and Amazons,[23] so that the women are here associated with outsiders and invaders of Athens. At the same time, as Calonice points out, Lysistrata's plan to sacrifice into a shield is inappropriate when peace is in question (189f.), and the pouring of wine instead of blood befits the end of hostilities. However, *spondai* were usually poured onto the ground and not down the throat, so that once again there is, in this anomaly, a negative element, which is complemented by the women's reluctance to accept the oath to give up sex, which accompanies the *spondai* (215f.).

War has paradoxically forced the women to 'declare war' in order to make peace, but they console themselves for the loss of sex, to which they are supposed to be addicted, by drink, to which they are traditionally partial. The conflicting sacrificial codes underline the paradoxes. In the opening of hostilities and the refusal of sex, these younger women are subverting that normality in which marriage is the goal of life for a girl as war is for a boy, and as in *Clouds* and *Wasps*, the reversal is marked by an actual rite. Complementarily, the Old Women have seized the religious centre of the city, the Acropolis, 'by appearing to be sacrificing' (179), an activity normally associated with men. In acting thus, the women invite comparison with other races of women who have similarly arrogated male power to themselves, to two of whom the Old Men make specific reference.

[21] Burkert 1985: 271; also 201.

[22] *Septem* 42–56. Compare also X. *Anab.* 2.2.9, an oath sworn by Greeks and barbarians over a bull, wolf, boar and ram slaughtered over a shield.

[23] Greece: *Il.* 23.171f. (Achilles at Patroclus' pyre, though the horses are thrown in, not sacrificed in the normal way); Plut. *Pelop.* 22 (at Leuctra); Paus. 3.20.9 (a horse is sacrificed and Helen's suitors, standing on the pieces, swear to defend her future husband); cf. Keller 1909–13: I 252–4. Scythians: Hdt. 1.216.4, 4.61.2; Lucian, *Scyth.* 2. Persians: X. *Cyr.* 8.3.12, 24; cf. E. *Hel.* 1258; Henderson 1987a: 92f. Amazons: A. R. 2.1175f.; Ps.-Callisthenes 3.25.

The women

Amazons

In Athenian mythology, the most famous attempt by women to take power was the attack by the Amazons, who seized the Pnyx, but were defeated when they tried to seize the Acropolis, by the Athenian culture-hero Theseus.[24] According to Plutarch, their graves were to be seen around the foot of that hill and there were shrines to them near the Peiraeus gates; an 'ancient sacrifice' was made to them on the day before the Theseia, and by the fourth century at the latest, there was an Amazoneium on the Areopagus.[25] This myth was frequently depicted on monuments: it was on the Parthenon, the shield of Athena Parthenos, the Theseum and in the paintings by Micon in the Painted Stoa.[26] Their defeat was one of the myths that represented the victory of 'cosmos' over chaos; it was frequently portrayed alongside the Battles of the Gods against the Giants, the Greeks against the Trojans and the Greeks against the Persians. Reasons for viewing the women's coup in terms of this myth are given by the Old Men: 'If the women ever turn to horse-riding, I write the Cavalry off. A woman's a good rider and knows how to stay on: she wouldn't slip off even at a gallop. Look at those Amazons Micon painted, fighting on horse-back against those men' (676–9).

By seizing the Acropolis, the women have achieved something the Amazons never did. They create a state of affairs that resembles those representations of the Amazons in which the women dominate politics and sexuality. For instance, Diodorus describes an Amazon society that reverses aspects of normal Greek life: the men do all the female tasks and have no freedom of speech, whilst the women rule and are the warriors.[27] So, in *Lysistrata*, Cinesias has to look after his own child in Myrrhine's absence (845ff.), and the men are forbidden access to the city's symbolic centre. This having been said, however, the women are, on closer inspection, rather far from being typical 'man-slaying' Amazons. The nearest they come to killing anyone is dressing the Proboulos as a corpse (599ff.). They do rout the Chorus of old men and the Scythian archers, but they do not kill them. Their

---

[24] E.g. A. *Eum.* 685ff.; Hdt. 9.27.4; Isoc. 4.70; Plut. *Thes.* 26–8. For the Amazons, Carlier 1979; Tyrrell 1984.   [25] Diod. 4.28.2f.; Cleidemus, *FGH* 323 F 18 (*ap.* Plutarch, last note).
[26] Von Bothmer 1957.   [27] 3.52ff.

seizure of the Acropolis is carried out to secure not their own power but peace and normality; there is to be no looting (461) and an account is given of how the treasury moneys will be looked after (488–96). Sexual relations are taken over by the women, but this too is done in the interests of peace. The Amazons did not perform the classic female tasks of spinning and weaving, but, even if the men use the verb *huphainein* ('weave') to describe the women's actions as cunningly leading to tyranny (630), Lysistrata is more accurate when she takes as her image for what she is trying to do that of carding and spinning wool to make a cloak for the demos (574–86).[28] Once again, therefore, we have an ambivalent picture of the women: they attack the city like Amazons, but are bent on the peaceful restoration of normal life.

In fact, this ambivalent picture is closer to that given of the Sauromatae by Herodotus,[29] than to Diodorus' Amazons. Defeated in battle by the Greeks, the Sauromatae were taken across the sea, but massacred their captors on the voyage. Ignorant of navigation, they floated to Scythia, where, quite peaceably, they took the sons of the locals as 'husbands', though they refused to spin and weave and rejected the usual conditions of marriage. Eventually, they took their husbands away from their homeland, in a reversal of the standard practice whereby wives went to their husbands' homes. These Sauromatae thus mediate between the 'radical' Amazons described by Diodorus and the 'civilising' ones who are not infrequently connected with the foundation of cities, especially on the Asia Minor coast: Homer tells of Myrine who invaded the Troad and gave her name to an Aeolic city.[30] In the same way, Lysistrata's women are radical in their actions, but concerned ultimately with the return of peaceful civilisation in Greece. Any attempt by the men in the Chorus or indeed in the audience to castigate the women's action by simply comparing it to the Amazons' attack on the city is thus effectively deconstructed by the play itself.

---

[28] For weaving not war as women's work, see Euelthon's insistence on giving Pheretima a golden spindle and distaff but not the army she requested (Hdt. 4.162). As is acknowledged by Lysistrata (137), weaving is close to trickery: Jenkins 1985.

[29] 4.110–17.

[30] *Il.* 2.814 (see Eustathius *ad loc.*); cf. Ephorus, *FGH* 70 F 114a; Diod. 3.53ff.; Chirassi 1968: 18f. Similar tales are told of Ephesus, Smyrna, Cyme (cf. Ephorus *loc. cit.*), Pitane, Priene, Mytilene (Diod. 3.55).

Lemnians

The men have, however, a second model which they invoke
and which provides a more thorough-going parallel to Aristophanes'
women, that of the Lemnian Women. For Aeschylus, it was the worst
of all crimes committed by women,[31] and he, like Sophocles and
Euripides, wrote a tragedy on it; it was also the subject of a comedy
by Aristophanes, and of later comedies by Nicochares and Anti-
phanes.[32] As they bring the fire to burn the women out of the
Acropolis, the men complain: 'How dreadfully this smoke bites my
eyes, like a mad bitch, as it pours from the pot. It really is *Lemnian*
fire, otherwise it wouldn't be savaging my eye-sores (*lemai*) like
this!' (296–301). The pun is very laboured, but here, as elsewhere in
Aristophanes, the feeble joke draws attention to an important point
which can be used to understand what the play is trying to do.

The myth of the Lemnian Women has very close structural
similarities to the New Fire festival on Lemnos, for which it provides
an aetiology.[33] The myth may be summarised and divided into
'mythemes' as follows. (a) Aphrodite, angered for some reason by the
women, afflicted them with a noxious smell, so that (b) their husbands abandoned them in favour of Thracian slave-girls. In retalia-
tion, (c) the women massacred their husbands and all the men on the
island, apart from (d) king Thoas, whom his daughter Hypsipyle
saved, either by hiding him in a coffin and throwing him into the sea,
or by dressing him as Dionysus and leading him to the sea-shore
dressed herself as a Bacchante. All of this happened (e) at night. (f)
The women set up a gynaecocracy. (g) When the Argonauts arrived,
(h) they married the women at a licentious festival, involving (i)
games at which a robe was the prize. (j) The town where this
happened was called Myrine, after the wife of Thoas.

The festival proceeded as follows. The women were not called
upon to smell but (a) the pungent herb rue appears to have played a
role in the festival.[34] At the end of the year, (b) the women and men

---

[31] *Cho.* 631f.; cf. Hdt. 6.138 for a second event on that island that confirmed its reputation.

[32] On knowledge of this myth in Athens, R. P. Martin 1987: 101–5.

[33] On this myth and its ritual, see especially Burkert 1970; also Dumézil 1924; Detienne 1977:
90–8.

[34] Uncertain: a marginal note to Antigon. *Hist. Mir.* 118 (which tells of the smell of the
Lemnians, and quotes Myrsilus, *FGH* 477 F 1b) refers to rue, but this does not relate to
anything in the text of Antigonus, and so may be the remains of some fuller treatment of the

gathered together in separate places. Obviously, there was no (c) massacre, but the dislocation of domestic life in reality corresponds to the massacre in myth. In the absence of evidence, one can only speculate that, as at other such festivals, (f) male political activity stopped: in Athens, as Mikalson writes, 'with very few exceptions meetings of the Ekklesia did not occur on monthly or annual festival days. Likewise meetings of the Boule did not occur on annual festival days'.[35] All fires on the island were extinguished (e), thus symbolically bringing all civilised activity to an end.[36] At the end of the festival, (g) new fire was brought by ship. Gloom was then replaced by (h) joyous reunion of husband and wife. The literary and mythical evidence suggests (i) that there were games with a robe as prize. (j) The two principal towns on Lemnos were Hephaestia and Myrine

The play has a comparable structure and repeats many of these elements; they will be taken in order, with reference to evidence from comparable myths and festivals where appropriate.

(a)   Bad smell

Spices and perfumes were a means of communicating with the gods, and in ritual the existence of bad smells was used to mark the fact that normality had been disrupted.[37] At the Scira garlic, and at the Thesmophoria garlic, *Vitex agnus-castus* and spurges were employed.[38] In the same way, in *Peace* and *Ecclesiazusae* bad smells, especially excrement, are used to emphasise disorder and are then replaced by sweet perfumes. This will explain what seems at first sight to be a somewhat obscure and frigid joke, made by Calonice when the women first begin to arrive (66–8):

> Cal. And here comes another group. Ugh! (*Holds nose.*) Where do
>   they come from?
> Lys. From Anagyrus.
> Cal. I'll say. Someone *has* shaken the *anaguros*!

---

subject (by Myrsilus?). Rue is an antaphrodisiac and contraceptive (schol. Nic. *Alex.* 410a; Plin. *NH* 20.142f.; Plut. *Mor.* 647B). *Vitex agnus-castus* was used in a similar fashion at the Thesmophoria. The prevalence of smells in such rites suggests Jackson 1990: 81 is wrong to detach the smell of the women from the Lemnian fire-ritual.

[35] 1975: 203.   [36] On fire generally in Greek religion, Furley 1981.

[37] Detienne 1977: 72–98 and next note.

[38] Garlic at the Scira: Philochorus, *FGH* 328 F 89; at the Thesmophoria: *IG* 2².1184.15 (mid-fourth cent.); other antaphrodisiacs at this festival were *Vitex agnus-castus*, *konuza* and *kneoron* (Fehrle 1910: 153).

The *anaguros* is the stinking bean-trefoil and 'to shake the *anaguros*'
was, according to the scholiast, a proverbial way of saying that
someone had got themselves into trouble. Here however the point is
that smell in the play has the same meaning as smell in the rituals: the
gathering of the women and the existence of bad smells indicates that
something unusual is afoot. There is then something of a paradox in
the fact that Myrrhine, who arrives after this joke about smells, takes
her name from the fragrant myrtle. In the topsy-turvy world of
Lysistrata, perfumes do not smell sweet, as Cinesias is to complain:
'By Apollo, this perfume doesn't smell at all sweet. It smells of delay
and of nothing to do with marriage!' (942f.). It is in terms of smell that
the old men characterise what the women are doing: 'All of this seems
to smell of greater and more weighty matters. I can distinctly smell
the tyranny of Hippias' (616–18). And they themselves are no more
sweet-smelling, with their onion-breath (798).

(b), (f) Separation and gynaecocracy

As in the festivals, the separation of the sexes brings about a
disruption affecting both domestic and political life, through the
sex-strike and seizure of the Acropolis respectively: the sexual and
political aspects of their action are linked in the play's imagery.

The calling of a sex-strike against men who are away at war is a
paradox in the play which has occasioned much comment,[39] but a
consideration of other myths of gynaecocracy will suggest an explanation for it. There are a number of versions of the Amazon-myth in
which women seize power when the men have been killed in battle
or are absent on a military expedition. Ephorus[40] tells how the
Amazon women were maltreated by their husbands; they waited
until most of the men were away at war, and then slew those who
were left behind and refused entry to the men when they returned.
In Trogus,[41] the Scythian women became warriors to avenge their
husbands' deaths, and killed all the surviving men so that they
should all be husbandless. In Stephanus of Byzantium,[42] the Amazons take control and mutilate their sons after the deaths of their
husbands in war. In *Lysistrata* too, the men are absent at war, leaving
behind a residue of older men, who are deprived of power by the
women. It is the absence of the politically dominant group from the

---

[39] Hulton 1972; Vaio 1973; Rosellini 1979; Loraux 1980; Moulton 1981; Foley 1982.
[40] *FGH* 70 F 60a.   [41] Fr. 36 Seel (p. 42.54ff.).   [42] s.v. *Amazones*.

city which marks times of the year or whole nations as abnormal: in myth, this may be the result of war; in ritual, it is represented by the cessation of political activity. Aristophanes combines this motif of the 'absence' of men with the motif of the disruption of normal sexual relations, and thus produces what in 'realist' terms is a paradox, but in mythological and ritual terms is a standard feature: there is disruption *both* in the civic sphere (men absent from political centre) *and* in the domestic (suspension of sexual relations).

This situation of dissolution of normal bonds may be characterised by two items in the text. First, there is the Old Men's reminiscence of their days as *Leukopodes* ('white feet', 665) at Leipsydrium, on the borders of Attica. The exact point of the pun on *Lukopodes* ('wolf feet'), the actual name the Alcmaeonids gave themselves during their exile at Leipsydrium, is not clear, but the reference to the exile of the opponents of Hippias' tyranny reflects the Old Men's displacement from power by the women. It also contains echoes of the idea of 'withdrawal' which is associated with marginal periods, in the mention of wolves,[43] in the movement to a fort on the margins of the land[44] and, possibly, in the reference to unconventional footwear, which was a feature of initiations in Greece and elsewhere.[45]

Equally appropriate to this world where communication between the sexes is by blows are the stories which the two semi-choruses fling at each other in the choral interlude at 781ff. The men tell of Melanion, who shunned marriage in favour of a huntsman's life with nets and dog because of his hatred of women (785–96):

> There once was a youth called Melanion, who fled into the desert to avoid marriage, and dwelt in the mountains. He hunted hares with nets he had woven and had a dog, and never came home again because of his hatred. That's how much he detested women, and we wise men hate them no less than Melanion.

A youth of this name we have already met in the myth of the Apaturia, and here too it belongs to an ephebic figure, this time one who refuses to leave his nets, dog and hunting in the wilds for

---

[43] The men select for special treatment the wife of Lycon (270).

[44] Apparently on Mt Parnes; cf. *PMG* 904 for a scholion commemorating the event.

[45] Cf. Jason 'with one sandal' in an ephebic context in Pi. *Py.* 4.75; cf. also Frazer 1927: 311ff. For the textual problems here, Hopper 1960; Edmunds 1984; Henderson 1987a: 159; Sommerstein 1990: 191.

marriage. We have also seen that people of this kind, such as Atalanta and her husband, also called Melanion, tend in mythology to suffer for their refusal to follow the normal course of life, so that the men's praise of Melanion's treatment of women marks once more the abnormality of the situation they are in. One may note too that it suggests their own attitude is questionable in the way it prolongs a situation that is anomalous in terms of normal human life.

A similar implication is also conveyed by the women's story of Timon, who like Melanion took to the wild countryside and lived in a manner reminiscent of the *kruptos*: 'homeless, hidden in a trackless thicket, with his face concealed, a scion of the Furies' (809–11). They create a version of his story in which his isolation from society was caused by hatred, not of all men but of evil ones, like those in the male semi-chorus; to women he was 'most friendly' (820). In contrast to the men's Melanion, Timon's withdrawal had legitimate causes, and ones which could easily be remedied if the men would behave appropriately and abandon war.

Finally, a rite celebrated at Hermione in honour of Demeter casts some light on why it is that it is the *old* women who disrupt politics by seizing the Acropolis. This rite took place 'in summer-time' and indeed has the characteristics of one which marked the end of the year.[46] Four frisky cows were driven one after the other into the sanctuary of Chthonia, where they were slaughtered by old women using sickles. The running loose of the cows, the fact that women carry out the sacrifice and that it is inside the shrine rather than outside, the use of the sickle and the manner of the sacrifice are all deviations from normal practice and characterise this rite as one belonging to an abnormal period. Old women do not normally carry out important sacrifices for the city. Thus the sex-strike, the 'absence' of the men, the control taken by women and the activities on behalf of the city by the old women all have their counterparts in the myths and rituals associated particularly with liminal times, not solely those of the Lemnian Women.

(d)   Disappearance of the king

In the Lemnian story, Thoas is dressed up by his daughter as the effeminate, 'marginal' god Dionysus, or put into a coffin, in order

---

[46] Paus. 2.35.4–8. Further on old women in antiquity, Bremmer 1985; Henderson 1987b.

that he may escape.[47] To this correspond the scenes between the women and the Proboulos (387–613). This Athenian official, one of those appointed after the Sicilian disaster,[48] is dressed in the corresponding *pnigos* and *antipnigos* of the *agon*, first as a woman (532–6):

> *Lys.* Take this veil from me and put it round your head, then shut up.
> *Wo.* And this basket.
> *Lys.* Then gird yourself and card the wool,

(the modesty, wool-working and silence are all characteristic of the 'ideal' Athenian woman), and then as a corpse, with his coffin, garland and honey-cake (599–607):

> *Lys.* Can't you see you've got to die? Your burial place is ready:[49] you'll buy yourself a coffin, and I'll knead you a honey-cake. Take this garland and put it on.
> *1st Wo.* And receive these from me.
> *2nd Wo.* And this garland from me.
> *Lys.* What's missing? What do you want? Get into the ship: Charon is calling you, and you're holding up the departure.

In other words, the two versions of the Thoas story are combined. There is a difference between the intentions of the women in the play and Hypsipyle in the myth, but this should not disguise the fact that their actions have the same meaning and function. In each, the legitimate male figure of authority is removed from power, and this removal is symbolised by the way he is disguised as the opposite of his normal self.

Thoas is sent across the sea, but new life returns from the sea in the shape of the Argonauts: Jason replaces Thoas each year. So in the play, the figure of male authority may be 'feminised' and 'killed',[50] but the male domination will return at the end.

(e) Fire extinguished

The Lemnian massacre took place at night and it is not unlikely that darkness played a role in the New Fire festival, when all the

---

[47] Coffin: A. R. 1.620–6 (with scholia); disguise: Val. Flacc. *Arg.* 2.242–310. The age of this last tradition is uncertain, but as Burkert says the 'general pattern, the *apopompe* of the semi-divine king, the way to the sea, the tossing of the *larnax* into the water surely goes back to very old strata' (1970: 7f.; cf. 11 on the comparable *apopompe* of Erechtheus).

[48] Thuc. 8.1.3; [Arist.] *Ath. Pol.* 29.2.

[49] I follow Sommerstein's interpretation (1990: 185).

[50] Cf. the use of *tumbos* of the male chorus in 372.

lamps on the island were extinguished.[51] In *Lysistrata*, the motif of
extinguishing fire appears when the women put out the fire, which
the men explicitly describe as 'Lemnian', by pouring water on them
(374f., 381). The women, whose normal job it is to tend the fire of the
hearth, are now by a reversal extinguishing it. The language they use
of this act of extinguishing is also ironic: they refer to the water as a
'bridal bath' (378), to help the men grow (384f.), which in the context
of the separation of the sexes underlines the dissolution that now
prevails. If the same extinction of fire has happened at Sparta (as it is
reasonable to suppose), we have another paradox like the one in
which the sweetly-perfumed 'Myrtle' smelt of the foul *anaguros* (66–
8): the woman who extinguishes the Spartan fires is Lampito, 'the
Lady of the Lamp'.[52]

(g) New fire

New fire was brought to Lemnos from 'outside'. In the myth
this was represented by the arrival of the Argonauts, but in the
festival the fire was presumably brought by Lemnians. Burkert
suggests there may have been a version of the myth in which the
gods of the island, the Cabiroi, who fled at the time of the massacre,
returned with the new fire.[53] In *Lysistrata*, normality is restored
when foreigners arrive in the form not of Argonauts but of the
Spartans. In fact, there are two arrivals of 'foreigners', since the
women offer to treat not only the Spartans but also their own
husbands as *xenoi* (1184), guests from without. As in the festival,
therefore, the outsiders are really insiders, and Lysistrata reminds
the men of the days when Athenians and Spartans were not divided
as they are now (1137–56): it is almost as if in her newly pacified
world the Spartans are insiders too. In the closing scene of the play, it
is made clear in suitably comic fashion that fire has returned through
the threats to burn hair with a torch (1217): the frequent motif of
torches at the end of Old Comedies is here given a more specific
meaning in terms of the framework of ideas that inform the play.

---

[51] There was a similar absence of fires at the Thesmophoria in Eretria (Plut. *Mor.* 298B–C), and
possibly also at Lyrcea in the Argolid (Paus. 2.25.4). Burkert 1970: 11 suggests the eternal
lamp in the Acropolis may have been extinguished and rekindled at the Panathenaea (cf.
Paus. 1.26.6f., and the rekindling of fire at Plataea after the Persian invasion (Plut. *Arist.*
20.4f.)).

[52] In 1003, the Spartans walk about 'like men carrying lamps', but, in the absence of the
women to tend the lamps, this can indeed be only a simile.   [53] 1970: 9.

(h)   Reunion

The reunion begins when the women reclothe the men and remove the gnat from their eyes (1014–34), and culminates in the songs at 1189ff., where the Chorus, which has been divided throughout the play, comes together to sing and to tease the audience with the prospect of non-existent riches. The command for reunion is given by Lysistrata at 1186f.: 'Everyone of you will go home taking his wife with him.' Shortly afterwards, she sums up what has been her aim all the time: 'Let husband stand by wife, and wife by husband, and then, because of our good fortune, let us dance for the gods and take care that in future we do not make the same mistake again' (1275–8). This new-found unity of husband and wife is complemented by that between Athenian and Spartan.[54] The Athenian delights in the song and dance of the Spartans (1246), which recalls the old alliance against Persia; either he or Lysistrata concludes with a request for a song,[55] which the Spartan sings to Athens' great goddess, but in her guise as Athena Chalcioecus ('Of the Bronze House'), patroness of Sparta's acropolis.

(i)   Games and the robe

We have no evidence that the actual Lemnian festival included games, but there is literary evidence for mythical games: Pindar and Simonides refer to games which had a robe as a prize, and Apollonius mentions three robes given by the Lemnians to the Argonauts, of which the most significant is that which was symbolic of power on Lemnos[56] and passed from the Graces to Dionysus to Thoas to Hypsipyle and was eventually given to Jason.[57] Images of clothing play a not unimportant part in the play. Lysistrata's great image for what the women are doing is the extended one of making a *chlaina* for the demos (574–86), and the reunion of husband and wife begins when the women put clothes on the old men of the Chorus (1019ff.).

[54] The forthcoming peace is symbolically prepared for: the Spartan herald's phallus begins as a spear (985), but becomes the staff of the herald sent to discuss peace (991).

[55] Sommerstein 1990: 221f. gives this speech to Lysistrata with the MSS. His arguments have force, but resolution of the problem depends partly on whether the men have so regained control of affairs that it would be inappropriate for a woman here to be playing so central a role: see below in text.

[56] In Apollonius (4.430), its 'divine fragrance' contrasts with the earlier stench of the women.

[57] *Py.* 4.252f.; *PMG* 547; A. R. 4.423ff. (cf. 2.30–2, 3.1204–6); a *chlaina* was the prize at the Hermaea at Pellene (schol. Pi. *Ol.* 7.156).

Lysistrata reminds the Athenians how the Spartans once helped them to replace the servile *katonake* with the free man's *chlaina* (1155f.).[58] In the myth, the donning of a robe marks the return of normal human family life, and so it does in the play. There are a number of mythical parallels for this idea. In Pherecydes of Syrus, Zas gave Chthonie a flowered robe on their marriage and she became Ge; West plausibly suggests that the gift marks the establishment of the cosmos as it is now, and that the change in Chthonie's name marks a move from death to fertility.[59] Penelope's weaving in the Orphic poem called *The Robe* may also be taken to represent the establishment of the present order of the cosmos.[60] For an Athenian, of course, the giving of a robe to mark a new beginning could not but have evoked the robe given to Athena at the Great Panathenaea.

(j)   Myrrhine

This helper of Lysistrata bears a heavy load of symbolism, which once again underlines the ambivalent nature of the women's actions. That Myrine was the name of a town on Lemnos is important,[61] but more so is the reminder, first made by Papademetriou, that Myrrhine was the name of the priestess of Athena Nike in 411.[62] Lewis later added that Lysistrata recalls in form and meaning the name of the priestess of Athena Polias, Lysimache;[63] at 554, Lysistrata predicts that if the women are successful they will in future be known as 'Lysimaches'. The women in *Lysistrata* are led therefore by people with names that evoke the priestesses of the city's most important goddess in her role as Nike and Polias, aspects connected with the city's very centre. At the same time, the myrtle and words from its root are regularly used of the female sexual organs,[64] and the

---

[58] Cleomenes' humiliation is marked by his having to leave the Acropolis clad only in a *tribonion* (278).   [59] 1971: 9–11, 15–20.

[60] M. L. West 1983: 10f.; the 'weaving' of the cosmos is a Near Eastern idea (cf. West 1971: 53–5; Richardson 1974: 83f.). A robe was also the *anakalupteria* gift from Cadmus to Harmonia at their marriage attended by the gods (Apollod. 3.4.2).

[61] The names were surely sufficiently close in pronunciation for the audience to have noticed the parallel; on these names, Heubeck 1949–50.

[62] Papademetriou 1948–9 on *SEG* 12.80. I have adopted this association despite the arguments against it of Henderson 1987a: xl–xli and Sommerstein 1990: 5 n. 31.

[63] 1955; for the fame of Lysimache, see Frazer on Paus. 1.27.5.

[64] Henderson 1975: 134f. (cf. Paus. 1.22.2, 2.32.3 for a myrtle tree whose leaves were punctured by Phaedra); Chirassi 1968: 17–38; Detienne 1977: 62f.; Burkert 1985: 371 n. 66; also Rogers on *Peace* 1154.

plant, sacred to Aphrodite, was used in the garlands of bridal couples.[65] When the myrtle goes on sex-strike normality is indeed suspended. Finally, we have seen that Myrine was the name of an Amazon, and the reason our Myrrhine gives for being late is that she could not find her girdle (72): the girdle of the Amazon queen was sought by Heracles during his labours.[66] Myrrhine is at once therefore the ambiguous Amazon, a symbol of sexuality and of the protection of the city: in other words, a symbol of women.

Lysistrata thus has a structure that closely resembles those of the myth of the Lemnian Women and of the festival of New Fire . This again underlines its ambiguity: if the crime of Lemnian Women is the worst of crimes, the Lemnian festival is a harmless rite which brings new life and order to the city. The women seem to be located between these horrors of Lemnos and the paragons of female virtue to be found, for instance in Plutarch's *Mulierum Virtutes*,[67] who may show fortitude, kill tyrants and encourage their failing husbands, but seldom do anything to scandalise them.

Hippias

The final model for the women's actions offered by the play is an historical event of great importance in democratic mythology, the sequence of events surrounding the ending of the tyranny of Hippias, the tyrant *par excellence* for fifth-century Athens.[68] As Aristophanes' plays show, the charge of attempting to institute tyrannical rule was always available to politicians and others in the late fifth century.[69] The *Arai* ('Commination') that preceded Assembly meetings cursed any who tried to bring back tyranny. Alcibiades was intriguing with the Persians and 411 was to be the year of the oligarchic coup,[70] so the political climate was one in which such references to tyranny would have struck a troubling note for many in the audience: they are no cliché. We have already noticed that the men smell the tyranny of Hippias in the actions of the women (619), but much greater stress is laid on this period of Athenian history: the

---

[65] Stes. 187; *Birds* 160f.   [66] Elderkin 1940: 394.

[67] *Mor.* 242E–263C; cf. Stadter 1965: 7f. on such collections.

[68] On the tyrant in the fifth century, Berve 1967: I 190–206 (esp. 198ff., post-Periclean attitudes) and II 625–9 (references in fifth-century literature); Tuplin 1985; Rosivach 1988.

[69] E.g. *Wasps* 463–507.

[70] On the chronology of events, see especially Sommerstein 1977 (and 1990: 1–3); Henderson 1987a: xv–xxv.

crucial events from the story are mentioned at various places in the text, in the same way as were features of the Lemnian story.[71]

(a) Hippias' tyranny was relatively benevolent until the murder of his brother by Harmodius and Aristogeiton. This deed gave rise to a famous scholion,[72] which the Old Men quote when claiming that they will not submit to tyranny: 'In future I shall carry my sword in a myrtle-branch, and follow Aristogeiton to the agora with my weapons, standing beside him like this' (632–4).

(b) The Alcmaeonids, the enemies of the Peisistratids, suffered a disastrous siege at Leipsydrium, to which, in a passage we have discussed, the men refer shortly after their quotation of the scholion: 'Come you "White-feet", who went to Leipsydrium when we were still fit men. Now, now we must be young again' (665–7).

(c) Under Cleisthenes, the Alcmaeonids secured Spartan aid. The Old Men express the fear that the Spartans may now be intriguing in 'Cleisthenes' house' (620–5), in which remark there are two jokes. First, there is the comic reversal whereby, instead of being on the side of the Alcmaeonid Cleisthenes, the men fear treachery from a contemporary with the same name; secondly, there is the comic appropriateness of this effeminate Cleisthenes as mediator between the women and the Spartans, who are to be characterised by homosexual proclivities.[73]

(d) The Spartan king Cleomenes came and besieged the Peisistratids in the Acropolis. They were forced to leave within five days, when their children were captured on their way to safety and displayed below the walls. In *Lysistrata*, five days after the women's occupation of the Acropolis (881), Myrrhine's child is displayed to her below the Acropolis in a wretched condition, but she shows herself to be made of sterner stuff than the Peisistratids, because having gone down to trick her husband, she is happy to see the child continue to suffer his incompetent ministrations. At 1149ff., as part of her speech of reconciliation, Lysistrata reminds the Athenians of Cleomenes' help to them in this incident.[74]

(e) Cleomenes occupied the Acropolis again, this time in response to the appeals of Isagoras, Cleisthenes' rival, but was himself besieged by the people and forced to leave after two days. Early in

---

[71] The principal sources are set out in Jones 1967: 50–5 (esp. Hdt. 5.62ff.; Thuc. 6.53.3ff.; [Arist.] *Ath. Pol.* 17–20).   [72] *PMG* 893–6.

[73] So Rogers *ad loc.*; compare Cleisthenes' role in *Thesm.* 574ff.

[74] For the comical inappropriateness of her examples here and in 1137–46, Wilson 1982.

the play, when they have learnt what the women have done, the old men fondly recall what they did to Cleomenes on this occasion: 'Huffing and puffing in the Spartan manner, he handed his weapons to me and left, wearing only a light cloak, dirty, ragged, unkempt – he'd not washed for six years' (276–80).

(f) There is a final parallel: Myrrhine was the name of the wife of Hippias.[75]

The portrayal of the women in terms of Hippias makes a clear political comment, but there is also a barely submerged sexual pun. In comedy, reference to 'riding' and horses often indicates the reversed sexual position.[76] For instance, in Wasps 500–2, this joke is used with specific reference to Hippias: 'Yes, and this tart I visited yesterday, when I asked her to ride, got all steamed up and said I was trying to set up the tyranny of Hippias.'

In Lysistrata, this joke also appears in connection with the Salaminian women and their keletes: 'They'll have been working over on their pinnaces well before daylight' (59f.); and with the Amazons in 676–9 (quoted above).[77] This joke is introduced by a similar one about the female warrior Artemisia, in which appear the verbs naumachein and plein, which are regularly used of the upper partner.[78] Artemisia was an ally of the Persians who infuriated the Greeks by fighting against them though a woman.[79] The attempt to imitate Hippias therefore implies not only a political but also a sexual 'revolution', as is pointed out in the crowning joke, the response of one of the women to Lysistrata's oracle (770–3):

> Lys. When the swallows cower in one place, in flight from the
>   hoopoes, and keep themselves away from the coots (phaletes),
>   there will be an end to troubles, and Zeus who thunders on high
>   will place what is under above . . .
> Woman. Oh! Will we lie on top in future?

The evocation by the men of the Lemnian Fire introduced a schema which enabled the audience to see the ambivalences in what the women are doing and in the men's reactions. The references to

[75] Lemnos acts as a marginal place where suffer those who have angered the gods: curiously, Aelian fr. 74 says that Hippias fled to Lemnos after the Persian defeat and died there diseased, blind and with blood flowing from his eyes, a divine punishment for his attempts to enslave his country to the barbarian: cf. too Hephaestus (Il. 1.590–4) and Philoctetes.

[76] In general, Henderson 1975: 164–6; Ar. fr. 721.

[77] Keles carries the same double entendre as the verbs for 'riding'; cf. Eccl. 38 for such jokes against the Salaminians. The brilliant translation is Sommerstein's.

[78] Henderson 1987a: 160 on 674–7.   [79] Hdt. 8.93.

Hippias work in the same way. In presenting their attack on the
women as the equivalent of defending the democracy, the men make
another claim that rings hollow on examination. It is neither Cleomenes nor the Peisistratids who are in the Acropolis, but their own
wives, and the murder of these people would hardly be the same as
ejecting a Spartan king or protecting democratic power, especially as
their aim is peace for everyone.

   Lysistrata, therefore, is broadly structured in the same way as
myths about the occupation of the city by people who do not belong ·
in power, be they tyrants or women. These myths provide filters
through which the actions of the play may be judged. Characters in
the play suggest that viewing the women as Amazons or Lemnians or
tyrants is indeed correct, but at the same time the play makes it clear
that this is a very partial analysis: the women do not conform well to
the stereotypes of female violence which the men put forward, and it
is the women's actions which lead to the re-establishment of that
normality in which the men may resume control. Their anomalous
deeds are designed solely to bring about peace, and women are not
acting so strangely in involving themselves in matters of war.
Lysistrata acidly points out, in reply to the Proboulos' claim that
women have nothing to do with war (588–92),[80]

> on the contrary, you devil, we have more than a double dose of
> it, first because we bear children and send them out as hoplites –
> *Prob.* Be quiet – don't raise unpleasant memories.
> *Lys.* – then, when we should be enjoying ourselves and profiting
> from our youth, we have to sleep alone because of the
> campaigns.

Evocation of festivals like the Lemnian Fire and of other, Athenian
ones where they gather together for the benefit of the city also
provides positive ways of considering what they do.

   At the same time, the characteristics traditionally given to
women in mythology are not obliterated. The prospect of a drink
determines the nature of their initial sacrifice and the Old Women are
as violent as the Old Men. Furthermore, some of the younger women
soon find the pressures of a sex-strike insupportable, as we can see

---

[80] Women's relationship to the production of sons who are to be hoplites is figured on vases:
the mother (or Athena) hands over the armour, but at the sacrifice and hieroscopy at
departure, she assumes a subordinate position: 'while she plays a role in the arming, she
apparently does not participate in the decision [to fight] or the action itself' (Lissarrague
1989: 43–50; quotation, 50).

from their attempts to escape and their plausible excuses offered for leave of absence (720ff.). This passage is in the form of a complex image, in which there is a sequence of escape, sex and parturition. Lysistrata begins with complaints about what has happened: 'I caught the first picking open a hole by the grotto of Pan, another suspended from a cable and a third trying to make off; yesterday I pulled one back by the hair as she planned to fly off down to Orsilochus' on a sparrow' (720–5). After this reference to using Aphrodite's bird to go to a brothel, another woman appears who wishes to go home to spread fleeces on a bed, and yet another who wants to strip her flax, both transparently sexual images.[81] The sting is in the tale: a sixth woman comes out, claiming to be pregnant, but she is carrying not a child but the helmet of Athena.[82] This image can be read in a number of ways. It can be taken to show that sex leads to war: hence the use of the sex-strike to bring peace. Alternatively, the production of a helmet and not a baby could stand for the sterility created by war and the absence of husbands. At the same time, the helmet is that of the city's protectress, who must be armed to carry out her duties: the deity herself, at once defender of her children, occupant of the hearth and yet warrior, is in part suggestive of the ambiguous role of women in the play, but also highlights the apparent contradictions between the treatment of women in the city and the representation of that city's main divinity, who is very different from her mortal counterparts, despite her female sex. This contradiction provokes speculation on what role the female should play in any society, and why what Lysistrata and her women do should be seen as so anomalous: Athena, in the foundation-myth, challenged the male authority of Poseidon and met his force with force,[83] and, despite this challenge the citizens, that is in fifth-century terms the male citizens, chose her as the city's patroness. That the heroine should bear the name of the chief priestess of Athena serves to keep the goddess ever before one's mind's eye.

The men

So far the analysis has been carried out by considering the validity of the models suggested by the structure of the play or by

[81] Henderson 1975: 167f.

[82] On the pun *kuein/kune*, Bodson 1973: 10–17; Whitman 1964: 206.

[83] Note the reference to the snake, hypostasis of her champion, in 758f.

the male characters in it. To complete the analysis, we need to look at
the characterisation of the men themselves. What stands out is that
even as they complain about the women being Amazons and Lemnians, they reveal themselves to be the same kind of disruptive,
dangerous and lustful figures that they use to portray women in their
mythology. Thus, it is the men who, by making war, have disrupted
households: 'Don't you long for the fathers of your children now that
they are away at war? I know that the husband of every single one of
you has gone' (99–101). It is they who threaten the city's continuity
by making women grow old without marriage (593–7):

> *Lys.* The way young women grow old in their chambers bothers
> me.
> *Prob.* Don't men grow old too?
> *Lys.* That's not the point; you're not talking of the same thing.
> When a man gets back from war, even if he's a greybeard he's
> soon married to a young girl: but a woman's time for action is
> short, and if she doesn't seize it, no one wants to marry her and
> she sits reading the tea-leaves.

It is also the men who have brought madness into politics (507–28)
and they who planned the Sicilian expedition. The Proboulos may
complain of the drunken woman singing at the Adonia, when the
expedition was being discussed (387–98), but a few drinks at a semi-
official festival pale into insignificance beside the events in Sicily.
The men too, by invading the agora in armour, have brought
violence and chaos into an area dedicated to the commercial and
religious life of the city (557–64):

> *Lys.* Now they go around the pottery- and vegetable-stalls in the
> market carrying their weapons just like Corybantes.
> *Prob.* So they should – they're brave lads.
> *Lys.* All right, but it's ridiculous to see a man with a Gorgon on his
> shield buying sprats.
> *Woman.* Yes, the other day I saw a long-haired officer on his horse
> putting gruel he'd bought from an old woman into his bronze
> helmet. And then there was a Thracian, shaking his shield and
> spear like Tereus; he scared off the fig-lady and ate up the tree-
> ripened ones.

Finally, and most strikingly, it is the men who attack Athena's
Acropolis with fire and her own olive-wood (255), which makes their
actions rather close to those of the mythical Amazons, to whom they
compare the women. Indeed, one might say that in this play the
comic phallus is not just a traditional item of costume, but a constant

reminder of male lustfulness and desire for control, especially in its erect form in the second part of the play.[84]

At the back of all this male violence there lies another piece of male mythology, the battle of Marathon, which plays such an important role in Athenian self-definition.[85] All the major battles of the Persian Wars are mentioned in the course of the play, except Plataea: Marathon, Salamis (675), Artemisium and Thermopylae (1247ff.). Should they fail to defeat the women, say the men, 'may my trophy no longer stand in the Tetrapolis' (285). This Tetrapolis consisted of Marathon, Probalinthus, Oenoe and Tricorythus, and so it can be no coincidence (nor simply the result of a desire for a pun on *koris*, 'bug') that the gnat removed by the women from the men's eyes as reconciliation begins should have come from Tricorythus (1032): excessive pride in the victory at Marathon has blinded the Old Men to realities and the need for peace.

Male mythology is thus turned against men: they cannot set up stereotypes of wild, undisciplined women and then behave in this way themselves, without incurring the comedian's mockery. The stereotypes they use to describe women are in truth merely a transcription of the nature of men, who are after all the ones who wage war and control sexuality in Athens. They wish to present the women as a threat to the city, but in their wrath, they themselves turn to actions which were constitutionally forbidden in Athens. They wish to destroy all their wives on a pyre together through a single vote of the Assembly (270). Not only was this use of a single vote illegal,[86] but such a simultaneous massacre of spouses is all too reminiscent of – the crime of the Lemnian Women.

Reconciliation

It has been said all along that the ending of the play brings about the restoration of normality, but that normality is not simple: it

---

[84] The phallus plays a significant role also in *Acharnians*. A similar satyriasis afflicted men in Athens when they refused to acknowledge Dionysus when he was brought by Pegasus from Eleutherae (schol. *Ach.* 243a; Paus. 1.2.5); this was an aetiological myth for the place of the phallus in the procession of the Rural Dionysia.

[85] E.g. *Ach.* 181, *Kn.* 1334, *Clouds* 986, *Wasps* 711, fr. 429. For the pride elicited by Marathon, compare Aeschylus' epitaph, which omitted mention of his poetry and participation at Artemisium and Salamis in favour of a single reference to Marathon (Paus. 1.14.5; in general, Loraux 1986: 155–71).

[86] X. *Hell.* 1.7.34f. (Arginousai); Lys. 12.52 (The Thirty): by the decree of Cannonus, a separate vote was to be taken for each accused (Hsch. s.v. *Kannonou*).

too is depicted in a way that unmasks its real nature. The women bring about the peace they have so desired, but ironically what they also achieve is the restoration of that male control of the two areas of sexuality and politics which caused all their problems in the first place. This restoration is symbolised in the scene with Reconciliation. The discussion of her body by the Athenian and Spartan men recalls the earlier admiration by the women of the bodies of Lampito, Ismenia and the Corinthian girl, and Lampito's complaints at being treated as a sacrificial victim (78ff.). Now we have the same treatment by men of a mute and passive female, and the symbolism of the scene and indeed of the change from female admirers to male should be clear. Reconciliation's body is divided up in terms of geographical features of Greece, each of which evokes a sexually desirable part of the female body (1162–72):

> *Spartans.* We'll make peace, if we can have this round part here.
> *Lys.* Which is that?
> *Sp.* Pylos. We've wanted it and been groping for it for ages!
> *Athenians.* By Poseidon, you're not getting that.
> *Lys.* Please give it to them.
> *Ath.* But what are we going to poke our – noses into then?
> *Lys.* Ask them for some other place in return.
> *Ath.* Give us . . . give us this Hedgehog first of all, the Melian Gulf round the back and the Megarian Legs.
> *Sp.* By the gods, you're not getting all that, my friend.
> *Lys.* Go on, don't squabble over a pair of legs.

This division can be decoded as the re-establishment of male control of sex (Reconciliation's body) and politics (the Greek world). At the end of the play, we will see men alone making decisions about the future of international relations.[87] The general exclusion of the women may be contrasted with Plutarch's tale of the Celtic women, who stopped a civil war between their menfolk and were subsequently consulted by them on peace and war, a reward that is significantly lacking in *Lysistrata*.[88]

If 'normality' is being restored, then we would expect to find this return of men to power: it is what happens after the Thesmophoria and the Lemnian massacre. Since this is comedy, which is

---

[87] Rosellini 1979: 20. On 1273–end, Henderson 1987a: 213f.; Sommerstein 1990: 221f.

[88] *Mor.* 246B–C; though note the grim variant in *Paradox. Vat. Rohdii* xlvi (= O. Keller, *Rerum nat. scr. gr. min.*, vol. I, Leipzig 1877, 112) in which the women paid with their heads if the men lost a war they had recommended.

supposed to deal in fantasies, we might expect too that the negative elements of the characterisation of the men would disappear in the final happy situation. This, however, is not the case. The scene with the body of Reconciliation shows the persistence of the male lustfulness and hunger for power, and when peace is concluded both sides are looking forward to characteristic forms of sexual indulgence (1173f.):

> *Ath.* I want to strip off and get down to some ploughing.
> *Sp.* Then by god I'll go off first and work in the dung.

The squabbling suggests also that the violent element in men is still prevalent, and this is confirmed in 1216–46, where violence is being offered to people outside the doors: the attempt by one group to get through a door and the threats by others to burn their hair are a repetition of the earlier attempt by the men to get through the gates of the Acropolis and the threat to burn the women's hair (1217f., 1222; cf. 381).[89] The 'new fire' torches are being put to disorderly use. Finally, there is drunkenness. This is much used in comedy to characterise female disruption, but here it is to be institutionalised as a necessary condition of (male) diplomacy (1229–35):[90]

> If the Athenians take my advice, we will carry out our diplomacy everywhere drunk. As it is, whenever we go to Sparta sober, we immediately look around to see what trouble we can make. Consequently, we don't hear what they say, and we guess at what they don't – not that we ever bring back a coherent report anyway!

In other words, the men have not changed, and are not likely to: drink and coherence do not go happily together.

Aristophanes' 'normality', therefore, like his men and women, is two-sided. He is once again exploiting the gap between 'reality' and the 'normality' supposedly restored in myth and ritual. In 'reality', men go to war, get drunk and control sexuality for their own ends; in ritually re-created 'normality', the presumed violence, drunkenness and lust of women is evoked in order to be suppressed, everything is supposed to be ordered, (the) cosmos is renewed and society is put into an ideal state. By making the end of his play not only reflect the kind of euphoria that is associated with the conclusion of rituals dramatising periods of chaos, but also emphasise the

---

[89] There are problems about what exactly is happening here: cf. Henderson 1987a: 208.
[90] This was a Persian or German custom (Hdt. 1.133.3f.; Tacitus, *Germ.* 22).

reality of life (with a certain comic exaggeration), Aristophanes draws attention to the gap between what rituals involving for instance women in power are supposed to achieve and what they actually achieve. It is in this gap that a good deal of the humour of *Lysistrata* is created. The women, in gaining one thing they desire, actually leave the way open for a repetition of the very problem they appear to have solved. If the play provides a critique of male ideology of the relationship between the sexes, it is by no means simply a 'feminist' drama as has sometimes been claimed. Its recognition of the power of women lasts for at most two days longer than the Thesmophoria's.

9

Thesmophoriazusae

Thesmophoriazusae and Thesmophoria

Ritual

If *Lysistrata* represented an 'illegal' seizure of control by the women of the city, *Thesmophoriazusae* makes use of a particular festival which officially 'dramatised' female control for the benefit of the city. The Thesmophoria, dedicated to Demeter and Persephone, was one of the most widespread festivals of the Greek world.[1] Although it was celebrated in secret by the women, it would be wrong to think that no man knew anything about what happened or that we cannot meaningfully discuss the play in terms of the festival, because of an inability to reconstruct its ritual and significance. It was financed by the men and its smooth running was guaranteed by them,[2] and those aspects that were truly secret were presumably, as at the Eleusinian Mysteries, not necessarily sensational actions, knowledge of which is essential to the understanding of the whole festival, but rather revelations of certain objects or gestures. There is in fact a good deal of circumstantial evidence about the festival,[3] and anything that was truly secret and unknown to Aristophanes and the men is naturally irrelevant to the reading of the play.

We have already seen that, in contrast to the general restrictions on women's activities in Athenian society, at the Thesmophoria

---

[1] See Farnell 1896–1909: III 75–112 and 326–8; Deubner 1932: 50–60; Dahl 1976: 104–48 for sources on the festival, of which the principal is schol. Lucian, *Dial. Mer.* 2.1 (p. 275 Rabe; from Apollodorus of Athens' *De Dis*, according to Jacoby, *FGH* 3b (Suppl.) 2.204). See also Parke 1977: 82–8; Detienne 1979b; Brumfield 1981: 70–103; R. C. T. Parker 1983: 81–3; Simon 1983: 17–22; Burkert 1985: 242–6; Sfameni Gasparro 1986: 223–83.

[2] Isaeus 3.80; Men. *Epitr.* 749f.; *IG* 2².1184 (Cholargus, 334/3), and 1177 (Peiraeus, 4th cent.).

[3] Certain aspects could be revealed (Ael. fr. 44; Hdt. 2.171.2). In *Thesm.* 472 and *Eccl.* 442–4 the women pride themselves on keeping quiet about the festival.

their role as guarantors of the continuity of *oikos* and *polis* was formally recognised and celebrated. According to the scholiast to Lucian, the festival was concerned 'with the generation of crops and the procreation of mankind'. It took place around the crucial time of the autumn sowing, on 11–13 Pyanopsion,[4] and legitimately married wives alone seem to have been permitted to attend,[5] having kept themselves from sexual intercourse for three days.[6] The fundamental aspect of the festival was to permit the women to occupy areas that were normally the preserve of men,[7] principally in politics,[8] sacrifice,[9] overt sexuality and certain aspects of death. The difference from the situation in *Lysistrata* is clear, but in the traditions and thinking surrounding the Thesmophoria, the potential violence of the women is still acknowledged. According to Herodotus, the Danaids brought these rites of fertility to Greece, after the mass-murder of their husbands,[10] and this ambivalence is reflected, as we shall see, in the myths, which represent the women who worship Demeter both as the safe, domestic 'Bee' and as attackers of men.[11]

This trespass onto male space can be most clearly seen in the case of politics. The law courts and the Assembly did not sit, so that when the women gathered at the Thesmophorion on the Pnyx, they were symbolically replacing the men at the political centre of the

---

[4] Cf. Brumfield 1981: 88–95. Pritchett 1979: 165 calculates that the Thesmophoria would have fallen at various times from 12 September to 5 December (on Meritt's table), and criticises the link with the sowing; cf. Burkert 1983a: 293–7 for a suggested pre-agricultural origin.

[5] Which women were permitted to attend is uncertain: perhaps unmarried women (Detienne 1979b: 197 n. 2), slaves (*Thesm.* 293f.) and concubines were excluded. Cf. R. C. T. Parker 1983: 82 n. 35 and add Isaeus 8.19f.

[6] So Schol. Lucian, *Dial. Mer.* 2.1, but see R. C. T. Parker 1983: 82 n. 33.

[7] For the idea of a women's festival, cf. Sokolowski 1969: no. 36.8–12 and *Thesm.* 834f., and for women's role in religion, E. *Mel. Desm.* fr. 6.12–22 von Arnim (all quoted by R. C. T. Parker 1983: 82 n. 34).

[8] Cf. Semus, *FGH* 396 F 21 and Hsch. s.v. *chalkidikon diogma*, a Thesmophoric rite celebrating the flight of the enemy towards Chalkis after prayers of the women, and so another example of female involvement in martial affairs regularly associated with abnormal times of the year (Graf 1984)? See further Detienne 1979b: 199–201.

[9] For the involvement of women in sacrifice, Detienne 1979b: esp. 186–91, 194–6, 202–9: 'il semble que la figure d'une femme-sacrificateur tenant l'égorgeoir se tienne à la limite du possible cultuel' (206); no male *mageiros* is cited until Pherecrates fr. 70 in the fourth century.

[10] 2.171, discussed by Detienne 1979b: 212.

[11] Detienne 1979b: 211; on Demeter's 'Bees', Apollodorus, *FGH* 244 F 89; Bodson 1978: 25–7; Williams 1978: 92–4.

city.[12] This political aspect of the festival is found elsewhere: in Thebes, king Cadmus and his descendants used to live in the Thesmophorion,[13] and on Thasos the sanctuary contained the altars of Zeus, Artemis, Athena and the Nymphs, to whom the leading families sacrificed;[14] at Mylasa in Caria, a third-century inscription contains the phrase 'the women decided . . .', using the usual formula for male assemblies.[15] There were officials called *archousai* who corresponded to the male *archontes*.[16] As a general rule, men performed sacrifices for the city's welfare, but here it became the responsibility of the women: it is not certain whether they performed the actual killing themselves or whether, as we know was the case at such festivals in other cities, for instance Delos[17] and Mylasa,[18] a male *mageiros* was employed for the purpose;[19] the myths to be discussed below certainly put sacrificial implements into the hands of the women,[20] but this may be no more than a symbolic representation of the meaning of the festival. Whatever the truth, the fact remains that the main sacrifices in the city on the days of the festival were conducted essentially by the women alone.

The women's contact with sexuality and death was expressed by the activities of the first day. At Athens, this was known as the *Anodos* ('Way Up'), when the women ascended to the Thesmophorion.[21] The timing of events at the festival is unclear, but it seems most likely that it was on this day that models of snakes and male genitals

---

[12] In most cities, the Thesmophorion was outside the walls (Richardson 1974: 250); its situation in Athens on the Pnyx thus gave it an unusual centrality: cf. 658 with scholia; H. A. Thompson 1936; Simon 1983: 18. For the suspension of public business in Athens, cf. X. *HG* 5.2.29 of Thebes, where 'The *Boule* met in the stoa in the agora because the women were holding the Thesmophoria in the Cadmeion.'   [13] Paus. 9.16.5.

[14] Rolley 1965.   [15] Sokolowski 1955: no. 61.5.

[16] Sokolowski 1962: no. 124.3; Isaeus 8.19f. See further on political aspects of the festival Detienne 1979b: 197–200 and Vian 1963: 135–9.   [17] Bruneau 1970: 272f.

[18] Sokolowski 1955: no. 61.5–10.

[19] There is uncertain evidence for a male *mageiros* at the Scira in Sokolowski 1962: no. 10.A.25–7 (403–399), if Sokolowski is right to ascribe it to that festival (it is for the month of Scirophorion) and to restore the word *mageiros*. Cf. Detienne 1979b: 207–9; Berthiaume 1982: 29–31.

[20] Compare the way the spits have found their way into the hands of the slaves who guard their master in *Wasps*.

[21] *IG* 2².1177.23; *Thesm.* 281, 623, 657, 893; cf. 585. There are problems about what happened on which day; since they are somewhat intractable and do not affect my argument, I omit discussion of them here.

made from dough were handled (as were branches of pine, a fertile
plant), and that the women indulged in *aischrologia* ('obscene language') in imitation of Iambe whose obscene behaviour made
Demeter laugh.[22] All of this would have marked the break with
everyday existence. The most striking event of the day was the
ascent from underground chambers of the *Antletriai* ('Balers') bearing the rotten remains of pigs which had been thrown down there at
some earlier date; these were placed on the altars, whence they were
taken to fertilise the fields by being mixed with the seed-corn. The
second day was *Nesteia* ('Fasting'),[23] which Plutarch describes as the
most 'grim-faced day' when they 'fasted beside the goddess'[24] sitting
on the ground[25] on piles of antaphrodisiac *Vitex agnus-castus*.[26]
These activities represented the grief of Demeter at the loss of her
daughter, and her own refusal to eat. On the final day, the celebrations of Persephone's return began. It was called *Kalligeneia* ('Fair
Birth') and involved 'the eating of meat' and the 'ritual slaughter of
pigs'.[27] Normal life is thus restored as rotten carcasses give way to
cooked food, and gloom and the public handling of sexual objects to
rejoicing and a new fertility.[28] Hermogenes says it was the custom to
release prisoners at the Thesmophoria;[29] this would obviously be
relevant to the play, but it is not known whether this was done in the
fifth century.

   Reference to a number of these aspects of the Thesmophoria is
made in the play, such as the restriction to citizen women (293f.,
329–31), the closure of the courts (76–80), fertility (in Mnesilochus'
parodic prayers to Demeter and Persephone for a good marriage for
his children (286–91)), and the fasting on Nesteia (947–9, 984). At the
Thesmophoria, the ritual actions of the women are designed to help
the fertility and well-being of the city; in the second part of this

---

[22] Apollod. 1.5.1, and *H. Dem.* 203–5; also at Pellene (Paus. 7.27.9) and in Sicily (Diod. 5.4.7).
[23] Diod. 5.4.7, talking of the Sicilians, says that on this day the women enacted the 'old life'
    before civilisation.   [24] *Dem.* 30.   [25] Plut. *Mor.* 378D
[26] Plin. *NH* 24.59. On this herb and women, King 1983: 122f.; it was an antaphrodisiac at the
    festival of Hera on Samos, 'a time of reversed order which establishes the *thesmos*, the order
    of normal life, all the more securely when the goddess is then returned, purified, to her
    ancient house' (Burkert 1985: 135; cf. Athen. 672A–3D = Menodotus, *FGH* 541 F 1; Anac.
    352; R. C. T. Parker 1983: 83 n. 36).
[27] Schol. *Frogs* 338. There were similar activities on Delos (Bruneau 1970: 285–90; Detienne
    1979b: 192f.).   [28] For the idea of a festival as creating fertility, Hes. *Op.* 735f.
[29] *Staseis* 31: a slave freed by a woman; this was also the custom at the City Dionysia and
    Panathenaea (Dem. 22.68 with schol.).

chapter we shall see that the women have a similarly beneficial effect on the city (with additional benefits for its drama). Equally importantly, the play is structurally related to the festival's ideology: the movement of the women onto male 'space' is mirrored in the play's action. This is symbolised by the ever increasing presence of 'the female' on stage. We begin with two adult males in Euripides, nearly seventy at the time and far from his youthful habits (173f.), and Mnesilochus, the comic old man (146). The female is introduced in Agathon's effeminate servant, and increased by Agathon himself, who, dressed as a woman, sings both the male and female parts of his lyric. There is a further increase through Mnesilochus' depilation and disguise as a woman. During the 'rites', the female naturally dominates (the male intruder Cleisthenes is, like Agathon's servant, womanish), until the final scene in which everyone except the Scythian archer either is a woman or is dressed as one.

As at the festival, the women are put in contact with areas normally closed to them. The early part has a strong political flavour. The festival is referred to as an 'Assembly' (84, 277 etc.), in which 'orators' (292) address the demos of the women (335, 353, 1145) to discuss *psephismata* ('proposals') and *nomoi* ('laws', 361). This lengthy scene in the Assembly opens in an elaborately formal manner (which contrasts with the haste in the opening Assembly in *Acharnians*), with prose and verse prayers for the city. In 373–9 there is a parody of the actual form of the minutes of the Boule.[30] There is also a parody of the *Arai* ('Comminations') which were formally recited at the start of an Assembly or Boule meeting (332ff.).[31] The traditional curses on political crimes, such as treating with the Mede or setting up a tyranny, are mixed with poetical ones of treating with Euripides and sexual ones of standing in the way of adultery etc., thus creating a blend of areas of life which will be important for the understanding of the play as a whole. In having the women put Euripides on trial, Aristophanes is once again pushing the logic of the Thesmophoria's ideology to comic limits: the festival is one of reversal and the male courts close, so why should not the women usurp the judicial function too? No matter that a highly civilised

---

[30] E.g. Thuc. 4.118.11. The names of the officers may have been specially chosen: Lysicles (cf. *Kn.* 765) and Sostratus (cf. *Clouds* 678) at least were notorious effeminates.

[31] See Rogers on 331; Rhodes 1972: 37.

institution like the lawcourts sits uneasily on the Nesteia's day of the
'old life'.

The women's involvement with sacrifice is represented, albeit
in a highly distorted image, in the scene of Mnesilochus' seizure of
the wine-skin child (689ff.). Indeed, given the nature of the Nesteia,
it is unlikely that there was any normal sacrificial activity on that
day: a male *mageiros* may have carried out the slitting of the throat at
the Thesmophoria, but it is unlikely that he did it on the Nesteia, a
day of abstention from meats, or in the manner of Mnesilochus'
ritual. A human sacrifice would be unusual at any time, but this one
is not made any less anomalous by the fact that the 'child' is in fact a
wine-skin. Mnesilochus 'sacrifices' the wine-skin so that the wine
flows over the thigh-bones (693f.), thus combining the ideas of
splashing the blood over the altar (usually done before the cooking),
lifting the sacrificial victim above the altar for slaughter, and pouring
wine over the burning meats. The attempted denial of sanctuary to
one who has fled to an altar, and the manner in which Mnesilochus
himself combines the roles of victim and sacrificer are both unusual.
What are we to make of this confusion of sacrificial codes? It could be
described as merely farcical, but as with the sacrifice in *Lysistrata*, it
would be unwise to stop at that. As in that play it is more likely that
this sacrifice parodies the practice of having, at festivals like the
Thesmophoria, the Buphonia and that of Demeter Chthonia at Hermione, sacrifices which are themselves 'parodies' and reversals of
normal practice. The second-order parody serves both to make the
audience laugh and to mark the unusualness not only of the Thesmophoria but also of *this* Thesmophoria, in which the women drink
wine on the Nesteia.[32]

The unusual licence offered the women in matters of obscenity
and sexuality is as boldly marked in the play as the events enacted at
a fertility festival like the Thesmophoria and the conventions of the
comic genre would lead one to expect. The tone is set by Mnesilochus, as he goes up to the Thesmophorion, with his somewhat saucy
prayers to Demeter and Persephone that the *choiros* of his daughter

---

[32] Demeter refuses wine during her mourning (cf. *H. Dem.* 206–8) preferring a *kukeon* of
'barley and water'. On this drink, in general Delatte 1955; Richardson 1974: 344–8: 'it
belongs to an intermediate stage between that of eating the grains (or offering them to the
gods) whole, and the introduction of fine milling and baking' (344), the liminal stage, in
other words, between the abnormalities of the festival and the normalities of civilised life.

should find a rich husband,[33] and that his son, *Posthaliskos*, 'Little Tommy', should have intelligence and wit (286–91). There is, as we have seen, a certain amount of *aischrologia* in the initial prayers at the Assembly, which call down curses on those who prevent sexual misdemeanours (339–46), but it is the debate that provides the best examples. In complaining of the effect of Euripides' tragedies on their husbands' perception of domestic life, the First Woman catalogues a number of female activities which his plays have made problematic. It is constantly assumed by the men that there are adulterers in the house, so that love affairs are more difficult than before, and it is impossible to bring in suppositious children: 'As soon as they come back from their seats in the theatre, they look suspiciously at us and immediately search to see that there isn't an adulterer hidden in the house: we can't do anything of the things we used to in the good old days' (395–9; cf. 399–409). The Second Woman complains in 'unintentionally' ambiguous language of Euripides' adverse effect on her trade in garlands (446–52):[34]

> My husband died in Cyprus, you see, leaving me five little kids, whom I've been struggling to feed by weaving garlands in the perfume-market. In the past, it's true, I didn't do it too badly, but now this character with his tragedies has persuaded men that there are no gods, so that I can't sell them even at half-price.

Shameful speech is most obvious in the disguised Mnesilochus' scandalous catalogue of female sexual misbehaviour, which he introduces with these provoking words: 'Since we're alone together, we must speak frankly – there's no-one to tell tales. Why are we constantly accusing Euripides and complaining if he uses his knowledge to talk of two or three of our misdemeanours, when we've committed tens of thousands of them?' (471–5). He goes on to give an account of 'his own' life, which has involved, after only three days' marriage, an affair with a man who had deflowered him at seven: the husband is fobbed off with a story about stomach-ache (476–88). His catalogue then runs through affairs with slaves and muleteers, tactical consumption of garlic, adulterers hidden under skirts, suppositious children, and, as the women advance on him, stealing corn, taking meat for their panders from the Apaturia, axings, poisonings,

---

[33] For this pun, Radermacher 1940.

[34] For the sexual overtones, Henderson 1975: 134f.; the making of garlands has become a suspicious activity anyway (400f.).

and patricide. Mnesilochus is, however, no Baubo or Iambe, and the women do not laugh.

After seizing hold of him, they set about determining his true sex and there follows the pursuit of Mnesilochus' errant organ (643–8):

> *Cleisth.* Stand up straight. Where are you pushing your cock down
>   to?
> *Woman.* It's peeped out here – and a good colour it is too!
> *Cleisth.* Now where is it?
> *Woman.* It's round the front again.
> *Cleisth.* Well it's not on this side.
> *Woman.* No – it's come back here again!
> *Cleisth.* It's as if you had an isthmus, my friend: you're pushing
>   your cock up and down more often than the Corinthians go
>   back and forth!

This bout of the handling of sexual objects provides an amusing parallel for the similar handling ascribed to the festival.

Myths

It is not only the details and structures of the festival that the play imitates. Also relevant are two kinds of myth, first, those warning of the perils awaiting men trying to infiltrate festivals like the Thesmophoria,[35] and second, the myth associated with the festival itself. In its punishment of Euripides and Mnesilochus, *Thesmophoriazusae* conveys the same message as myths of improper male involvement in Demeter's rites. The goddess is as dangerous as Dionysus in this respect, as Mnesilochus unwittingly reminds us, when he questions Agathon in a parody of Aeschylus' *Edonoi*, a play about the punishments of Lycurgus for his attack on Bacchic rites (134ff.).[36] The earliest attested myth of this sort is in Herodotus.[37] Miltiades of Athens was advised by Timo, a priestess of Demeter and Persephone, that if he wished to capture Paros he should enter the shrine of Demeter Thesmophoros. This he did, 'perhaps to tamper with things it is sacrilege to tamper with', but once over the wall he was seized with such panic that he shattered his leg in his haste to

---

[35] Detienne 1979b: 184f.; modern parallels in Brumfield 1981: 125 and Tarsouli 1944: 194 (I owe this to John Petropoulos).

[36] Cf. A. frr. 57–67 (*TGF* 3.178–85); Apollod. 3.5.1; West 1991: 27–32. Richard Seaford (pers. comm.) draws attention to the similarities between the treatment of Mnesilochus in this play, Pentheus in Euripides' *Bacchae* and Lycurgus in this trilogy.   [37] 6.134–6.

leave. Back in Athens, he was fined fifty talents for his failure to capture the island and died shortly afterwards of gangrene-poisoning. Aeneas Tacticus[38] and Plutarch[39] tell closely similar stories about Peisistratus at Eleusis and Solon at Colias. In their war with Athens for Salamis, the Megarians attempted to capture the Athenian women at the Thesmophoria festival one night. In each case, the attempt ended in disaster: in Plutarch, youths were disguised as women to massacre the Megarians with sacrificial implements; in Aeneas, Peisistratus ambushed the Megarians and sailed with some of the women to Megara, where the leading citizens were attacked as they came to welcome what they took to be their own men returning with a cargo of prisoners. The tale of the hero of the Messenian resistance, Aristomenes, links political and sacrificial elements. He tried to capture the women at Demeter's temple in Aegila, but, with his men, he was wounded by the sacrificial knives and spits wielded by the women; beaten with torches, he was tied up and escaped only because the priestess was in love with him.[40] A worse fate befell Battus of Cyrene, who, not satisfied with seeing 'the first things of the Thesmophoria, display of which brought no harm to the viewer or the displayer', insisted on looking at 'the secret things it is better not to see'. He was attacked by the *sphaktriai*, 'female sacrificers', who had naked swords and bloody faces and attempted to castrate him.[41] The repeated motif of the abnormal use of sacrificial instruments should be noted.

Mnesilochus' attempt to infiltrate the festival represents a failure similar to that of the mythical examples. Like Aristomenes, he is tied up by the women, and the Old Woman who guards him threatens with her torch anyone who tries to free him (916f.). Despite admiration for his anatomy (644), none of the women is sufficiently in love with him to wish to liberate him, and his condign punishment for having tried to become a woman is to be exposed to public ridicule in a saffron dress.

Mnesilochus, however, suffers little more than temporary discomfort and ridicule. By contrast, Euripides, the instigator of the

---

[38] 4.8–11.   [39] *Sol.* 8   [40] Paus. 4.17.1.

[41] Ael. fr. 44. For other similar tales, Hdt. 6.16.2 (and 6.75.3); Parthen. *Erot. Path.* 8.1: Diod. 32.10f. For the exclusion of men from festivals of Demeter, Wächter 1910: 130f.; Sokolowski 1955: no. 61.8–9 (Mylasa, 3rd cent.); 1969: no. 63.10 (Laconia); R. C. T. Parker 1983: 179 n. 193.

crime, undergoes a more radical punishment. At the start of the play, he has two significant characteristics: he is an adult male, who, unlike Agathon, no longer goes in for dressing as a woman to write his female parts (173f.), and he is a playwright noted for his attacks on women. Towards the end of the play, after being forced to take the female role of Echo behind the scenes, he makes a final appearance on stage dressed in comic guise as an old woman with a dancing girl; he has then to make a truce with the women whereby he will write no more plays about their misdemeanours. Both of his characteristics therefore, of masculinity and anti-woman playwright, are lost to him, and one might say that, in a manner reminiscent of Battus, he suffers something of a symbolic castration, both as a man and as an artist.

Turning to the mythology of the festival itself, we find that the play follows closely if grotesquely the pattern of the story of Demeter and Persephone.[42] In the myth, Persephone is taken away by Hades; with her descend the pigs of Eubuleus, animals which are representative of fertility and constituted the main sacrificial victim for Demeter.[43] Fertility fails in the world, causing famine and a breach in sacrifice to the gods,[44] while Demeter, bearing a torch, searches for Persephone.[45] In the *Homeric Hymn*, she disguises herself as an old woman before meeting the daughters of Celeus at the well.[46] Persephone is finally released when Demeter strikes a bargain with the gods that normal fertility will be resumed, so long as her daughter is returned to spend part of the year on earth. There was a version in which Demeter herself went down to Hades.[47] This version is given explicitly in some sources,[48] and is implied by others.[49] It is not found before the Hellenistic age, but the possibility that it existed in earlier Orphic tradition remains: Orphic versions of the Demeter and Persephone myth do not use the motif of the famine which forces the

---

[42] E.g. Förster 1874; Richardson 1974: esp. 74–86; on the *Homeric Hymn*, R. C. T. Parker 1991.

[43] Bruneau 1970: 269–90; Richardson 1974: 82; Orph. fr. 49.41.   [44] *H. Dem.* 305–13.

[45] *H. Dem.* 48, 61; cf. 52. Was there a torch-lit search for Persephone at the Thesmophoria as at Eleusis (Richardson 1974: 162)? The only evidence is *Thesm.* 655–85, which would then be another parody of an aspect of the festival.

[46] 94–111; cf. Paus. 1.39.1 (from Pamphos).   [47] Harrison & Obbink 1986.

[48] E.g. *H. Orph.* 41.5 Quandt; schol. Pi. *Ol.* 6.160a; Olympiod. *In Pl. Phd.* 67c8–9; Hygin. *Fab.* 257; schol. Ar. *Plutus* 431 (referring it to a *barathron* in Attica).

[49] Especially stories concerning Ascalabus: Lact. *Comm. Stat. Theb.* 3.511 (Jahnke); Philicus, *H. Dem.* (*SH* 676–80; 3rd cent.) would be the earliest if *agou* in 48 means 'bring her up yourself'.

negotiated settlement, so they must have had another means of raising Persephone.[50]

Euripides too loses a relative, and one who has characteristics of Persephone about him. Mnesilochus, who is in the play only referred to as 'relative' (e.g. 1165), is dressed as a woman in the *krokotos* robe associated with Demeter (253), and takes the part of a comic Persephone.[51] In his guises as Telephus threatened with death by the Greeks, as Palamedes who was unjustly done to death by them, as Helen in the clutches of Theoclymenus, a man whose name has chthonic associations, and as Andromeda awaiting death at the jaws of the sea-monster, he plays roles not unlike that of Persephone in the grasp of Hades.

Pigs accompanied Persephone to the Underworld, and appropriately enough, having agreed that he will go himself, if Agathon cannot, Mnesilochus is prepared not only as a woman, but also as a sacrificial pig.[52] The point is made three times. When he cries out at being cut with Agathon's razor by Euripides, the tragedian tells him 'shut up, or I'll put a peg in your mouth' (221f.). This butchers did before sacrifice to see that the pig's tongue was not measly and the pig therefore impure.[53] Then, on being singed, he says he will become a *delphakion* ('sucking pig', 237): the scholiast comments that these animals were singed after sacrifice to make them smooth.[54] At 239, in an obscene pun, he is warned to watch his *kerkos* ('pig's tail') as the flames come near to singe him.[55]

Like Demeter, Euripides goes in search of his relative (if Demeter's descent to Hades was known, the parallel would be particularly close), and he too eventually disguises himself as an old

---

[50] Richardson 1974: 84, 156, 259.

[51] For the *krokos*, Demeter and the underworld, S. fr. 451 and Richardson 1974 on *H. Dem.* 6, 19, 428. As a garment, the *krokotos* 'characterises both the strongly sexual female and the sexually somewhat ambivalent' (Sourvinou-Inwood 1988: 128, and in general 119–35; see also passages collected at Headlam 1922: 384 on Herod. 8.28). Crocon was son of Demeter's lover Triptolemus (Paus. 1.38.1f.; Hsch. s.v. *Rheitoi*; Bekker, *Anec. Gr.* 1 273; Töpffer 1889: 101–10).

[52] He also speaks of becoming a *psilos*, 'smooth-shaven' or a 'light-armed warrior', i.e. a non-hoplite and even non-citizen (232).   [53] Rogers on *Kn.* 375.

[54] There may be an echo here of Demeter's other great festival, the Eleusinian Mysteries, where initiation involved having a torch brought up to the initiand from below (Burkert 1985: 459 n. 7).

[55] This union of piglet and woman will later be picked up in the pun used to threaten Mnesilochus with punishment for his slander, 'we'll pluck his *choiros*' (537f.).

woman (1199).[56] Finally, as in the myth, it is through a bargain that he frees Mnesilochus: in return for his liberty, Euripides undertakes not to reveal any more of the women's iniquities on his stage, just as Demeter agrees to restore fertility to the earth in return for her daughter. At the last, just as the divinities returned home, so do the women (1228f.), and Mnesilochus (1204).

In fact, the mythical events of *Kalligeneia* are doubly represented at the end of the play, because there is a double visual joke on the person of Persephone. Her role is split between Mnesilochus, the lost relative disguised as a woman, and Teredon, the alluring young dancing girl. This equivalence between play and myth is then splendidly confirmed when, in answer to the Chorus's most insistent prayer to the Thesmophoroi to attend their rites – 'Appear, come, we beseech you, two Thesmophoroi, mighty goddesses, if ever before you harkened and came, come now, approach us too here, we beseech you' (1155–9) – there appear on stage an old woman and a nubile young girl, in an irreverent parody of the reunion of divine mother and daughter.

We can now tie up the relationships between play, rites and myths. Allowing for the comic distortions introduced by having a mature man play a young girl, there is a fourfold homology between the actions of the women at the festival, the fate of Persephone in the myth, the changing use of the pigs in the ritual, and Mnesilochus in the play. In the ritual, wives move abnormally into male space, take on male roles and involve themselves in death, infertility and corruption, before returning to their normal way of life. In the myth, a girl, ripe for fertile marriage, is united not with a young husband but with the god of death, for a period which entails general sterility, before returning to a newly productive earth. The pigs follow a similar pattern. In the first stage, 'raw' pigs, like the 'raw' Persephone, are thrown into underground caverns, where they rot in a fruitless fashion: the pig does not belong in the earth. This rotting, which is a natural form of cooking, acts as an intermediate stage between the raw pigs and the cooked ones with which the ceremony ended,[57] and the rotten remains play their part in restoring fertility

[56] Called Artemisia, like the Carian warrior-queen whose naval prowess caused Xerxes to remark 'My men have become women, my women men' (Hdt. 8.88.3).

[57] Cf. for this opposition of 'raw' and 'cooked' the Eretrian cemetery where those who had not reached maturity were inhumed, while the mature were cremated, and the cremation of adult Athenians but inhumation of Plataeans and slaves after Marathon (Vidal-Naquet 1981c: 173).

when they are mixed with the seed-corn for the next year.[58] Mnesilochus, similarly, is to be found 'in the wrong place', suffers role-reversal in his disguise as a woman and *psilos*, is represented as a pig, indulges in obscene talk and has his *schemata* handled (643–8); he too, as will become clearer later in this chapter, has a hand in the restoration of fertility and returns at the end to his normal place 'in the manner of a man' (1204), when the women's dispute with Euripides is resolved.

Thesmophoria and Euripidean tragedy[59]

Before we can discuss the point of the parodies of the Thesmophoria in the play, we must consider a second set of relationships, those between Euripidean tragedy and this festival.[60] We have already seen that the fundamental notion behind the Thesmophoria could be described in terms of the crossing of boundaries by the women and it is this which provides the link between Euripides and Thesmophoria. As the women at the festival have moved into male areas, so Euripides has not only infiltrated a women's rite, but will also be shown to have transgressed in his tragedies over two further boundaries: first, that between tragedy and comedy, and second (and complementary to the first), that between what is and is not appropriate subject-matter for tragedy. For both of these condign punishment is forthcoming, this time at the hands not of the women but of Aristophanes.

The first transgression: onto comic space

Euripidean tragedy is remarkable for the boldness with which it introduces its innovations. For instance, the conventions of the *deus ex machina* may be exploited by putting it in the middle of the play rather than the end, as happens in *Heracles*, where the arrival of

---

[58] A similar intermediate phase is attested for Eretria, where the women at the Thesmophoria cooked their meat in the sun, not the fire (Plut. *Mor.* 298B). Compare too the *panspermia* made without milling and baking on the Chytroi day of the Anthesteria (Bremmer 1983a: 120f.).

[59] A number of the ideas found here are also in Zeitlin 1981; they were arrived at independently. She should be consulted for matters only touched on here. On the tragic parodies, Rau 1967: 42–89; 98–114.

[60] The parallelism between poetry and festival is suggested by the use of prayers at the start both of the scene of tragic parody (39ff.) and of the parody of the Thesmophoric Assembly (295ff.).

Iris and Lyssa is not used to bring a disturbed action to a close but to start the events on a new and terrible course, just when it appeared that all was well. Again, in the *Troades*, when the chorus use the *ea! ea!* formula that normally introduces the *deus*, it is a sign of the final hopelessness of the Trojans' position that it is not a god that appears but Talthybius with commands for the final destruction of the city. In *Helen*, Euripides makes play with the recognition scene, by having Helen and Menelaus twice get to what one expects to be their mutual recognition (565f., 588f.), but then delaying the actual recognition until we have embarked on what we expect to be a lengthy messenger speech.

More relevant however to our purposes is his use of comic features in his tragedies. *Helen*, produced the year before *Thesmophoriazusae* with the *Andromeda*, is also one of those tragedies that are remarkable for the way in which they introduce elements more associated with comedy, thus blurring the relatively sharp distinction that was maintained in Athens between the two genres.[61] The scenes where the shipwrecked Menelaus comes on stage and meets the Old Woman guarding the door are straightforwardly comic, although Euripides skilfully prevents them becoming farce or burlesque. The scene is framed in a way that again makes comic use of questions of identity and recognition. Menelaus enters just after Helen has complained in her song that she has 'destroyed the Achaeans who are dead' (385), and when he leaves the Chorus immediately comes out to confide to the audience that they've heard from a prophetess that Menelaus is not dead. Menelaus enters in rags like the best Euripidean kings, but Euripides writes parts of the scene as if he wished himself to make fun of this habit of so dressing his heroes, when Menelaus is made to draw attention to his rags in a way that shows an odd concern for couture (414–24). Menelaus' entrance has been similarly unusual, when he began his monologue with a comically over-poetic curse on his grandfather, which soon mutates to petty arrogance as the recital of his genealogy reminds him who he is (386–96). When he confronts the Old Woman, Menelaus is roundly abused by her and treated with complete scorn in a scene that, though good comic knock-about stuff, nevertheless manages to generate a certain pathos.

[61] On this boundary, Winnington-Ingram 1969; Knox 1979: 250–74; Seidensticker 1982; Taplin 1986.

We may note here other ways in which *Helen* has features of importance to the *Thesmophoriazusae*. In it, Helen describes herself in terms that recall the rape of Persephone, saying that she was snatched away when picking flowers (241–51), and there is a long chorus which associates Demeter in a striking way with Cybele (1301–68). Furthermore, *Helen* makes much use of features from the *Odyssey*. It is modelled on Menelaus' own story in *Odyssey* 4 of his voyage to Egypt, though it blends this with Stesichorus' version in which Helen was hidden there while her phantom was sent to Troy. Menelaus does not have to wrestle with Proteus, but that is the name of the father (4) of the dangerous Theoclymenus with whom he has to deal and whose name is also chosen from the *Odyssey*; in dealing with Theoclymenus he gets help from his opponent's sister Theonoe, who was formerly known as Eido (11), just as he did in the *Odyssey* from Proteus' similarly-named daughter Eidothea. This help from the seer Theonoe parallels the various advantageous prophecies and helpful tellers of the future (like Theoclymenus) who aid Odysseus and Telemachus. The *Odyssey* is itself a work much concerned with disguise, identity problems and recognition: the skilful way in which Homer avoids Odysseus' recognition by Penelope in *Odyssey* 19 has obvious similarities with Euripides' play with recognition discussed above.[62] Both works concern a husband's ultimately successful attempts to secure his wife once again in the face of violent suitors.[63]

In its use of comic motifs and material, its play with and subversion of tragic conventions, its use of illusion and recognition, and its complex intertextual relationships with a famous predecessor which it 'parodies', *Helen* is a striking and unusual play, which, as the struggles of commentators to deal with it show, is stretching the bounds of tragedy and using many things which comedy might have felt to be its own trade-marks.

I want to suggest that Aristophanes in *Thesmophoriazusae* is replying in kind to this *démarche* by the tragedian, in which he had expanded tragedy's range by incorporating comic features. Aristophanes produces a similar blend of the two genres using similar techniques and devices, so as to demonstrate not only that the range

---

[62] Cf. most recently Goldhill 1991: 1–68.
[63] Compare too Theonoe's account of the *concilium deorum* (876ff.), which has its predecessors in *Od.* 1.19ff. and 5.1ff.

of comedy can be likewise extended, but also to submit tragedy and tragic conventions to a radical critique, in which a comparison of the two genres reveals comedy's much greater flexibility and potential. The play thus becomes a continuous demonstration in various spheres of the superiority of comedy as a dramatic form, and inflicts upon Euripides, for this transgression onto comic territory, a punishment no less severe than that he suffers for his meddling with the Thesmophoria.[64]

The first area where comedy's superiority is shown is in the matter of language. The early scenes of the play imply a preciosity in tragic language which not only distances it from 'plain', everyday speech but also renders it incapable of tolerating the intrusion of certain kinds of words: by contrast, it is in just such words which are destructive of tragic discourse that comic language revels. Mnesilochus is confronted in Euripides' opening lines with the opacity shown by tragic diction even when it involves simple words (5–9):

> *Eur.* But it is not necessary for you to hear all you will straightway see in person.
> *Mnes.* How do you mean? Tell me again. It's not necessary for me to hear?
> *Eur.* Not at any rate what you are going to see.
> *Mnes.* So I mustn't see either?
> *Eur.* No, not at any rate what you must hear.
> *Mnes.* What are you advising me? It's awfully clever.

His incomprehension is not lessened when the style is raised for the description of the creation of eye and ear in 14–18, which brilliantly catch the tone of Euripidean expository passages: 'When Aether first was made discrete and gendered living things within her, for sight first created he the eye, in imitation of the sun's round disk, and th' ear for hearing, as a funnel bored.' Further up the stylistic scale, the epicene Servant's prayer similarly draws cries of 'What's he saying?' and 'Rubbish' (45): 'Let all mortal flesh keep silence, and seal their lips; for the choir of the Muses dwells in the halls of the master-singers. Let the windless aether halt its blasts, and the wave of the sea keep still' (39–44). This language finally provokes Mnesilochus into going on the offensive and adding to the Servant's climactic words in

---

[64] Devastating as this critique may turn out to be, the play is in many ways a tribute to Euripides through its acknowledgement of the remarkable broadening that he brought to the tragic genre.

49f. 'Our sweet-voiced leader, Agathon, is on the point of . . .' the obscenity 'not – be *fucked* surely?' (50): the tragic discourse collapses but the comic comes to life. This point is reinforced by the complementary joke of Mnesilochus' use of the poetic 'windless aether' (51), which causes laughter in his vulgar mouth in a way that it did not in the lyric context of the prayer (43). The technique of juxtaposing colloquial and high-flown, comic and tragic language then persists through the scenes with Agathon to establish this opposition as a key to the understanding of the play, and to show how fragile tragic language is compared with comic.

It was traditional to talk of poetic composition in metaphors drawn from other crafts,[65] but when Aristophanes has the Servant sow these metaphors by the sack, the gap that in fact exists between metaphor and subject yawns comically, as Mnesilochus tarnishes their quasi-Pindaric grandeur (52–62):

> *Serv.* He comes to lay the props for the framework of his song, and
>   bends the novel arches of the words; some parts he turns as on a
>   lathe, others glues he; thoughts he moulds, and alters names;
>   like wax he pours them, rounds them off and funnels . . .
> *Mnes.* And fellates![66]
> *Serv.* What bumpkin to our coping comes?
> *Mnes.* One who having turned it round and twisted it up, under the
>   coping of you and your sweet-voiced poet will fix his cock in
>   the mould!

The gap is equally apparent when the Servant himself is permitted to reduce the metaphors to a fatuously concrete state with his lines: 'It's winter, so it isn't easy to bend the strophes, unless he puts them out of doors in the sun' (67–9).

After language, the play shows that in matters of illusion too tragedy is, in comparison with comedy, generally deficient.[67] The importance of illusion has been signalled in the prologue, where, as we saw, Euripides and Mnesilochus discuss perception and its organs, and Mnesilochus is reduced to bold statements that he can certainly see something, which have immediately to be qualified, as in 26f. 'Indeed, at least I think so', and more strikingly in 34, with its double qualifying particle *ge*: 'Certainly not – at least as far as I at any

---

[65] Harriott 1969: 92–104; Murray 1981: 98f.

[66] Once again, an obscenity invests these craft images with an unexpected sexual orientation. On this word in comedy and elsewhere, Jocelyn 1980; Bain 1991: 74–7.

[67] For the illusion of tragedy, cf. Grg. 82 B 23 DK; *Diss. Log.* 3.10 (Diels & Kranz 1951: II 410f.).

rate know.' This is picked up later when he is uncertain whether he sees Agathon or Cyrene (97f.), or himself or Cleisthenes (235). The verbs *horan* ('see') and *akouein* ('hear') are emphasised in the prologue and are scattered in a greater than usual profusion through the early part of the play.[68] These ideas are, as we have seen, important in *Helen*, and also in *Andromeda*, where the Echo scene involves hearing one who is not there to be seen.

The First Woman in the Assembly complains at Euripides' revelation to husbands of women's various transgressions:[69] common, everyday occurrences, like weaving a garland or dropping a jug, take on a sinister significance when viewed in the emotionally charged light of a Euripidean tragedy (400–4). However, Mnesilochus demonstrates from his own 'experience' that Euripides is only very partially informed on such matters (474f. quoted above): for knowledge of female wickedness, one must consult comedy, since tragedy is a poor reflection of life in the *oikos*.

In the parodies, Aristophanes demonstrates that the very idea of tragic drama is only possible if its audience suspends disbelief and accepts, on tragedy's own terms, the artificial conventions and the illusion of reality: tragedy requires the protective environs of the theatre in order to operate. Thus in the parodies of *Telephus* and *Palamedes*,[70] Mnesilochus finds that the devices used for escape in tragedy cannot cope with certain 'extra-dramatic realities' of the comic stage. As Telephus, he seizes the woman's child, only to discover it is a wine-skin: in tragedy women suckle babies, in 'reality' they will do anything for a drink. As Oiax from *Palamedes*, he decides to send a message on oar-blades, but, as he soon realises, such stage-properties are not simply lying around in normal life: 'Like Oiax, I'll write on oar-blades and throw them around – but the oar-blades aren't here!' (770f.).

The parodies of *Helen* and *Andromeda* establish the point more graphically. When a 'spectator' like the Old Woman or the Scythian

---

[68] Seeing and hearing are precisely the things the men must not do at the Thesmophoria.

[69] The women wish to have their cake and eat it: they complain that Euripides reveals their wrong-doing and makes it impossible for them to misbehave. Note that their reaction to Mnesilochus' speech is not one of denial but of outrage that any woman should expose these deeds 'openly' (525).

[70] There is a thematic link between these two stories, in that Palamedes also seized a child, Telemachus, to prove Odysseus' sanity: *Cypria*, *EGF* p. 18 Kinkel; Hygin. *Fab.* 95; Lucian, *De Domo* 30; Apollod. *Epit.* 3.7. On Euripides' play, Scodel 1980: 43–63.

refuses to co-operate and see the actors as Helen or Menelaus, but insists on treating the drama as part of their own everyday reality, then tragic drama collapses. The *Helen* cannot be played if the Old Woman warns one of the characters not to be taken in by the role played by another (892–4), confuses the mythical Proteus with the recently deceased Athenian Proteas (874–6), or complains at the reference, perfectly reasonable for tragedy, to the theatre's altar as a tomb (886–8). *Andromeda* becomes a farce if the Echo-scene is over-played or the Scythian views the *innamoramento* of 'Perseus' and 'Andromeda' as a rather unappetising homosexual romp: presumably the fact that every tragic love affair is 'homosexual', because all the actors are men, was normally suppressed in the minds of the audience, but here the reality is brusquely revealed. After bumping along their rocky course (and it must have been very difficult to play these tragic lines with the interruptions of the Old Woman and Scythian and the laughter of the audience), the 'tragedies' eventually collapse before the further realities of the Prytanis and the Archer with his sword (923). Even plays like *Helen*, therefore, which make apparently clever use of illusion cannot display the bravura use of it that comedy is able to. As the tragedies are falling apart under the assault of the non-believers, the comedy is succeeding brilliantly. Furthermore, Aristophanes takes on an especially difficult task in choosing for parody a scene from the *Helen* which is itself highly comic: he must produce in effect a parody of a parody. For good measure, Aristophanes even permits the actors to puncture their own illusion-making by a joke about the herbs of Euripides/Menelaus (909f.):

> *Eur*. You look just like Helen.
> *Hel*. And you like Menelaus, as far as I can tell from your lavender.

But we are not finished with illusion in the play. When Mnesilochus seizes the child, the play becomes an overt parody of *Telephus*, but a moment's thought shows that we have been in a play very like it for some time: as we saw on *Acharnians*, in *Telephus*, the king, disguised as his opposite, a beggar, infiltrated the hostile Greek camp and made a speech in self-defence; he was forced to seize Orestes when a messenger brought news of the presence of a spy in the camp and a search was started. Nearly one hundred lines before Mnesilochus seizes the child (689), Cleisthenes has come in to warn

the women (574), who institute a search (656ff.); before that Mnesilochus has infiltrated the Thesmophoria in disguise and made a speech
of self-justification. The slightest of hints that we are in a '*Telephus*' is
given in a quotation from that play in the last line of Mnesilochus'
scandalous speech (519),[71] but this is scarcely sufficient to alert many
to the double nature of the action.

Again, the audience came to see a comedy, but they get instead
a series of tragedies, at which, however, they can legitimately laugh.
The comedy, furthermore, is remarkable because, apart from the
parabasis (where it is normal), *Thesmophoriazusae* in general avoids
the rupture of the dramatic illusion caused by referring to itself as a
play, thus imitating a characteristic of tragic drama. The play begins
as an ostensible defence of Euripides' plays about women, but ends
as a massive critique; it pretends to defend Euripides from the charge
of slandering women, yet makes much use of *Helen* which actually
rehabilitates this most slandered of heroines. The hopes the spectator
may have had of seeing the women at the Thesmophoria are also
disappointed, since all they see is a comic reflection of their own
Assembly. This is carried out by women, but even these are in fact
men dressed up as women. All of this play with illusion and
contradiction functions without problem in comedy, whereas in
tragedy it runs the risk of changing the nature of the genre, as many
may have felt Euripides had done in *Helen*. Comedy's flexibility is
emblematised in Mnesilochus, a man, dressed as a comic character
disguised as a woman, who plays a variety of tragic parts, male and
female. The persistent triumph of comedy over tragedy is finally
symbolised in Euripides' abandonment of tragic stratagems in favour
of disguise as a comic bawd with a dancing girl.

If comedy can do all that tragedy can and more, what further
need have we of tragedy? Not much perhaps, and even less when it is
realised that *Thesmophoriazusae* is made up of four plays of Euripides
– *Telephus*, *Palamedes*, *Helen* and *Andromeda* – plus a comic coda
involving a bawd, a dancing girl and a comic policeman. Is this not
exactly the pattern during the Peloponnesian War of a day at the City
Dionysia, with its three tragedies, satyr-play and comedy?[72] It will
rightly be objected that *Andromeda* was not a satyr-play, but the

---

[71] = E. fr. 711. The other parodies are clearly sign-posted (a relatively unusual procedure for
Aristophanes): 134f., 769–71, 851f., 1010–2, 1059–64.

[72] Pickard-Cambridge 1988: 66, 79f.

obscenity with which Aristophanes invests it, in the unappetising love-scene between Mnesilochus and Euripides and the sexually explicit language of the Scythian, who is soon to suffer from satyriasis when he sees the girl, is not inappropriate to that genre's predilection for such matters.[73] Not only therefore is comedy a much more flexible and versatile genre than tragedy, it can even save us from having to sit through long stretches of tragedy by abbreviating a whole festival-day's drama into a single play; only the Birds could offer as much.[74] Finally, in *Alexandros–Palamedes–Troades* Euripides appears to have revived the idea of composing three connected tragedies on aspects of the Trojan story, that is, a trilogy of the type now represented only by the *Oresteia*.[75] In *Telephus–Palamedes–Helen*, Aristophanes has done the same, by dramatising aspects of the story which, as in Euripides, relate to events occurring before, during and after the Greek victory respectively. Anything Euripides can do . . .

The second transgression: onto female space

Euripides' second transgression in his plays correlates with his transgression onto the women's festival and consists in his tragedy's improper involvement in women's affairs. This transgression is largely reflected in the subject matter of Euripides' plays.

If one may speak broadly, tragedy is supposed to deal with the affairs of the *polis*; but Euripides has transferred his attention to the *oikos*, and more particularly to that most private part, the *gunaikeion*, whose secrets were not the business of other men. In the words of the complaint in *Frogs* 969, he brings *oikeia pragmata* ('affairs of the *oikos*') onto the stage. His attempt to infiltrate the festival is thus an attempt to use one crime to solve the problems caused by another. The indictment is begun by the First Woman: 'He calls us adulteresses, nymphomaniacs, drunkards, traitresses, gossips, unclean, a great evil to mankind' (392–4). When husbands see these characters on stage, they immediately suspect the same of their wives. The effect of this is that normal domestic life is disrupted, as old men fail to marry young girls(!). Most significantly, store-houses are now firmly locked against the women. If locking up the women's quarters

---

[73] Seaford 1984: introduction, esp. 38f. with n. 109, and Pl. IV; for homosexuality in this genre, cf. S. *Ach. Erast.* fr. 149, 153; fr. 756; Achaeus, *TGF* 10 F 26.
[74] *Birds* 786–9.   [75] Scodel 1980: 64–79.

and keeping dogs against adulterers is forgivable (414–8), the same
cannot be said for the following (418–28):

> we're no longer able to look after ourselves by getting away with
> taking corn and oil and wine from the store-cupboards, because
> our husbands now carry around their own horrible Spartan keys
> with secret patterns and three teeth. Before now, all we had to do
> was make ourselves a signet-ring and we could open the doors. But
> now this house-destroyer Euripides has taught them to carry seals
> with complex, worm-eaten patterns.

In other words, Euripidean tragedy has effected a complete revolution in the ways of the *oikos*, whereby men take over the supervision
of the store-houses and their keys, tasks which were usually the
province of the women.[76]

Euripides is thus well called a 'house-destroyer' (426) for
having caused an upheaval in the relationships in the *oikos* that is as
fundamental as the assumption of male roles by the women at the
Thesmophoria. Now, the Thesmophoria brought to an end a period
of abnormality and reversal, in which the married women abstained
from sexual relations, and involved themselves in politics, *aischrologia* and other things they should not touch. Can something similar be
said of the play *Thesmophoriazusae*? I think it can. Euripides had
strayed onto space belonging to women and to comedy, so that the
period of these plays was an anomalous period like that of the
Thesmophoria. As is made (somewhat hyperbolically) clear in the
scene of the Assembly, his 'anti-women' plays constitute a Thesmophoric time. He is accused of putting on stage all of the obscenity,
domestic disruption, tension between men and gods, 'disordered
fertility' or even infertility caused by adultery, mariticide, suppositious children and so on, which the women bring up. Some of the
complaints echo specific Thesmophoric prohibitions: the unwillingness of the Athenians, complained about by the Second Woman, to
wear garlands would parallel their presumed absence on the day of
fasting; and it might even be possible to correlate the inability of the
women to steal from the store-houses barley, oil and wine, the foods
of civilisation, with the fasting on the Nesteia, when these foods were
denied them.

Euripidean tragedy has, as it were, created one big, city-wide
Thesmophoria. Thus, by imposing on Euripides the promise not to

[76] X. *Oec.* 7–9; Fraenkel 1950: 2.302f.

slander women again, the play has in effect restored normality to Euripidean tragedy and so to the city in the same way as the festival was designed to. *Thesmophoriazusae* has brought to an end this period of 'abnormal' tragedy as effectively as Calligeneia replaced Nesteia at the festival: at the end of the play, normal relationships are re-established in the city and Mnesilochus returns 'like a man' home to his wife and children (1204). This return to the usual state of affairs is foreshadowed by the normal, healthy desire of the Scythian for the dancing girl, which threatens no marital harmony. There is also a hymn to Athena, described as *Kleidouchos*, 'Key-holder' of the city (1142), as a woman should be of the store-rooms of her *oikos*.[77] The *Thesmophoriazusae* is thus as efficacious as the Thesmophoria.

There is however a catch. If comedy has purified and regenerated Euripidean tragedy, it may be said to have silenced the source of knowledge of women's wickedness: it was this knowledge that enabled men to control their misdemeanours. But all is not lost. Though there will be no more help from Euripides (nor from Agathon and the younger tragedians, where illicit perversion is still presumably to be found), a new champion has arisen, whose plays, as Mnesilochus the comic hero proceeds to demonstrate in his great speech (466ff.), will give a much more accurate and fulsome picture of female villainy. Aristophanic comedy has thus purged and defeated tragedy, shortened the Great Dionysia's lengthy performances, executed the role of the Thesmophoria – and slighted women in a way beyond anything that Euripides has done. It is as if Euripides' transgression onto female and comic space were a single transgression: it is the function of comedy to slander women. But then, does Euripidean tragedy really slander women?

---

[77] The political element discussed above now returns in the references to the demos of the women (1145) and to Athena's hatred of tyrants (1143f.).

10

Frogs

Frogs and Eleusis?

At 159, Xanthias says 'I'm the ass at the Mysteries.'[1] The precise point of this jest is unfortunately not yet recovered, and at this stage in the play it seems to be a gratuitous remark prompted from Xanthias by Heracles' reference to the Mystae and by exasperation. So far the play has given us Dionysus, on his way to Hades to fetch back Euripides, dressed in a bizarre combination of clothes appropriate to himself and to Heracles, two dialogues in which the derelict state of comedy and tragedy has been lamented, and a description of the various ways of completing a *katabasis* or journey to Hades. Heracles' account of the travails on the journey to Hades culminates in the promise of the music, lights and dancing of the Mystae, the Eleusinian Initiates, but at this point we do not know what, if any, part they are to play in the drama.

The *Frogs* continues to generate much scholarly writing,[2] which has not excluded discussion of its relationship to the Eleusinian Mysteries. However, much work has recently been done on these Mysteries, so that a further consideration is not entirely otiose. There have been attempts to deny a connection specifically with the Eleusinian Mysteries, and to see rather the Lesser Mysteries at Agrae, which were preparatory to the Greater,[3] or the processions at the Lenaea.[4] My argument will be that this Chorus is indeed composed of

[1] See Stanford 1971: 86 for interpretation.
[2] Gelzer, *RE* Supplbd. 12.1488; add Elderkin 1955; Graf 1974: 40–50; on questions of unity, Segal 1961; Fraenkel 1962: 163–88; Hooker 1980; on ritual matters, Konstan 1986 and Moorton 1989. An admirably full and important treatment of the play in terms of Dionysus' functions in Greek culture is being prepared by Lada (forthcoming).
[3] Tucker 1906: xxviii–xxxiv; see Segal 1961: 219 n. 44.
[4] Tierney 1935; see the review by Deubner 1936 for the difficulties in his arguments. Guarducci 1982 is no more convincing.

Eleusinian Initiates who, having achieved the posthumous happiness promised by their initiation,[5] are continuing to practise a form of their cult: the scene is after all Hades, not Athens.

Indeed, the attempt to disprove Eleusinian connections seems doomed from the beginning, partly because for an Athenian, 'the Mysteries', with no other qualification, meant the Eleusinian Mysteries, and partly because the Eleusinian colouring is in fact so pervasive.[6] The use of the words *mustikotatos* ('most mystic', 314) and *memuemenoi* ('initiated', 318) in a context containing Iacchus would surely have made an Athenian think of the Eleusinian Mysteries? Iacchus, mentioned fourteen times in one hundred lines, was the deity whose statue, crowned with myrtle (330) and accompanied by torches (313, 340), was in the procession that went from Athens to Eleusis.[7] The meadow (326) is a standard piece of Eleusinian infernal geography.[8] Xanthias smells pig-meat (338), and the pig, regularly sacrificed to Demeter, played an important role in the Eleusinian rite: on the day *Halade mustai* ('Initiates to the Sea'), those about to take part in the Mysteries bathed in the sea with a piglet which was subsequently sacrificed.[9] In 354ff. there is the parodic equivalent of the Prorrhesis, the proclamation of the restrictions on those who could attend: 'Whoever has no experience of these doctrines and is not pure in heart must keep holy silence and stand apart from our choruses' (354f.). Some of the Mystae go off to a *pannuchis* (371, 448), which we know to have taken place on arrival at Eleusis,[10] and in 452 the Chorus describe their dancing as *kallichorotaton*, which Richardson compares to the dancing around the well Callichoron at that

---

[5] Lobeck 1829: 1.69ff.; Foucart 1914: 361ff.; Graf 1974: 79–94. Earlier references include *H. Dem.* 480ff.; Pi. frr. 129–131 (referred to Eleusis by Clement *Strom.* 3.17.2); S. fr. 837; Isoc. 4.28; cf. also Pl. *Rep.* 365A, *Phd.* 69C. For initiates celebrating their rites in Hades, e.g. the Hipponion gold-leaves and Plut. *Mor.* 1105B.

[6] For the ancient sources on the Eleusinian Mysteries, Farnell 1896–1909: III 343–62. For modern discussions, principally Foucart 1914; Deubner 1932: 69–91; Mylonas 1961; Boyancé 1962: 460–82; Graf 1974; Bianchi 1976; Dowden 1980b; Simon 1983: 24–35; Burkert 1983a: 248–97, 1987a; Bérard 1989b: 114–20.

[7] The refrain of 403 etc. echoes the use in later inscriptions of *propempein* of the Ephebes who accompanied the image: *IG* 2².1006.9, 1008.8, 1011.8, 1028.9 (Graf 1974: 44 n. 24).

[8] Pi. fr. 129.3; [Pl.] *Axioch.* 371C; Diod. 1.96.5; Plut. fr. 178; also Orph. fr. 32 f 6 (?fifth cent.), 222; Philodamus, *Delphic Hymn to Dionysus* 3.29f. (*CA* 166) and the Niinion tablet (Graf 1974: 46–50, 90f.).

[9] Plut. *Phoc.* 28.3; schol. Aeschin. 3.130; *IG* 1³.84.35f. (418/17).

[10] E. *Ion* 1074ff.; Richardson 1974: 215. The metre of 441–6, the 'Euripidean', sung before the *pannuchis*, was used by Callimachus for a *pannuchis*-poem (fr. 227).

pannuchis.[11] Then there are the hymns to Iacchus, described as 'discoverer of the festival's song' (399f.), which recall Herodotus' description of him as the *mustikos Iacchos* that rang out supernaturally when the phantom Eleusinian procession appeared before Salamis.[12] Indeed, 'Iacchus, O Iacchus' (316) is most likely the cry of the Eleusinian procession. In 402f., Iacchus is called up to show how easily he can make the journey; though there are echoes here of the ease of travel enjoyed by the Bacchic initiate,[13] in the context of the other indications, would not the audience have taken this to be a reference to the twenty-mile journey to Eleusis, which they had so often made (even if Iacchus' avatar, Dionysus, may in this play find the reference ironic after his own journey)? There are hymns too to Persephone as Soteira and Demeter as Basileia.[14] In the latter, the Chorus pray to Demeter that they may be able 'having won, to wear a garland' (395), which can be referred both to the victor's garland with its streamers and to the similar garland worn by the Initiates.[15] We shall come to other aspects in due time. The recital of details such as these does no more than support the usual contention that the Eleusinian Mysteries are in question; for our purposes we need to consider the whole question of the relationship between play and festival in a much more all-embracing, structural fashion.

Orpheus, Dionysus and Eleusis

In his book, *Eleusis und die orphische Dichtung Athens*, Fritz Graf argued convincingly that, by the end of the fifth century, the Eleusinian Mysteries had taken on elements not only from Orphic

---

[11] Richardson 1974: 215 and esp. 326–8: Call. *Hy.* 6.15, fr. 611; Nic. *Ther.* 486; Paus. 1.38.6; Apollod. 1.5.1. The well is still there: Mylonas 1961: 97ff., fig. 4 no. 10, fig. 33.

[12] 8.65.   [13] E. *Ba.* 64ff, 161ff.

[14] One of Tierney's arguments against the Eleusinian Mysteries as model for *Frogs* was the absence of a hymn to Core in the parodos (1935: 205f., 216): *Soteira* in 378 must be Demeter because she is the subject of the hymn starting in 384a. However, Core and not Demeter is called 'Soteira' in cult (Usener 1896: 37, 219f., 223f.). Furthermore, in the rest of the parodos a single metre is used throughout for each topic, whereas 378–83 (to Soteira) and 386–95 (to Demeter) are in different metres. Again, the Chorus tend to mark each change of subject not only by a change of metre but also by phrases such as *nun, ag' eia* (372, 378, 384, 396, 420, 445), so that *age nun* in 384 would suggest such a change.

[15] Clinton 1974: 106 with n. 49; Maass 1922: 258; also Theo Smyrn. p. 15 Hiller. For beribboned statues of Demeter and Persephone, Paus. 10.35.10 and 8.31.8; for the ribbon as mark of athletic victory, Thuc. 4.121 and Frazer on Paus. 6.20.19.

religion,[16] but also from Dionysiac.[17] That this should be the case need be no cause for surprise: given the popularity of these other cults, it would have made sense for the *polis* to incorporate elements of them in the great city mystery cult, and thus provide 'mystic' experiences that were under its control and not the control of *goetes* or other marginal figures. In discussing *Frogs*, therefore, we should perhaps not confine ourselves solely to parallels with the Eleusinian Mysteries, but also widen the discussion to include Orphic cult and, with due care, Athenian mystery cults in general, especially, given the presence in the play of the god, the Dionysiac mysteries.

The similarities between the Eleusinian Mysteries and Orphism can be seen in such things as infernal geography: there is a striking similarity between the picture of the Underworld ascribed by Plutarch to the Eleusinian Mysteries, that ascribed by Diodorus to Orpheus, that in a fragment of Pindar and that on South Italian gold-leaves: sunshine, flowers and the enjoyment of festivals are found in them all. The Mysteries turned to the Orphic poems to give colour to the literary presentation of their beliefs.[18] We also find that Orphism has influence upon the content of those beliefs. In the *Homeric Hymn*, Demeter makes the following promise: 'Happy the mortal man who has seen these things. He who has not been initiated into these holy rites and has no part of them, will never share in the same things when he dies and goes beneath the mouldy darkness' (480–2). That is, in the Eleusinian Mysteries, what matters is whether or not one has been initiated; it is initiation that provides one with 'better hope' for the afterlife. The Orphics, in a slight variation, made moral character also a determinant, as in Pindar's *Olympian* 2.61–7:

> with equal nights and equal days, the good enjoy the sun and have a life without toil; they do not trouble the earth with the strength of their hand nor the sea's water in search of food that does not satisfy. Those who rejoiced in keeping their oaths have a tearless life beside the honoured ones of the gods. But the others suffer toils unbearable to look upon.

Plato makes the point with explicit reference to Musaeus and his son Eumolpus, who put 'the holy ones' in a symposium and the

[16] Cf. also Burkert 1985: 296–301.

[17] For Dionysiac mysteries, Cole 1980; Seaford 1981; Casadio 1982, 1983; Burkert 1985: 290–5; 1987a: 22 n. 49, 34 n. 17.

[18] Graf 1974: 92. He suggests (chh. 4 and 5) that the influence came from Orphic poems, especially those dealing with Orpheus' *katabasis*.

'unholy ones' in mud.[19] The closing words of the Mystae in the
parodos provide a variation and amplification of this idea:[20] 'We
alone have the sun and the holy light, who have been initiated and
behave in a pious way towards *xenoi* and private citizens' (454–9). By
combining the straightforward Eleusinian view with the Orphic
emphasis on moral rectitude Aristophanes appears to be reflecting
current Eleusinian beliefs; the song of the Mystae is then 'ein
Umgangsstadium'.[21] There would have been an interaction between
Eleusinian poems about Demeter explaining individual aspects of the
Mystic rites, and the Orphic poems, providing mythical expression
of the feelings of the Mystae.[22] In *Frogs*, Orpheus and Musaeus are
specifically mentioned as two of the poets who have benefited
mankind: 'Orpheus revealed mystery rites to you and taught you to
keep away from slaughter [for food]; Musaeus taught you cures for
diseases and oracles' (1032f.). Verse 355 (quoted above) with its
reference to the man who is 'unacquainted with these words (*logoi*)'
and is not 'purified' (*katharos*) also has Orphic resonances.[23]

The relationship between Dionysus and the Mysteries has long
been problematic, but it is now fairly clear that such a relationship
did exist.[24] It can best be seen in the way he is associated with
Iacchus as early as the end of the fifth century, an association no
doubt aided by the homophony of 'Bacchus' and 'Iacchus', and also
by the fact that the Eleusinian procession had an ecstatic character.
The earliest evidence is uncertain. In Berlin, there is a black-figure
lecythus of about 500, which shows a bearded Dionysus with the
inscription *IAKXNE*, which may be a miswriting for *IAKXE*.
Later in the century, there is much more compelling, literary evidence. The famous ode in *Antigone* addresses Dionysus with reference both to Eleusis 'you rule over Eleusinian Deo's glens which
receive all' (1119–21), and to Iacchus, whose name is the last word of

[19] *Rep.* 363C–D.
[20] For what follows, Graf 1974: 79–126; R. C. T. Parker 1983: 323f.
[21] Graf 1974: 120. Cf. also Nilsson 1955: 667 who argues that this moral element was implicit in the Mysteries.
[22] Graf 1974: 183: the *katabasis* story at Eleusis created 'einen Mythos zum dichterischen Ausdruck dessen, was der Myste als Effekt der Zeremonien erfuhr'. In general, Burkert 1987a: 89ff.
[23] *Logos* is regularly used of the Orphic texts: Hdt. 2.81; Kern 1922: 140ff. For *katharos*, Pl. *Phd.* 69C; *Rep.* 364E; Orph. fr. 32c (gold-leaf from Thurii, fourth or third cent.) etc.
[24] Graf 1974: 40–78; also Metzger 1944–5; Mylonas 1961: 275–8; Bérard 1974: 94 n. 2; Richardson 1974 on *H. Dem.* 489; Burkert 1983a: 279 n. 23; Simon 1983: 32.

the ode.[25] The description of Iacchus in *Frogs* 342 as 'bright star of the nocturnal ritual' recalls *Ant.* 1146ff., where, in the same hymn to 'polyonymous' Dionysus, Iacchus is invoked as 'chorus-leader of the fire-breathing stars, guardian of the voices of the night', a passage which the scholiast describes as 'in accordance with some mystic *logos*'. In another, unknown play, Sophocles speaks of Dionysus' place of nurture, Nysa:[26] 'I saw ecstatic Nysa, famed among mortals, which the ox-horned Iacchus counts as his sweetest motherland.' In *Bacchae* 725f., the messenger describes the Maenads as 'calling as one on Iacchus, the son of Zeus, Bromius'.

There is also evidence from cult. At the Lenaea, the Daduchus cried 'Call on the god' and the people replied 'Son of Semele, Iacchus giver of wealth',[27] and the Lesser Mysteries at Agrae contained an 'imitation of the things about Dionysus', though we do not know what about Dionysus.[28] It would seem reasonable therefore to see Dionysus and Iacchus as deities who in an Eleusinian context could be identified with each other.[29]

That the parodos and entry of the Mystae in *Frogs* contains a number of strikingly Dionysiac elements should perhaps be put down not only to the presence of the god when it is sung, but also to the influence of Dionysiac cult. Thus the metre of the opening strophe is basically ionics *a minore*, which is characteristic of Dionysiac cult-hymns, such as those in Euripides' *Bacchae* and Philodamus' Delphic Hymn.[30] The Chorus refer to themselves as 'members of a *thiasos*' (327; cf. 156), a word more appropriate to Dionysiac than Eleusinian affairs.[31] This is reinforced by the subsequent words, which are reminiscent of descriptions of rites in Euripides' *Bacchae*,

[25] 1151f.   [26] Fr. 959.1–3.   [27] Schol. *Frogs* 482.

[28] Steph. Byz. s.v. *Agra kai Agrai*; Simon 1966: 78ff.; Graf 1974: 68; Parker 1989. Already in the *Axiochus* (371E), there is the story of Dionysus' initiation before his descent to Hades. For Dionysus' connection with Demeter and Persephone elsewhere, Paus. 8.54.5 and Stroud 1968: 328f.

[29] Graf 1974: 54. A vase from Apollonia shows them separately: Venedikov *et al.* 1963: 92ff., plates 13ff.; Bérard 1974: 94f.

[30] Dodds 1960: 71–4; M. L. West 1982: 124–7 and 142–5. Ionics are rare in Euripides outside *Bacchae* and in Sophocles, but more common in Aeschylus, especially in *Persae*. They appear to be connected with cult-songs of eastern origin: e.g. Sappho 140; Varro, *Sat.* 540 (Adonis); Heph. p. 38.15 C.; Choerob. p. 246.1 (Cybele). For Dionysiac songs, cf. Philodamus (*CA* 165ff.) and Siron of Soli (*PMG* 845 = *SH* 312), who used the metre for a song in which Demetrius of Phaleron was acclaimed in a Dionysiac procession of 308. See also Festugière 1956: 76–8.

[31] Tierney 1935: 201f.; though see LSJ s.v. *thiasos* II for more general usage.

for instance: 'Come shaking your rich garland, bursting with myrtles on your head, beating out with bold steps the lively, playful dance honouring the god' (328–34). The same may be said for the rejuvenating qualities in 345–50, which recall the effects of Dionysus on Cadmus and Teiresias,[32] and also for the reference to the ease of the god's travelling in 401f., which recalls Teiresias' remark that 'the god will lead us there without toil'.[33] In the Prorrhesis (354ff.), excluded from membership of the chorus is the man who does not know the 'Bacchic rites of bull-eating Cratinus' (357): Cratinus is given a cult-title of Dionysus, recalling the devouring of the bull in the rites of Dionysus–Zagreus.[34] Finally, also excluded is the rhetor who cannot bear being mocked 'in the traditional rites of Dionysus' (368). In Hades, therefore, as in Athens, these Mysteries happily blend aspects of all three cults.

Frogs and Mysteries

We move now from the discussion of Eleusinian details to the question of how the Mysteries function in the play. Dionysus' journey to Hades takes up a good part of the play, but this is not merely because of its comic potential. In Eleusinian and other mystery cults, the journey was a standard image for the process of initiation: wandering, tribulation and uncertainty led to the bright lights at the end of the initiatory tunnel.[35] Plutarch speaks of the journey as follows:[36]

> wanderings astray in the beginning, tiresome walkings in circles, some frightening paths in darkness that lead nowhere; then immediately before the end all the terrible things, panic and shivering and sweat, and amazement. And then some wonderful light comes to meet you, pure regions and meadows are there to greet you, with sounds and dances and solemn, sacred words and holy views; and there the initiate, perfect by now, set free and loosed from all bondage, walks about, crowned with a wreath,

---

[32] E. Ba. 187–90.   [33] Ibid. 194.

[34] S. fr. 668 for *taurophagos* of Dionysus; for Zagreus, Call. fr. 643 (with Pfeiffer's note); Burkert 1985: 298.   [35] O. Becker 1937; Tierney 1937: 18f.; Burkert 1987a: 92f.

[36] Fr. 178. Cf. Apuleius, *Met.* 11.23.6–8 'I approached the frontier of death, I set foot on the threshold of Persephone, I journeyed through all the elements and came back, I saw at midnight the sun, sparkling in white light, I came close to the gods of the upper and the nether world and adored them from near at hand.'

celebrating the festival together with the other sacred and pure people; and he looks down on the uninitiated, unpurified crowd in this world in mud and fog beneath his feet.

That Dionysus should begin by visiting his brother Heracles is appropriate, since Heracles was the 'mythical archetype of the Eleusinian initiate':[37] he had been purified by Eumolpus and initiated into the Mysteries before his descent to the Underworld in search of Cerberus.[38] There are many parallels between the two descents, which figure, in their different ways, the experiences of the initiand.[39] Both crossed with Charon, as the initiand and initiate crossed the Cephisus river to go to Eleusis.[40] On landing, both encountered monsters of one kind or another;[41] something similar happened to the initiands.[42] Heracles was frightened by the ghost of Medusa, until told she was only a shade; Dionysus 'sees' Empusa, a shape-changing demon with a bronze leg.[43] Both encountered mud and the punishment of sinners. Dionysus then meets the Mystae. There seems to have been no comparable episode in Heracles' case, but Pindar and Virgil, who seem to be using the same source for Heracles' journey, both refer to the lights and music. Persephone received Heracles well, as she does Dionysus in *Frogs*; she is roasting an ox for his arrival, which gives a comic twist to Heracles' sacrifice of an ox to give blood to the ghosts. Pluto permits Dionysus to take Aeschylus away with him, just as Heracles was allowed Cerberus, as

[37] Burkert 1983a: 257; cf. 254 n. 26, 266, 267 n. 11; so on vases, Bérard 1989b: 117f. with figs. 160a, 161f.   [38] E. *HF* 613; [Pl.] *Axioch.* 371E.

[39] Cf. Lloyd-Jones 1967 for the details of this paragraph; also Graf 1974: 139–50; Robertson 1980. On *katabaseis* generally, Bérard 1974.

[40] Charon's cry in 185f. echoes the notion of initiation as a freedom from toil (Thomson 1935: 22).

[41] When Dionysus meets the Frogs, they sing of when 'at the holy Chytroi the hung-over crowd of people goes to my temple' (217–19), thus evoking the time when spirits wandered the city as Dionysus is about to enter the Underworld (Moorton 1989: 315f.).

[42] On the Frog in antiquity, Keller 1909–13: II 305–8; little evidence comes from Greece in the massive study of Deonna 1951. It is not a chthonic animal until later (e.g. Rev. 16.13; Juv. 2.150). For similar tribulations caused by frogs, *Batrachom.* 187ff.; Ael. *NA* 3.37; Plin. *NH* 8.227; [Arist.] *Mir. Ausc.* 70; Ant. Caryst. 4; for a story of Demeter, Persephone and frogs, Serv. *Geo.* 1.378; *Myth. Vat.* 2.9.

[43] On *phasmata* at the Eleusinian Mysteries, Seaford 1981: 259 n. 68; at Dionysiac mysteries, Orig. *Cels.* 4.10; Burkert 1983a: 288 n. 64. Given the difficulties of staging Empusa's changes in broad daylight, if Heracles' Gorgon was merely a shade, Dionysus' Empusa was probably not there at all. Idomeneus (*FGH* 338 F 2) says Aeschines' mother, a priestess of Sabazius, appeared in the darkness to the initiands as Empusa: *Vita Aeschin.* III p. 268.1ff. W.; but see Jacoby, *FGH* 3b 86.24ff.; Brown 1991.

Aeacus remarks in *Frogs* 467f. The initiand is treated to bright
lights,[44] welcomed and symbolically reborn.

The journey-image also represented the way in which in
initiatory rites things were done to the initiand which were intended
to jolt him out of his normal psychological state, to render him
susceptible to receive the new sensations and to purify him of his
earlier less satisfactory condition: Dionysus' journey has both these
functions.[45] The scaring of the initiand was done in a variety of ways
involving darkness, loud noise, curious ritual activity, dressing in
animal skins and so on. There seems to be an element of this in *Frogs*.
The test to determine whether Dionysus or Xanthias is the god is
administered by flogging, with the one who makes a noise first being
the loser. The need for silence is a frequent requisite in the course of
mysteries and after them.[46] In the literature on mystery cults there is
mention of flogging in the initiations; in the famous paintings from
the House of Mysteries at Pompeii, a figure with a whip stands beside
a women with her back bared. As Burkert notes, however, the figure
is winged and so not of this world, and it would appear that
references to flogging should often be read symbolically. Flogging
was however a recognised method of purification:[47] leeks and onions
had purificatory properties,[48] but Xanthias is keen, for other reasons,
that they should not be used here (621f.). There is no evidence
whatsoever, nor indeed any reason to believe, that beating featured
at Eleusis, but this does not mean that the scene cannot be considered
in this light: the beating and the disorientation of the constant
changing of identity would provide a comic refraction of this idea for
those who knew the symbolism and indeed for those whose cults
may have offered such activities.

---

[44] Hippol. *Ref.* 5.8.40; Burkert 1983a: 276.

[45] Cf. Burkert 1987a: 102–4; the scholiast on *Wasps* 1363b says 'before the Mysteries, the
Initiated cause fear in those intending to be initiated'; cf. Pl. *Phd.* 107D–8c; *Phdr.* 246Dff.

[46] In general, Casel 1919 (I owe the reference to Richard Seaford). For Eleusis, S. *OC* 1048–53;
also A. fr. 316; Thomson 1935: 20f; Tierney 1937: 12; Richardson 1974: 171, 218, 307f.
Konstan 1986: 307 discusses the passage in terms of 'le langage comme secret', but actual
silence seems to be more relevant.

[47] Burkert 1987a: 168 n. 94 quotes Hsch. *katharthenai: mastigothenai*; cf. R. C. T. Parker 1983:
231f. Note also the beating of ephebes at the Sicilian Sciereia festival, dedicated to Dionysus
(Theoc. 7.106–8 and schol.; Nilsson 1906: 408), the later rite by the altar of Artemis Ortheia,
and perhaps also the *agon* and *skillomachia* in Priene (*Inscr. Priene* 112.91, 95 (84 or later)).

[48] Hp. *MS* 2.21f.

Aristotle said that the initiand did not 'learn' (*mathein*) but 'experienced' (*pathein*) in order to undergo a change of state of mind (*diathenai*),[49] and the image of the journey from tribulation to salvation was in part a metaphor for a change in the nature of the initiand. Dionysus clearly has identity problems in the early part of the play. Segal 1961 noted that he seems at various points not to recognise aspects of his own cult, which suggests some kind of incompleteness in him. Furthermore, during the play, there are places where his identity seems, at moments of fear and crisis, to be in doubt.[50] When they encounter Empusa, he begs Xanthias not to call him by his name 'Heracles', let alone 'Dionysus'. On meeting the denizens of Hades, he exchanges identities with Xanthias so frequently that a test has to be set up to settle the matter once and for all. The first and clearest indication, however, of this uncertainty of identity is the extraordinary garb which Dionysus has adopted for his journey – the lion-skin and club of Heracles worn over his own saffron robe and boots. The combination is obviously comic at a rather basic level because of its incongruity.[51] At the same time, in Dionysus' own mystery cults, the wearing of animal-skins was common: we find it in the messenger's speech in the *Bacchae* and in a specifically initiatory context in Demosthenes' description of Aeschines' activities in his mother's cult of Sabazius: 'You dressed the initiates in fawn-skins . . .'[52] Transvestism too is common in Dionysiac cults.[53] Thus, the wearing of garments that signified the opposite of 'man' marked for the initiand, like the ephebe, the period of his rite of passage. There are many examples from ritual, as we have seen.[54] Dionysus, therefore, comes on stage in a comic version of the kind of marginal attire which is associated with status-transition and

---

[49] Fr. 15.   [50] Goldhill 1991: 201–22 for the implications of this scene.

[51] Cf. Aesop's ass who put on a lion-skin to terrify all around but was betrayed by his unconvincing braying (*Fab.* 199 H.–H.; cf. Aphthonius 10; Themist. *Or.* 21.245b; Lucian, *Fug.* 13, *Necyo.* 8 (Menippus takes symbols of Heracles, Orpheus and Odysseus to Hades to use at different times)). On comic portrayals of Dionysus, Pascal 1911: 25–67, esp. 61; Segal 1961: 208f.; Cantarella 1974: 301 n. 46.   [52] 18.259.

[53] Seaford 1981: 258f. In the Eleusinian myth, Demeter, whose experiences reflect those of the initiate, disguised herself as an old woman during the period of Persephone's absence (*H. Dem.* 101ff.).

[54] It is not clear whether special clothing was worn at the Eleusinian Mysteries. Schol. *Plutus* 845 says 'pure new garments' were used, and that the clothes in which one had been initiated were dedicated to the goddesses (Deubner 1932: 79 n. 7). Others however (e.g. Stanford 1971: 109) take 'rags' in *Frogs* 404ff. to mean that old clothes were worn.

initiation, and from which we expect him to change at the end of his 'initiation'.[55]

This doubleness in Dionysus is also represented in his literary sensibilities. At the start of the play, he is keen to keep the tone up by avoidance of the typically crude jokes on which comedy is presumed to rely. In his scene with Heracles, he appears to be a man of some literary culture, with a wide range of poetic vocabulary and tragic quotation at his disposal, in contrast to Heracles with his coarse suggestions and need for the analogy of soup (62–5) to comprehend Dionysus' desperate 'desire' for Euripides (53). At the same time, it is made fairly apparent that this desire for Euripides is not, in fact, to be seen as a symptom of sound critical judgement, since he is a playwright whom even the gluttonous Heracles can see is pretty poor stuff: 'That's cobblers, and you know it' (104) he says when faced with 'the foot of time' and other such gems. His critical powers are, therefore, like his dress, somewhat confused: the desire for a 'creative' poet (96) who will save tragedy and (the city) is a sound one, but the choice of Euripides questionable: why not Sophocles, for instance, a less contentious choice (76f.)? Once he has been recognised by Pluto and Persephone, he doffs the skin to resume, however improbably, his traditional role as arbiter of the poetic *agon*,[56] and at the end he makes a 'correct' poetical decision in choosing the noble Aeschylus. The mystic torches then blaze up at the true end of his 'initiation'.

Frogs and politics

Dionysus' journey therefore and the Eleusinian Mysteries have a similar end in view: salvation. But what then of the political element in the play? Until the arrival of the Mystae, the play has proceeded as if the troubled state of poetry were its most important aspect: Dionysus' search for the creative poet was not given any specifically political colouring. This begins to change with the lines of the Chorus in 354–7:

[55] Cf. two comparable figures dressed in a 'double' manner indicating marginal status, Paris in *Il.* 3.16–20 and Jason in Pi. *Py.* 4.79–83 (Vidal-Naquet 1986: 130f.). In a cultic example, on the Amyclaean throne Apollo is depicted with helmet, bow and spear: god of ephebic transitions between the world represented by these latter two weapons, he stands upon the tomb of his youthful lover Hyacinthus (Paus. 3.19.2).

[56] As in the cases of Agoracritus and of Peisetaerus and Euelpides, a character is named or recognised at the point where he is to play a role in his own right.

we must have holy silence and there must stand apart from our choirs whoever has no experience of these words and is not pure in thought, has neither known nor danced in the rites of the noble Muses and has not been initiated into the Bacchic rites of the tongue of Cratinus the bull-eater.

These words echo the actual Prorrhesis, which forbade entry to those who could not speak Greek or were not ritually pure;[57] here the Chorus go on to list a number of more or less serious crimes which debar people from joining their mystic chorus. In Athens, anyone who had been declared to have forfeited his rights as a citizen was banned from *ta hiera* ('holy rites') generally, and sometimes the Eleusinian Mysteries are specifically mentioned.[58] A number of the crimes mentioned in the Prorrhesis of *Frogs* are just such as would have attracted the penalty of *atimia*: for instance, treason and the overthrow of democracy (359, 362ff.),[59] theft of public property (360),[60] bribery (361),[61] and misconduct in office (367).[62] Political crimes are thus set in an Eleusinian context.

This ribaldry on political themes continues in 420ff., where the Chorus, still acting as if they were on a journey, sing jokes in iambic metre against contemporary figures. One is tempted to see in this a reference to the *gephurismoi*, the insults hurled by hooded figures at notable citizens as the Eleusinian procession crossed the bridge over the river Cephisus, which formed a boundary between Athens and Eleusis.[63] The men on the bridge were hooded, the Chorus masked. In *Frogs*, as Tierney argued when opposing the Eleusinian interpretation of the play, it is the procession itself that fires the abuse, rather

---

[57] Isoc. *Paneg.* 157 'At the rite of the Mysteries, because of our hatred of [the Persians], the Eumolpidae and Ceryces make an announcement forbidding entry to the other barbarians as well, as to murderers'; cf. Lucian, *Demon.* 34, *Alex.* 38; Pollux 8.90; Lobeck 1829: 114ff. The Lesser Mysteries were created so that Heracles, a foreigner and polluted with the blood of the Centaurs, could satisfy the requirements of the Proclamation (Dowden 1980b: 420).

[58] Hansen 1976: 54–98, esp. for exclusion from the *hiera* 62 n. 9 (*IG* 1³.5 A 32 (before 460)); Andoc. 1.33, 71, 132; Lys. 6.9, 24, 52 (reference to Eleusis); Dem. 21.58f., 22.73, 24.181; Aeschin. 3.176 with schol. Also Rhodes 1981: Index s.v. *atimia*.

[59] [Plut.] *Mor.* 834A; Idomeneus, *FGH* 338 F 1; *SEG* 12.87 (336); [Arist.] *Ath. Pol.* 16.10. For this and the next three notes, see Hansen 1976: 72–4.   [60] Andoc. 1.74.

[61] Ibid.; Dem. 21.113.   [62] [X.] *Ath. Pol.* 3.13; Aeschin. 3.44; *SEG* 12.87.11ff.

[63] Hsch. s.v. *gephuris, gephuristai*; Wüst 1921: 26–45. *Wasps* 1362f. perhaps suggest there was a more general mockery amongst those in the procession. For iambics and jesting in Demeter's cult, Richardson 1974: 213–17; *IG* 2².1078.29; Plut. *Alc.* 34.4; the Chorus' prayers to jest worthily of Demeter's festival (393) suggest more than traditional comic abuse is involved. *Paizein* ('play') and *skoptein* ('jest') recur frequently in this part of the play (390, 394, 409, 413, 419, 421, 446, 453); cf. *H. Dem.* 203; Plut. *Mor.* 1105B.

than figures on a bridge, but this is to be somewhat pedantic in the
face of theatrical conventions: the Chorus stand here by synecdoche
for the procession and those associated with it; in the context I
cannot see that it is incredible that the many in the audience, who
had regularly been in the procession, would have connected the
two.[64] Again, the insults levelled against the three men they choose
to attack concern activities which would be likely to leave their
objects open to loss of citizen rights: Archedemus is accused of being
a *xenos* and 'the height of wickedness' (419–25);[65] Cleisthenes
laments his dead male lover (426–31), echoing the prohibition on
male prostitution by citizens;[66] and Callias squandered his patri-
mony (432–4).[67]

The connection between the Mysteries and political misdemea-
nour then comes into sharper focus in the parabasis. The lyric
portions attack two contemporary politicians in a somewhat baroque
and obscure way: the meaning of the final sentence in each case is not
entirely clear,[68] but once again an Eleusinian perspective is fruitful.
Cleophon is attacked first:[69] 'on whose lips of mongrel speech a
Thracian swallow makes horrible din as it sits on a foreign leaf; he
sings the mournful nightingale's lament, since he will perish even if
the votes are equal' (679–85). It is the barbarity of his speech that is
important here: his speech is incomprehensible like that of the
Thracian swallow, to which the Greeks likened the speech of barbarians.[70] He is accused of being not just a foreigner but one of barbarian
speech, and as such he too, like the politicians in the gephyristic
Prorrhesis, would have been forbidden entry to the Mysteries
because he breaks the ban on those who could not speak Greek.

[64] Scholia *Plutus* 1013f. speak of the women 'insulting each other on the way' in carriages in
the procession.   [65] Dem. 59.52; Hansen 1976: 91.

[66] Aeschin. 1.19–21, 160, 164, 188; Dem. 22.30 etc. (Hansen 1976: 74 n. 20; R. C. T. Parker
1983: 94f.).

[67] Aeschin. 1.30–2, 94–105, 154; Hansen 1976: 73. Callias' lion-skin, effeminacy and sea-battle
uncomfortably mirror those of the watching Dionysus, who now comes forward, as if on
cue.

[68] Even if oddly prophetic in the case of Cleophon, who was next year to be condemned to
death under a law specially passed for the purpose.

[69] Tr. follows Stanford, as does the next.

[70] Fraenkel on A. *Ag.* 1050. Plato Comicus' *Cleophon*, produced alongside *Frogs*, showed him as
a foreigner, stupid and a Thracian (Tzetzes schol. on *Frogs* 676a; that on 681 (Dind.) says his
mother was brought on stage by Plato 'speaking in barbarian fashion'). Plato Comicus fr. 64
uses *maragna*, apparently borrowed from Old Persian and so appropriate to Cleophon or his
mother. Cf. also Aeschin. 2.76.

The case of Cleigenes is more problematic: 'Not long will bother us that troublesome monkey little Cleigenes, that most wretched bathman and as many as be ash-watering lords of the impure detergents and the Cimolian earth' (709–13). He is portrayed as a fraudulent bath-house attendant, the marginal status of which profession is clear from the end of *Knights*, where Paphlagon is sent to be insulted by them and by prostitutes in the not very desirable district of the Ceramicus.[71] The quality of his soaps and fulling-earth cannot, apparently, be relied upon, but his failing cannot be simply that he does not give value for money in his bath-house:[72] in the light of his involvement in the removal of citizenship privileges, such a charge would hardly have made him blush. Should we perhaps view his failing as one that is complementary to Cleophon's and so one with consequences for Cleigenes' own participation in the Eleusinian Mysteries? The second prohibition on attendance affected those who were impure, ritually unclean. Is Cleigenes' crime therefore that he has an effect on the cleanliness of the city, which was essential to the proper conduct of religious affairs? The reference to soaps and fuller's earth most naturally refers to the washing of people and clothes,[73] but these substances were also used not only in medicine but more importantly in pollution and purification.[74] Earth, ash, dirty clothes and failure to wash are found as forms of self-pollution connected with mourning, and complementary substances like mud are common materials in religious purifications: earth was used in the cleansing of a house after death on Ceos;[75] Aeschines purified his mother's initiates with mud; and Lemnian earth was also used in rites.[76] To approach the gods one needed not only to be unpolluted in the metaphysical sense, but also in the physical, of having washed and donned clean clothes. The Eleusinian Mysteries prescribed a ritual bath in the sea, it is true, but may not Aristophanes be

---

[71] For the lowly status of these people, cf. also the scholion in Athen. 15.695E; Diogenianus, *CPG* 1.227; Suidas, Hsch. s.v. (see Ginouvès 1962: 212f. and 183–229 on the *balaneion* generally; the first public baths in Athens were built outside the walls by the Dipylon Gate).

[72] For the adulteration of Cimolian earth, Plin. *NH* 35.36.

[73] Athen. 8.351E and Galen 12.180 K. (Ginouvès 1962: 142; cf. 219 n. 11).

[74] On ritual cleanliness, Moulinier 1952 and R. C. T. Parker 1983: esp. 224–34. On the importance of ritual cleanliness in mystery-cults, Ginouvès 1962: 375–404, esp. 375–86.

[75] Sokolowski 1969: nos. 97.16 (fifth cent.), and 64.16 (Messenia, 191).

[76] Dem. 18.259; S. fr. 34; Plut. *Mor.* 166A; Galen 12.176f. K.; Lemnian earth: Dsc. 5.97.1f. Cf. Maass 1922: 257–71.

comically suggesting that Cleigenes' bath-houses that do not measure up to the standards of Her Majesty's inspectors pose a threat not just to personal hygiene but also to the purity of the city? It would have been to these baths that most Athenians would have turned to remove the pollutions attaching to everyday life.

If this be allowed, the 'holy chorus' of Mystae here pillory two men whose political activities are precisely the ones which would, by the terms of the Hierophant's Prorrhesis, have excluded them from the Mysteries. A similar point is made in a different way in the famous coin-simile of the antepirrhema. The well-minted Athenian coinage has been driven out and coins badly made yesterday have taken over (718–26):

> We've often thought the city has the same problems with regard to its best citizens as it does with the old coinage and the new gold one. We don't use at all that coinage of sterling quality, the most excellent kind of all that alone is properly struck and tried and tested amongst Greeks and barbarians everywhere, but these wretched bronze ones struck from the worst dies yesterday or the day before.

There is a similar Gresham's law amongst the politicians: instead of those with traditional Greek virtues and a gymnastic and musical education there are red-headed foreigners,[77] wretched 'johnny-come-latelies', whom the city would not have found satisfactory as *pharmakoi* (730–2). In politics, therefore, the incomprehensible, the unclean and the barbarian have replaced the Athenian.

So far, this idea of politicians being excluded from Eleusis by their corruption has seemed little more than a joke, extending the Eleusinian insults neatly to two currently prominent political figures. It is in the epirrhema of the parabasis that we see that it is in fact crucial to the meaning of the play and has pertinent and poignant reference to the contemporary situation in Athens. Here the Chorus, still speaking as Mystae ('the holy chorus', 686), comment on the recent award of Plataean status to slaves who had fought at Arginusae (687–99):[78]

---

[77] Adamantius, *Physiogn.* p. 394 F. for the violence of the red-haired. For the ethical use of coinage terms, Neil 1901: 206; Radermacher 1954: 246. For a numismatic commentary on the passage, Kroll 1976.

[78] The rigorous process of *dokimasia*, membership of deme and tribe and recording of the names on stone is given in [Dem.] 59.104–6.

> First of all we think we should make the citizens equal and take
> away their fears. If anyone has made a mistake, tripped up by
> Phrynichus' manoeuvres, I think those who slipped up then
> should be allowed to state their case and free themselves from their
> former errors. Then, no-one should be without his citizen rights in
> the city. For it is a shame that those who fought but one sea-battle
> should become both Plataeans and masters instead of slaves. Not
> that I could deny that this was well done – I commend it: it's the
> only sensible thing you've done. But besides this, it's reasonable
> that you should forgive those who have (like their fathers) fought
> in many sea-battles and are our kith and kin this one mistake when
> they beseech you.

With the city 'in the arms of the waves' (704) it would make more
sense if all were 'both in possession of their rights (*epitimoi*)',[79] and
'citizens' (702). There have been jesting remarks about this earlier:
because Xanthias did not fight in the sea-battle,[80] he has not the
freedom to speak to Dionysus as he wishes (33) and must walk
around the lake (195); at 48ff., Heracles listens incredulously to
Dionysus' account of the battle. Significantly, the issue of the
relationship between slave and master dominated the scene immediately before the parabasis, where whips were taken out to discover
who was who. The kind of confusion between master and slave that
we have seen as a result of Dionysus' cowardly behaviour is reflected
in the current political state of Athens: true citizens by a miscalcula-
tion are now worse off than former slaves, though these have it is
true, like Xanthias, displayed a bravery that deserves its reward. The
relationship between Dionysus and Xanthias in the play thus
provides an articulation of the relations between citizens and non-
citizens in the state, though any obvious one-to-one allegorical
reading is prevented by the fact that Xanthias did *not* fight in the
battle and Dionysus the god has no meaningful counterpart among
the citizenry.

Here we may begin to see the relevance to the contemporary
circumstances of the Athenians of Aristophanes' choice of the
Eleusinian Mysteries as a structural element in this play. The *atimoi*,
we have said, were not permitted to approach *ta hiera*, and many of
those involved with Phrynichus had fled the city.[81] Thus the

---

[79] On *epitimia*, see Hansen 1976: 55.

[80] Failure to play one's part in a sea-battle was an offence punishable by *atimia* (Andoc. 1.74,
with MacDowell 1962 *ad loc.*).

[81] Their return was one of the stipulations of the terms of peace in 404: X. *HG* 2.2.20 and other
references in Rhodes 1981: 430.

emphasis which is placed by the play on the happiness of the Mystae greatly enhances the plight of those who were tripped by Phryni-chus and so lost their citizenship: we are reminded that they are excluded not only from political life, but possibly also from partici-pation in the Mysteries and so from access to the eternal happiness promised by that festival. We can feel here too something else of the force of these lines when read in this fashion, because the procession to Eleusis had taken place only once since 413. To extend Aristo-phanes' metaphor, everyone is in the same boat, in that even those who have citizen rights have not been able to attend. Everyone therefore should be able all the more to sympathise with those whose 'one error' has led to their exclusion.

In the first part of the play, therefore, the Eleusinian Mysteries are evoked as a way of thinking about participation in and ordering of the state.[82] There is room for all, slave and free alike:[83] the very first piece of advice in the parabasis is 'make the citizens equal' (688). The movement of the procession from Athens to Eleusis, linked and thus acknowledged the importance of both the centre and the margins.[84] The copper-headed barbarian, the polluted and those whose moral and political crimes are such as to exclude them from civilised society and the temples of the gods could not take part. This is just, but the Chorus of Mystae plead that one political error should not be sufficient to deprive good citizens of their rights to citizenship and *epopteia*. Everyone now knows what it is like to suffer this for a short time: would they condemn fellow-citizens to it for ever? The final words of the parodos sum up what is required, initiation and good political behaviour towards *xenoi* and citizens (455–9; quoted above).

Mysteries and poetic *agon*

The Eleusinian Mysteries therefore bulk large in the construc-tion of the sense of the first part of the play. But what significance

---

[82] Cf. Isoc. *De Bigis* 6 for the idea that revealing the Mysteries could be viewed as tantamount to overthrowing the democracy.

[83] Richardson 1974: 214f.; Osborne 1985a: 171. It is tempting to see the narrowing of the bridge to prevent carriage traffic as another measure of equality: carriages, like Xanthias, had to go round the long way (*IG* 1³.79.11ff. (422/1)).

[84] The processions at the Scira and Panathenaea followed the same trajectory; see further, Osborne 1985a: 154–82, esp. 170ff. on the Arcteia and on Eleusis.

have they to the extended poetic *agon* of the second part? The Eleusinian colouring of the second part of the play is less overt than in the first, but it does continue. The Chorus are not again referred to as Mystae, but we have no reason from the text to presume that they have changed their dress or nature and they still frame the action. Since the first part has put the audience in 'an Eleusinian frame of mind', it will be of interest to look at the *agon* through similar mental filters. We receive some encouragement in this from the dialogue which opens the second part. As the slaves discuss the pleasures of behaving as slaves do, there is the following exchange (745):

> *Xa.* Do you *really* like doing it?
> *Slave.* Yes, indeed I seem to enjoy the *epopteia*.

The Slave employs the word used of viewing the culminating ritual of the Eleusinian Mysteries: the *epoptes* was the higher rank to which the *mustes* graduated.[85]

In the preceding scenes, we have seen how references to ritual, politics and poetry are closely bound together and here too the language of poetry and of politics is mixed (760ff.): the quarrel between the two poets is a *stasis* caused by the *nomos* that the best practitioner of each craft should enjoy the *sitesis* in the Prytaneum.[86] The supporters on each side are also described in political terms ('demos', 779; 'the good element', 783). The idea that tragedy is to be 'tested' (802) by various means recalls Aeacus' attempts to discover the god and also the political metaphor of coin-testing from the parabasis.[87] The two codes of the play, the quality of poetry and politics, are thus brought together for an *agon* in which the poet to save the city is chosen.

Like the *agon* in *Wasps*, this one is inaugurated by an offering to the gods, this time of incense (871–3), followed by a hymn of invocation and prayers to the Muses. The act of judging is thus marked as significant, since the correct decision is vital, involving

---

[85] This word is played upon again in 1138ff. There is nothing particularly Eleusinian about the context but the repetition helps keep the Eleusinian *schema* in the audience's mind (cf. Thomson 1935: 23f. for the similar use of this word in *Oresteia*).

[86] Cf. the *prohedria* offered to the Mystae in [Pl.] *Axioch.* 371D and D. L. 6.39.

[87] There are elements in this part of the play reminiscent of the judgement of souls in Hades: Ruhl 1903; Graf 1974: 121–6. For the 'weighing' of lines, cf. the solemn *psuchostasiai* of *Il.* 8.69–72 and 22.209–13; in Aeschylus' *Psuchostasia* Thetis and Dawn disputed for the lives of their sons beside Zeus' scales (fr. 279–80a); *Frogs* 1266 is taken from that play. The image of weighing had appeared in Eupolis' *Demes* (fr. 130).

the state of tragedy in both the upper and lower worlds. When the contestants are called upon to make their prayers before they begin, Aeschylus turns to the goddess of the main festival of his home town: 'Demeter who nourishes my thought, may I be worthy of your Mysteries' (886f.). This may seem to characterise Aeschylus as the pious tragedian, beside the sophistic Euripides who prays to 'other gods' such as Ether, Pivot of the Tongue and Intelligence, but as Charlesworth 1926 argued, if we are to believe the charge of revealing the Mysteries which was brought against Aeschylus (the source is Aristotle) and of which he was acquitted on pleading ignorance of his crime, this would be not the pious prayer of the model poet, but an appeal which most inopportunely recalls a charge of grave seriousness in any circumstances, but especially so in a play which makes these Mysteries a central part of its design.[88]

The contestants have already been introduced by four stanzas in which the epic flavour of the first three lines is deflated by a trochaic lecythion (814–29). Perhaps as an indication of the final result, the imagery is kaleidoscopic to an Aeschylean degree, but by the end, a fairly clear opposition has developed. Both are characterised in terms of animals from Homeric similes and of epic warriors and chariot races, but it is interesting that Aeschylus tends towards the more monstrous:[89] in 'loud-roarer' (814) the same stem is used of him as was applied to Cleophon (680), and he makes a noise like a bull (823); like a giant, he will hurl huge words about (823–5). When his anger breaks out, Dionysus calls for a black lamb to sacrifice 'because a hurricane is on its way' (847f.).[90] He may be given the epithet used earlier of Iacchus, 'much-honoured' (324, 398), but there is something barbaric, or even barbarian in his monstrosity, and the reference to the hurricane (*tuphos*) brings with it echoes of Typhoeus, the instrument of chaos. Beside this, Euripides' sophistry might seem almost Greek: one thinks of a Sausage-Seller before a Paphlagonian or an Odysseus before the Cyclops perhaps, cunning facing a rock-throwing giant. The negative elements of characterisation are not, therefore, all on Euripides' side.[91]

---

[88] Arist. *NE* 1111a9; Anon. *in* Arist. *CAG* 20.145.23ff. (Heylbut) says five plays were involved. For other references, cf. A. *TGF* T 93. I can see no reason to reject this testimony, but one could wish it were clearer. Aeschylus certainly makes use of Eleusinian ideas and imagery in the *Oresteia* (cf. Thomson 1935; Tierney 1937; Bowie 1993b: 15–17).

[89] Sheppard 1910; Tarkow 1982.   [90] Radermacher 1954: 272.

[91] This imagery of giant vs. Sophist is recapped as the *agon* is about to begin (900–4).

In these references to Aeschylus' roaring speech, one begins to hear again echoes of the Eleusinian Prorrhesis, and the suspicion is not a little confirmed by the complaints about the incomprehensible nature of Aeschylus' language which Euripides is soon making (923–6, 928–30 (my emphases)):

> When he'd talked all this nonsense, and the play was half over, he'd come out with a dozen ox-like words, with eyebrows and crests, terrifying things with faces like bogeys; they were quite *unintelligible to the audience* ... He *wouldn't say anything that was clear*, but it was all Scamanders or moats, or bronze-beaten griffin–eagles on shields and beetling phrases that were *difficult to work out*.

His words were like the monsters on Persian hangings (938). The barbaric quality of Aeschylus' language is thus given a negative flavour when viewed against the Eleusinian prohibition which the parabasis has brought before the audience's attention.

There are also Eleusinian overtones to Euripides' very first criticism, of the way in which his distinguished predecessor cheated his spectators (909). Consider 911–20:

> First of all, he'd sit someone on stage, having covered them up – an Achilles or a Niobe – and he wouldn't show their face: it was a pretence at tragedy, because they wouldn't say a thing ... The Chorus would grind out four strings of songs, one after another – but the characters would stay silent ... He did this out of devilment so that the spectator would sit guessing when Niobe would say something. Meanwhile, the drama would drag on.

This description bears a resemblance to the manner of initiation at Eleusis, in the *thronosis*. The clearest evidence is found in artistic representations of the mythical initiation of Heracles, such as the Torre Nova sarcophagus and Lovatelli urn. Heracles sits on a fleece laid on a chair, with his head veiled, as a priestess approaches with either a winnowing-fan or a torch. This is closely similar to the description of Demeter in the *Homeric Hymn* (194–201):[92]

> She waited in silence with her fair eyes down-cast, until subtle Iambe put out for her a jointed chair, and threw over it a white fleece. There she sat holding her veil before her in her hands. For a long time she sat silent with grief on the chair and greeted no-one with word or with gesture, but she sat not laughing nor taking food or drink, pining with longing for her deep-girdled daughter.

[92] Richardson 1974: 211ff.

We do not know much of what was said and done at this and other initiations, but it seems reasonable to suppose that, even if some of the evidence, such as Socrates' initiation of Strepsiades, is comic burlesque, the proper state of mind was induced in the initiand by ritual activity going on around him. Seaford, in an important discussion of what was said at such times, argues that it is likely that 'the central event of the ritual was presented to the initiand, in the ritual itself, in riddling language', which was designed to produce the fear and terror we have spoken of.[93] We do not know when, at Eleusis, the *sunthema*, or password, was pronounced, but its past tenses might suggest it came at the climax of the rite of initiation and its riddling language would also make it suitable: 'I fasted, I drank the *kukeon*, I took out of the covered basket, I worked and laid back into the tall basket, and from there into the other basket.'[94] Aeschylus' representation of his characters on stage as veiled and silent whilst strange language is sung around them is thus a close copy of the Eleusinian initiation ritual. The silence of Niobe in the play is obviously the silence of grief, but it remains striking that Aristophanes should have chosen this aspect of Aeschylus' drama which relates so well to the Eleusinian initiation. Furthermore, Demeter, like Niobe, was grieving for her child when she sat in veiled silence.

Can this 'Eleusinian' analysis also be applied to Euripides' dramaturgy, at least as conceived in *Frogs*? The connection is much less obvious, but it may not be going too far to suggest that Eleusinian ideas are also relevant to the representation, or at least that viewing this representation of Euripides through Eleusinian filters reveals a significant contrast with Aeschylus viewed in the same way. Euripides boasts of the way that his work was 'highly democratic' (952),[95] in that everyone could speak, be they slave, master or woman (950); he introduced 'affairs of the household' (959), which all could understand and could use to 'run their homes better' (975), and generally to take a more intelligent view of their lives. Dionysus reduces this idea *ad absurdum* (980ff.), but it offers us, in place of Aeschylus' incomprehensible barbarisms, tragedies that are open and beneficial to all, slave and free, in which they may be said to

---

[93] 1981: 254f., quoting e.g. the Thurii gold-leaves; Pl. *Phd.* 69c; Demetrius, *De Eloc.* 100f.

[94] Clement, *Protr.* 21.2 finally revealed this secret; cf. also Delatte 1955: 12–23. It is, however, far from certain when the *sunthema* was said: Richardson 1974: 22f.

[95] This is of course weakened by Dionysus' remark in 952f.

resemble the Mysteries. Gaining knowledge that led to salvation was a central feature of Mystic initiation.[96]

Discussion of the lyric passages of the two men reinforces this distinction: Euripides again complains of Aeschylus' obscurity and Aeschylus shows that trivial, everyday objects can always be fitted into Euripides' iambics. If Euripides' lyrics are wildly dithyrambic and on banal subjects (1309ff.), Aeschylus' are repetitive and full of the mumbo-jumbo of *tophlattothrat* (1264ff.).

The evocations of Eleusinian parameters in this way serve, like those of the Gigantomachy, to introduce from the outset of the *agon* an element of ambiguity into the representation of the two contestants. Aeschylus is marked out as the potential victor by the conventional respect of Attic comedy for the past, by the reputation and treatment of Euripides in Aristophanes, and by the fact that Euripides speaks first in the *agon*,[97] and yet Aeschylus is presented to us in ways which, in an Eleusinian context, give us pause for thought. If he is incomprehensible, then he breaks the Eleusinian prohibition on the *barbaros* (and one wonders how he will save the city through his tragedies). If he puts on stage figures in an Eleusinian mode, then we are made to wonder whether this is not another example of his 'revealing the Mysteries'.

This ambiguity is a feature of the different contests that follow, so that it is hard to disagree with the authors of *Hypotheses* 1 and 4, who say that Aeschylus' victory comes 'unexpectedly'.[98] When Aeschylus is finally persuaded to reply to Euripides' criticisms (1006ff.), he attacks the effects of Euripidean tragedy, arguing that while he himself produced warriors Euripides produced talkers; this would be a stronger argument if it had not been the enemies of Athens, the Thebans and Persians, who had been made more warlike (1022–7). Aeschylus contrasts his warriors with Euripides' Stheneboeas and Phaedras (1039ff.). Were the stories not true? Yes, but such things should be suppressed (why, we are not told). Euripides accuses Aeschylus of teaching useless things, which Aeschylus defends with a stylistic argument, but one which borders on the

---

[96] Seaford 1981: 253f.

[97] Neil 1901: 53. This is borne out by e.g. *Clouds*, whose *agon* is similarly constructed to that of *Frogs* (cf. Dover 1968a: 209f.).

[98] Line 27 in each case. There is no clear sign of victory, such as the theft of the hare and the revelation of the oracle in *Knights*.

bathetic: 'Anyway, it's quite right that heroes should use grander words, because they wear more august clothing than we do' (1060f.). This not surprisingly introduces a joke about the effect Euripides' beggar-kings have on the rich Athenians' willingness to pay liturgies, and the catalogue of his ill effects of this kind reaches its climax with Dionysus' description of a man made unfit by Euripidean tragedy putting in a pathetic performance in the Panathenaic torch-race (1089–98). The play lingers on these Euripidean faults, but the consideration of the truth of the first complaint is not attempted, and the second is a 'religious' ill effect for which a parallel has already been given in the case of his opponent. The constant slippage from one criterion of literary and civic excellence to another leaves the question of who has won constantly deferred. After the stylistic competitions, there is the penultimate test, the weighing, which uses a similar slippage. Euripides has earlier boasted of how he slimmed down the overweight Aeschylean drama (939–44); now 'weighty' comes to mean, first the physical weight of the objects mentioned, then, 'grievous', and finally physical weight again, each change being designed to ensure that Euripides is always one step behind.[99] That Dionysus cannot decide the matter after this weighing is a sign of the ambiguous result that ensues from this as from the earlier contests.

The distinction between obscurity and clarity returns in the final, political questions which Dionysus puts to the two poets. The first round is equal, Aeschylus showing wisdom, Euripides clarity (1424–34). In the second,[100] Euripides gives some fatuous advice but then, after one and a half lines of almost Aeschylean obscurity (1443f.), says very much what Aristophanes has said in the parabasis: 'If we mistrust the politicians that we now trust, and make use of those we don't make use of, perhaps we might be saved. If we're now in difficulties in the present circumstances, how would we not be saved if we did the direct opposite?' (1446–50). Aeschylus is again only slightly less obscure than normal (1458–65).

That Euripides should give the same advice as Aristophanes is striking, and, coupled with the fact that Dionysus has come for him, opens up the enticing but unlikely possibility that Dionysus might

---

[99] On stylistics and weighing, Radermacher 1954: 287.
[100] There are major textual difficulties here. I follow MacDowell 1959. Cf. Dörrie 1956–7 for earlier views.

take him after all. But it is not to be. Dionysus gets out of his oath to take Euripides (1469f.) by parodying the famous line of the *Hippolytus*, 'My tongue swore, my heart was unsworn' (612), and the reasons for this are swallowed up in Euripidean outrage and parody. The Chorus of Mystae state their preference with some force, and, as was done at Mystic initiations, pronounce a *makarismos* of Aeschylus,[101] in which they praise his 'accurate intelligence' and the benefits it will bring him and his city (1482ff.). This makes an appropriate climax for the play, but it is also notable that 'intelligence' is one of Euripides' gods (1483, 1490; cf. 893).

The play ends with the blaze of torches, summoned by Pluto's command. This exodos, in which the Mystae, led by the Coryphaeus as Hierophant, escort with their torches Aeschylus and Dionysus–Iacchus, brings back the torch-lit procession of earlier in the play: *propempein* (1525) is the technical term for the Mysteries.[102] We may possibly be intended to recall the end of the *Oresteia*, which, as we have noted, makes much use of Mystic imagery. The ending presumably carried something of the same meaning as the climax described by Plato in the *Phaedrus*:[103]

> Then resplendent beauty was to be seen, when together with the blessed chorus we ... saw a blessed view and spectacle ... and were initiated in initiations which may rightly be called most blessed, and which we celebrated as perfect beings ... encountering, as *mustae* and *epoptai*, happy apparitions in pure splendour, and were pure ourselves.

Dionysus is no longer curiously dressed and isolated from his religious rites, and one of the great Athenian dead ascends to save his city, while those of the living who would be better in Hades are summoned below (1504–14; note the reference to Cleophon): order on and below earth is restored. The resurrection of Aeschylus and the *katabasis* of the wicked reflects the idea that initiation involved a symbolic death and rebirth which is common in ancient mystery cults.[104] The evidence for Eleusis is slight: we hear of the birth of a

---

[101] Dirichlet 1914: 62–4; Seaford 1981: 260 n. 70.

[102] Seaford 1981: 267f. on the pattern *pompe – agon – komos* of the Eleusinian Mysteries in the *Bacchae*; in *Frogs* the same pattern is found.

[103] 250B–C; cf. *Rep.* 560D–E; and in general, Burkert 1987a: 89–114.

[104] For instance, the mysteries of Isis are 'in the form of a voluntary death' from which the initiand is *renatus*; he says 'I set foot on the threshold of Persephone' (Apuleius, *Met.* 11.21, 23; Burkert 1987a: 99–101).

divine child and Sophocles describes the two goddesses as 'nurturing solemn rites'.[105] To quote Burkert, 'There are other suggestions and images as well, which seem to be parallel codes to express the paradox of life in death: Persephone carried off by Death personified and still coming back as a joy for gods and men; the ear of grain, cut to provide seed; the child in the fire, burned to become immortal.'[106] Dionysus' journey to Hades to bring back to life a poet to save the city would therefore express a similar idea.

If in the second part of the play, therefore, the Eleusinian references have been used in a more allusive way than in the first, none the less, taking the play as a whole, we can see a pattern of a mystic initiation. In the first part, there are *prorrhesis*, the 'journey' and tribulation culminating in the procession of the Mystae, *gephurismos*, arrival and *pannuchis*, things which even the uninitiated could know and partake in; and in the second part, there are the *thronosis*, further 'trials', attainment of knowledge and rebirth. The god regains his identity, as the *mustes* underwent the process of the dissolution of his personality and the creation of a new one. Aristophanes thus offers both the taste of the dances, ceremonies and benefits of the festival, and also the prospect of the city's salvation through a great poet. It is not therefore only the politicians like Alcibiades who can revive the Mysteries, which were, after all, a gift of poets like Orpheus and Musaeus in the first place (1032).[107] The Mysteries have acted as a model for stable life in a *polis*: they are open to slave and free alike; they offer justice and proper treatment and equality to all, as well as happiness in the afterlife; they exclude the incomprehensible barbarian and polluted criminal. They even offered peace in time of war: a truce from war of fifty-five days was traditionally declared.[108]

Fantasy in Aristophanes, as we have seen, however, is always put at the service of a greater understanding of the nature and indeed unavoidability of reality, so one must not be too carried away by the triumphal ending. After all, Aeschylus is dead, and in any case has certain features like his incomprehensibility and his uncertain victory that render his usefulness suspect. One might console oneself with the thought that there is another great poet, who has shown,

---

[105] *OC* 1050.   [106] 1987a: 100.
[107] [Dem.] 25.11; Ephorus, *FGH* 70 F 104; Graf 1974: 22–39.
[108] Mylonas 1961: 244; Clinton 1980: esp. 263, 275–8.

both here and in *Thesmophoriazusae*, how he can encompass the tragic dramaturgy of both Aeschylus and Euripides, who can give us the Mysteries, but in truth even his drama can be no more than a *proschema* (913) of them. Nor should one have too simplistic a view of the Mysteries as a model of the Athenian state: Athenian society was not open to all, and the apparent equality of the Mysteries was restricted to the period of their celebration; it was a kind of ideal, whose fulfilment is easier at a ritual or on the comic stage than in the face of the brute reality of war and social relations. There is, in the final procession, no Xanthias, over-burdened or otherwise. And yet, because this is the stage, he has become a citizen after all – his actor is, of course, now playing Euripides or perhaps, even better, Aeschylus.[109]

[109] Segal 1961: 216.

II

Ecclesiazusae

Because of its similarities of subject matter and treatment shared with *Lysistrata* and *Thesmophoriazusae*, *Ecclesiazusae* can be treated at rather less length than the other plays we have looked at. It begins in a manner very similar to *Lysistrata*. A single woman is on stage complaining that her friends have not appeared as promised; these friends then arrive and we are told the details of the women's unprecedented plot to seize power.[1] Again, because it is early in the morning and the women are gathering, the suggestion is that something odd is afoot. Like *Lysistrata* and *Knights*, *Ecclesiazusae* is structured around festivals concerned with the dissolution and regeneration characteristic of the year-end, and there are again specific references to those festivals; like *Thesmophoriazusae*, it uses a festival period in which women were permitted greater scope for public activity.[2] There are however differences between *Ecclesiazusae* and these three other plays. In *Knights*, the festival sequence leads to a return to the great days of Athens under Miltiades and Aristeides; in *Lysistrata*, the women's seizure of power is only temporary and brings about the re-establishment of a world at peace but once more controlled by men; and in *Thesmophoriazusae* the women take matters into their own hands in order to put right a situation which a man has reduced to chaos. In *Ecclesiazusae* by contrast the women assume power completely and for good (458ff., 1024f.), as the model of the *oikos* is imposed upon the *polis*. Their use of the constitutional method of a vote in the Assembly is more

[1] For its unprecedented quality, 456f.; for its impracticality, Pl. *Legg.* 838E–9D. On the question of the relationship between the 'communism' of *Ecclesiazusae* and that of the philosophers, Ussher 1973: xiii–xx.

[2] For a different account of the relationships of *Ecclesiazusae* and *Lysistrata*, Foley 1982.

legitimate than the seizure of the Acropolis by the old women, but is closer to the 'anomalous' arrogation to themselves of legal powers by the women at the Thesmophoria. Of course, the fact that the three plays about women all take place in or are associated with festivals marking periods of 'dissolution' gives a certain comic justification for women playing out roles normally reserved for men. *Ecclesiazusae* can be 'dated' to the period of dissolution that fell between the Scira, where the women hatched their plot, and the Panathenaea which is parodied in Chremes' parade of his household goods at 730ff. As in the earlier plays, the new world created by the end of the drama is by no means perfect. *Ecclesiazusae* combines at its close the role of women as providers of food and drink to their menfolk, and as creators of just that kind of wild sexual disorder that mythology predicates of women: any sympathy one may have for the more equal distribution of property is somewhat qualified by the ambivalent attitudes the extraordinary results of the sexual policies provoke.

The play opens with a hymn to the lamp Praxagora is carrying. This becomes an emblem for the take-over by the world of women of the world of men. The lamp is apostrophised in ways which characterise it as the equivalent in the female sphere of several aspects of the male: it stands for an internal world that is opposed to the external world of the men but at the same time complementary to it.[3] Praxagora begins by addressing the lamp in a manner appropriate to addresses to the sun: her opening words, 'O bright eye . . .', fit the sun and the association is made explicitly in 5: 'You perform the bright duties of the sun.' She then tells how it is 'giving the agreed signs' (6), so that it becomes like the beacons used in the military world of men. One may compare the way in which Clytaemestra in *Agamemnon* steps outside the *oikos* in order to arrange the mighty chain of beacons which alert her to the impending return of her husband whose death and the usurpation of whose power she is planning. The lamp also plays the role of the sun in the inner world of the women, shining on lovers in the intimacy of their bedroom (8). The love-making there is described in terms of wrestling, a male activity performed in the sun:[4] the lamp acts as a *parastates* (9), a word from the hoplite vocabulary,[5] and an *epistates*, a word from

---

[3] Bérard 1989a: 90–3, for this idea on vase-paintings.

[4] Women's internal work is described in a similar athletic metaphor in X. *Oec.* 10.11ff.

[5] LSJ s.v. II.1, 2.

athletic and political usage.[6] It is used in the private act of depilation, when it looks into the women's 'secret recesses' (*muchoi*, 12f.). Of *muchos* Padel writes that, 'if in its hiddenness it was emblematic of the space enclosed within women, as well as being the space which enclosed them, then also in its darkness it was emblematic of darkness ascribed by men to the female interior'.[7] The lamp also stands guard whilst the women pilfer the food and wine from the storerooms, which were themselves deep inside the house.[8] Praxagora calls the store-rooms 'stoas' and the word is significant, because 'stoa' is not found of the store-rooms of houses, but always of the large public ones:[9] again, male and female, external and internal worlds are linked together. In her example of a speech to the Assembly, Praxagora will argue that because the women are 'stewards' and 'treasurers' in their house, they should be given the chance to run the city in the same way (211f.). Finally, there is one difference between the lamp and the sun. Whereas the sun was a regular witness and reporter of men's deeds,[10] the lamp tells nothing of what it sees (16). This secrecy, a feature of the general representation of women in mythology, is one of the boasts of Praxagora and her fellow-conspirators: if the men reveal the secrets of the Boule, the women would never reveal those of the Thesmophoria (442–4), being people of principle (446–51). Thus, that this secret domestic world of the lamp will come to dominate the outdoor world of the men is prefigured by the way that, in the dark of morning, it is the woman's lamp moving out of the *oikos* and addressed as the sun, and not the sun itself, which 'comes out' to signal the start of the day's activities. This reversal is especially paradoxical given that the play takes place at the time of year when the sun was at its hottest.[11]

Because the lamp is the guardian of the women's secrets, Praxagora says she will tell it what the women have planned (17f.). She refers here and again at 59, in language of an official tone, to 'the decisions made at the Scira', thus early directing our attention to the year-end festivals. During the Scira, the women met together in a

---

[6] LSJ s.v. II.2 and III.

[7] 1983: 10; see also Hes. *Op.* 523; *H. Dem.* 113–7; X. *Oec.* 7.3ff.; Walker 1983; Vernant 1983: 148f.   [8] Walker 1983: 87.

[9] The scholiasts say that the storerooms of houses were the same shape as the public ones, but this is wrong (Ussher 1973: 74).   [10] Richardson 1974: 156.

[11] On the 'thesis that the culminating point of summer constituted a threat to sexual life and marital relations', Detienne 1977: 99–131.

special temple 'according to ancestral custom', and had their own organisation as at the Thesmophoria.[12] The seizure of power at the Assembly is thus a comic representation of what took place symbolically at the festival. In the scene where Praxagora leads the women in a practice for their behaviour in the Assembly, various 'errors' are made, which, as in *Thesmophoriazusae*, correspond to the nature of the changes about to be wrought. The *oikos*, the sphere of the women, is about to take over the *polis*, so the domestic weasel rather than the pig normally used is borne round the 'Assembly' (128); because there are garlands to be worn, the women think in terms of the private symposium (131ff.); another proposes to card wool while in the Assembly (88–92).

This gathering together of people not normally so found is underlined by Chremes' remarks on the unusual composition of the Assembly that day: 'when we saw them we all thought they looked like leather-workers; indeed, the Assembly seemed remarkably full of pale folk' (385–7; cf. 'the leather-working crowd', 432). Workers in such crafts were of very low status, and Xenophon notes that they were not only characterised by their indoor life, which rendered them pale, but also by the fact that they had little time for politics and little inclination to fight:[13] pallor also stood as the opposite to the sun-tan associated with masculinity. Pale and unpolitical, they thus make a good parallel for the occupation of the Assembly by women.

Part of the women's plan to assume male power is to steal their husbands' clothes for their disguise in the Assembly. Much emphasis is laid on the usurpation of their husbands' cloaks, shoes and sticks, the putting on of beards, and the cultivation of a sun-tan. Transvestism, as we have seen, is a common feature of rites of transition, but there is no sound evidence for anything of this sort at the Scira.[14] There is however a nice parallel for the reciprocal interchanging of clothes in the Argive Hybristica, a festival marking the temporary assumption of military power by the women under the leadership of the poetess Telesilla. She dressed them in men's clothes to defend the city, and in commemoration of this event each year men and women

---

[12] *IG* 2/3².1177.

[13] *Oec.* 4.2f., 6.6f. Cf. the proverbs in schol. vet. *Peace* 1310 and Macarius 5.55, with Leutsch *ad loc.*; also *Frogs* 1092, *Thesm.* 191; Pl. *Rep.* 556D, *Phdr.* 239C–D; Vernant 1983: 169 n.103.

[14] Cf. Vidal-Naquet 1981b: 156f.; for vases with sun-shades and transvestite figures which might be connected with the Scira, Deubner 1932: 49f.; Beazley 1954: 55–61.

exchanged clothes.[15] So, in a symmetrical reversal in the play, Blepyrus is forced to don his wife's saffron dress and Persian shoes (311ff.). The Hybristica took place in midsummer and so at a similar time of the year to the Scira.[16]

This exchange of clothing between men and women is not the only sign of dissolution exhibited by the Athens of *Ecclesiazusae*. In discussing the *Lysistrata* and the Lemnian Women, we saw that malodorous smells, death and infertility were used to mark the period of female domination. There is something similar in *Ecclesiazusae*, except that here these three things are all associated with the men. Indeed, it is notable that until the women's triumph the men in the play tend to be old and weary in contrast to the more dynamic women. It is as if the sexes have exchanged not only clothes but also the physical powers traditionally ascribed to them.

Perhaps the men's most striking characteristic is malfunction of the bowel. We are first introduced to this in the figure of the flatulent Lamias (78), but the most obviously excremental scene is that where Blepyrus comes on stage to relieve himself (311–72). In these sixty lines, there are some sixteen references to ordure as Blepyrus gives us a rather precise account of the nature of his complaint. When the countrymen demur at the proposal to give power to the women, their reaction is described in terms of intestinal rumbling (433), and when Chremes is describing the pleasures that will accrue to men when the women are in power he does not forget the internal organs: 'You will stay at home farting with nothing to grumble at' (464). At 595, Praxagora accuses Blepyrus of being so keen to prevent her in everything that 'You'll eat shit before I do.' Blepyrus expresses his fears of what children will do to old men when they do not know who their real father is with the words 'They'll surely shit on us?' (640), and the Man has recourse to similar language in his ironic remarks about the likelihood of Antisthenes' contributing his goods to the common fund (807f.): 'It would suit his tune much better to shit for thirty days or more.' Finally, the Young Man tries to escape from the Second Hag by expressing his desire to relieve himself (1059–62). Male reactions thus seem regularly to be of an excremental nature, with the excrement marking the disturbance of normality.

---

[15] Plut. *Mor.* 245C–F; see Saïd 1987 on *travestissements* generally.
[16] Though in the Argive calendar Hermaeus was the fourth not the last month of the year: Daremberg & Saglio 1904: II 829.

We may compare the way that Homer contrasts the disorder in the palace of Odysseus with the glories of those of Menelaus and Alcinous in part by placing at his door a heap of dung with the dying dog Argos on top.[17]

The infertility of the male world is made apparent through two juxtaposed and complementary scenes. At the end of Blepyrus' constipation scene, he prays to Eileithuia for release, though not from the pains of the usual parturition: 'O Lady Eileithuia, do not ignore me bursting and bunged up as I am; I don't want to become a comic commode' (369–71). In the corresponding scene, Praxagora claims to have been visiting a pregnant friend, who successfully gave birth to a male child (549). This is a lie, but it is none the less significant that the text gives us in this formally balanced way a man who has great trouble being productive, and a woman who succeeds. The infertility is also to be seen in Blepyrus' fears first that old men like himself may not be able to satisfy the women's sexual demands (and may therefore miss breakfast (465–72)) and secondly that the old men may have nothing left for the pretty women, now to be held in common, after they have satisfied the less favoured (619ff.). This infertility and the general feebleness of the men accords well with the Greek idea that at the height of summer, as Hesiod puts it, 'women are at their most wanton and men at their weakest'.[18]

Finally, in a passage reminiscent of the 'death' of the Proboulos in *Lysistrata*, Blepyrus complains that Praxagora left him behind as if he were a corpse laid out for burial but in an incomplete state of preparation, being bereft of the traditional garland and oil-bottle (537f.).

These male characteristics are summed up in a joke made slightly later in the scene about the plant *kalaminthe*. Blepyrus expresses his horror at the prospect of certain children claiming that he is their father, but Praxagora points out that there are worse fears (647f.):

> *Prax.* If Aristyllus were to kiss you and say you were his father.
> *Blep.* He'd be in trouble if he did.
> *Prax.* And you'd smell of *kalaminthe*.

[17] *Od.* 17.291–327; cf. Austin 1975: 169f. On death and filth, *Il.* 22.414f., 24.163–5, 639f.; Macleod 1982: 103; Sourvinou-Inwood 1983: 37f, 46f. quoting Heracl. fr. 96 DK 'Corpses are more worthless than dung.'

[18] Hes. *Op.* 582–8; [Arist.] *Prob.* 879a26ff.; Detienne 1977: 120–2.

Clearly, *kalaminthe* is used for a pun on *minthos*, 'dung' / *minthe*, 'mint', but this variety of wild mint was also evil-smelling,[19] and associated with Hades and with impotence.[20] In mythology, Mintha was a lover of Hades who was displaced by Penelope and turned into the plant either by her or Demeter. An Orphic fragment tells how the grieving Demeter once saw this flourishing plant and condemned it to sterility.[21] On Mt Mintha in south-east Elis, there was a rare *temenos* to Hades.[22] The medical writers give mint a double function: it provokes lust but also prevents procreation, making women sterile and destroying or preventing the coagulation of male semen.

All of this excrement, infertility and death, the references to the inadequate way in which men run the political life of the city (e.g. 132ff., 300ff.) and also to their effeminacy (e.g. 102–14, 165–8) show the men to be excellent embodiments of dissolution. Indeed, Blepyrus, dressed in his wife's saffron cloak and shoes, left like an unburied corpse, liable to smell of *kalaminthe* and unable to 'bring forth' is a concise emblem of the disorder staged by *Ecclesiazusae*. Furthermore, he also represents the confusion of inside and outside we discussed above. He tells how, as he looked unsuccessfully for his clothes, the 'dung-collector was already knocking at the door' (315–7). This 'door' may at first blush be taken as the house-door, but one soon realises that it is in fact Blepyrus' own 'back door' that is meant: where normally the dung-collector would come from outside to collect the dung, here he is inside trying to get out.

In *Lysistrata*, the difference between the violent men and the peaceful women was important; the women had, it is true, some negative traits, such as lustfulness, but in general they were represented in a better light. In *Ecclesiazusae*, by contrast, the women's take-over is rendered more natural not just because the men are feeble but also by the many similarities between the women and their husbands: the women can as easily assume male roles in public life as adopt their clothing.[23] The shared features are of various sorts. The names of the women who begin to appear at the start of the plot express virtues associated with male discourse: Cleinarete, Sostrate, Philainete, Geusistrate, embody the ideas of *kleos* ('fame'), *arete* ('virtue'), and military success; the *-agora* element in Praxagora

---

[19] Schol. *ad loc.*; Ael. *NA* 9.26.
[20] Detienne 1977: 72–98; for Aristyllus in a similar context, cf. *Plutus* 313f.
[21] Fr. 44 Kern.   [22] Strabo 8.3.14.   [23] Cf. esp. Saïd 1979.

points to her involvement in the male sphere of the market-place, as in Agoracritus.[24] Some are comically trivial, such as the fondness for drink shared by each sex, or the fact that women have 'beards' (97). There are also the comic insults in which both men and women in politics are referred to as followers of banausic trades: men are like builders' labourers in their civic life (310), Cephalus is accused of being a mere potter (252f.), while the women are referred to as a 'gang of leather-workers' (432). Others contain more serious charges. Praxagora argues at length that women are better keepers of tradition than the men who would normally have been expected to uphold it (214ff., 301ff., 442–5). Men are regularly associated with mal-practice in city politics, and Praxagora mentions at an early stage the women's delight in stealing from the 'stoas' of the house (14f.). The men especially look to politics to provide them with meals (185–8, 206–8, 304–10), and Blepyrus complains to Praxagora that his failure to attend the Assembly has cost him eight quarts of wheat (547f.); since women regularly looked after the household and provided their husbands with meals, it is an easy step for them to do this on a city-wide scale (cf. 211f.).

The normal sexual roles of women also fit them for political life.[25] When one of the women asks how they will handle public speaking, Praxagora replies: 'We'll do it very well. They say that those of the youths who are buggered the most are the best speakers – and we get that a-plenty' (111–14). After all, the women's ability to speak at length is not in doubt: 'Which of us *doesn't* know how to chatter?', says one of them (120). This point is developed in the puns of 256–60:

> *Woman.* What if they interfere with you?
> *Prax.* I'll move with the blow: I'm used to a lot of interference.
> *Woman.* But we've not considered what you'll do if the archers drag you off.
> *Prax.* I'll put my elbows out like this; I'll not be taken round the middle.

The key verb is *hupokrouein*, which not only means 'interrupt', of e.g. an orator, but is also a wrestling term, as in 259f., and a sexual one much used in the play,[26] as here in 'move along with'. The

---

[24] On the names in the play, Paganelli 1978–9.
[25] On sex and rhetoric in the play, Rothwell 1990: 77–101.
[26] 588, 596, 618, 989–91, 1017f.

effeminacy of male politicians renders Praxagora's assumption of power entirely reasonable. Look at Agyrrhius: 'He got away with wearing Pronomus' beard, though he was a woman before. Now, as you see, he's a big noise in the city' (102–4). Thus it is no great task for the women to assume power and Praxagora sums up her intentions by saying that each individual *oikos* is to be subsumed in a single, city-wide entity: 'I tell you I will make the city into a single household, breaking down all the walls to create a single house' (673f.). As in *Lysistrata*, the women's power is exercised in the spheres both of politics and of sexuality.

In the festivals, the return of the women to the homes they had left marks the end of the abnormal period. As if the normal pattern were being followed, *Ecclesiazusae* similarly emphasises at some length the return of the women, and their replacing of the items of male attire they had stolen (479–513), but this new phase of life for the city is to be far from normal. The Panathenaea closed the sequence of year-end festivals and inaugurated the new year with its refreshed normality, and it is a parody of the procession at that festival which marks the start of the new regime in the play.[27] At 730–45, Chremes (if it is he) lines up his household goods, as if they were the members of the Panathenaic procession, in order to take them to the Agora and the communal pile.

> Fair Flour-Sieve, first of my household goods, march out finely, to be a powdered Basket-Bearer; many is the sack of flour you've gobbled down. Where is the Chair-Bearer? Pot, come out here – by heavens, you're black, more than if you'd used Lysicrates' hair-dye! – stand by her. Come here, the maid. Pitcher-Bearer, bring that pitcher here. Out you come, musician, your ill-timed morning chorus has often got me up for the Assembly at night. Let the one with the bowl come forward. Bring the honey-combs, put the branches near by and bring out the tripod and oil-flask. The small pots and the bits and pieces you can send out now.

The *kanephoros*,[28] *diphrophoros*,[29] *hudriaphoros*,[30] *skaphephoros*[31] are found among the members of the Panathenaic procession, and the branches point to the *thallophoroi*, the distinguished older men who also marched.[32] The emphasis on the beauty of the *kanephoros*

---

[27] Cf. the 'circular chorus' of pots and pans in X. *Oec.* 8.19f.

[28] *Lys.* 646.   [29] *Birds* 1552.   [30] Harp. s.v. *skaphephoroi*.

[31] Hsch. s.v.; Photius s.v. *skaphas*.   [32] X. *Symp.* 4.17; schol. *Wasps* 544.

accords with the emphasis placed on physical attractiveness for the choice of members of the procession.

The household that was disrupted by the departure of the wives is now given a new order, but in this case the surprise is that the old order is not restored. This Panathenaic procession is not composed of representatives of all sections of the community, whose presence together displays the unity of the city, but of kitchen-ware. These items symbolise the future dominance of the *oikos* over the *polis* and of the life of dining that Athenians will henceforth enjoy. The use of the domestic implements is reminiscent of the way the items of household furniture form parts of the lawcourt, which effects Philocleon's passage from city to *oikos* and the symposium. Aspects of the *polis* are 'domesticated': there will be no trials, as punishment will be the simple withholding of food (657–72), and the lawcourts, stoas, and rostrum will become *andro__nes*, dining-rooms, where in the past men alone gathered;[33] the *kleroteria*, the machines which used to allot men to the various courts, will now determine where they eat (675–88).

Chremes' domestic Panathenaea thus inaugurates the new age. If the festival schema points to an improved world, Aristophanes' earlier plays and the fact that the procession is composed of household goods suggest something different. There are signs of rejuvenation, as in the skittish behaviour of Geron, 'Old Man' and his 'young' friend (848f.), and indeed in the behaviour of the Old Women. The smells are sweeter too: perfume-sellers now stand by every table (841f.) and the tipsy slave-girl announces herself with the words 'I've perfumed my hair with perfumes' (1117), and extols the bouquet of the Thasian wine (1118–24). However, as in the case of Dicaeopolis' realm, Philocleon's new life and Peisetaerus' empire, one does not have far to look for problems. It is not even certain that all the men will accept the new utopian conditions. There is a long scene between Chremes and a Man in which the latter is most reluctant to give up his property, not least because he is sure that there will be plenty of others with the same reservations; the Athenians are more prone to take than to give, and there is even divine sanction for such an attitude: 'The gods are just the same. You can tell by the hands on statues: when we pray that they will give us

[33] Ussher 1973: 171.

good things, they stand there with their cupped hand outstretched, not like people about to make a gift but in order to get something themselves' (779–83). He goes off to work out how to get his dinner and avoid contributing, his private enterprise not only leaving a small question mark over the success of the whole idea, but also showing why such radical action was needed to improve the city.

As befits a world dominated by the *oikos*, it is in nutritional and sexual matters that the results of the women's coup are most fully represented. In each case, however, there are features which prevent one accepting the changes as simply beneficial. In place of corrupt politicking there is copious eating, summed up in the great compendious word-feast of 1169–75, the longest extant word in ancient Greek. This word provides a splendid closural device, but can be read as more than merely a virtuoso joke:[34]

> this word-feast (*mot-repas*) describes in effect a feast that is nothing but a word ... It is also a *mot-pâtée* or even a *mot-merde*, since all the food-stuffs are so mixed together there as to lose their identity ... The consumption of everything by everybody reveals also its true nature: a return to a general lack of differentiation and to chaos.

Furthermore, Praxagora has decreed sexual communism and, in an attempt to give all a share in this new-found licence, proclaims that the ugly shall have first refusal. However egalitarian this may appear at first sight, the complications that it involves are rapidly made plain in the scene between the Young Girl, the Old Women and the Young Man (877ff.). If the new feasting is unproblematic in a world that seems sealed from outside interference, the sexual revolution gives one pause for thought. Normal sexuality is made almost impossible, as the natural coupling of young male and female is always to be prefaced by the union of young and aged, so that the Youth is faced with the same problems of sexual inadequacy as beset Blepyrus earlier: 'If I die at your hands first, how will I be able to approach this pretty girl?' (1079f.; cf. 465ff.). The Girl will be reduced to desperation or Lesbianism (906–10, 918–20). As she says to the First Old Woman, the new laws will produce a strange breed: 'You'd be a better mother to him than wife. If you establish this law, you'll fill the whole land with Oedipuses' (1040–2). Add to this the chaos that is produced as the old women compete to be the ugliest,

[34] Saïd 1979: 55, 60.

and it is clear that Praxagora's new legislation has produced at least as much disorder as existed before.[35]

Significantly, the themes of sterility and death recur from the first part. Young men are bedded with old women, and associate them with death: the First Old Woman is 'death's darling' (905); the significantly named Geres (932) is her only suitable lover, though the Young Man suggests the best painter of funerary vases would do as well (995f.). When she insists he follow her, the resulting exchange grimly confuses the paraphernalia of weddings and funerals (1030–5):

> *Young Man.* Well then, spread first the oregano and lay down four crushed vine branches; put on the ribbons and set out the oil-flasks; set the pot of water by the door.
> *O.W. And* you'll buy me a garland too.
> *Y.M.* Indeed I will, so long as it's a wax one:[36] I think you're going to fall to bits in there.

The Second Old Woman is an Empusa (1056f.), a chthonic horror linked with Hecate, and the Third has risen from the 'majority', the dead (1073), and swears by Hecate (1097).[37] The Young Man's joke ultimately turns sour on him, and his last words are instructions for his own rather surreal funerary-monument: 'Bury me at the very mouth of the harbour, and on the top of the tomb put this woman, alive; fix her feet in pitch, and pour lead round her ankles to set her up in place of the lecythus' (1107–11). One is reminded of Blepyrus' complaint to Praxagora that she did not provide him with a lecythus: death has not been banished from the new utopia, and now it is the vitality and fertility of the young that is threatened.

This scene is sufficiently obscene and disconcerting for some scholars to feel that it throws a curious light over the rest of the action.[38] It makes the subsequent speech of the Heraldess, 'O blessed people' ring somewhat hollow, and even the gift of youthful attendants to Blepyrus (1137f.) seems tainted by what has gone before and is a pale reflection of similar scenes in plays such as *Acharnians*, *Knights*, *Peace*, and *Birds*. Others prefer to see it as the 'gross triumph

---

[35] On these songs, Olsen 1988.
[36] Used at funerals: Artemid. *Oneir.* 1.77 (p. 85.16–18 Pack).
[37] Hecate is 'always a goddess of private rather than public cult' (M. L. West 1966: 277).
[38] E.g. Saïd 1979: 58–60.

of comic energy'.[39] One should probably not choose either pole here, as there is a danger of reacting in a culturally determined fashion. Obviously, the Old Women are represented as very grotesque, but in many societies when women get beyond child-bearing age they are permitted much greater freedom in matters where younger women are strictly controlled.[40] The type of the lewd old woman is common in Greek literature,[41] and she is a comic exaggeration of the greater liberty that old women had for appearing in public, for lascivious talk, for publicly taking part in the orgiastic rites of deities like Sabazius and so on.[42] This consideration should mitigate too horrified a reaction to the scene.

One may ask whether the scene has any ritual analogues that could give us an insight into how the Athenians may have understood it. Its meaning in terms of the reversal of normal sexual relations is clear, but there may perhaps have been further echoes for an Athenian audience. Unfortunately this paragraph must be very speculative because of the uncertainties involved, but the suggestion is put forward only as a possible schema that the Athenians may have used. The sexual licence that is inaugurated by Praxagora, for all the rules which hedge it about, has something of a parallel in the Adonia, a festival which was not one of the 'official' city festivals and whose wantonness contrasted with the usual strict control of sexual relations in the city, and drew unfavourable comment in some quarters. Something of the rituals and the attitude to them can be seen from the passage in *Lysistrata* (387–98, discussed above), where the Proboulos complained of the laments for the dead Adonis sung from the rooftop (389, 395) by a drunken woman during the debate on the Sicilian expedition. Whether we can see an allusion to this in our scene depends in part on how we imagine it staged. Fraenkel, following Wilamowitz in his notion that a flat roof was normal for tragedy and comedy, argued that the most effective staging would be for the Old Woman to be standing on the roof: 'The love songs of the old hag become much funnier if she is whirling round on the roof than if she were only allowed to accompany her excited stanzas by nodding and waving her arms from the window.'[43] He quotes Pollux to the effect

---

[39] Konstan & Dillon 1981: 382; cf. also Sommerstein 1984: 320; Henderson 1987b: 118f.

[40] Apte 1985: 79f.   [41] Oeri 1948.

[42] Bremmer 1985: 276–86; Dem. 18.259f.; Hyperides, fr. 205 Jenson: 'A woman who leaves the house should be at the stage of life when those who meet her ask not whose wife but whose mother she is.'   [43] 1936: 265.

that 'in comedy, pimps, old women and women (*gunaia*) look down from the roof', as Dicaeopolis' wife did at his Rural Dionysia.[44] He would like the Young Woman to be on the roof too: 'In all probability the striking symmetry of the speeches and songs of the two women is to be emphasized by a corresponding symmetry of action.'[45] If Fraenkel is right and the women are together or singly on their roofs until 975, then lascivious singing and dancing on a roof might well have provoked thoughts of the Adonia in the audience.[46] In 1040, the Young Woman tells the Old that she 'would make a better mother than a wife' to the handsome Young Man, which could also be said of Aphrodite in her affair with the new-born and irresistible Adonis.[47] More adventurous spirits may even have seen in the competition between the Old Women for the youth a reflection of the dispute for Adonis between Aphrodite and Persephone,[48] and in the elaborate preparations for the laying out of the bier for the 'death' of the Young Man the laying out for burial of the dead Adonis and the casting of his statue into the sea: Plutarch tells us that there were 'images everywhere like laid-out corpses; the women imitated his funeral, beating their breasts and singing laments'.[49] The time of the year would also be right: the Adonia was a summer festival.[50]

If one may view this scene in terms of the Adonia, then the play juxtaposes the sequence of official year-end festivals with an unofficial one that took place at roughly the same time, in a manner reminiscent of *Lysistrata*, which situated the women between Thesmophoria and Adonia. Praxagora's reforms not only impose the model of the *oikos* on the *polis* but also alter the nature of *polis* festivals, making them domestic: the Adonia was celebrated at home. *Ecclesiazusae* thus uses the freedom of action by the women in the year-end period and the sequence of festivals to create a reversed world, an opposite of the normal. It is up to the audience to relate this new world which follows Chremes' Panathenaic parade of pots to the normality felt to be restored after the city's Panathenaea.

[44] Pollux 4.129; *Ach.* 262; Call. *H.* 6.4f.; E. *Ph.* 88ff. [45] 1936: 265.
[46] However, the most recent discussion of this scene rejects Fraenkel's suggestions: Mastronarde allows that the Young Woman may be up high, but prefers to see her at a window; the Old Woman he does not think is upstairs (1990: 257f., 282, 285). [47] Also [Bion] 1.24.
[48] Panyassis *ap.* Apollod. 3.14.4; according to this version, Adonis' time was divided between three people, Zeus, Aphrodite and Persephone. For sex at this festival, Men. *Samia* 39–45.
[49] *Alc.* 18, cf. *Nic.* 13; also Theoc. 15.8off.; [Bion] 1.68ff. Others, of course, may have demanded a reference to gardens or lamentations before they would accept this suggestion.
[50] Weill 1966.

Plutus

Economic and social circumstances

Plutus is Aristophanes' last surviving play, produced shortly before his death in 388. Its subject is wealth and its place in society. After the defeat in the Peloponnesian War, Athens' economy naturally suffered a severe decline, but there is a tendency now among economic historians to avoid painting too black a picture of the early decades of the fourth century.[1] True, she had lost the great revenues that accrued to her from the empire, her supplies of corn had been interrupted, many slaves had fled from the city in the last years of the war and the Laurium mines were no longer worked, but within a decade of the crucial defeat at Aegospotami Athens was once again involved in a major war and was clearly once again a power to be reckoned with. The big economic problems which beset the rest of Greece seem to have affected Athens less,[2] and as a result the tensions between rich and poor seem to have been less traumatic. There were indeed those who made a great deal of money very quickly after the defeat, and these are pilloried in the orators;[3] there was too a concentration of wealth in the hands of certain people,[4] and a disinclination on the part of the rich to contribute to the costs of the city;[5] the poorer citizens had either to work if they could to make a living,[6] or to depend on state-aid which provided only a minimal existence.[7] None the less, one does not get the impression of a city

---

[1] Mossé 1962, with the revaluation of the evidence in Mossé 1972; David 1984; Sommerstein 1984; Strauss 1986: 42–69; M. Dillon 1987b; Burke 1990.
[2] For Isocrates' grim picture of Greece in the fourth century, Fuks 1972.
[3] Lys. 19 (esp. 28f., 39f., 42f., 46–8), 20, 22, 27, 32.   [4] Mossé 1962: 147.
[5] Mossé 1972: 144.   [6] E.g. X. *Mem.* 2.7.
[7] For the minimal nature of state-aid, *Wasps* 303–6; Andoc. *Areop.* 54; Dem. 3.33.

riven by disputes between the haves and have-nots, or plagued by endemic poverty. One should not therefore read the economic situation at Athens straight from the *Plutus*, which is not simply a response to economic disparities, as has often been thought.

Furthermore, as Dillon has shown, Aristophanes is careful to avoid too much in the way of specific references to contemporary people and conditions: there are very few allusions to individuals and 'the very brevity of the allusions, even the most important, deprives them of thematic weight';[8] we hear nothing of the charges of profiteering or of the burdens the rich were becoming less willing to bear. The play is thus constructed in a way that makes it more than just a comment on the society of its time. Dillon ascribes the absence of topicality also to the 'decreasing interest in political engagement on the part of the public at large' compared with earlier periods.[9] There are obvious dangers in seeing too close a relationship between changes in political and social life and changes in literary genres, since there is no reason why one should follow the other *pari passu*; furthermore, *Ecclesiazusae*, produced not many years before, differs from *Plutus* in that it still operates more at the level of the city, at least in its first part, than does the later play. None the less, there is evidence to suggest a 'loosening of the close bond between citizen and state', with politics being left more to 'professionals', who can come to be closely identified with the sycophants.[10] The increasing use of mercenary soldiers in place of the old citizen militias also played its part, since a vote for war now did not necessarily mean going home to get one's helmet. We shall return to the significance of this point later.

Plutus

The eponymous hero of this play is the product of the union of Demeter with Iasion, with whom she consorted in a thrice-ploughed field.[11] Since he was engendered in an agricultural context, the wealth he stands for is not unnaturally often expressed in agricultural terms, as for instance in Hesychius' glosses, 'wealth: fertility of

---

[8] 1987b: 167.   [9] Ibid. 174; cf. 174–83 in general.   [10] Ibid. 176; Lévy 1976: 233–8.
[11] *Od.* 5.125–8, without reference to Plutus, first found in Hes. *Th.* 969–74 (M. L. West 1966: 422f.); cf. *H. Dem.* 489; *PMG* 885; *Thesm.* 295–8. Plutus is regularly depicted sitting on Demeter's lap: Richardson 1974: 316–21.

seed, *panspermia'*, and 'an opulent basket: they used to call wealth abundance of barley and corn'.[12] He is connected with the god of the Underworld, Pluto, with whom he is identified in 727; Plato says Pluto is so called 'because wealth comes up out of the ground'.[13] He is regularly depicted as blind.[14] In our period, he appears in a restricted number of rituals. For the Athenians, the most important would have been the Eleusinian Mysteries, where his birth featured as part of the climax of the secret rites: 'His chief role is as the young child of Demeter, the guarantor and bringer of prosperity, and so of men's hopes for happiness in the present life, balancing their expectations of a better fate after death.'[15] The blind wanderings and tribulations of Plutus followed by the restoration of sight to his eyes could be related to the initiates' journey to the light that shines out in the darkness in the Telesterion,[16] but, unlike *Frogs*, the play does not make great use of Eleusinian imagery. The restoration in the dark of his sight (737–40) and the placing of a cloth over his head (730–2) have obvious Eleusinian resonances, but the principal schema here, as we shall see, is the cult of Asclepius; furthermore, there is a gap in time between the restoration of sight and the shining forth of the light of day (743f.): had the two come together then evocation of the Mysteries to explain the scene would be much more compelling.

One other rite involving Plutus merits mention. At Chaeronea, 'there is a traditional rite of sacrifice, which the Archon performs at the common hearth (of the city) and everyone else at home, called "the driving out of Bulimus" [hunger]. Striking one of the servants with branches of agnus castus, they drive him out of doors shouting "out with Bulimus, in with Plutus and Health".'[17] We do not know how prevalent this ritual was elsewhere, but there are a number of literary texts which talk of inviting Plutus into one's home, which may suggest that Chaeronea was not alone in having such a 'first-

---

12 Cf. Hsch. s.vv. *ploutos, euplouton kanoun*; Hes. *Op.* 22–4, 30–4, 299–301; schol. Hes. *Th.* 971.

13 *Crat.* 403A.   14 First in Hippon. 36.1, then Timocr. *PMG* 731.1.

15 Richardson 1974: 320; cf. 318; this idea is opposed by Mylonas 1961: 213, 307f.; cf. also Burkert 1983a: 289.

16 For a discussion of the play in terms of rites of passage, Paradiso 1987.

17 Plut. *Mor.* 693Eff. For this type of festival, Mannhardt 1904–5: I 251ff. *Agnus castus* is used again at the liminal times of the Thesmophoria. Compare also the Aristophanic compound *plouthugieia* (*Kn.* 1091, *Wasps* 677, *Birds* 731). Words connected with health are frequently used in the play to express the fact that things are in some way disordered: 37, 50, 274, 355, 356, 362, 364, 507, 870, 1060, 1066; cf. also 2, 8–12, 366, 903.

footing' rite.[18] In 374, when the cult of Peace was instituted at Athens, Cephisodotus created a statue of her holding the child Plutus.

As a youth, Plutus was blinded by Zeus because of the benefits he brought to just mortals: 'Zeus did this to me because he was jealous of mankind. When I was small I boasted that I would consort with the just, wise and upright alone, but he made me blind so that I wouldn't recognise any of them: such is his jealousy of the good' (87–92). There is nothing exceptional in this idea of divine *phthonos*: Pindar regularly prays that it will not beset his victors because of their great happiness, and Solon described the divinity as 'jealous and disruptive'.[19] As Buxton has shown, the punishment of blinding was characteristic of cases where there is 'a specific infringement of the boundary between god and man'.[20] There are many examples. Similar to the plight of Plutus is Apollonius of Rhodes' tale of how Phineus was blinded for abusing Apollo's gift of prophecy because he revealed to men the 'sacred mind' of Zeus.[21] The Harpies defiled his food and left him 'like a lifeless dream, bowed over his staff; . . . as he moved, his limbs trembled with weakness and age; his parched skin was caked with dirt, and nothing but the skin held his bones together'.[22] His one consolation was an oracle saying the sons of Boreas would free him of the Harpies.[23] At 635f., Aristophanes quotes from one of Sophocles' treatments of this story. Unfortunately, it is far from clear which versions of Phineus' story were used by Sophocles, but there are traditions that Phineus was blinded either by Zeus or the Argonauts for blinding his sons;[24] it was on curing his sons that Asclepius was struck by Zeus' thunderbolt.[25] Seers, men with superhuman knowledge of the future, are regularly blind, as are poets like Homer or, in a case involving transgression, Stesichorus, who was blinded because of a poem he wrote of Helen

[18] Hes. *Op.* 377; Hom. *Epigr.* 15.3; *H. Dem.* 488; Sappho 148.1; Hippon. 36; S. fr. 273; Chaeremon, *TGF* 71 F 36; Phoenix fr. 2.8 (*CA* 233). So in the play at 41–3, 230–3, 234–44 etc.

[19] Hdt. 1.32.1; Ranulf 1933–4; Pötscher 1958.

[20] 1980: 27; cf. also Esser 1939. There is a mass of material in Deonna 1965.

[21] 2.178ff.; in the earlier version, perhaps from the Hesiodic *Catalogue* (fr. 157), Apollo (or Helios) blinded him because he preferred a blind but prophetic existence over a sighted one (Buxton 1980: 28f.). [22] 2.197–201; cf. S. fr. 712 for Phineus as 'an embalmed corpse'.

[23] A. R. 2.234f. Plutus too is comforted to know that Apollo is aware of what is happening (212–4).

[24] Hygin. *Fab.* 19; Apollod. 3.15.3; schol. Ov. *Ibis* 265, 271; Pearson 1917: II 311ff.; *TGF* 4.484–9. [25] S. fr. 710; Phylarchus, *FHG* 1.338, fr. 17.

and only regained his sight when he repented through his 'palinode'.[26] Seeing a divinity albeit involuntarily was a common cause of blindness, most famously perhaps in the case of Teiresias' seeing Athena bathing.[27] There is a 'historical' example in Herodotus, where Epizelus, an Athenian warrior saw a *phasma* at the battle of Marathon and lost his sight.[28] Other transgressions were similarly punished, as in the case of Lycurgus, whom Zeus blinded for his opposition to Dionysus,[29] or Thamyrus, who challenged the Muses to a musical competition and suffered similarly.[30] Even crimes against mortals, especially sexual ones, can bring about blindness, perhaps, as Buxton suggests, because 'in so far as the gods are guarantors of human morality, such crimes are, at one remove, infringements of the divine order.'[31] In comparison with these tales, the blinding of Plutus stands out as anomalous. Some of the mortals who are blinded are clearly blameless, in that they meant no harm, but even they are not punished for their desire to help good men, which in normal ideology is the province of Zeus. One could just about argue that Plutus has transgressed onto Zeus' territory in deciding to look after the good, but it would be a transgression that, in comparison with the others mentioned here, scarcely deserves the name. Zeus, who is described as being jealous of mankind, would appear to be immediately placed in a questionable position.

Another structure shared by this play with myth and ritual is that of the return of a god to his full powers after a period of withdrawal. In Plutus' case, of course, the 'return' is to a place which seems to be above that of Zeus;[32] the result is similar to that in *Birds*, but less dramatic. We have already discussed this type of myth in connection with *Peace*. Plutus' conflict with Zeus is close to stories of divine figures who fell foul of Zeus' anger and were punished before returning to their former positions. Thus Hephaestus tells of being thrown by Zeus from heaven down to Lemnos, where the Sinties nursed him back to health,[33] and, perhaps in a reference to the same story, Zeus reminds Hera of how she was hung from heaven with

---

[26] Buxton 1980: 27–30.   [27] Call. *H*. 5.   [28] 6.117.   [29] *Il*. 6.130ff.   [30] Hes. fr. 65.
[31] 1980: 32, put forward 'with diffidence', but eminently plausible.
[32] Cf. 1188–90. From the scholiast onwards, many scholars have taken 'Zeus the Saviour' here to be Plutus himself, but 'the Priest could not have rejoiced at the good tidings had he received no tidings at all': he knows Plutus is in Chremylus' house, which is why he has decided to abandon Zeus to 'settle here' (Rogers 1187); his delight is surely that he need not abandon his god, because that god has already gone over to Plutus?   [33] *Il*. 1.589–94.

anvils around her feet, because of her attempt to damage Heracles.[34] More pertinently in the context of *Plutus*, when Zeus killed Asclepius, Apollo avenged his son by killing in turn the Cyclopes; only Leto's intervention saved him from death, instead of which he was sent to serve the mortal Admetus as a slave for a year, before he could again take up his place in Olympus.[35] Apollo's reduction to the condition of servitude is repeated in the way Plutus has been reduced to a miserable condition as a result of his wanderings (80, 265–7), during which misers have buried him underground and profligates have thrown him naked out of the house (237–44). The blindness and separation from the good men who are his natural milieu also mark his removal from his proper position. The ragged nature of Odysseus in *Odyssey* and of Philoctetes on Lemnos, who also suffers a debilitating physical wound, provide parallels for this period of marginalisation.

The significance of the evocation of Asclepius, and indeed of that other helper of mankind who is also an important figure for understanding the play, Prometheus, is a subject to which we will return after a discussion of how the play conducts its examination of the role of wealth in the workings of society. Two main problems are involved. First, there are the relationships between one man and another and between man and god which are expressed through the notion of *charis*, that moral concept whereby any benefaction entailed an obligation to repay it.[36] Second, it concerns the effect on those relationships of removing the stimulus of poverty.

Charis

We have seen that the reason behind Zeus' blinding of Plutus was his desire to consort with good men (87–92). In so directly failing the good, Zeus does two things. First, by allowing the wicked to flourish like the green bay-tree and the just to languish in poverty, he has, as it were, broken his side of the bargain whereby those who follow the laws of the gods are rewarded, and so he undermines the

---

[34] Ibid. 15.18–24.   [35] Hes. frr. 50–8.

[36] The idea is fundamental to Greek ideology. Cf. e.g. Gould 1989: 85: 'The "reciprocity model" is Herodotus' most serious model for explaining not merely human and divine behaviour, but also . . . physical phenomena . . .' The importance of this concept can be seen in e.g. Hes. *Th.* 503–6, *Op.* 349ff.; Pi. *Ol.* 1 and the speeches of Thuc. 3.

whole system of morals which is supposed to be guaranteed by the gods. In this way, secondly, he removes any reason for mortals to follow the laws of the gods. As a result, he threatens his own position: it is the just alone who honour him (93f.). By allowing the blind circulation of wealth to rupture the presumed natural connection between justice and prosperity, Zeus has created an unstable situation which will be resolved in favour of his rival, since only the just will be helped by Plutus and consequently they will sacrifice to him alone. This danger is realised at the end when the priest of Zeus Soter is out of a job, because no-one needs to sacrifice for the success of a business venture (1171–84): that he should choose a commercial example to make his point is symptomatic of the general obsession with *virtus post nummos*.

This absence of any correlation between justice and prosperity is the mainspring of the action, as Chremylus makes clear (28–31):

> *Chr.* Though I'm a devout and just man, I was doing badly and was poor.
> *Carion.* Don't I know it.
> *Chr.* But sacrilegious politicians, sycophants and villains were prosperous.

Chremylus is depicted (or depicts himself) as a model man; he keeps his oaths (61) and the golden mean (245), and there is none better than he for moral behaviour (104–6) or in money matters (247f.). But the problem is not confined to him: 'There are many wicked men who are rich and who have gained their wealth by unjust means, but there are many perfectly good men who are in a bad way and are poor' (502–4). It is for this reason that Blepsidemus insists at such length that Chremylus must have acquired his wealth by criminal means (352–90). That this situation should obtain flies in the face of what is obvious to anyone, that the good should prosper and the wicked suffer (490f.), and Chremylus promises that natural justice will be restored by Plutus and himself, so that the just will flourish (386–8; cf. 495–7).

For Chremylus, this state of affairs has reached the point where he wonders whether his son should abandon traditional moral behaviour in favour of a life of crime, since this appears to be the only way to prosperity (35–8); he himself is too old to change, but he feels the problem for his son is sufficiently acute for him to consult the Delphic oracle. If Zeus is not prepared to let the just prosper, then why should one continue to be just? Carion's interpretation of the oracle as meaning that the son should follow 'the local custom' (47), a transparent reference to criminality, serves to emphasise the depressing state to which things have sunk.

The scene between Carion and Hermes emphasises in a more comic fashion this breakdown in relationships between men and gods (1097ff.). Much of the banter revolves around the question of whether the god has helped Carion sufficiently in the past to be able to demand in return admission to Plutus' realm. When Hermes, like the priest, complains about the lack of sacrifice, Carion makes the crucial reply: 'And no-one *will* sacrifice to you, because you looked after us badly in the past' (1116f.). Carion is not impressed by Hermes' comparison of his present hunger with the past, when tavern-women would bring him dainties, and comments again that the god has not kept his side of the bargain: 'It's right that you should be hungry, because, though you got those presents, you did damage to those who gave them' (1124f.). Undeterred, Hermes asks whether Carion will not help a *philos* ('friend', 1134) and there follows a comic debate on reciprocity (1139–45):

> *Herm.* Well, whenever you stole a pot from your master, I always
> saw to it that you weren't noticed.
> *Ca.* Only on condition that you got a share as well, you burglar,
> because you always got a rich cake done to a turn.
> *Herm.* Then you ate the lot yourself.
> *Ca.* That's because you didn't share the blows I got when I was
> caught red-handed.

Even Hermes' reminder of Thrasybulus' magnanimity after the fall of Phyle does not persuade Carion to give him something for nothing; Hermes has to prove his usefulness (1152), which Carion eventually grudgingly agrees he has, when he offers to put on celebratory games for Plutus as Hermes Agonios (1161–3).

It is not only between a god and his worshippers that relationships of *charis* have broken down. Three further scenes from the end of the play make this point repeatedly. Amongst mortals, the fact is revealed most clearly in the scene with the Just Man (823–49). Having inherited a decent sum of money from his father he used it to help his friends, because he thought this the wisest way of life (829–31). When the money ran out, however, his friends did not reciprocate and only the accession of Plutus has freed him from penury.

Unlike his friends, however, the Just Man brings a gift of thanks to the god, the cloak and shoes in which he suffered. These are described as 'pleasing indeed' by Carion (849), which should not be taken as merely ironic or mocking; such an attitude might be hinted at by the actor saying the lines, but it should be remembered that it was normal practice for, for instance, sailors to hang up the garments in which they were saved from shipwreck as votive-offerings to the god who saved them[37] and for patients to bring bandages,[38] prisoners fetters and so on.[39]

A more complex evaluation is given in the most substantial scene concerning *charis*, that between Chremylus, the Old Woman and the Young Man (959–1096). That a young man should have to sell himself to an old woman may be a sign of the abnormal times caused by Plutus' blinding. What is less clear however is the attitude that the reader is to take to the antagonists in the debate, not least because of the bizarre nature of the affair and their ambiguous personal qualities. The text contrives to complicate the matter to the point where it does not permit a preference for one argument over another, thus bringing out the complexities of the *charis*-system. The youth is presented at the outset in a sympathetic light, because he is described in terms reminiscent of Chremylus and the other deserving poor (976f.; cf. 28f.), and the woman paints a picture of an arrangement that appears to benefit both sides: 'If I wanted anything, he'd do everything for me in a nice gentlemanly way, and I gave him all he needed' (977–9). Natural suspicions that all could not be so simple are confirmed by the Old Woman's description of the youth's exorbitant demands for money (981–6). As she recounts his kindnesses to her, Chremylus' foolish remarks constantly point up the suspicious nature of the youth's real intentions. So long as the Old Woman was happy with this state of affairs, however, the youth's greed is merely disagreeable, but now he has achieved wealth from another source, and no longer wishes the relationship to continue. This prompts the Old Woman to protest in language that echoes the fundamental question of the play: 'By Zeus, it's right to compel the one I benefited to benefit me in return' (1028f.). The justice of this is not seriously undermined by Chremylus' obscene suggestion that the youth had

[37] Rouse 1902: esp. 187–239; *AP* 6.245; Hor. *C.* 1.5.14 (with Nisbet & Hubbard 1970: *ad loc.*).
[38] Herzog 1931: no. 6; Osborne 1985a: 170 on the dedication of clothes worn during childbirth and menstruation.   [39] Hdt. 1.66.2–4; Paus. 2.13.4, 8.47.2; Rouse 1902: 233.

fulfilled his obligation every night (1031). The Old Woman wishes to prolong the arrangement with her gift of cakes (999–1002), but the Young Man's refusal to respond brings up the questions of how long such exchanges of *charis* should continue and in what way they may be affected by circumstance. The scene closes with a series of remarkably cruel jokes at the expense of the Old Woman, which incline one to a certain sympathy: old bawd she may be, but is she any worse than a young gold-digger, even one who is repaying the god with an offering of his garlands (1088f.)? That he should be going to a *komos* with a young girl (1040f.) may be natural, and his concern for his mother and sisters laudable (984f.), but can the past be buried so easily? Significantly, the scene ends without the questions being resolved.

The scene with the Sycophant looks at the matter in more political terms (850–958), as Aristophanes shows that even the most unlikely figures partake in *charis*-relationships. Given the reputation of his class[40] it might be thought that the Sycophant would be hard to fit into any scheme of *charis*, but he has a case to make. His arrival appears to show yet again that Plutus' reign has righted human affairs, because a man 'of bad stamp' is faring badly (861f.), but he makes bold to claim that he is 'a lover of his city' and 'good' (900), in a complaint that echoes the language of Chremylus' original dissatisfaction at the way people were rewarded. His interlocutor (it matters little whether it is Carion or the Just Man, though the latter might be more appropriate in a discussion of city affairs) is amazed, but the Sycophant uses standard arguments from the lawcourts.[41] He is a 'benefactor' of the city and a guardian of its laws (911–15). He is the man who avails himself of the right created by Solon that 'anyone who wished' could instigate a prosecution: how else is the city's legal system to work? (916–19). It is interesting that the *Athenaion Politeia* calls this provision one of the three 'most democratic' aspects of Solon's legislation.[42] The Sycophant's democratic concerns are also evinced in his complaint that Plutus has acted unconstitutionally in not going before the Boule or Assembly, thus threatening the democratic process (945–50), no feeble argument in a democracy that saw these as fundamental features of its political system and which had survived a number of attempts to bypass or radically alter the

[40] Lofberg 1914; Lévy 1976: 233–8.   [41] Dover 1974: 288–301 for examples.
[42] 9.1; Rhodes 1981: 159f.

nature of the two bodies. Few can have felt much *charis* for a
Sycophant, but his case is not entirely specious by any means nor is it
founded merely on special pleading. Furthermore, in his favour it
must be said that, though it may surprise us, he does what he does
because he believes in it and not for money: not Plutus himself nor all
the silphium in Cyrene would make him give up what he sees as
benefiting the city and its democracy (924f.). Since he cannot be
reproached for his greed, unlike many of the other rich and bad, his
polupragmosune is attacked, but this was a protean concept, which
could be talked of as a good thing, as showing a proper interest in the
city's affairs, or a bad one, as meddling in the affairs of others. At a
time when politics was becoming more of a profession, 'being a
"sycophant"' was taking on a new meaning. To quote Lévy:[43]

> thus the sycophants appear henceforth as the representatives of
> the radical democracy and of political activism. At the same time,
> this showed the effects of the hatred of the sycophant and the fear
> of extremism: eventually, the choice is no longer between involve-
> ment in political life or showing oneself to be of no use to the city,
> but between staying 'quiet' or acting as a sycophant.

He is therefore too ambiguous a figure to be simply written off as a
villainous buffoon, even if he is used as the post on which they hang
the Just Man's old cloak and shoes (935–43), and then sent to take the
Just Man's place amongst the poor by the bath-house stove, in a
reversal reminiscent of Paphlagon's change of place with the Sausage-Seller at the end of *Knights*. He has benefited the city in the past
and now expects his reward.

Plutus, Asclepius, Prometheus, Hermes

The involvement of Apollo in prophesying Plutus' return,[44] the
reference to the Cyclops Polyphemus in a scene of burlesque dance
(290ff.), and the role of Apollo's son, Asclepius, in healing Plutus all

---

[43] 1976: 237.
[44] Apollo tells Chremylus to follow the first person he meets on leaving the sanctuary (41–3).
This motif of the importance of the first person met is widespread (Thompson 1955–8:
motifs P.17.1 and C.664; and Index s.v. 'first'; e.g. Jephthah (Judges 11.29–40); Idomeneus
(Serv. *ad Aen.* 3.121); Archilochus' father (*AP* 14.113 = Parke & Wormell 1956: II no. 231;
Müller 1985); Xuthus (E. *Ion* 534–6)). A closer parallel to *Plutus* is *Inscr. Magn.* 17.36ff. =
Parke & Wormell 1956: II no. 381. Compare the oracle of Hermes Agoraeus at Pharae (Paus.
7.22.2f.; cf. 9.11.7).

point to the conflict between Apollo and his father over Asclepius' restoration of a dead man to life. The account of the cure of Plutus given by Carion in 653ff., for all its burlesque and irreverence, corresponds closely to the accounts of cures given on the inscriptions which were set up in the shrine at Epidaurus.[45] Before the cure, Plutus is purified in the sea.[46] The cure is carried out by incubation.[47] The god arrives with a slave carrying his medicine chest[48] and wipes Plutus' eyes with a clean cloth;[49] his daughter Panacea covers Plutus' head[50] with a purple cloth[51] and, at a signal from the god, two snakes appear,[52] who slip under the cloth and lick his eyes.[53]

In his essentially benevolent intentions towards mankind, Plutus also bears comparison not only with Asclepius, but also with two other benefactors, Prometheus, last met in *Birds*,[54] and Hermes. Both of these figures are given crucial though differing roles in the establishment of the human condition as it is, and in their cases, as in that of Asclepius, a limit is set explicitly or implicitly to their benefactions by Zeus.

We have seen that Prometheus, through his tricky handling of the sacrifice at Mecone, established current practices in sacrifice, caused the separation of men and gods, stole and introduced to mankind civilising fire, and thus brought the mixed blessing of Pandora and women. Prometheus, as a Titan, is a figure separated from though linked with the Olympians. A complementary situation characterises Hermes, who is an Olympian but one with a close connection with the world of men, through his role as messenger of the gods and his involvement with many aspects of human life, such as weddings, guiding souls to Hades and so on.[55] He too acts a role as a helper and, as with Prometheus, trickery plays an important part.

---

[45] These are to be found in Herzog 1931; cf. also Edelstein & Edelstein 1945; Festugière 1954: 85–104; Kee 1982; Burkert 1985: 214f. Blindness and eye-complaints account for ten of the seventy cures preserved. For the god's cruelty to the wicked (cf. 716ff. on Neocleides, Herzog 1931: nos. 7, 22, 47, 55).

[46] According to the scholiast on 656f., this was the general custom.   [47] Deubner 1900.

[48] Hp. *Ep.* 15; Edelstein & Edelstein 1945: I 258f., no. 448.

[49] Herzog 1931: no. 53.   [50] Ibid. no. 31.   [51] Ibid. no. 37.

[52] The snakes are an important feature of the inscribed cures: ibid. nos. 17, 33, 39, 42, 44f.; also Paus. 2.10.3, 11.8, 3.23.6f.

[53] Herzog 1931: nos. 17, 45 for snake cures.

[54] For the parallelism of Plutus and Prometheus, Newiger 1957: 168, 176; L. Kahn 1978: 50–6; Burkert 1984: 840–3; Strauss-Clay 1987: 228f.

[55] For the 'social' aspects of Hermes, Toutain 1932; Watkins 1970.

Hermes' story is found in the *Homeric Hymn to Hermes*, and I give here the points of it which are relevant to our discussion.[56] On the evening of the first day of his life, having created the lyre from a tortoise-shell, he spirits away the immortal cattle of Apollo, marching them backwards to leave no trail to be followed and covering his own tracks with a pair of cunning sandals. By the Alpheus, he makes fire with a fire-drill, then throws two of the cattle onto the ground and pierces their spines, before cooking and dividing the meats into twelve equal portions and putting a portion of honour (*geras*) on each. When he and Apollo make up their quarrel, Hermes gives Apollo the lyre and says that he will pasture on the hills the cattle, which 'will bring forth in union with the bulls a mixture of male and female offspring' (491–4).

Once again, fire and a sacrifice involving a particular division of the parts is used to establish an aspect of human life. Burkert sees in Hermes here and in Prometheus the divine 'trickster' who is responsible for the creation of civilisation. Being a god, Hermes is, unlike the Companions of Odysseus,[57] able to get away with the killing of the 'immortal' cattle of Apollo, compounding their deaths with the new life they will have through ordinary reproduction. By breaking this taboo, Hermes becomes one of those divine intermediary figures who transfer power over animals from the gods to men, and then effect a reconciliation with the divine 'master' or 'mistress' of the animals.[58] The way is then open for mortals to imitate this divine example, which permits them to kill animals for food and yet not bring down divine wrath on themselves. Burkert concludes:[59]

> The order of the world, which is realised particularly in the equal distribution to gods and men of 'honorific gifts' seems to find . . . its legitimacy in the sacrifice. Power, violence, killing, opposition are subordinated to a just and eternal order. From this derives the idea of transgression, of the breaking of taboo, through trickery and force, in which the 'la condition humaine' is realised.

Strauss-Clay emphasises the importance of Hermes' division of the parts for human society, because the equal nature of the division

---

[56] L. Kahn 1978: 41–73; Burkert 1984; Strauss-Clay 1987 for three rather different recent treatments of this story. For our purposes, it does not matter too much whether Hermes' rite is an 'anti-sacrifice', an actual though elsewhere unrecorded Arcadian rite, or a more general *dais*, as the three authors respectively suggest.

[57] For the contrast, Burkert 1984: 842.

[58] Burkert 1984: 842f. and 1979: 83–98.   [59] 1984: 845.

corresponds to the equal division of meats at human meals. Though Hermes joins the immortals, 'as "companion of the feast"', *daitos hetairos* (line 436), he continues to 'participate in the human *dais* he has founded'.[60] The Old Man whom Hermes meets Strauss-Clay interprets as 'an emblem of post-Promethean man, separated from the gods and reduced to a level of solitary brutishness. According to the *Hymn* it is not Prometheus, but Hermes whose *techne* will alleviate that state.'[61] She compares him to the Cyclopes as a pre-agricultural man.

The myths of Prometheus and Hermes both therefore give an account of how sacrifice came about, was justified and operates now. There is a contrast between the two. L. Kahn makes much of the hybristic nature of Prometheus' actions as opposed to the civilising nature of Hermes': 'Hermes' fire is indeed a fire of craft ('feu technique'), created by *techne* and produced by *metis*, and is opposed to the stolen fire of Prometheus.'[62] Strauss-Clay states that Prometheus' trick separated man and gods for ever, unlike Hermes': 'His new *dais*, far from being an instrument of separation, becomes a means of uniting men into social communities through the fundamental human institution of commensality.'[63] It is not without significance that the Olympian benefits man without there being the kind of cost entailed by the help of the Titan: 'While man's loss of intimacy with the gods arises from Prometheus' hybristic challenge, Hermes' beneficent actions are in complete harmony with the mind of Zeus (cf. line 10).'[64] In fact, Kahn and Strauss-Clay are being a little unfair to Prometheus in considering only Hesiod's version: in *Prometheus Vinctus*, there is a much more sympathetic picture of the Titan, who appears as humanity's champion against a Zeus who, for no reason that the text gives, decides to take no account of mortals and to replace them with another race.[65] The tragedy makes no mention of Pandora or of the sacrifice at Mecone.

Against the myths of these two benefactors, we can set the case of Plutus. As in the case of Prometheus, an oracle plays an important part. Like Prometheus, Plutus is lauded as a discoverer of civilising skills (160ff.) and is fêted as one who will turn a world that is intolerable for men into a happier one. Just as Prometheus is punished by Zeus because of his help to mortals so Plutus is blinded,

[60] 1987: 233f.   [61] 1987: 231.   [62] 1978: 52.   [63] 1987: 231f.
[64] 1987: 232.   [65] *PV* 228–41.

and both spend a time in acute discomfort. Prometheus knows how Zeus can be deposed, and Plutus is said to be the reason Zeus is in power (124ff.) and is used to bring him down. In *Prometheus Vinctus*, Zeus' reasons for taking the attitude to men that he does are not given; in *Plutus*, it is his envy (*phthonos*, 92) of good men. The results of this attitude are comically touched upon in the scene with Penia. She argues that Zeus is poor: 'If he were rich, how was it that when he himself put on the Olympic games, to which he gathers all the Greeks every four years, he began garlanding the victors he announced with wild olive? If he were rich, it ought rather to have been a garland of gold' (583–6). Chremylus replies that he does this because he so loves gold that he fobs the victors off with rubbish, which provokes Penia to say: 'You're trying to accuse Zeus of something worse than poverty, saying he's rich but ungenerous and greedy' (590f.). Penia appears not to believe this, but Chremylus surely has a point?

However, in contrast to the Titan's myth, in *Plutus* a veritable Golden Age is restored rather than lost as a result of the hero's efforts: comedy reverses mythology's more serious pattern. The presence of the gods residing once again on earth amongst mortals recalls the situation in the Golden Age, and Carion's description of the changes in the household furniture echoes this period too (802ff.).[66] The passage derives in part from Sophocles' *Inachus*, in which were described the rich blessings bestowed on Argos when Zeus came to visit Io:[67] there is thus an implicit contrast between Zeus' bestowal of wealth in the pursuit of successful philandering and Plutus' far more disinterested act. Precious metals abound: vessels have filled with silver and gold or perfume; the cruets and other parts of the dinner-service have turned to bronze, and the fish-plates to silver; slaves play with gold coins not knuckle-bones; the *ipnos*, be it oven, lantern or dung-heap, has turned to ivory. The earth is giving its produce without human labour: the well has filled with oil and the loft with figs; the grain tubs are full of white barley and the amphorae with sweet-smelling wine. In achieving this glorious work, Plutus finds himself nearer to Hermes, but surpasses even him, who gave men animals to sacrifice for their communal meals, but then took his place

---

[66] The smoke and the three victims (820f.) recall the *trittus*, in which the portions offered to the gods were burnt (Stengel 1886). Plutarch notes a holocaust to Bubrostis, 'Ravenous Appetite' in Smyrna (*Mor.* 694A–B, after discussion of the Chaeronea rite (= Metrodorus, *FGH* 43 F 3)).   [67] Cf. frr. 273, 275, 278; also 276, 286.

among the Olympians, visiting men rather than living with them; if their lives improved over that of the Old Man of Onchestus, they did not receive from Hermes the kind of blessings Plutus has wrought. Hermes' actions had the approval of Zeus and the other gods, and it is intriguing that Chremylus should tell Blepsidemus that Plutus will come to his house 'if the gods wish it' (405). What Apollo thought when he gave the oracle we do not know, but by abandoning Zeus for better conditions of service elsewhere (1148–70), Hermes perhaps suggests that dissatisfaction with Zeus may not be limited to men: at least, there is no embassy from Olympus to put Zeus' case as in *Birds*.

Both Prometheus and Hermes face worlds in which there is an imbalance whereby mortals are disadvantaged, either through lack of civilising *technai* or absence of sacrificial animals. The complaint in *Plutus* against Zeus and the financial system operating under his control is that only the unscrupulous profit while the just suffer poverty: there is trickery and theft (the Greek word *kleptein*, used of both Prometheus' and Hermes' actions, means both), but some mortals are using them to benefit themselves at the expense of others; a divine trickster is needed to put matters to rights. Once he has found Plutus, Chremylus' initial reaction is to get him to reward only the just, though this plan eventually gives way to the idea of universal wealth.[68] We have thus another aspect of the break-down of the *charis* relationships discussed above: the problem is that the *distribution* of wealth is not being properly handled; sacrifices are being made but the gods are not keeping their side of the bargain. As in *Birds*, the way in which this will be rectified is through the withholding of sacrifice, although this time it is not given the unpleasant overtones of 'Melian hunger' (137–43):

> *Chr.* No man would go on sacrificing an ox, a cake or anything, if you did not wish it.
> *Pl.* How?
> *Chr.* How? He'll have no way of buying any offering, unless you're there to give him the money; so that you alone can destroy Zeus' power, if he causes trouble.
> *Pl.* What do you mean? They sacrifice to him for me?
> *Chr.* Yes.

Chremylus' arguments are proved correct by the end of the play: it is the absence of people wishing to use his services for sacrifice that

[68] On this shift, Konstan & Dillon 1981.

drives the impoverished Priest of Zeus to Chremylus' house (1178–84). The problem of the unequal distribution of riches has been solved by the wholesale enrichment of all. Hermes made an equal distribution of the sacrificial meats, and Chremylus' plan is that everybody should have 'an equal portion' of Plutus (225f.; cf. 510).

Wealth versus Poverty

The generally cheerful picture given by these mythical correlates needs to be qualified by one important scene which has so far been neglected, that with Penia. The four closing scenes of the play that we discussed above showed that, though the correlation between just behaviour and divine approbation has been restored by Plutus' regaining his sight, there remain problems, such as the desire of some people to put their political views before the possession of wealth and the insistence of others that past relationships of *charis* cannot be merely forgotten when better times come along. More fundamental problems caused by the absence of the need to work to create wealth are raised in the scene with Penia. This has caused considerable problems to critics, who have perhaps been too keen to examine the validity of the arguments as if a philosophical tract were in question, and to presume either that Penia is not to be taken seriously[69] or that it is in fact she who embodies the real truth which the play is trying to convey.[70]

I propose to examine the scene with the presumption that Penia is to be listened to and that, whether or not Chremylus can find a satisfactory opposing argument, her words should be read as an alternative discourse to the apparently unquestioning acceptance of the desirability of the effortless procurement of wealth for the just which is shown by most characters. There may be flaws and inconsistencies in her arguments, but this is not a reason for rejecting them wholesale as meaningless. As does the Sycophant, she presents her arguments in the language of paradox, and there are similarly unsatisfactory aspects in the contrary arguments of Chremylus and Blepsidemus. Furthermore, there are a number of arguments pro-

---

[69] The best statement of this position is by Sommerstein 1984.

[70] So those who see the play as essentially ironic, with Penia's speech subverting the play's happy ending, e.g. Flashar 1967 and Hertel 1969; that this 'ironic' quality is not an 'Eigenart' only of the last two plays I hope this book makes clear.

pounded by Penia with which the less affluent majority of the audience would have felt some sympathy, as when, for instance, she claims that she makes men lean, wasp-like and implacable to the enemy, whereas wealth makes them gouty and pot-bellied, with fat legs (557–61). Attractive too would have been the claims that she brings *sophrosune*, as opposed to the hybris to which the wealthy are prone (563f.),[71] and that politicians are men of justice when poor, but become unjust and undemocratic when they become wealthy (567–70). Even Chremylus has to admit that: 'None of what she says is false – even if she is a monster' (571). Indeed, these poorer Athenians might perhaps have taken less than kindly to Chremylus' suggestion that poverty leads to crime (565).[72]

When Penia rushes in (415), she is depicted negatively in two ways: through her awful appearance, and through the mockery to which she is subjected; she is at once horrific and ridiculous. This, and the fact that no man would *prima facie* willingly support poverty against wealth, combine to generate an adverse reaction to her. None the less, she soon lays claim for herself to qualities Chremylus had attributed to the blind god, thus setting the stage for the debate. Compare 468–70 of Penia, 'If I show that I alone am responsible for all your good things . . .' with 182f. of Plutus, 'You alone are responsible for all things bad and good.'

The debate between Penia and Chremylus begins in earnest at 489. Chremylus begins by restating the problem. In 489–98, he notes that everyone would agree that the good should prosper and the wicked and impious should not; if Plutus could see again, he would put to flight the latter and make everyone good, rich and pious. He then complains that the opposite is currently the case (500–6): the wicked enjoy unjust prosperity, while the good starve. Penia does not contest this remark directly. Instead she points to a flaw in the utopian scheme proposed by Chremylus: she argues that if people are to be wealthy merely at the cost of being just, then no-one will work and all the services that workers provide will cease to be available, since, if she were absent, it would mean that 'no man would practise any craft or skill' (511f.). Her references to bronze-working, ship-building, leather-working and laundry-keeping also recall that earlier passage (513f., cf. 162–7). In effect, therefore, all human skills and

---

[71] For this idea, Dover 1974: 109–12, who quotes Thuc. 3.45.4; X. *Cyr.* 8.4.14; Dem. 21.182; Lys. 7.13f.   [72] Dover 1974: 109f.

wisdom will cease, since no-one will need to work to make his living now that everyone can live a life of idleness (516). Penia is able to reinforce her point when Chremylus says that slaves will do all the jobs currently done by workers: no-one will risk his neck to get slaves, because he will have no need to sell them. Commerce will then cease, and each man will be forced to do everything for himself; what is more, there will be no luxuries, no beds, pillows, carpets, perfumes, so that wealth will be pointless: 'What use will extra wealth be if you lack these things?' (531). Penia thus claims that civilised life and the social and economic exchange that characterises it will cease; men will live in wealthy isolation, and civilised society will be no more.

It is interesting to compare Aristotle's remarks on the 'first form of human association' (*koinonia*), the *oikos*:[73]

> it is obvious that there is no purpose to be served by the art of exchange (*chrematistike*) ... The members of the household had shared all things in common: the members of the village, separated from one another, had at their disposal a number of different things, which they had to exchange with one another, as need arose, by barter – much as many uncivilised tribes still do to this day.

Even this basic form of exchange will be absent in Chremylus' new world. That this is not a meaningless point is confirmed by Carion's remark to Hermes, who has suggested he might be allowed to join Chremylus' household in his guise as 'Empolaios': 'But we're rich; why do we need to feed a Hermes of petty commerce?' (1155f.). For the same reasons, normal commerce between men and gods comes to an end and temples become public lavatories (1178–84).

There is a good parallel for this situation in the Homeric picture of the Cyclopes.[74] They live in a land where everything grows 'without sowing or ploughing',[75] and the caves are replete with dairy produce.[76] On the other hand, they do not constitute a proper society: they have no 'agoras where debate is held' nor 'laws',[77] and they live in isolated units on the mountain tops:[78] 'Each man gives ordinances to his wife and children, and they pay no heed to each other.' Aristotle quotes this line as evidence for the scattered nature

---

[73] *Pol.* 1257a19–25; tr. Barker.   [74] Austin 1975: 143–9; Vidal-Naquet 1981a.
[75] *Od.* 9.109; cf. 123.   [76] Ibid. 219ff.   [77] Ibid. 112; cf. 189, 215, 428.
[78] Ibid. 114f.

of the life of primitive man.[79] The lack of communication between them is symbolised in the failure of Polyphemus to make his neighbours understand his plight and their reluctance to stay to find out what is happening.[80] Throughout the episode, there is a contrast between the cleverness of Odysseus and the stupidity of the Cyclops,[81] and this absence of wisdom combined with the lack of cohesive social grouping among the Cyclopes is his downfall. Penia has said, similarly, that men will no longer practise wisdom (511). She also warned of the disappearance of skills, and in this too the Cyclopes are deficient: in addition to the absence of ploughing,[82] 'The Cyclopes nation possess no red-prowed ships; they have no shipwrights in their country to build sound vessels to serve their needs, to visit foreign towns and townsfolk as men elsewhere do in their voyages by sailing to the cities of men.'

That there should be such a parallel with the Cyclopes gives significance to the scene between Carion and the Chorus at 290ff.[83] To celebrate the fact that Plutus is coming to make them rich (285), Carion pretends that he is the Cyclops and they are his flocks:[84] 'Now I want to imitate – threttanelo! – the Cyclops, and lead you off swinging my feet like this. But come, my children, clamouring incessantly and bleating the songs of sheep and malodorous goats' (290–4). The anti-social world of the Cyclopes is an example of the kind of society that Penia fears for mortals. This idea is then reiterated in the second pair of stanzas. The Chorus played along with Carion's view of themselves as flocks, before transforming themselves into Odysseus' men and threatening to blind him (296–301). He now becomes Circe and threatens to turn them into animals: 'And I in every way shall Circe, the mixer of poisons, imitate, who once persuaded the companions of Philonides in Corinth that, being boars, they should eat the kneaded dung she prepared for them' (302–6). In the *Odyssey*, Circe is more civilised than the Cyclops but is

---

[79] *Pol.* 1252b22–4.   [80] *Od.* 9.399–414.   [81] Especially ibid. 403–24.

[82] Ibid. 125–9 (tr. Shewring).

[83] The primary source of this passage is the *Cyclops* of Philoxenus of Cythera (schol. *Plutus* 298; Diod. 15.6; Athen. 6F; Pickard-Cambridge 1927: 61–4). The Homeric intertext is also likely to have been operative: Homer was more familiar than Philoxenus to a fifth-century audience.

[84] For the use of such 'tableaux' as keys to the understanding of a play, cf. above p. 175 on the four Choruses of fabulous peoples and sights in *Birds*.

far from being in normal society. She lives with four servants surrounded by animals who were once men, and her island is prosperous but lacks the 'works of mortals':[85] she has 'unfailing meat'.[86] She too therefore is emblematic of the life that Penia sees for mortals: prosperous perhaps, but isolated and with more than a touch of the animal.

It is possible that there is also a hint of this problem in Carion's words to the Chorus immediately before these Odyssean exchanges; he assures them of the truth of his good news about Plutus (286f.):

> *Cho.* Will it really be possible for us all to be rich?
> *Ca.* Yes, and Midases, if you get asses' ears.

Two stories about Midas are alluded to here: first, his great wealth,[87] and second, his asses' ears won because he preferred Apollo's opponent in a musical contest.[88] If we could include here the story of his request to Dionysus, that all he touched should turn to gold, and his subsequent problem that he could not eat, because the food became gold, he would encapsulate Penia's warnings about wealth, animality and the problems of limitless wealth.[89] It must be said, however, that though this tale incorporates a fairy-tale motif,[90] the earliest evidence for it is in Ovid, *Met.* 11.85ff. None the less, the reference to Midas' asses' ears won by a mistaken judgement may possibly pass a silent comment on the choice made by the men in the play.

Penia's prognostications are not to be quite accurate as far as the play is concerned, but Chremylus does not here refute them (it is characteristic of this *agon* that he and Penia do not so much engage in detailed refutation of each other's arguments as juxtapose one set against another). Instead, he gives a scathing description of the miseries of poverty. This is indeed a potent indictment of what great poverty does to people, but its force is somewhat blunted by Penia's insistence that he is not describing the life she stands for, but that of beggary (548). This is a very fair riposte. It may be dangerous to generalise attitudes to poverty in any society, but it is important to note that *penes* (literally 'poor man') did not mean 'poverty-stricken':

[85] *Od.* 10.147.   [86] Ibid. 468, 477.   [87] Hdt. 8.138.
[88] Ibid. 146ff.; Hygin. *Fab.* 191.
[89] For the ambiguity of Greek views of early life, as both idyllic and grim, Vidal-Naquet 1981a.
[90] Bolte & Polívka 1915: 213.

the Greek definition [of wealth and poverty] was quite different: the two categories did not correspond to two extremes, on the contrary they touched each other and could even overlap. The criterion was not a given standard of wealth but the need for work. A Greek was wealthy if he could live without having to work, poor if he did not have enough to live on without working. From this point of view the majority of people in Greece were 'poor' since they had to work.[91]

In so far as Penia is describing the existence of the majority of the audience as *penetes*, it would have been hard for them to deny all validity to her arguments. Furthermore, poverty is one of the merits of many of the heroes of Old Comedy.

Penia's life-style is essentially one of *autarkeia* ('self-suf-ficiency'), an ideal of both individuals and states.[92] Aristotle echoes the standard Greek view when he says 'self-sufficiency is the goal and a great good';[93] the *polis* is the 'final and perfect association . . . which may be said to have reached the height of full self-suf-ficiency'.[94] He makes a point later which recalls Penia's forecast of the absence of skills. A perfect state must perform certain services and must contain elements to perform those services: food, arts and crafts, arms, property, religion, a system of justice are all essential, for 'If any of these services is missing it cannot be totally self-sufficient.'[95] Self-sufficiency for Aristotle, therefore is an ideal that a state and its parts must aim at; being part of a *polis* means playing one's role as a whole, and man is a 'political animal'. By contrast, 'The man who is isolated – who is unable to share in the benefits of political association, or has no need to share because he is already self-sufficient – is no part of the *polis*, and must therefore be either a beast or a god.'[96] In the play, the Sycophant will make a similar point. Asked whether he would not rather live a life of ease, he says this would be the 'life of a beast' (922). It is this that Penia's self-sufficiency is designed to avoid.

With the discussion nearing its end, it begins to lose something of its serious element as Chremylus is forced to resort to the common-sense claim that wealth is better than poverty; the futility of this part

---

[91] Austin & Vidal-Naquet 1977: 16.   [92] See esp. 553f.   [93] *Pol.* 1253a1.
[94] Ibid. 1252b27–9.   [95] Ibid. 1328b2–23; cf. 1281a1; 1326b26–30.
[96] Ibid. 1253a27–9; cf. 1253a3f.

is marked by his statement 'You won't persuade me, not even if you persuade me' (600). And so it is. Penia is discomfited and Chremylus' plan is put into operation. The new world is indeed magically wonderful. In a change reminiscent of the Chaeronea rite, Plutus is welcomed in and poverty driven out, so that the *bulimia* affects the Sycophant (873). Plutus will reverse his former policies, and Zeus the Saviour has left Olympus for Chremylus' house.

It is through Penia that *Plutus* conveys its critique of the apparently natural desire for wealth and ease. Her arguments reflect Greek thinking on topics like the Golden Age, poverty and wealth and self-sufficiency and express a viewpoint which the average *penes* in the audience could feel sympathy with, however much he might fantasise about being truly wealthy. As such, her arguments provide an alternative picture of a life where the *penes* is just, a good fighter and self-sufficient economically, which is an ideal that is rather more 'realistically' obtainable than the situation which Chremylus creates. In other words, Penia's case, significantly placed before the changes wrought by Plutus' reign, provides a deconstruction of the fantasy before it takes place. She makes us aware of the contradiction in Chremylus' position: he is worried that the *charis*-system has broken down, but wishes to introduce another world which would also have no place for the relationships characteristic of the observance of *charis*; the general availability of wealth and the lack of the need to work in the people of his world would mean that no social or economic interchange would be required. That her warnings do not come true does not mean that they are irrelevant: they simply point up not only the fantasy involved in the notion of universal wealth but also its cost and even undesirability.

One aspect of the ending of the play provides corroboration for this reading. This is the fact that so much emphasis is placed upon the entry of Plutus into the *house* of Chremylus. One can contrast this with the way in which Peace is handed over to city institutions. Again, in *Knights*, Demos' house stands for the city of Athens by synecdoche, but there is no suggestion that this is the case with Chremylus'; he is clearly just an ordinary citizen. It is true that at the very end preparations are made for the *hidrusis* of Plutus in the *opisthodomos* of Athena's temple, so that the play closes with a *polis*-centred act, but this receives curiously less emphasis than the induction into Chremylus' house, as if the latter were somehow more significant. The induction into the house is carried out in terms of the *katachusmata*. These were small gifts poured, in a *rite d'agrégation*, over newly-purchased slaves and newly-weds, whose entry into the house needed to be propitiously marked; Chremylus' wife says she will throw them 'as if over the newly-purchased eyes' of Plutus (769).[97] Plutus is most insistent that this should be carried out inside by the hearth, 'as is the custom' (795): there is thus no suggestion that this act is to stand as one carried out publicly as a rite integrating Plutus into the city. Chremylus' house appears to be an important space to which the inhabitants of Olympus repair and from which the crucial changes in the world emanate. Not only have the Boule and Assembly of the city been circumvented, as the Sycophant complains (945–50), but control of the universe has passed from the palaces of Olympus to the house of one just man. The change of focus from the earlier plays is striking, and creates an air of unreality about the events, less dramatic but scarcely less potent than that of plays where more fantastic means are employed. This shift from *polis* to *oikos* reflects the warnings given by Penia of the destruction of normal social relations in a world of general prosperity.

The play ends with a pun symbolizing the way things have been turned upside down. In return for a visit from her Young Man, the Old Woman (*graus*) agrees to carry the pots in the *hidrusis* procession; Chremylus notes that normally the *graus* ('froth') sits on top of the pots (1197–1207). This 'inversion' may be read as marking the way things in the universe have been turned upside down, but in this newly reversed world of general prosperity it does not perhaps matter where Plutus is installed: all will be wealthy anyway and the distinction *polis/oikos* will be collapsed into an undifferentiated world of whose dangers Penia has warned.

Once again, therefore, Aristophanes has allowed the fantasy of a solution to an intractable problem to range until a new world is created, but has done so whilst at the same time indicating that the fantasy has sides to it to which an unthinking pursuit of notions of a golden age may blind the audience. Aristophanic comedy at least is not prepared cheerfully to indulge in fantasy, nor to let its audience do so – if they have eyes to see.

[97] Schol. 768; Paradiso 1987: 255–60.

Conclusion

So ends our *tour d'horizon* of what the structural study of Greek myths and rituals can tell us about the interpretation of Aristophanic comedy. A number of points may be briefly highlighted. The most crucial perhaps is the importance of not trying to impose or deduce a single structure for the reading of these plays, either individually or as a group. Although there may be certain broad structures, such as initiation or men/women, which can be detected in a number of plays, on closer inspection each play is different from the others, and will itself admit of discussion in terms of a number of different structures: I have not exhausted the possibilities here.

We have seen how, though the titles or details of the play may more or less explicitly invite discussion in terms of certain mythical or ritual structures, as in the case of *Thesmophoriazusae*, the Mysteries in *Frogs* or the reference to the 'Lemnian fire' in *Lysistrata*, attention must also be paid to structures not so indicated by the play, but identifiable by the critic from consideration of other aspects of Greek culture, as, say, the *ephebeia* in *Wasps* or divine 'returns' in *Peace*. The plays share features with other cultural constructs, and they throw mutual light upon each other even where there is no overt gesture from one to the other. There is more work to be done here, especially on comedy and the iconography of vase-painting, a notable absence from this book.

Important too are the references in the texts to individual myths and festivals which do not so much structure the plays as provide the means of commenting on the action and deconstructing the more triumphalist aspects of the portrayal of the hero's actions: the meaning of the Diasia in *Clouds* is important for understanding what Strepsiades is doing whatever he or others may claim; the same is true of Telephus and the Anthesteria in *Acharnians*. Such references are not there only for the humorous purposes of the scene they occur in.

We have seen that though the plays have plots which are original in their story-lines rather than being dependent on traditional mythology, at the level of their structures they relate to pre-existing story-patterns, as is regularly the case with traditional literatures. A comparative study of comedy's and tragedy's techniques in the use of myth and ritual would be useful.

One thing which I hope has become clear is that these are dramas that should be taken 'seriously'. They have much to say about conditions and affairs in ancient Athens, and indeed elsewhere, and the fact that they use comedy should not be a reason for underestimating the power of analysis and realistic sense of the world that we find in them. They engage with the problems of Athenian democracy as much as, indeed one might say more than, tragedy, because they treat them more directly; and, while making hay mercilessly with the faults in that democracy, none the less remind their audiences that there are other forms of political control that are, from a democratic point of view at least, even less desirable and, what is more, do not exist only in the fantastic worlds created by the comic poets. But this is not something which is rammed home, or preached; it is not 'the message' of the plays. Rather it has to be worked out by the reader attentive to all aspects of the plays: nothing is there 'for its own sake'.

'Aristophanes' may now, I venture to hope, be freed from debates about his personal views, political, social and sexual orientation, attitude to intellectual matters, changing attitudes to Athenian life with the passage of time, and so on, and be allowed to see his name become synonymous with his texts. I am not, of course, denying that he had personal views, but I am not convinced that Lenaea and Dionysia were the vehicles for their dissemination. If Aristophanes did try so to use the festivals, we can only be thankful that he was unable to make those views plain and uncontroversial, and instead produced texts whose meanings are complex and challenging, and not just because modern literary theory would have it so. Whatever Aristophanes may have thought, close study of his plays which we have, rather than of him whom we do not, is likely to be more interesting – and fruitful.

BIBLIOGRAPHY

Adcock, F. & Mosley, D. J. 1975: *Diplomacy in Ancient Greece*, London.
Adkins, A. W. H. 1970: 'Clouds, Mysteries, Socrates and Plato', *Antichthon* 4:13–24.
Adrados, F. R. 1972: 'Los coros de la "Paz" y los "Dictiulcos" y sus precedentes rituales', in *Studi classici in onore di Q. Cataudella*, Catania, 173–85.
Alexiou, M. 1974: *The Ritual Lament in Greek Tradition*, Cambridge.
Ambrosino, D. 1983: 'Nuages et sens. Autour des Nuées d'Aristophane', *QS* 9:3–60.
Anderson, C. A. 1989: 'Themistocles and Cleon in Aristophanes' *Knights*', *AJP* 110:10–16.
Anderson, J. K. 1970: *Military Theory and Practice in the Age of Xenophon*, Berkeley and Los Angeles.
Apte, M. L. 1985: *Humor and Laughter: an anthropological approach*, Ithaca and London.
Arnould, D. 1981: *Guerre et paix dans la poésie grecque de Callinos à Pindare*, New York.
Arrowsmith, W. 1973: 'Aristophanes' *Birds*: the fantasy politics of Eros', *Arion* 1:119–67.
Atallah, W. 1966: *Adonis dans la littérature et l'art grecque*, Paris.
Auger, D. 1979: 'Le théâtre d'Aristophane: le mythe, l'utopie et les femmes', in Auger, Rosellini and Saïd 1979.
Auger, D., Rosellini, M., & Saïd, S. 1979: *Aristophane, les femmes et la cité*, Fontenay-aux-Roses.
Aurenche, O. 1974: *Les Groupes d'Alcibiade, de Léagros et de Teucros. Remarques sur la vie politique athénienne en 415 avant J.C.*, Paris.
Austin, M. M. & Vidal-Naquet, P. 1977: *Economic and Social History of Ancient Greece: an introduction* (tr. M. M. Austin), London.
Austin, N. 1975: *Archery at the Dark of the Moon: poetic problems in Homer's Odyssey*, Berkeley, Los Angeles and London.
Bain, D. 1991: 'Six Greek verbs of sexual congress', *CQ* 41:51–77.
Barkan, I. 1935: *Capital Punishment in Ancient Athens*, diss. Chicago.
Baumgarten, A. I. 1981: *The Phoenician History of Philo of Byblos: a commentary*, Leiden.

Beavis, I. C. 1988: *Insects and Other Invertebrates in Classical Antiquity*, Exeter.

Beazley, J. D. 1954: *Attic Vase Paintings in the Museum of Fine Arts, Boston*, vol. II by L. D. Caskey and J. D. Beazley, Oxford and Boston.

1956: *Attic Black-figure Vase-Painters*, 2nd edn, Oxford.

1963: *Attic Red-figure Vase-Painters*, 2nd edn, 3 vols., Oxford.

1971: *Paralipomena: additions to Attic Black-figure Vase-Painters and to Attic Red-figure Vase-Painters*, 2nd edn, Oxford.

Becker, O. 1937: 'Das Bild des Weges und verwandte Vorstellungen im frühgriechischen Denken', *Hermes Einzelschriften* 4.

Becker, W. A. 1880: *Charicles, or Illustrations of the Private Life of the Ancient Greeks* (tr. F. Metcalfe), 5th edn, London.

Benveniste, E. 1932: 'Le sens du mot *KOLOSSOS* et les noms grecs de la statue', *RPh.* 118–35.

Bérard, C. 1970: 'L'Hérôon à la porte de l'Ouest', in K. Schefold (ed.), *Etruria, fouilles et recherches*, Berne 1970.

1974: *Anodoi: essai sur l'imagerie des passages chthoniens*, Rome.

1987: *Images et société en Grèce ancienne: l'iconographie comme méthode d'analyse*, Lausanne.

1989a: 'The order of women', in Bérard *et al.* 1989: 88–107.

1989b: 'Festivals and mysteries', in Bérard *et al.* 1989: 108–20.

Bérard, C. & Bron, C. (eds.) 1986: *L'Association dionysiaque dans les sociétés anciennes: coll. de l'école française de Rome* 89, Rome.

Bérard, C. and Bron, C. 1989: 'Satyric revels', in Bérard *et al.* 1989: 130–49.

Bérard, C., Bron, C., Durand, J.-L., Frontisi-Ducroux, F., Lissarrague, F., Schapp, A. & Vernant, J.-P. 1989: *A City of Images: iconography and society in ancient Greece* (tr. D. Lyons), Lausanne.

Berthiaume, G. 1982: *Les Rôles du mágeiros: étude sur la boucherie, la cuisine et le sacrifice dans la Grèce ancienne*, Leiden.

Berve, H. 1967: *Die Tyrannis bei den Griechen*, 2 vols., Munich.

Bianchi, U. 1976: *The Greek Mysteries*, Leiden.

(ed.) 1986: *Transition Rites: cosmic, social and individual order*, Rome.

Binder, G. 1964: *Die Aussetzung des Königskindes Kyros und Romulus*, Meisenheim am Glan.

Binder, J. 1984: 'The west pediment of the Parthenon: Poseidon', in *Studies Presented to Sterling Dow on his Eightieth Birthday*, ed. K. J. Rigsby, Durham, N.C., 15–22.

Blech, M. 1982: *Studien zum Kranz bei den Griechen*, Berlin.

Boardman, J. 1972: 'Herakles, Peisistratos and sons', *RA* 57–72.

1989: 'Herakles, Peisistratos, and the Unconvinced', *JHS* 109:158f.

Bodson, L. 1973: 'Gai, gai! Sauvons-nous. Procédés et effets du comique dans *Lysistrata* 740–52', *AC* 42:5–27.

1978: *Hiera Zoa*, Brussels.

Boegehold, A. L. 1967: 'Philocleon's Court', *Hesp.* 36:111–20.

Boersma, J. S. 1970: *Athenian Building Policy from 561/0 to 405/4 B.C.*, Groningen.

Bolte J. and Polívka, G. 1915: *Anmerkungen zu den Kinder- und Hausmärchen der*

Brüder Grimm, vol. II, Leipzig.

Bolton, J. D. P. 1962: *Aristeas of Proconnesus*, Oxford.

Bömer, P. 1969: *P. Ovidius Naso: Metamorphosen*, vol. I, Heidelberg.

Bonanno, M. G. 1972: *Studi su Cratete comico*, Padua.

1987: 'Paratragoidia in Aristofane', *Dioniso* 57:135–67.

Bond, G. W. 1963: *Euripides: Hypsipyle*, Oxford.

1981: *Euripides: Heracles*, Oxford.

Bonner, R. J. 1933: *Aspects of Athenian Democracy*, Berkeley.

Bonner, R. J. & Smith, G. 1930: *The Administration of Justice from Homer to Aristotle*, 2 vols., Chicago.

Borthwick, E. K. 1968: 'The dances of Philocleon and the Sons of Carcinus in Aristophanes' *Wasps*', *CQ* 18:47–51.

1992: 'Observations on the opening scene of Aristophanes' *Wasps*', *CQ* 42:274–8.

Bothmer, D. von, 1957: *Amazons in Greek Art*, Oxford.

Bouché-Leclerq, A. 1880: *Histoire de la divination dans l'antiquité*, vol. III, Paris.

Bowie, A. M. 1979: 'The poetic dialect of Sappho and Alcaeus', diss. Cambridge.

1981: *The Poetic Dialect of Sappho and Alcaeus*, New York.

1982a: 'The parabasis in Aristophanes: prolegomena, *Acharnians*', *CQ* 32:27–40.

1982b: Review of Sommerstein 1980a and 1981, *LCM* 7:8.111–15.

1983: 'The end of Sophocles' *Ajax*', *LCM* 8.8 (Oct.):114f.

1984: '*Lysistrata* and the Lemnian Women', *Omnibus* 7:17–19.

1987: 'Ritual stereotype and comic reversal: Aristophanes' *Wasps*', *BICS* 34:112–25.

1993a: 'Oil in ancient Greece and Rome', in *The Oil of Gladness*, ed. M. Dudley and G. D. Rowell, London and Collegeville, 26–33.

1993b: 'Religion and politics in Aeschylus' *Oresteia*', *CQ* 43.

Bowie, E. L. 1989: 'Who is Dicaeopolis?', *JHS* 108:183–5.

Boyancé, P. 1962: 'Sur les mystères d'Eleusis', *REG* 75:460–82.

Bravo, B. 1980: 'Sulân. Représailles et justice privée contre les étrangers dans les cités grecques', *ASNP*³ 10.3:675–987.

Brelich, A. 1958: *Gli eroi greci: un problema storico-religioso*, Rome.

1969: *Paides e parthenoi*, Rome.

Bremmer, J. 1978: 'Heroes, rituals and the Trojan War', *SSR* 2:5–38.

1980a: 'An enigmatic Indo-European rite: paederasty', *Arethusa* 13:279–98.

1980b: 'Marginalia Manichaica', *ZPE* 39:30f.

1983a: *The Early Greek Concept of the Soul*, Princeton.

1983b: 'Scapegoat rituals in ancient Greece', *HSCP* 87:299–320.

1985: 'La donna anziana; libertà e indipendenza', in G. Arrigoni (ed.), *Le donne in Grecia*, Rome 1985: 275–98.

(ed.) 1987: *Interpretations of Greek Mythology*, Beckenham.

Brickhouse, T. C. and Smith, N. D. 1989: *Socrates on Trial*, Oxford.

Brixhe, C. 1988: 'La langue de l'étranger non-Grec chez Aristophane', in R. Louis (ed.), *L'Étranger dans le monde grec*, Nancy, 113–38.

Brock, N. van 1959: 'Substitution rituelle', *RHA* 17 (65):117–46.

Brock, R. J. 1986: 'The double plot of Aristophanes' *Knights'*, *GRBS* 27:15–27.

Brommer, F. 1963: *Die Skupturen der Parthenon Giebel: Katalog und Untersuchung*, Mainz.

Brown, C. G. 1991: 'Empousa, Dionysus and the Mysteries: Aristophanes, *Frogs* 285ff.', *CQ* 41:41–50.

Brown, N. O. 1947: *Hermes the Thief: the evolution of a myth*, Wisconsin.

Brumfield, A. C. 1981: *The Attic Festivals of Demeter and their Relation to the Agricultural Year*, New York.

Bruneau, P. 1970: *Recherches sur les cultes de Délos à l'époque hellénistique et à l'époque impériale*, Paris.

Bryant, A. A. 1907: 'Boyhood and youth in the days of Aristophanes', *HSCP* 18:73–122.

Bugh, G. R. 1988: *The Horsemen of Athens*, Princeton.

Burford, A. 1972: *Craftsmen in Greek and Roman Society*, London.

Burke, E. M. 1990: 'Athens after the Peloponnesian War: restoration efforts and the role of maritime commerce', *Cl. Ant.* 9:1–13.

Burke, U. P. 1978: *Popular Culture in Early Modern Europe*, London.

Burkert, W. 1962: '*Goes*. Zum griechischen "Schamanismus"', *RM* 105:36–55.

1966: 'Kekropidensage und Arrhephoria: vom Initiationsritus zum Panathenäenfest', *Hermes* 94:1–25.

1970: 'Jason, Hypsipyle, and new fire at Lemnos. A study in myth and ritual', *CQ* 20:1–16.

1972: *Lore and Science in Ancient Pythagoreanism* (tr. E. L. Minar, Jr), Cambridge, Mass.

1975: 'Apellai und Apollon', *RhM* 118:1–21.

1979: *Structure and History in Greek Mythology and Ritual*, Berkeley, Los Angeles and London.

1982: 'Craft versus sect: the problem of Orphics and Pythagoreans', in Meyer and Sanders 1982: 1–22.

1983a: *Homo Necans: the anthropology of ancient Greek sacrificial ritual and myth* (tr. P. Bing), Berkeley, Los Angeles and London.

1983b: 'Apokalyptik im frühen Griechentum: Impluse und Transformationen', in D. Hellholm (ed.), *Apocalypticism in the Mediterranean World and the Near East*, Tübingen, 235–54.

1984: 'Sacrificio-sacrilegio: il trickster fondatore', *Stud. Stor.* 25:835–45.

1985: *Greek Religion: archaic and classical* (tr. J. Raffan), Oxford.

1987a: *Ancient Mystery Cults*, Cambridge, Mass., and London.

1987b: 'Oriental and Greek mythology: the meeting of parallels', in Bremmer 1987: 10–40.

Buxton, R. G. A. 1980: 'Blindness and limits: Sophocles and the logic of myth', *JHS* 100:22–37.

1982: *Persuasion in Greek Tragedy: a study in peitho*, Cambridge.

1987: 'Wolves and werewolves in Greek thought', in Bremmer 1987: 60–79.

Byl, S. 1980: 'Parodie d'une initiation dans les Nuées d'Aristophane', *RBPh.* 58:5–21.

1988: 'Encore une dizaine d'allusions éleusiniennes dans les *Nuées* d'Aristophane', *RBPh*. 66:68–77.

Cairns, F. 1979: *Tibullus: a Hellenistic poet at Rome*, Cambridge.

Calame, C. 1977: *Les Chœurs de jeunes filles en Grèce archaïque*, 2 vols., Rome.

Cameron, A. and Kuhrt, A. (eds.) 1983: *Images of Women in Antiquity*, London and Canberra.

Cantarella, R. 1974: 'Dioniso. Fra *Bacchanti* e *Ranes*', in *Serta Turyniana: studies in Greek literature and palaeography in honour of A. Turyn*, ed. J. L. Heller and J. K. Newman, Urbana, Chicago and London, 291–310.

Carlier, J. 1979: 'Voyage en Amazonie grecque', *A. Ant. Hung.* 27:381–405.

Carrière, J. C. 1979: *Le Carnaval et la politique: une introduction à la comédie grecque suivie d'un choix de fragments*, Paris.

Carter, L. B. 1986: *The Quiet Athenian*, Oxford.

Cartledge, P. 1990: *Aristophanes and his Theatre of the Absurd*, Bristol.

Casadio, G. 1982, 1983: 'Per un'indagine storico-religiosa sui culti di Dioniso in relazione alla fenomenologia dei misteri', 1: *SSR* 6:209–34; 2: *SMSR* 7:123–49.

Casel, O. 1919: *De philosophorum Graecorum silentio mystico*, Giessen.

Cassio, A. C. 1981: 'A "typical" servant in Aristophanes (Pap. Flor. 112, Austin 63, 90ff.)', *ZPE* 41:17f.

1985: *Commedia e partecipazione*, Naples.

Chadwick, J. 1976: *The Mycenaean World*, Cambridge.

Chantraine, P. 1968–80: *Dictionnaire étymologique de la langue grecque*, 4 vols. in 5, Paris.

Charlesworth, M. P. 1926: *CQ* 40:4f.

Chirassi, I. 1968: *Elementi di culture precereali nei miti e riti greci*, Rome.

Chirassi-Colombo, I. 1979: 'Paides e gynaikes: note per una tassonomia del comportamento rituale nella cultura attica', *QUCC* 30:25–58.

Clark, R. J. 1968: 'Trophonios: the manner of his revelation', *TAPA* 99:63–75.

Clinton, K. 1974: *The Sacred Officials of the Eleusinian Mysteries*, Philadelphia.

1980: 'A law in the City Eleusinion concerning the Mysteries', *Hesp.* 49:258–88.

Cole, S. G. 1980: 'New evidence for the Mysteries of Dionysus', *GRBS* 21:223–38.

Connor, W. R. 1987: 'Tribes, festivals, and processions; civic ceremonial and political manipulation in archaic Greece', *JHS* 107:40–50.

Cook, A. B. 1914–40: *Zeus: a study in ancient religion*, 3 vols. in 5, Cambridge.

Cook, R. M. 1987: 'Pots and Pisistratan propaganda', *JHS* 107:167–9.

Cornell, T. J. 1983: 'Gründer', *RLAC* 12:1107–71.

Cornford, F. M. 1914: *The Origin of Attic Comedy*, Cambridge.

Craik, E. M. 1987: 'One for the pot: Aristophanes' Birds and the Anthesteria', *Eranos* 85:25–34.

Dahl, K. 1976: *Thesmophoria. En graesk kvindefest*, Copenhagen.

Daremberg, C. and Saglio, E. 1904: *Dictionnaire des antiquités grecques et romaines*, Paris.

Daux, G. 1963: 'La Grande Démarchie: un nouveau calendrier sacrificiel d'Attique (Erchia)', *BCH* 87:603–34.

1983: 'Le calendrier de Throikos au Musée de J. Paul Getty', *AC* 52:150–74.

David, E. 1984: *Aristophanes and Athenian Society of the Early Fourth Century B.C.*, *Mnem.* Suppl. 81, Leiden.

Davies, J. K. 1971: *Athenian Propertied Families 600–300 B.C.*, Oxford.

Davies, M. & Kathirithamby, J. 1986: *Greek Insects*, London.

Delatte, A. 1932: *Les Conceptions de l'enthousiasme chez les philosophes présocratiques*, Paris.

1955: *Le Cycéon, breuvage rituel des mystères d'Eleusis*, Paris.

Delcourt, M. 1959: *Oreste et Alcméon: étude sur la projection légendaire du matricide en Grèce*, Paris.

1961: *Hermaphrodite* (tr. J. Nicholson), London.

Denniston, J. D. 1966 (1954): *The Greek Particles*, 2nd edn., Oxford.

Deonna, W. 1951: 'L'ex-voto de Cypsélos à Delphes: le symbolisme du palmier et des grenouilles', *RHR* 139:162–207 and 140:5–58.

1965: *Le Symbolisme de l'œil*, Berne.

Detienne, M. 1977: *The Gardens of Adonis: spices in Greek mythology* (tr. J. Lloyd), London.

1979a: *Dionysos Slain* (tr. M. and L. Muellner), Baltimore and London.

1979b: '"Violentes eugénies". En pleines Thesmophories: des femmes couvertes de sang', in Detienne and Vernant 1979: 183–215.

1981a: 'The "Sea-Crow"', in Gordon 1981: 16–42.

1981b: 'Between beasts and gods', in Gordon 1981: 215–28.

1986: 'Dionysos en ses parousies: un dieu épidémique', in Bérard and Bron 1986:53–83.

Detienne, M. & Svenbro, J. 1979: 'Les loups au festin ou la cité impossible', in Detienne and Vernant 1979: 215–37.

Detienne, M. & Vernant, J.-P. 1978: *Cunning Intelligence in Greek Culture and Society* (tr. J. Lloyd), Hassocks and New Jersey.

Detienne, M. and Vernant, J.-P. (eds.) 1979: *La Cuisine du sacrifice*, Paris.

Deubner, L. 1900: *De incubatione capita quattuor*, Leipzig.

1932: *Attische Feste*, Berlin (2nd edn by B. Doer, 1969).

1936: review of Tierney 1935, *Gnomon* 12:506.

Diels, H. & Kranz, W. (eds.) 1951: *Die Fragmente der Vorsokratiker*, vol. I, 6th edn., Berlin.

Dieterich, A. 1893: 'Ueber eine Scene der aristophanischen Wolken', *RM* 48:275–83.

Diggle, J. 1984: *Euripidis Fabulae*, vol. I, Oxford.

Dillon, J. E. M. 1989: 'The Greek hero Perseus: myths of maturation', diss. Oxford.

Dillon, M. 1987a: 'The *Lysistrata* as a post-Deceleian peace play', *TAPA* 117:97–104.

1987b 'Topicality in Aristophanes' *Ploutos*', *Cl. Ant.* 6:155–83.

Dindorf, G. 1827: *Aristophanis Comoediae*, vol. III, Oxford.

Dirichlet, G. E. 1914: *De veterum macarismis*, Giessen.

Dobrov, G. 1990: 'Aristophanes' *Birds* and the metaphor of deferral', *Arethusa* 23:209–33.

Dodds, E. R. 1951: *The Greeks and the Irrational*, Berkeley and Los Angeles.

(ed.) 1960: *Euripides: Bacchae*, Oxford.

Dörrie, H. 1956–7: 'Aristophanes' Frösche 1433–67', *Hermes* 84:296–319.

Douglas, N. 1928: *Birds and Beasts of the Greek Anthology*, London.

Dover, K. J. 1963: 'Notes on Aristophanes' *Acharnians*', *Maia* 15:6–25 (repr. in Dover 1987: 287–306).

(ed.) 1968a: *Aristophanes: Clouds*, Oxford.

1968b: 'Portrait-masks in Aristophanes', in *Komoidotragemata: studia Aristophanea Viri Aristophanei W. J. W. Koster in honorem*, Amsterdam, 16–28 (repr. in Dover 1987: 266–78).

1970: 'Lo stile di Aristofane', *QUCC* 9:7–23 (Eng. tr. in Dover 1987: 224–37).

1972: *Aristophanic Comedy*, Berkeley and Los Angeles.

1974: *Greek Popular Morality in the Time of Plato and Aristotle*, Oxford.

1978: *Greek Homosexuality*, London.

1987: *Greek and the Greeks: collected papers*, vol. I, *Language, Poetry, Drama*, Oxford.

Dowden, K. 1979: 'Apollon et l'esprit dans la machine: origines', *REG* 92:293–318.

1980a: 'Deux notes sur les Scythes et les Arimaspes', *REG* 93:486–92.

1980b: 'Grades in the Eleusinian Mysteries', *RHR* 197:409–27.

1988: *Death and the Maiden: girls' initiation rites in Greek mythology*, London.

Duchemin, J. 1957: 'Recherches sur un thème aristophanien et ses sources religieuses: les voyages dans l'autre monde', *LEC* 25:273–95.

Dumézil, G. 1924: *Le Crime des Lemniennes: rites et légendes du monde égéen*, Paris.

1929: *Le Problème des Centaures*, Paris.

1975: *Fêtes d'été et d'automne, suivi de dix questions romaines*, Paris.

Dümmler, F. 1897: 'Sittengeschichtliche Parallelen', *Philol.* 56:5–32.

Durand, J.-L. & Schnapp, A. 1989: 'Sacrificial slaughter and initiatory hunt', in Bérard *et al.* 1989: 53–70.

Easterling, P. E. 1988: 'Tragedy and ritual: cry "Woe, Woe", but may the good prevail', *Métis* 3:87–109.

Edelstein, E. J. and Edelstein, L. 1945: *Asclepius: a collection and interpretation of the Testimonies*, 2 vols., Baltimore.

Edmunds, L. 1980: 'Aristophanes' *Acharnians*', *YCS* 26:1–41.

1984: 'Thucydides on monosandalism (3.22.2)', *Studies Dow* (see J. Binder 1984), 71–5.

1987a: *Cleon, Knights and Aristophanes' Politics*, Lanham.

1987b: 'The Aristophanic Cleon's "disturbance" of Athens', *AJP* 108:233–63.

(ed.) 1990: *Approaches to Greek Myth*, Baltimore and London.

Ehrenberg, V. 1947: 'Polypragmosyne: a study in Greek politics', *JHS* 67:46–67.

Eitrem, S. 1909: 'De Mercurio Aristophaneo', *Philol.* 68:344–67.

1915: *Opferritus und Voropfer der Griechen und Römer*, Christiania.

Elderkin, G. W. 1940: 'Aphrodite and Athena in the *Lysistrata* of Aristophanes', *CP* 35:387–96.

1955: *Mystic Allusions in the Frogs of Aristophanes*, Princeton.

Eliade, M. 1961: *Images and Symbols: studies in religious symbols* (tr. P. Mairet), London.

1964: *Shamanism: archaic techniques of ecstasy*, rev. ed. (tr. W. R. Trask), London.

1965: *The Myth of the Eternal Return: or Cosmos and History* (tr. W. R. Trask), Princeton.

Eliot, C. W. J. 1962: *Coastal Demes of Attika: a study of the policy of Kleisthenes*, Toronto.

Esser, A. A. M. 1939: *Das Anlitz der Blindheit in der Antike*, Stuttgart.

Farnell, L. R. 1896–1909: *Cults of the Greek States*, 5 vols., Oxford.

Fehrle, E. 1910: *Die kultische Keuschheit im Altertum*, Giessen.

Ferguson, J. 1971: 'Dinos', *Phronesis* 16:97–115.

1972–3: '*Dinos* on the stage', *CJ* 68:377–80.

1978–9: '*Dinos* in Aristophanes and Euripides', *CJ* 74:356–9.

Ferguson, W. S. 1938: 'The Salaminioi of Heptaphylai and Sounion', *Hesp.* 7:1–74.

Festugière, A. J. 1954: *Personal Religion among the Greeks*, Berkeley and Los Angeles.

1956: 'La signification religieuse de la Parodos des Bacchantes', *Eranos* 54:72–86.

Filippo Balestrazzi, E. di 1980–1: 'L'Agyieus e la città', *CRDAC* 11:93–108.

Finley, M. I. 1975: *The Use and Abuse of History*, London.

Fisher, N. R. E. 1993: 'Multiple personalities and Dionysia festivals: Dicaeopolis in Aristophanes' *Acharnians*', *G&R* 40:31–47.

Flashar, H. 1967: 'Zur Eigenart des Aristophanischen Spätwerks', *Poetica* 1:154–75 (= Newiger 1975: 405–34).

Foley, H. P. (ed.) 1981: *Reflections of Women in Antiquity*, New York.

1982: 'The "female intruder" reconsidered: women in Aristophanes' *Lysistrata* and *Ecclesiazusae*', *CP* 77:1–21.

1988: 'Tragedy and politics in Aristophanes' *Acharnians*', *JHS* 108:33–47.

Fontenrose, J. 1959: *Python: a study of the Delphic myth and its origins*, Berkeley, Los Angeles and London.

Forbes Irving, P. M. C. 1990: *Metamorphosis in Greek Myths*, Oxford.

Forrest, W. G. 1963: 'Aristophanes' *Acharnians*', *Phoenix* 17:1–12.

Förster, R. 1874: *Der Raub und Rückkehr der Persephone*, Stuttgart.

Foucart, P. 1873: *Des associations religieuses chez les Grecs, thiases, éranes, orgéons*, Paris.

1914: *Les Mystères d'Eleusis*, Paris.

Fraenkel, E. 1936: 'Dramaturgical problems in the *Ecclesiazusae*', in *Greek Poetry and Life: essays presented to Gilbert Murray on his seventieth birthday*, Oxford, 257–76.

1950: *Aeschylus: Agamemnon*, 3 vols., Oxford.

1962: *Beobachtungen zu Aristophanes*, Rome.

Frazer, J. G. 1921: *Apollodorus: the Library*, 2 vols., Cambridge, Mass., and London.

1927 (1911): *Taboo and the Perils of the Soul*, 3rd edn., London.

Frontisi-Ducroux, F. 1989: 'In the mirror of the mask', in Bérard *et al.* 1989: 150–65.

Frye, N. 1957: *The Anatomy of Criticism*, Princeton.

Fuks, A. 1972: 'Isocrates and the social-economic situation in Greece', *Anc. Soc.* 3:17–44.

Furley, W. D. 1981: *Studies in the Use of Fire in Ancient Greek Religion*, New York.

Gardiner, E. N. 1910: *Greek Athletic Sports and Festivals*, London.

Garvie, A. L. 1986: *Aeschylus: Choephori*, Oxford.

Gatz, B. 1967: *Weltalter, goldene Zeit und sinnverwandte Vorstellungen*, Hildesheim.

Gauthier, P. 1976: *Un commentaire historique des 'Poroi' de Xénophon*, Geneva.

Geddies, A. G. 1987: 'Rags and riches: the costume of Athenian men in the fifth century', *CQ* 37:307–31.

Geissler, P. 1925: *Chronologie der altattischen Komödie*, Munich.

Gennep, A. van 1909: *Les Rites de passage: étude systématique des rites*, Paris (tr. M. B. Vizedoni and G. L. Caffee, *The Rites of Passage*, London 1960).

Gernet, L. 1981: *The Anthropology of Ancient Greece*, Baltimore and London.

Ginouvès, R. 1962: *Balaneutikè: recherches sur le bain dans l'antiquité grecque*, Paris.

Golden, M. 1979: 'Demosthenes and the age of majority at Athens', *Phoenix* 33:25–38.

Goldhill, S. D. 1986: *Reading Greek Tragedy*, Cambridge.

1987: 'The Great Dionysia and civic ideology', *JHS* 107:58–76.

1991: *The Poet's Voice: essays on poetics and Greek literature*, Cambridge.

Gomme, A. W. 1938: 'Aristophanes and politics', *CR* 52:97–109.

1956a: *A Historical Commentary on Thucydides*, vol. II, books II–III, Oxford.

1956b: *A Historical Commentary on Thucydides*, vol. III, books IV–V.24, Oxford.

Gomme, A. W., Andrewes, A. & Dover, K. J. 1970: *A Historical Commentary on Thucydides*, vol. IV, books V.25–VII, Oxford.

1981: *A Historical Commentary on Thucydides*, vol. V, book VIII, Oxford.

Gordon, R. L. (ed.) 1981: *Myth, Religion and Society: structuralist essays by M. Detienne, L. Gernet, J.-P. Vernant and P. Vidal-Naquet*, Cambridge and Paris.

Gould, J. P. A. 1980: 'Law, custom and myth: aspects of the social position of women in classical Athens', *JHS* 100:38–59.

1985: 'On making sense of Greek religion', in P. E. Easterling and J. V. Muir (eds.), *Greek Religion and Society*, Cambridge, 1–33.

1989: *Herodotus*, London.

Graf, F. 1974: *Eleusis und die orphische Dichtung Athens in vorhellenistischer Zeit*, Berlin.

1979: 'Apollon Delphinios', *MH* 36:2–22.

1981: 'Milch, Hönig und Wein: zum Verständnis der Libation im griechischen Ritual', in *Perennitas: studi in honore di A. Brelich*, Rome, 209–21.

1984: 'Women, war, and warlike divinities', *ZPE* 55:245–54.

1985: *Nordionische Kulte*, Rome.

Griffin, J. 1980: *Homer on Life and Death*, Oxford.

Griffith, M. (ed.) 1983: *Aeschylus: Prometheus Bound*, Cambridge.

Griffith, R. D. 1987: 'The hoopoe's name: a note on *Birds* 48', *QUCC* 55:59–63.

Guarducci, M. 1982: 'Le Rane di Aristofane e la topografia ateniese', in *Studi in onore di A. Colonna*, Perugia, 167–72.

Guthrie, W. K. C. 1935: *Orpheus and Greek Religion: a study of the Orphic movement*, London.

1950: *The Greeks and their Gods*, London.

1969: *A History of Greek Philosophy*, vol. III: *The Fifth-century Enlightenment*, Cambridge.

Hadzisteliou-Price, T. 1978: *Kourotrophos: cults and representation of the Greek nursing deities*, Leiden.

Hall, E. 1989: *Inventing the Barbarian: Greek self-definition through tragedy*, Oxford.

Halliday, W. R. 1909–10: 'A note on Herodotos VI.83, and the Hybristika', *BSA* 16:212–19.

1928: *The Greek Questions of Plutarch*, Oxford.

Halliwell, S. 1991: 'The uses of laughter in Greek culture', *CQ* 41:279–96.

Hamdorf, F. W. 1964: *Griechische Kultpersonifikationen der vorhellenistischer Zeit*, Mainz.

Hamilton, R. 1985: 'The well-equipped traveller: *Birds* 42', *GRBS* 26:235–9.

Handley, E. W. 1985: 'Comedy', in P. E. Easterling and B. M. W. Knox (eds.), *The Cambridge History of Classical Literature*, vol. I: *Greek Literature*, Cambridge, 355–425.

Handley, E. W. & Rea, J. 1957: *The Telephus of Euripides*, *BICS* Suppl. 5, London.

Hani, J. 1975: 'Le mythe de Timarque chez Plutarque et la structure de l'extase', *REG* 88:105–20.

Hansen, M. H. 1976: *Apagoge, Endeixis and Ephegesis against Kakourgoi, Atimoi and Pheugontes: a study in Athenian administration of justice in the fourth century B.C.*, Odense.

Hanson, V. D. 1991: *Hoplites: the classical Greek battle experience*, Leiden.

Harriott, R. 1969: *Poetry and Criticism before Plato*, London.

Harrison, G. & Obbink, D. 1986: 'Vergil, Georgics 1 36–39 and the Barcelona Alcestis (P. Barc. Inv. no. 158–161) 62–65: Demeter in the Underworld', *ZPE* 63:75–81.

Harrison, J. 1908: *Prolegomena to the Study of Greek Religion*, 2nd edn., Cambridge.

Harry, J. E. 1910: 'Plato *Phaedo* 66B', *CR* 23:218–21.

Hartog, F. 1988: *The Mirror of Herodotus: the representation of the other in the writing of history*, Berkeley.

Harvey, F. D. 1981: '*Nubes* 1493ff.: was Socrates murdered?', *GRBS* 22:339–43.

Havelock, E. A. 1978: *The Greek Concept of Justice: from its shadow in Homer to its substance in Plato*, Cambridge, Mass.

Hawtrey, R. S. W. 1976: 'Plato, Socrates and the Mysteries: a note', *Antichthon* 10:22–4.

Headlam, W. 1906: 'The last scene of the *Eumenides*', *JHS* 26:268–77.

1922: *Herodas: the Mimes and Fragments* (ed. A. D. Knox), Cambridge.

Heath, M. 1987a: *Political Comedy in Aristophanes*, Göttingen.

1987b: 'Euripides' *Telephus*', *CQ* 37:272–80.

Heberlein, F. 1980: *Pluthygieia: zu Gegenwelt bei Aristophanes*, Frankfurt am Main.

Hedrick, C. W. 1988: 'The temple of Apollo Patroos in Athens', *AJA* 92:185–210.

Heeger, M. R. 1889: *De Theophrasti qui fertur peri semeion libro*, Leipzig.

Heinimann F. 1945: *Nomos und Physis: Herkunft und Bedeutung einer Antithese im griechischen Denken des 5. Jahrhunderts*, Darmstadt.

Helbig, W. 1902: *Les Hippes athéniens*, Paris.

Hemberg, B. 1952: 'Die Idaiischen Daktylen', *Eranos* 50:41–59.

Henderson, J. 1975: *The Maculate Muse*, New Haven and London.

  1987a: *Aristophanes: Lysistrata*, Oxford.

  1987b: 'Older women in Attic Old Comedy', *TAPA* 117:105–29.

  1990: 'The *demos* and the comic competition', in Winkler and Zeitlin 1990: 271–313.

Herington, C. J. 1955: *Athena Parthenos and Athena Polias*, Manchester.

Hertel, G. 1969: *Die Allegorie von Reichtum und Armut: ein Aristophaneisches Motiv und seine Abhandlungen in der abendländischen Literatur*, Nuremberg.

Herter, H. 1966: 'Das Königsritual der Atlantis', *RM* 109:236–59.

Herzog, R. 1931: *Die Wunderheilungen von Epidauros*, *Philologus Supplbd.* 22.

Heubeck, A. 1949–50: 'Smyrna, Myrina und Verwandtes', *BN* 1:270–82.

Hofmann, H. 1976: *Mythos und Komödie: Untersuchungen zu den Vögeln des Aristophanes*, Hildesheim and New York.

Hooker, J. 1980: 'The unity of Aristophanes' Frogs', *Hermes* 108:169–82.

Hopper, R. 1960: 'A note on Aristophanes, *Lysistrata* 665–70', *CQ* 10:242–7.

Horn, H. 1970: *Gebet und Gebetsparodie in den Komödien des Aristophanes*, Nuremberg.

Hulton, A. O. 1972: 'The women on the Acropolis: a note on the structure of the *Lysistrata*', *G&R* 19:32–6.

Hunter, R. L. 1983: *Eubulus: the Fragments*, Cambridge.

Immerwahr, W. 1891: *Die Kulte und Mythen Arkadiens*, Leipzig.

Jackson, S. 1990: 'Myrsilus of Methymna and the dreadful smell of the Lemnian Women', *ICS* 15:77–83.

Jameson, M. 1960: 'A decree of Themistokles from Troizen', *Hesp.* 29:198–223.

  1965: 'Notes on the sacrificial calendar from Erchia', *BCH* 89:154–72.

  1980: 'Apollo Lykeios in Athens', *Archaiognosia* 12:213–36.

Jeanmaire, H. 1913: 'La cryptie lacédémonienne', *REG* 26:121–50.

  1939: *Couroi et Courètes: essai sur l'éducation spartiate et sur les rites d'adolescence dans l'antiquité hellénique*, Lille.

Jenkins, I. 1985: 'The ambiguity of Greek textiles', *Arethusa* 18:109–32.

Jocelyn, H. D. 1980: 'A Greek indecency and its students: *laikazein*', *PCPS* 26:12–66.

Jones, A. H. M. 1967: *Sparta*, Oxford.

Just, R. 1989: *Women in Athenian Law and Life*, London.

Kadeletz, E. 1980: 'The race and procession of the Athenian Oschophoroi', *GRBS* 21:361–71.

Kahn, C. H. 1960: 'Religion and natural philosophy in Empedocles' doctrine of the soul', *AGP* 42:3–35.

Kahn, L. 1978: *Hermès passe ou les ambiguités de la communication*, Paris.

Kannicht, R. 1969: *Euripides: Helena*, 2 vols., Heidelberg.

Kany, R. 1988: 'Dionysus Protrygaios: pagane und christliche Spuren eines antiken Weinfestes', *JbAC* 31:5–23.

Kassel, R. 1981: '*Ene kai Nea*', *ZPE* 42:26.

Kearns, E. 1989: *The Heroes of Attica*, *BICS* Suppl. 57, London.

Kee, H. C. 1982: 'Self-definition in the Asclepius cult', in Meyer and Sanders 1982: 118–36.

Keller, O. 1909–13: *Die antike Tierwelt*, 2 vols., Leipzig.

Kern, O. 1900: *Die Inschriften von Magnesia am Maeander*, Berlin.

　　1922: *Orphicorum Fragmenta*, Zürich.

Killeen, J. F. 1986: 'What was the ancient Greek word for a "kite"?', *LCM* 11.2.31f.

King, H. 1983: 'Bound to bleed: Artemis and Greek women', in Cameron and Kuhrt 1983: 109–27.

Kinnier Wilson, J. V. 1979: *The Rebel Lands: an investigation into the origins of early Mesopotamian mythology* (with the assistance of H. Vanstiphout), Cambridge.

Kirk, G. S. 1970: *Myth: its meaning and functions in ancient and other cultures*, Cambridge, Berkeley and Los Angeles.

Kirk, G. S., Raven, J. E. & Schofield, M. 1983: *The Presocratic Philosophers: a critical history with a selection of texts*, 2nd edn., Cambridge.

Kiso, A. 1984: *The Lost Sophocles*, New York.

Kleinknecht, H. 1937: *Die Gebetsparodie in der Antike*, Stuttgart.

　　1939: 'Die Epiphanie des Demos in Aristophanes' *Rittern*', *Hermes* 74:58–65.

Klinz, A. 1933: *Hieros gamos: quaestiones selectae ad sacras nuptias Graecorum religionis et poeseos pertinentes*, diss. Halle.

Knox, B. M. W. 1979: *Word and Action: essays on the ancient theatre*, Baltimore and London.

Köhnken, A. 1980: 'Der Wolken-Chor des Aristophanes', *Hermes* 108:154–69.

Konstan, D. 1986: 'Poésie, politique et rituel dans les Grenouilles d'Aristophane', *Métis* 1:291–308.

　　1990: 'A city in the air: Aristophanes' *Birds*', *Arethusa* 23:183–207.

Konstan, D. & Dillon, M. 1981: 'The ideology of Aristophanes' *Wealth*', *AJP* 102:371–94.

Kopff, E. C. 1977: '*Nubes* 1493ff.: was Socrates murdered?', *GRBS* 18:113–22.

　　1990: 'The date of Aristophanes, *Nubes II*', *AJP* 111:318–29.

Krentz, P. 1985: 'The nature of hoplite battle', *Cl. Ant.* 4:50–62.

Kroll, J. H. 1976: 'Aristophanes' *ponera khalkia*: a reply,' *GRBS* 17:329–41.

Kurtz, D. C. and Boardman, J. 1971: *Greek Burial Customs*, London.

Labarbe, J. 1953: 'L'âge correspondent au sacrifice du *koureion* et les données historiques du sixième discours d'Isée', *BARB* 5me sér. 39:358–94.

Lacey, W. K. 1968: *The Family in Classical Greece*, London and Auckland.

Lada, I. (forthcoming): 'Initiating Dionysus: ritual and theatre in Aristophanes' Frogs', diss. Cambridge.

Lalonde, G. V. 1982: 'Topographical notes on Aristophanes', in *Studies in Athenian Architecture, Sculpture and Topography presented to H. A. Thompson*, Princeton, 77–81.

Lamprinoudakis, V. K. 1972: '*Ta Ekdusia tes Phaistou*', *AE* 99–112.

Landfester, M. 1967: *Die Ritter des Aristophanes: Beobachtungen zur dramatischen Handlung und zum komischen Stil des Aristophanes*, Amsterdam.

Lattimore, R. 1962: *Themes in Greek and Roman Epitaphs*, Urbana.

Lawler, L. B. 1964: *The Dance in the Ancient Greek Theatre*, London.

Leschhorn, W. 1984: '*Gründer der Stadt*'. *Studien zu einem politisch-religiösen Phänomen der griechischen Geschichte*, Stuttgart.

Lesky, A. 1925: 'Alkestis, der Mythos und das Drama', *SB Akad. Wiss. Wein, Phil.-Hist. Klasse* 203.2.

Lévy, E. 1976: *Athènes devant la defaite de 404: histoire d'une crise idéologique*, Paris.

Lewis, D. M. 1955: 'Notes on Attic inscriptions (II)', *BSA* 50:1–36.

   1958: 'When was Aeschines born?', *CR* 8:108.

   1977: *Sparta and Persia*, Leiden.

Lilja, S. 1972: *The Treatment of Odours in the Poetry of Antiquity*, Helsinki.

Linforth, I. M. 1944–50: 'The Corybantic rites in Plato', *UCPCS* 13:121–62.

Lissarrague, F. 1989: 'The world of the warrior', in Bérard *et al.* 1989: 39–52.

   1990: *The Aesthetics of the Greek Banquet: images of wine and ritual*, Princeton.

Littlefield, D. 1968: 'Metaphor and myth. The unity of Aristophanes' *Knights*', *SPh.* 65:1–22.

Lloyd, G. E. R. 1979: *Magic, Reason and Experience: studies in the origin and development of Greek science*, Cambridge.

   1983: *Science, Folklore and Ideology: studies in the life sciences in ancient Greece*, Cambridge.

Lloyd-Jones, P. H. J. 1967: 'Heracles at Eleusis: P.Oxy. 2622 and P.S.I. 1391', *Maia* 19:206–29.

   1983: 'Artemis and Iphigeneia', *JHS* 103:87–103.

Lobeck, C. A. 1829: *Aglaophamus sive de theologiae mysticae Graecorum causis libri tres*, Königsberg.

Lofberg, J. O. 1914: *Sycophancy at Athens*, diss. Chicago.

Loraux, N. 1980: 'L'Acropole comique', *Ancient Society* 11:119–50.

   1981: *Les Enfants d'Athéna: idées athéniennes sur la citoyenneté et la division des sexes*, Paris.

   1986: *The Invention of Athens: the funeral oration in the classical city* (tr. A. Sheridan), Cambridge, Mass., and London.

Lukas, F. 1984: 'Das Ei als kosmogonische Vorstellung', *Zeits. des Vereins für Volkskunde*, 4:227–43.

Maass, E. 1922: 'Segnen, Weihen, Taufen', *ARW* 21:241–86.

MacCarey, W. T. 1979: 'Philocleon Ithyphallos. Dance, costume and character in the *Wasps*', *TAPA* 109:137–47.

McCartney, E. S. 1929: 'Clouds, rainbows, weather galls, comets, and earthquakes as weather portents in Greek and Latin writers', *CW* 23:2–8 (clouds).

MacDowell, D. M. 1959: 'Aristophanes, *Frogs* 1407–67', *CQ* 9:261–8.

1962: *Andokides: On the Mysteries*, Oxford.

1963: *Athenian Homicide Law in the Age of the Orators*, Manchester.

1971: *Aristophanes: Wasps*, Oxford.

1983: 'The nature of Aristophanes' *Akharnians*', *G&R* 30:143–62.

Macleod, C. W. 1981: 'The comic encomium and Aristophanes' *Clouds* 1201–1211', *Phoenix* 35:142–4.

1982: *Homer: Iliad XXIV*, Cambridge.

Mainoldi, C. 1981: 'Cani mitici e rituali tra il regno dei morti e il mondo dei viventi', *QUCC* 37:7–41.

Malkin, I. 1987: *Religion and Colonization in Ancient Greece*, Leiden.

Mannhardt, W. 1904–5: *Antike Wald- und Feldkulte aus Nord-Europaeischen Überlieferung*, 2nd edn. W. Heuschkel, Berlin.

Martin, A. 1887: *Les Cavaliers athéniens*, Paris.

Martin, R. 1951: *Recherches sur l'agora grecque: études d'histoire et d'architecture grecque*, Paris.

Martin, R. P. 1987: 'Fire on the mountain: *Lysistrata* and the Lemnian Women', *CA* 6:77–105.

Marzullo, B. 1953: 'Strepsiade', *Maia* 6:99–124.

1970: 'L'interlocuzione negli "Uccelli" di Aristofane', *Philol.* 114:181–94.

Mastromarco, G. 1988: 'L'odore del mostro', *Lexis* 209–15.

Mastronarde, D. J. 1990: 'Actors on high: the skene roof, the crane, and the gods in Attic drama', *Cl. Ant.* 9:247–94.

Maxwell-Stewart, P. G. 1970: 'Remarks on the black cloaks of the Ephebes', *PCPS* 16:113–16.

Méautis, C. 1938: 'La scène d'initiation dans les Nuées d'Aristophane', *RHR* 118:92–7.

Meder, A. 1938: *Der athenische Demos zur Zeit des Peloponnesischen Krieges im Lichte zeitgenössischer Quellen*, diss. Munich.

Meiggs, R. 1972: *The Athenian Empire*, Oxford.

Meiggs, R. and Lewis, D. M. 1988: *A Selection of Greek Historical Inscriptions to the End of the Fifth Century BC*, rev. edn., Oxford.

Meineke, A. 1839–41: *Fragmenta Comicorum Graecorum*, 4 vols., Berlin.

Merkelbach, R. 1972: 'Aglauros: die Religion der Epheben', *ZPE* 9:277–83.

Mette, H. J. 1977: *Urkunden dramatischer Aufführungen in Griechenland*, Berlin and New York.

Metzger, H. 1944–5: 'Dionysos chthonien d'après les monuments figurés de la période classique', *BCH* 68–9:323–39.

Meuli, K. 1935: 'Scythica', *Hermes* 70:121–76.

Meyer, B. F. and Sanders, E. P. (eds.) 1982: *Jewish and Christian Self-Definition*, vol. III *Self-definition in the Greco-Roman world*, Philadelphia.

Michell, H. 1952: *Sparta*, Cambridge.

Mihailov, G. 1955: 'La légende de Térée', *Annuaire de l'univ. de Sofia, Fac. Lettres*, 50.2:77–208.

Mikalson, J. D. 1975: *The Sacred and Civil Calendar of the Athenian Year*, Princeton.

1976: 'Erechtheus and the Panathenaia', *AJP* 97:141–53.

1983: *Athenian Popular Religion*, Chapel Hill, N.C., and London.

Miller, S. G. 1978: *The Prytaneion: its function and architectural form*, Berkeley, Los Angeles and London.

Minns, E. H. 1913: *Scythians and Greeks: a survey of ancient history and archaeology on the north coast of the Euxine from the Danube to the Caucasus*, Cambridge.

Moessner, O. 1907: *Die Mythologie in der dorischen und altattischen Komödie*, diss. Erlangen.

Mommsen, A. 1891: 'Die attischen Skirabräuchen', *Philol.* 50: 108–36.

1898: *Feste der Stadt Athen im Altertum, ausgeordnet nach attischem Kalendar*, Leipzig.

Mondi, R. 1990: 'Greek mythic thought in the light of the Near East', in Edmunds 1990: 141–98.

Moorton, R. F., Jr 1989: 'Rites of passage in Aristophanes' *Frogs*', *CJ* 84:308–24.

Moreau, J. 1954: 'Sur les *Saisons* d'Aristophane', *La Nouvelle Clio* 6:327–44.

Mossé, C. 1962: *La Fin de la démocratie athénienne: aspects sociaux et politiques du déclin de la cité grecque au IVe siècle avant J.C.*, Paris.

1972: 'La vie économique d'Athènes au IVe siècle: crise ou renouveau?', in *Praelectiones Pataviniae* (ed. F. Sartori), Rome.

Moulinier, L. 1952: *Le Pur et l'Impure dans la pensée des Grecs d'Homère à Aristote*, Paris.

Moulton, C. 1981: *Aristophanic Poetry*, Göttingen.

Mullen, W. 1982: *Choreia: Pindar and Dance*, Princeton.

Müller, C. W. 1985: 'Die Archilochuslegende', *RM* 128:99–151.

Murray, G. M. 1924: *The Rise of the Greek Epic*, 3rd edn., Oxford.

Murray, O. 1980: *Early Greece*, London.

Murray, P. 1981: 'Poetic inspiration in early Greece', *JHS* 101:87–100.

Mylonas, G. E. 1961: *Eleusis and the Eleusinian Mysteries*, Princeton.

Naber, S. A. 1900: 'Observationes miscellaneae ad Plutarchi Moralia', *Mnem.* 28:85–117.

Nagy, G. 1979: *The Best of the Achaeans: concepts of the hero in archaic Greek poetry*, Baltimore and London.

1986: 'Pindar's *Olympian* 1 and the aetiology of the Olympic games', *TAPA* 106:71–88.

Neil, R. A. (ed.) 1901: *The Knights of Aristophanes*, Cambridge.

Neils, J. 1987: *The Youthful Deeds of Theseus*, Rome.

Nestle, W. 1925–6: '*Apragmosune* (zu Thukydides II.63)', *Philol.* 81:129–40.

Newiger, H.-J. 1957: *Metapher und Allegorie: Studien zu Aristophanes*, Munich.

1975: *Aristophanes und die alte Komödie*, Darmstadt.

Newman, W. L. (ed.) 1902: *The Politics of Aristotle*, 3 vols., Oxford.

Nilsson, M. P. 1906: *Griechische Feste von religiöser Bedeutung, mit Ausschluss der attischen*, Leipzig.

1952: 'Kultische Personifikationen: ein Nachtrag zu meiner Geschichte der griechischen Religion', *Eranos* 50:31–40.

1955: *Geschichte der griechischen Religion*, vol. I, 2nd edn., Munich.

Nisbet, R. G. M. and Hubbard, M. 1970: *A Commentary on Horace: Odes Book 1*, Oxford.

Nock, A. D. 1972: *Essays on Religion and the Ancient World* (selected and edited by Z. Stewart), 2 vols., Oxford.

Norwood, G. 1931: *Greek Comedy*, London.

Nussbaum, M. 1980: 'Aristophanes and Socrates on learning practical wisdom', *YCS* 26:43–97.

Oder, E. 1888: 'Die Wiedehopf in der griechischen Sage', *RM* 43:541–56.

Oeri, H. G. 1948: *Der Typ der komischen Alten in der griechischen Komödie*, diss. Basel.

Olson, S. D. 1988: 'The "love-duet" in Aristophanes' *Ecclesiazusae*', *CQ* 38:328–30.

1990: 'The new Demos of Aristophanes' *Knights*', *Eranos* 88:60–3.

Osborne, R. G. 1985a: *Demos: the Discovery of Classical Attika*, Cambridge.

1985b: 'The erection and mutilation of the Hermai', *PCPS* 31:47–73.

1987: *Classical Landscape with Figures: the ancient Greek city and the countryside*, London.

Otto, A. 1890: *Die Sprichwörter und sprichwörterlichen Redensarten der Römer*, Hildesheim.

Otto, W. F. 1933: *Dionysos: Mythos und Kultus*, Frankfurt.

Padel, R. 1983: 'Women: model for possession by Greek daemons', in Cameron and Kuhrt 1983: 3–19.

Paduano, G. 1973: 'La città degli uccelli e le ambivalenze del nuovo sistema etico-politico', *SCO* 22:115–44.

Paganelli, L. 1978–9: 'Blepyros nome parlante: Aristofane, *Eccl.* 327', *MC* 13–14:231–5.

Page, D. L. 1962: *Select Papyri*, vol. III *Literary Papyri: Poetry*, London and Cambridge, Mass.

Palmer, L. R. 1980: *The Greek Language*, London and Boston.

Papademetriou, I. 1948–9: 'ΑΤΤΙΚΑ I', *AE* 86–7:146–53.

Pappas, T. 1987: 'Contributo a uno studio antropologico della commedia attica antica: struttura e funzione degli esodi nelle commedie di Aristofane', *Dioniso* 57:191–202.

Paradiso, A. 1987: 'Le rite de passage du Ploutos d'Aristophane', *Métis* 2:249–67.

Parke, H. W. 1977: *Festivals of the Athenians*, London.

Parke, H. W. and Wormell, D. E. W. 1956: *The Delphic Oracle*, 2 vols. Oxford.

Parker, L. P. E. 1983: Review of Sommerstein 1980a, *CR* 33:11.

Parker, R. C. T. 1983: *Miasma: pollution and purification in early Greek religion*, Oxford.

1987a: 'Festivals of the Attic Demes', *Boreas* 15:137–47.

1987b: 'Myths of early Athens', in Bremmer 1987: 187–214.

1989: 'Dionysus at Agrai', *LCM* 14:10.154f.

1991: 'The *Hymn to Demeter* and the *Homeric Hymns*', *G&R* 38:1–17.

Pascal, C. 1911: *Dioniso: saggio sulla religione e la parodia religiosa in Aristofane*, Catania.

Pearson, A. C. 1917: *The Fragments of Sophocles*, 3 vols., Cambridge.

Pease, A. S. 1917: 'Notes on the Delphic Oracle and Greek colonisation', *CP* 12:1–20.

(ed.) 1955–8: *M. Tullius Cicero: de Natura Deorum*, 2 vols., Cambridge, Mass.

Pélékidis, C. 1962: *Histoire de l'éphébie attique des origines à 31 avant Jésus-Christ*, Paris.

Pembroke, S. 1967: 'Women in charge: the function of alternatives in early Greek tradition and the ancient idea of matriarchy', *JWI* 30:1–35.

1970: 'Locres et Tarente: le rôle des femmes dans la fondation de deux colonies grecques', *Annales ESC* 25:1240–70.

Petersen, C. 1848: *Der geheime Gottesdienst bei den Griechen*, Hamburg.

Piccaluga, G. 1968: *Lycaon*, Rome.

Pickard-Cambridge, A. 1927: *Dithyramb, Tragedy and Comedy*, Oxford.

1962: *Dithyramb, Tragedy and Comedy*, 2nd edn. revised by T. B. L. Webster, Oxford.

1988: *The Dramatic Festivals of Athens*, 2nd edn. (1968) revised by J. Gould and D. M. Lewis, reissued with supplement and corrections, Oxford.

Pieters, J. T. M. F. 1946: *Cratinus: Bijdrage tot de Geschiedenis der Vroeg-Attische Comedie*, Leiden.

Pigeaud, J. 1987: *Folie et cures de la folie chez les médecins d'antiquité greco-romaine: la manie*, Paris.

Platnauer, M. 1964: *Aristophanes: Peace*, Oxford.

Pohlenz, M. 1952: 'Aristophanes' Ritter', *NGG* 95–128.

Pollard, J. 1977: *Birds in Greek Life and Myth*, London.

Pötscher, W. 1958: 'Götter und Gottheit bei Herodot', *WS* 71:5–29.

Powell, B. 1906: *Erichthonius and the Three Daughters of Cecrops*, Ithaca.

Pritchett, W. K. 1979: *The Greek State at War*, vol. III: *Religion*, Berkeley, Los Angeles and London.

1985: *The Greek State at War*, vol. IV, Berkeley.

Radermacher, L. 1931: *Der homerische Hermeshymnus*, Vienna.

1940: '*Khoiros* "Mädchen"', *RM* 89:236–8.

1954: *Aristophanes' Frösche* (2nd edn. by W. Kraus), Vienna.

Raingeard, P. 1935: *Hermès Psychagogue*, Paris.

Rankin, D. I. 1987: 'Sokrates, an oligarch?', *AC* 56:68–87.

Ranulf, S. 1933–4: *The Jealousy of God and Criminal Law at Athens: a contribution to the study of moral indignation*, 2 vols., Copenhagen.

Rau, P. 1967: *Paratragodia: Untersuchungen einer komischen Form des Aristo-phanes*, Munich.

Reckford. K. J. 1987: *Aristophanes' Old-and-New Comedy*, vol. I: *Six Essays in Perspective*, Chapel Hill.

Reinmuth, O. W. 1952: 'The genesis of the Athenian ephebeia', *TAPA* 83:34–50.

Rhodes, P. J. 1972: *The Athenian Boule*, Oxford.

1981: *A Commentary on the Aristotelian Athenaion Politeia*, Oxford.

Richardson, N. J. 1974: *The Homeric Hymn to Demeter*, Oxford.

1983: 'Innovazione poetica e mutamenti religiosi nella antica Grecia', *SCO* 33:15–37.

Richter, I. 1858: *Aristophanes: Vespae*, Berlin.

Riedweg, C. 1987: *Mysterienterminologie bei Platon, Philon und Klemens von Alexandrien*, Berlin.

Ries, J. and Limet, H. (eds.) 1986: *Les Rites d'initiation*, Louvain-la-neuve.

Robertson, C. M. 1975: *A History of Greek Art*, 2 vols., Cambridge.

Robertson, N. 1980: 'Heracles' "Catabasis"', *Hermes* 108:274–300.

Roeger, J. 1924: *Aidos kunee: das Märchen von der Unsichtbarkeit in den homerischen Gedichten*, diss. Graz.

Rohde, E. 1925: *Psyche: the cult of souls and belief in immortality among the Greeks*, London.

Rolley, C. 1965: 'Le sanctuaire des dieux patrôoi et le thesmophorion de Thasos', *BCH* 89:441–83.

Roos, E. 1951: *Die tragische Orchestik im Zerrbild der altattischen Komödie*, Lund.

Roscher, W. H. 1896: 'Das von der "Kynanthropie" handelnde Fragment des Marcellus von Side', *ASAW* 17 no. 3.

Rosellini, M. 1979: '*Lysistrata*: une mise en scène de la féminité', in Auger, Rosellini and Saïd 1979: 11–32.

Rosivach, V. J. 1988: 'The tyrant in Athenian democracy', *QUCC* 30:43–57.

Rothwell, K. S., Jr, 1990: *Politics and Persuasion in Aristophanes' Ecclesiazusae*, Leiden.

Rouse, W. H. D. 1902: *Greek Votive Offerings: an essay in the history of Greek religion*, Cambridge.

Roussel, P. 1941: 'Les chlamydes noires des éphèbes athéniens', *REA* 43:163–5.

Ruhl, L. 1903: *De mortuorum iudicio*, Giessen.

Rusten, J. S. 1983: '*Geiton heros*: Pindar's prayer to Heracles (*N*. 7.86–101) and Greek popular religion', *HSCP* 87:289–97.

Rutherford, I. and Irvine, J. 1988: 'The race in the Athenian Oschophoria and an oschophoricon by Pindar', *ZPE* 72:43–51.

Saïd, S. 1979: '*L'assemblée des femmes*: les femmes, l'économie et la politique', in Auger, Rosellini and Saïd 1979: 33–69.

　　1987: 'Travestis et travestissements dans les comédies d'Aristophane', *CGITA* 3:217–48.

de Ste Croix, G. E. M. 1972: *Origins of the Peloponnesian War*, London.

Sallares, R. 1991: *The Ecology of the Ancient Greek World*, London.

Schachermeyr, F. 1950: *Poseidon und die Entstehung des griechischen Götterglaubens*, Berne.

Schefold, K. 1946: 'Kleisthenes: der Anteil der Kunst an der Gestaltung des jungen attischen Freistaates', *MH* 3:59–93.

Schmid, P. B. 1947: *Studien zu griechischen Ktisissagen*, Freiburg.

Schmitt, P. 1977: 'Athéna Apatouria et la ceinture: les aspects féminins des Apatouries à Athènes', *Annales ESC* 32:1059–73.

Schnapp, A. 1989: 'Eros the hunter', in Bérard *et al.* 1989: 71–87.

Schultz, W. 1909: 'Herakles am Schiedewege', *Philol.* 68:488–99.

de Schutter, X. 1987: 'Le culte d'Apollon Patrôos à Athènes', *AC* 56:103–29.

Scodel, R. 1980: *The Trojan Trilogy of Euripides*, Göttingen.

　　1987: 'The ode and antode in the parabasis of *Clouds*', *CJ* 82:334f.

Seaford, R. 1981: 'Dionysiac drama and the Dionysiac Mysteries', *CQ* 31:252–75.

— 1984: *Euripides: Cyclops*, Oxford.

Segal, C. 1961: 'The character and cults of Dionysus and the unity of the *Frogs*', *HSCP* 65:207–42.

— 1962: 'The Phaeacians and the symbolism of Odysseus' return', *Arion* 1.4:17–64.

— 1969: 'Aristophanes' Cloud-Chorus', *Arethusa* 2:143–61.

— 1981: *Tragedy and Civilization: a study of Sophocles*, Cambridge, Mass., and London.

— 1982: *Dionysiac Poetics and Euripides' Bacchae*, Princeton.

Seidensticker, B. 1982: *Palintonos Harmonia: Studien zu komischen Elementen in der griechischen Tragödie*, Göttingen.

Servais, J. 1984: 'La date des Adonies d'Athènes et l'expédition de Sicile (à propos d'Aristophane, *Lysistrata* 387–389)', in *Adonis (Coll. di studi fenici* 18), 83–93.

Sfameni Gasparro, G. 1986: *Misteri e culti mistici di Demetra*, Rome.

Shapiro, H. A. 1986: 'The Attic deity Basile', *ZPE* 63:134–6.

— 1989: 'Poseidon and the tuna', *AC* 58:32–43.

Sheppard, J. T. 1909: '*Tis estin he Basileia*; the last scene of the *Birds* of Aristophanes', in *Fasciculus Ioanni Willis Clark dicatus*, Cambridge, 529–40.

— 1910: 'Politics in the Frogs of Aristophanes', *JHS* 30:249–59.

Sichelen, L. van 1987: 'Nouvelles orientations dans l'étude de l'arréphorie attique', *AC* 56:88–102.

Sidwell, K. 1989: 'The sacrifice at Aristophanes: *Wasps* 860–90', *Hermes* 117:271–7.

— 1990: 'Was Philocleon cured? The *nosos* theme in Aristophanes' *Wasps*', *C&M* 41:9–31.

Siewert, P. 1977: 'The ephebic oath in fifth-century Athens', *JHS* 97:102–11.

— 1979: 'Poseidon Hippios am Kolonos und die athenischen Hippeis', in *Arktouros: Hellenic studies presented to Bernard M. W. Knox*, G. W. Bowersock, W. Burkert, M. C. J. Putnam (eds.), Berlin and New York, 280–9.

Sifakis, G. M. 1971: *Parabasis and Animal Choruses: a contribution to the history of Attic comedy*, London.

Silk, M. S. 1988: 'The autonomy of comedy', *Comparative Criticism* 10:3–31.

— 1990: 'The people of Aristophanes', in C. B. R. Pelling (ed.), *Characterization and Individuality in Greek Literature*, Oxford, 150–73.

Simon, E. 1955: 'Ixion und die Schlangen', *ÖJh* 42.5–26.

— 1960: 'La mission de Triptolème d'après l'imagerie athénienne', *Recueil C. Dugas*, ed. H. Metzger, Paris, 123–39.

— 1966: 'Neue Deutung zweier eleusinischer Denkmäler des vierten Jahrhunderts v. Chr.', *AK* 9:72–91.

— 1975: 'Versuch einer Deutung der Südmetopen des Parthenon', *JDAI* 90:100–20.

— 1983: *Festivals of Attica: an archaeological commentary*, Madison.

Smith, N. D. 1989: 'Diviners and divination in Aristophanic comedy', *Cl. Ant.* 8:140–58.

Sokolowski, F. 1955: *Lois sacrées de l'Asie Mineur*, Paris.

  1962: *Lois sacrées des cités grecques: supplément*, Paris.

  1969: *Lois sacrées des cités grecques*, Paris.

Sommerstein, A. H. 1977: 'Aristophanes and the events of 411', *JHS* 97:112–26.

  1980a: *Aristophanes: Acharnians*, Warminster.

  1980b: 'Notes on Aristophanes' *Knights*', *CQ* 30:46–56.

  1981: *Aristophanes: Knights*, Warminster.

  1983: *Aristophanes: Wasps*, Warminster.

  1984: 'Aristophanes and the Demon Poverty', *CQ* 34:314–33.

  1985: *Aristophanes: Peace*, Warminster.

  1987: *Aristophanes: Birds*, Warminster.

  1989: *Aeschylus: Eumenides*, Cambridge.

  1990: *Aristophanes: Lysistrata*, Warminster.

Sourvinou, C. 1971a: 'Theseus lifting the rock and a cup near the Pithos Painter', *JHS* 91:94–109.

  1971b: 'Aristophanes, *Lysistrata*, 641–647', *CQ* 21:339–42.

Sourvinou-Inwood, C. 1974: 'The votum of 477/6 BC and the foundation legend of Locri Epizephyrii', *CQ* 24:186–98 (= 1991: 147–88).

  1979: *Theseus as Son and Stepson: a tentative illustration of Greek mythological mentality*, *BICS* Suppl. 40, London.

  1983: 'A trauma in flux: death in the 8th century and after', in R. Hägg (ed.), *The Greek Renaissance of the Eighth Century B.C.: tradition and innovation*, Stockholm, 33–48.

  1988: *Studies in Girls' Transitions: aspects of the arkteia and age representation in Attic iconography*, Athens.

  1990: 'What is *Polis* religion?', in O. Murray and S. R. F. Price, *The Greek City from Homer to Alexander*, Oxford, 295–322.

  1991: *'Reading' Greek Culture: texts and images, rituals and myths*, Oxford.

Spyropoulos, E. S. 1975: 'Magnès le comique et sa place dans l'histoire de l'ancienne comédie attique', *Hellenika* 28:247–74.

Stadter, P. A. 1965: *Plutarch's Historical Methods: an analysis of the Mulierum Virtutes*, Cambridge, Mass.

Stanford, W. B. 1971: *Aristophanes: The Frogs*, 2nd edn. London.

Starkie, W. J. M. 1897: *The Wasps of Aristophanes*, London.

  1909: *The Acharnians of Aristophanes*, London.

  1911: *The Clouds of Aristophanes*, London.

Stengel, P. 1886: 'Die Farbe und Geschlecht der griechischen Opfertiere', *NJ Cl. Phil.* 133:329–31.

  1920: *Die griechischen Kultusaltertümer*, 3rd edn., Munich.

Stockmeyer, P. 1988: 'Hermes', *RLAC* 108–9:722–80.

Storetzki, N. 1954: *Motive in Grundungssagen*, diss. Leipzig.

Storey, I. C. 1985: 'The symposium at *Wasps* 1299ff.', *Phoenix* 39:317–33.

Strauss, B. S. 1986: *Athens after the Peloponnesian War: class, faction and policy 403–386 B.C.*, London and Sydney.

Strauss-Clay, J. 1987: 'Hermes' *dais* by the Alpheus: *Hymn to Hermes*, 105–141',

Métis 2:221–34.

Stroud, R. 1968: 'The Sanctuary of Demeter and Kore on Acrocorinth: preliminary report II (1964–1965)', *Hesp.* 37:299–33.

Sutton, D. F. 1980: *The Greek Satyr Play*, Meisenheim am Glan.

Sutton, R. F. 1981: 'The interaction between men and women portrayed on Attic red-figure pottery', diss. Chapel Hill.

Taillardat, J. 1962: *Les Images d'Aristophane*, Paris.

Taplin, O. P. 1986: 'Fifth-century tragedy and comedy: a *synkrisis*', *JHS* 106:163–74.

Tarkow, T. A. 1982: 'Achilles and the ghost of Aeschylus in Aristophanes' *Frogs*', *Traditio* 38:1–16

Tarsouli, G. 1944: *Songs from Methoni and Koroni*, Athens.

Taylor, A. E. 1911: *Varia Socratica*, first series, Oxford.

Thiercy, P. 1986: *Aristophane: fiction et dramaturgie*, Paris.

Thompson, D'A. W. 1936: *A Glossary of Greek Birds*, London.

   1947: *A Glossary of Greek Fishes*, London.

Thompson, H. A. 1936: 'Pnyx and Thesmophoria', *Hesp.* 5:151–200.

   1961: *AA* 76:224–31.

Thompson, S. 1955–8: *Motif-Index of Folk Literature*, Copenhagen.

Thomson, G. 1935: 'Mystical allusions in the *Oresteia*', *JHS* 55:20–34.

Tierney, M. 1935: 'The parodos of Aristophanes' *Frogs*', *Proceedings of Royal Irish Academy* 42C:199–218.

   1937: 'The Mysteries and the Oresteia', *JHS* 57:11–21.

Töpffer, J. 1889: *Attische Genealogie*, Berlin.

Toutain, J. 1932: 'Hermès, dieu social chez les Grecs', *RHPR* 12:289–99.

Traill, J. 1975: *The Political Organisation of Attica, Hesp. Suppl.* 14.

   1978: 'Diakris, the island trittys of Leontis', *Hesperia* 47:89–109.

Trencsényi-Waldapfel, I. 1957: 'The *Knights* of Aristophanes', *A. Ant. Hung.* 5.95–127.

Trumpf, J. 1958: 'Stadtgründung und Drachenkampf', *Hermes* 86:129–57.

Tucker, T. G. 1906: *The Frogs of Aristophanes*, London.

Tuplin, C. J. 1985: 'Imperial tyranny: some reflections on a classical Greek political metaphor', in P. A. Cartledge and F. D. Harvey (eds.), *Crux: essays in Greek history presented to G. E. M. de Ste Croix on his 75th birthday*, London, 348–75.

Tyrrell, W. B. 1984: *Amazons: a study of Athenian mythmaking*, Baltimore.

Usener, H. 1896: *Götternamen*, Bonn.

   1904: 'Psithyros', *RM* 59:623f.

Ussher, R. G. 1973: *Aristophanes: Ecclesiazusae*, Oxford.

Vaio, J. 1971: 'Aristophanes' *Wasps*. The relevance of the final scenes', *GRBS* 12:335–51.

   1973: 'The manipulation of theme and action in Aristophanes' *Lysistrata*', *GRBS* 14:369–80.

Venedikov, I., Gerassimov, T., Dremsizowa, C., Ivanov, T., Mładenova, J. & Velkov, V. 1963: *Apollonia: les fouilles dans la nécropole d'Apollonia en 1947–1949*, Sofia.

Vernant, J.-P. 1979: 'A la table des hommes: mythe et fonction du sacrifice chez Hésiode', in Vernant and Vidal-Naquet 1979: 37–132.

1980: *Myth and Society in Ancient Greece*, London.

1983: 'Hestia–Hermes: the religious expression of space and movement in ancient Greece', in *Myth and Thought amongst the Greeks*, London, 127–75.

Vernant, J.-P. & Vidal-Naquet, P. 1978: *Tragedy and Myth in Ancient Greece*, vol. I, Paris.

1979: *La Cuisine du sacrifice au pays grec*, Paris.

1988: *Myth and Tragedy in Ancient Greece*, New York 1988.

Versnel, H. S. 1990: 'What's sauce for the goose is sauce for the gander: myth and ritual, old and new', in Edmunds 1990: 23–90.

Vian, F. 1952: *La Guerre des Géants: le mythe avant l'époque hellénistique*, Paris.

1963: *Les Origines de Thèbes: Cadmos et les Spartes*, Paris.

Vidal-Naquet, P. 1981a: 'Land and sacrifice in the Odyssey: a study of religious and mythical meanings', in Gordon 1981: 80–94.

1981b: 'The Black Hunter and the origin of the Athenian *ephebeia*', in Gordon 1981: 147–162.

1981c: 'Recipes for Greek adolescence', in Gordon 1981: 163–85.

1981d: 'Slavery and the rule of women in tradition, myth and utopia', in Gordon 1981: 187–200.

1986: 'The Black Hunter revisited', *PCPS* 32:126–44.

1988: 'Sophocles' *Philoctetes* and the ephebeia', in Vernant and Vidal-Naquet 1988: 161–79.

Wächter, T. 1910: *Reinheitsvorschriften im griechischen Kult*, Giessen.

Waegeman, M. 1984: 'The gecko, the hoopoe ... and lice', *Ant. Class.* 53:218–25.

Walker, S. 1983: 'Women and housing in classical Greece: the archaeological evidence', in Cameron and Kuhrt 1983: 81–91.

Watkins, C. 1970: 'Studies in Indo-European legal language, institutions and mythology', in G. Cardona & H. Hoenigswald (eds.), *Indo-European and Indo-Europeans*, Philadelphia.

Weber, H. 1908: *Aristophanes Studien*, Leipzig.

Webster, T. B. L. 1967: *The Tragedies of Euripides*, London.

Weill, N. 1966: 'Adoniazusai ou les femmes sur le toit', *BCH* 90:664–98.

Welsh, D. 1979: '*Knights* 230–3 and Cleon's eyebrows', *CQ* 29:214f.

West, M. L. 1966: *Hesiod: Theogony, edited with prolegomena and commentary*, Oxford.

1971: *Early Greek Philosophy and the Orient*, Oxford.

1978: *Hesiod: Works and Days, edited with prolegomena and commentary*, Oxford.

1982: *Greek Metre*, Oxford.

1983: *The Orphic Poems*, Oxford.

1991: *Studies in Aeschylus*, Stuttgart.

West, S. R. 1982: 'Proteus in Stesichorus' Palinode', *ZPE* 47:6–10.

Westlake, J. D. 1954: 'Overseas service for the Father-Beater', *CR* 4:90–4.

Wheeler, E. L. 1988: *Stratagem and the Vocabulary of Military Trickery*, Leiden.

Whitehead, D. 1986: *The Demes of Attica 508/7–ca. 250 B.C.*, Princeton.

Whitman, C. H. 1964: *Aristophanes and the Comic Hero*, Cambridge, Mass.

Wilamowitz-Moellendorff, U. von 1893: *Aristotles und Athen*, 2 vols., Berlin.

1959 (1895): *Euripides: Herakles*, 3 vols., Darmstadt.

Wilkins, J. 1990: 'The young of Athens: religion and society in *Herakleidai* of Euripides', *CQ* 40:329–39.

Willetts, R. F. 1955: *Aristocratic Society in Ancient Crete*, London.

1962: *Cretan Cults and Festivals*, London.

Williams, F. (ed.) 1978: *Callimachus: Hymn to Apollo: a commentary*, Oxford.

Wilson, N. G. 1982: 'Two observations on Aristophanes' *Lysistrata*', *GRBS* 23:157–63.

Winkler, J. J. 1990: 'The ephebes' song: *tragoidia* and *Polis*', in Winkler and Zeitlin 1990:20–62.

Winkler, J. J. and Zeitlin, F. I. (eds.) 1990: *Nothing to do with Dionysus?: Athenian drama in its social context*, Princeton.

Winnington-Ingram, R. P. 1969: 'Euripides: *poiêtês sophos*', *Arethusa* 2:127–42.

Wood, E. M. 1988: *Peasant-Citizen and Slave: the foundations of Athenian democracy*, London and New York.

Wüst, E. 1921: 'Skolion und *gephurismos* in der alten Komödie', *Philol.* 77:26–45.

Wycherley, R. E. 1957: *The Athenian Agora*, vol. III, *Literary and Epigraphical Testimonia*, Princeton.

Zaganiaris, N. J. 1973: 'Le mythe de Térée dans la littérature grecque et latine', *Platon* 25:208–32

Zanker, P. 1965: *Wandel der Hermesgestalt in der attischen Vasenmalerei*, Bonn.

Zannini-Quirini, B. 1987: *Nephelokokkugia: la prospettiva mitica degli Uccelli di Aristofane*, Rome.

Zeitlin, F. I. 1978: 'The dynamics of misogyny in the *Oresteia*: myth and myth-making', *Arethusa* 11:149–84.

1981: 'Travesties of gender and genre in Aristophanes' *Thesmophoriazousae*', in Foley 1981: 169–217.

Zielinski, T. 1885a: *Die Gliederung der altattischen Komödie*, Leipzig.

1885b: *Die Märchenkomödie in Athen*, St Petersburg.

Zijderveld, C., Jr 1934: *Telete: bijdrage tot de kennis der religieuze terminologie in het Grieksch*, Utrecht.

INDEX

(References in italics are to the most important discussions of particular points.)

317